THE

GREAT LAKES READER

C A N A
Port Arthur
Ft. William
Michipicot
LAKE SUPERIOR
Two Harbors
Duluth
Superior
Ashland
Marquette
M I C H
Port Inland
Escanaba
Straits of
WISCONSIN
Green Bay
LAKE MICHIGAN
MISSISSIPPI RIVER
Milwaukee
IOWA
Chicago
ILLINOIS
INDIAN

THE
Great Lakes

ST. MARY'S RIVER
AND SOO LOCKS

D
A

GEORGIAN BAY

ckinac

LAKE HURON

lcite

lpena

Midland

Collingwood

Toronto

LAKE ONTARIO

Oswego

ST. CLARE RIVER

LAKE ST. CLARE

Hamilton

WELLAND CANAL

Buffalo

DETROIT RIVER

NEW YORK

A
Detroit

LAKE ERIE

Erie

Conneaut

Ashtabula

Z

Cleveland

Toledo
Sandusky

Lorain

OHIO

PENNSYLVANIA

RIKI

Books by Walter Havighurst

PIER 17 *1935*

THE QUIET SHORE *1937*

THE UPPER MISSISSIPPI (Rivers of America) *1938*

THE WINDS OF SPRING *1940*

NO HOMEWARD COURSE *1941*

THE LONG SHIPS PASSING *1942*

LAND OF PROMISE *1946*

SIGNATURE OF TIME *1949*

GEORGE ROGERS CLARK: Soldier in the West *1952*

ANNIE OAKLEY OF THE WILD WEST *1954*

WILDERNESS FOR SALE *1956*

VEIN OF IRON *1959*

THE MIAMI YEARS *1959*

LAND OF THE LONG HORIZONS *1960*

THE HEARTLAND *1962*

PROUD PRISONER *1963*

VOICES ON THE RIVER *1964*

With Marion Boyd Havighurst

HIGH PRAIRIE *1944*

SONG OF THE PINES *1949*

CLIMB A LOFTY LADDER *1952*

THE
GREAT LAKES READER

EDITED BY Walter Havighurst

COLLIER BOOKS
A Division of Macmillan Publishing Co., Inc.
New York

COLLIER MACMILLAN PUBLISHERS
London

Macmillan Publishing Co., Inc.
866 Third Avenue, New York, N.Y. 10022
Collier Macmillan Canada, Ltd.

Library of Congress Catalog Card Number: 66-15024
ISBN 0-02-080540-3 pbk.

First Collier Books edition 1978

The Great Lakes Reader is also published in a hardcover edition
by Macmillan Publishing Co., Inc.

Printed in the United States of America

The author wishes to thank the following publishers and individuals for their kind permission to reprint copyrighted material: The Bobbs-Merrill Company for an excerpt from *Lake Huron*, by Fred Landon, copyright 1944 by The Bobbs-Merrill Company, Inc. Chicago Historical Society for an excerpt from the *Journal* of Jacob Butler Varnum. Doubleday & Company for excerpts from *Northwest Passage*, by Kenneth Roberts, copyright 1936, 1937 by Kenneth Roberts. Mrs. Helen Hardie Grant for "Winter in the North." Harcourt Brace Jovanovich, Inc., for excerpts from *Seven Iron Men*, by Paul de Kruif, copyright 1929 by Harcourt Brace Jovanovich, Inc., renewed © 1957 by Paul de Kruif; and from *The Invasion*, by Janet Lewis, copyright 1932, copyright © 1960 by Janet Lewis. Holt, Rinehart and Winston, Publishers, for excerpts from *The St. Lawrence*, by Henry Beston, copyright 1942 by Henry Beston, copyright © 1970 by Elizabeth Coatsworth Beston; from *The Chicago*, by Harry Hansen, copyright 1942, © 1970 by Harry Hansen; from *Reminiscences*, by Raphael Pumpelly, all rights reserved. *Inland Seas*, quarterly journal of the Great Lakes Historical Society, for articles by Rowland W. Murphy, Ernest H. Rankin, and Julius Wolff, Jr. Macmillan Publishing Co., Inc. for an excerpt from *The Seaway Story*, by Carleton Mabee, copyright 1961 by Carleton Mabee. The Marquette County Historical Society for excerpts from *Landlooker in the Upper Peninsula of Michigan*. Meredith Press for an excerpt from *Stranger on the Island*, by Brand Whitlock. Mrs. William A. Murdoch for an excerpt from *Boom Copper* by Angus Murdoch, copyright 1943 by William A. Murdoch. Oxford University Press for excerpts from *The Great Lakes*, by Harlan Hatcher, copyright 1944 by Oxford University Press, Inc., renewed 1972 by Harlan Hatcher; and from *Land of the Crooked Tree*, by Ulysses Prentiss Hedrick, copyright 1948 by Oxford University Press, Inc., renewed in 1976 by U. P. Hedrick, III. Pickands Mather & Co. for Chief Folkert's report. William Ratigan for an excerpt from his book *Straits of Mackinac*. St. Anthony Guild Press for an excerpt from *By Cross and Anchor*. The Macmillan Company of Canada, Limited, for an excerpt from *Rivers of Canada*, by Hugh MacLennan, copyright © 1961 by Hugh MacLennan. The Society of Naval Architects and Marine Engineers for excerpts from "Current Trends in the Design of Iron Ore Ships," Vol. 70, 1962 *Transactions*. The Wayne State University Press for excerpts from *River of Destiny: The St. Marys*, by Joseph E. and Estelle L. Bayliss in collaboration with Milo M. Quaife. Jack C. Yewell for his story "North to Salt Water."

Acknowledgments

For various courtesies in the course of preparing this volume, I have become indebted to a number of people. I should like to make grateful acknowledgment of assistance from Miss Janet Coe Sanborn, editor of *Inland Seas*; Mr. Ernest H. Rankin of the Marquette County Historical Society; Mr. John Horton of the Cleveland-Cliffs Iron Company; Mr. E. J. Mapes of Pickands Mather & Co.; Mr. Jack C. Yewell of the Pittsburgh Steamship Division, United States Steel Corporation; Mr. William Ratigan of the Dockside Press, Charlevoix, Michigan; Mr. John Lochhead of the Mariners Museum, Newport News, Virginia; Mr. Oliver Burnham of the Lake Carriers Association; Mr. Paul M. Angle, director of the Chicago Historical Society; Rev. Gerald Dolan, O.F.M., of St. Anthony's Guild Press, Paterson, N.J.; Mrs. Helen Hardie Grant of New York City; Miss Agnes Hanson of the Cleveland Public Library; Miss Alice J. Pickup of the Buffalo and Erie County Historical Society; Captain W. W. Landers, U.S.N. (Ret.) of the Society of Naval Architects and Marine Engineers; J. L. Avesian, chief, Technical Liaison Branch, U.S. Army District, Detroit, Corps of Engineers; Mrs. Patricia Straker of the Oxford (Ohio) Branch of the Lane Public Library; and Mr. L. S. Dutton and members of the staff of the Miami University Library.

WALTER HAVIGHURST
Oxford, Ohio

Contents

VI STORM WARNING

VII   THE LONG SHIPS

VIII   CITIES AND SEAWAY

Illustrations

"Fountain of the Great Lakes," by Lorado Taft.
Buffalo harbor in the 1850s.
The pioneer steamboat *Walk-in-the Water*, 1820.
Milwaukee harbor, 1874.
Chicago commerce in the 1850s.
The *Lady Elgin* at Superior, Wisconsin, 1856.
The steamer *Japan*.
One of Alexander McDougall's whalebacks.
Passengers leaving Duluth, 1908.
One of the lake-built ocean freighters of World War I.
St. Marys Falls Canal celebration, 1905.
The steamer *Cliffs Victory*, towing through the Chicago River.
Ore fleet in the ice of Whitefish Bay.
International bridge and coffer dams at Sault Ste. Marie, 1963.
Mackinac Straits Bridge.
Navy Pier, Chicago.

Introduction

In his "Fountain of the Great Lakes," which he designed for the Chicago Art Institute, Lorado Taft portrayed five classic sisters, each holding a shell of flowing water. Above the rest stands Lake Superior, lordly and alone. From her scalloped vessel the endless stream falls into the twin basins of Michigan and Huron, which send it on to Erie whose shell pours into the brimming bowl of Ontario. That sister looks away from the others, unheeding the water's source; the Ontario current flows to the St. Lawrence and the sea.

It is nearly twelve hundred miles, the distance from London to Sicily or from Madrid to Berlin, from the head of Lake Superior to the mouth of Lake Ontario. The five lake basins are larger than the combined area of England, Scotland and Wales. Their eight thousand miles of shoreline include brooding wilderness and teeming cities, cliffs, capes and headlands, and long beaches where the breakers roll. Over the lakes pass fleets of freighters carrying a bulk commerce of coal, grain, oil, limestone and iron ore. At Sault Ste. Marie and Niagara the sea-seeking waters generate a massive hydroelectric energy. To the North American heartland the Five Sisters give beauty, wealth and power.

These living waters are a gift from the long ice age that sealed the land in a white silence. During thousands of years the great glaciers gouged out the lake basins and rimmed them with rocky coasts and shifting hills of sand. As it retreated the last glacier left moraines that blocked drainage to the south. The waters surged eastward, carving channels between the huge bowls, and Niagara began its plunge over the limestone ledges. Thirty thousand years ago the melting of the ice cover, ten thousand feet deep, left blue water overflowing the five basins.

Then, in a benign climate, forests darkened the lake shores, game animals multiplied, the waters swarmed with fish. Indian nations roamed lake-bordered hunting grounds, the Iroquois on Lake Ontario, the Algonquin on Lake Huron, the Menominee and the Chippewa in the far Northwest. Tribesmen followed the shores in bark canoes. They lived in the lake country like deer and foxes, leaving it unchanged by their possession.

Three and a half centuries ago the first white men found this realm of woods and water, and its history began. It was a rich country—rich in fish and furs, then in timber, then in copper and iron ore—and the lakes themselves were an incomparable highway for its commerce. As commerce grew, the barriers of Sault Ste. Marie and Niagara were skirted by canals. Much of the growing trade was contained in the lake basins, but some of it sought the sea. For more than a century small vessels moved to and from the lakes by the old St. Lawrence canals around the river rapids. At last came the Seaway, unlocking the lakes to ocean commerce.

A literature of the lakes has developed in the present century, especially since the rediscovery of America by the Federal Writers Project in the 1930s. Some of the literature is fiction; more is regional history—narrative, descriptive, interpretive, recalling a storied past. This rediscovery of the lakes led to the founding of the Great Lakes Historical Society in 1942, which quickened the rediscovery by the publishing of its quarterly *Inland Seas* and the establishing of its Wakefield Museum and Library at Vermilion-on-Lake Erie. Other societies and libraries at Toronto, Buffalo, Cleveland, Detroit, Chicago, Sault Ste. Marie, Marquette, Duluth and elsewhere have stimulated the study and writing of Great Lakes history.

The current literature of the lakes rests upon an older literature, the first-hand records of experience in times past. For 350 years men have left accounts of their discoveries and endeavors. The first voyage through the Straits of Mackinac, the launching of the first vessel above Niagara, the building of trading posts and mission stations, the portaging of schooners and steamers on log rollers around the rapids at the Soo—all are recorded.

The literature of the lakes begins heroically. A whole shelf of books, seventy-one volumes of the *Jesuit Relations*, tells the story of the explorer priests who crossed unknown waters and landed upon unmapped shores. Wrote the historian Bancroft: "Not a cape was turned, nor a mission founded, nor a river entered, nor a settlement begun, but a Jesuit led the way." Far from people of their kind, living with savages in a dark country, they suffered privation, persecution and sometimes death for the peculiar glory of their calling. With numb or bleeding hands, dipping a quill in ink made from melted snow and gunpowder, they recorded their voyages and discoveries, and the baptism of uncomprehending Indians.

The first Great Lakes writers were Claude Allouez and Claude Dablon in their long cassocks beaded with burrs and muddy from the portage paths. After the "black robes" the literature became various, as various as the men and motives in the wilderness. It includes the tales of Indian traders, field notes of geologists and surveyors, stories of landlookers and prospectors, records of Indian agents, the logs of schoonermen and steamboat captains, the diaries of travelers and emigrants, accounts of the building of canals and harbors and of the surging freshwater commerce. The great waters flow from the heartland to the sea, and the record goes on into the future.

In this *Reader* some of the narratives are from experience—set down by firelight on an upturned canoe or on a rock above the restless water. Some came from a burial place on the shore, from a ship's cabin, or an island camping place. Some were written beside the loud rapids, or to the sound of Indian drums, or in a choking mosquito smudge at a portage. The Great Lakes record includes accounts by historians and biographers who see their story in context and perspective. But original sources are the best, and the first aim of this *Reader* is to recall men and moments from the past. The moments are of landfall and arrival, of discovery and disaster, of contest with the lakes' danger and promise. The men are those who were there.

I

VOYAGEURS'
TALES

In France a *voyageur* was merely a traveler—on the way to the crossroad or the village, or perhaps to Paris—but America made it a heroic term. In the New World the *voyageur* was a finder of paths and of channels. He was a horizon-seeker, pushing deep into unknown country while the English colonists were clinging to their seacoast. Sault Ste. Marie is older than Philadelphia, and Green Bay had a settlement fifty years before the founding of Baltimore.

The empire-dreaming Frenchmen came to the Great Lakes by the northern rivers, being blocked in the south by the Niagara cataract and the hostile Iroquois. They mapped the northern waters before they had ever seen Lake Erie. By the French River and the Nipissing they entered Lake Huron and found the way between straits and islands to Lake Superior and Lake Michigan. Each lake looked to them like an ocean. Champlain called Lake Huron the South Sea, and he envisioned the Indies beyond it. Brulé called Lake Superior the Great North Sea, and Nicolet, crossing Lake Michigan, laid his course for China. But these were seas of sweet water (*Mer Douce* was the first name for Lake Huron) and the unknown continent stretched beyond them. In 1632, putting together the reports of his *voyageurs*, Champlain sketched the first map of the Great Lakes. It shows Lake Huron and Lake Superior with the Sault between them, but there is no hint of the Straits of Mackinac and only a forked river in the place of Lake Michigan. Two years later Jean Nicolet crossed the Lake of the Illinois (Lake Michigan), landing not in China but in the Winnebago country.

If not a route to the Orient, the lakes were a rich empire of their own. The French claimed it, building missions to convert the Indians and trading posts to gather peltry. They strung a necklace of names around the northern waters—Sault Ste. Marie, St. Ignace, L'Abre Croche, Bois Blanc, Les Chenaux, Gros Cap de Tour—linked with the old savage names Neebish, Manitoulin, Michipicoten, Michilimackinac. At each of these places civilization encountered savagery, the grace of the Cross met the superstition of a dark and primitive people. On the way to La Pointe in 1665 Father Allouez' box of letters and medicines (opium, sweet spices, cardoman, cinnamon, mace) was left behind at a portage where some wandering Ottawas found it. They rifled the papers and smelled and tasted the powders, and left the box open to the sun and rain. Then, fearing the white devils inside it, they brought the sodden chest to Allouez at his lonely station.

Of their long, hard and dangerous travels the *voyageur*- priests told quietly, with fewer words for their own ardor and endurance than for the wonders of their journeys. "Having then entered Lake Tracy [Lake Superior] we spent the whole month of September in coasting along its southern shore." Their carrier was the *canot du maître*. Thirty to forty feet long and seven feet wide, tapering to a point at each end, it was a sturdy, commodious and seaworthy craft. Over a cage of cedar ribs sheets of leathery birch bark were sewn with wiry spruce roots; the seams were caulked with pine pitch. Wholly a product of the north country, it was steered and propelled by cedar paddles. But the *voyageurs* brought European canvas; in fair wind and wide water they raised a cedar mast and a canvas sail.

This craft, manned by Indians and French *voyageurs,* traveled rivers, straits and open waters. Coasting the lake shores, free from portages, they made a hundred miles a day with full cargo. In the 1790s the great trader Simon McTavish of the North West Company set a record of seven and three-quarter days for nine hundred obstacle-strewn miles from the Sault to Montreal. A few years later twenty-year-old George Landon in a twenty-five foot canoe with nine picked paddlers, helped by a following wind on Lake Huron, made the run in seven days and six hours.

The *voyageurs* could travel from May to December; then the long northern winter locked the lakes in silence. For the Indians this was the time of storytelling. The animals were burrowed in the earth, fish lurked under the ice, the forest was white and still. Now it was safe to gossip of the West Wind, of the old and the new Moon, of the Great Turtle and the Great Hare. While snow deepened in the woods and the ghostly aurora shimmered overhead, they told of Manabazho the warrior hero and of how the great Manitou created the earth from a grain of sand which the little muskrat brought up from the bottom of the Big Sea Water. To these people the French brought new mysteries, the prayer beads and the crucifix and stories of the god that lived in their bark chapels.

The *voyageurs* traveled the lakes in the dawn of history, when forest darkened the shores and the smoke of an Indian camp was the only sign of man in all that country. But sometimes they had startling glimpses of the future. Wrote Louis Hennepin in 1680, traveling the lakes in their first commercial vessel: "It were easy to build on the sides of these great lakes an infinite number of considerable towns which might have communication one with another by navigation for five hundred leagues together, and by an inconceivable commerce which would establish itself among them."

Nicolet's Bold

Venture

Just a year after the founding of the Jamestown colony in Virginia, a permanent French settlement was planted in Canada. In 1608, under a great rock on the tidal St. Lawrence, Samuel de Champlain began the colony of Quebec. Westward led the St. Lawrence and westward into unknown distance stretched the mysterious wilderness.

Each year Indian brigades came down the rivers with bundles of beaver skins. To the Frenchmen's wonder they told of great waters in the wilderness. It took the explorers more than half a century, learning by their own journeys and the tales of the Indians, to map, even vaguely and crudely, the five Great Lakes. Champlain himself saw just two of them. In 1615, having passed up the Ottawa River, over Lake Nipissing and down the French River, he stood on the shores of Lake Huron's Georgian Bay; from there he descended the River Trent to Lake Ontario.

In the canoe brigades of 1629 came a tall Algonquin who laid at the governor's feet a lump of copper. Other Indians told of a hairless "People of the Sea" who lived on the far side of a wide water. To Champlain this sounded like the Orient, and desire inflamed his mind; the maps of New France and the sovereignty of the king must extend to that remote, rich country.

Five years later his man was ready. Jean Nicolet had lived among the Hurons, learning their lore and languages and their wilderness routes to the West. Now, in 1634, Champlain ordered him to explore the great western waters and to begin a trade with their people.

With Indian boatmen Nicolet went into country no white man had entered. He passed through the northern reach of Lake Huron, along the Manitoulin Islands, into a northward-leading river that led to a Chippewa town beside a rushing rapids. Here, at Sault Ste. Marie, he must have known of Lake Superior, though he did not see it opening beyond the riverhead. Instead he turned southward. With seven pad-

5

dlers he rounded Point Detour and passed the Straits of Mackinac. Westward, the waters widened like an ocean. Across that sea he came to shores he thought were China, but he found half-naked Winnebago tribesmen. He was still in America, with untold wilderness beyond.

After a winter with these people, Nicolet made the long voyage back to the St. Lawrence. He married a young French wife and became a fur trader at Three Rivers. On a stormy night in 1642, enroute from Quebec, he was drowned in the St. Lawrence. Three years later his wife's sister bore a son, named Louis Jolliet. In years to come he would follow his uncle's route to Mackinac, Lake Michigan and beyond.

Nicolet left no record of his venture, but he recounted his journey to the priests and Father Vimont recorded it briefly in the *Jesuit Relations.* Using all the French records, C. W. Butterfield, Wisconsin historian, wrote in 1881 his *History of the Discovery of the Northwest by Jean Nicolet,* from which these pages are taken.

I T W A S now that Nicolet, after all ceremonies and "talks" with the Hurons were ended, began preparations for his voyage to the Winnebagoes. He was to strike boldly into undiscovered regions. He was to encounter savage nations never before visited. It was, in reality, the beginning of a voyage full of dangers—one that would require great tact, great courage, and constant facing of difficulties. No one, however, understood better the savage character than he; no Frenchman was more fertile of resources. From the St. Lawrence, he had brought presents to conciliate the Indian tribes which he would meet. Seven Hurons were to accompany him. Before him lay great lakes; around him, when on land, would frown dark forests. A birch-bark canoe was to bear the first white man along the northern shore of Lake Huron, and upon Saint Mary's strait to the falls—"Sault Sainte Marie;" many miles on Lake Michigan; thence, up Green bay to the homes of the Winnebagoes: and that canoe was to lead the van of a mighty fleet indeed, as the commerce of the upper lakes can testify. With him, he had a number of presents.

What nations were encountered by him on the way to "the People of the Sea," from the Huron villages? Three—all of Algonquin lineage—occupied the shores of the Georgian bay, before the mouth of French river had been reached. Concerning them, little is known, except their names. Passing the river which flows from Lake Nipissing, Nicolet "upon the same shores of this fresh-water sea," that is, upon the shores of Lake Huron, came next to "the Nation of

Beavers," whose hunting-grounds were northward of the Manitoulin islands. This nation was afterward esteemed among the most
noble of those of Canada. They were supposed to be descended
from the Great Beaver, which was, next to the Great Hare, their
principal divinity. They inhabited originally the Beaver islands, in
Lake Michigan; afterward the Manitoulin islands; then they removed to the main-land, where they were found by Nicolet. Farther on, but still upon the margin of the great lake, was found
another tribe. This people, and the Amikoüai, were of the Algonquin family, and their language was not difficult to be understood
by Nicolet. Entering, finally, St. Mary's strait, his canoes were
urged onward for a number of miles, until the falls—Sault de Sainte
Marie—were reached: and there stood Nicolet, the first white man
to set foot upon any portion of what was, more than a century and a
half after, called "the territory northwest of the river Ohio," now
the States of Ohio, Indiana, Illinois, Michigan, and Wisconsin, and
so much of Minnesota as lies east of the Mississippi river.

Among "the People of the Falls," at their principal village, on
the south side of the strait, at the foot of the rapids, in what is now
the State of Michigan, Nicolet and his seven Hurons rested from
the fatigues of their weary voyage. They were still with Algonquins. From Lake Huron they had entered upon one of the channels of the magnificent waterway leading out from Lake Superior,
and threaded their way, now through narrow rapids, now across
(as it were) little lakes, now around beautiful islands, to within
fifteen miles of the largest expanse of fresh water on the globe—
stretching away in its grandeur to the westward, a distance of full
four hundred miles. Nicolet saw beyond him the falls; around him
clusters of wigwams, which two centuries and a half have changed
into public buildings and private residences, into churches and
warehouses, into offices and stores—in short, into a pleasantly-
situated American village, frequently visited by steamboats carrying valuable freight and crowded with parties of pleasure. The
portage around the falls, where, in early times, the Indian carried
his birch-bark canoe, has given place to an excellent canal. Such are
the changes which "the course of empire" continually brings to
view in "the vast, illimitable, changing West."

Nicolet tarried among "the People of the Falls," probably, but a
brief period. His voyage, after leaving them, must have been to him
one of great interest. He returned down the strait, passing, it is
thought, through the western "detour" to Mackinaw. Not very
many miles brought him to "the second fresh-water sea," Lake
Michigan. He is fairly entitled to the honor of its discovery; for no

white man had ever before looked out upon its broad expanse. Nicolet was soon gliding along upon the clear waters of this out-of-the-way link in the great chain of lakes. The bold Frenchman fearlessly threaded his way along its northern shore, frequently stopping upon what is now known as "the upper peninsula" of Michigan, until the bay of Noquet was reached, which is, in reality, a northern arm of Green bay. Here, upon its northern border, he visited another Algonquin tribe; also one living to the northward of this "small lake." These tribes never navigated those waters any great distance, but lived upon the fruits of the earth. Making his way up Green bay, he finally reached the Menominee river, its principal northern affluent.

In the valley of the Menominee, Nicolet met a populous tribe of Indians—the Menominee. To his surprise, no doubt, he found they were of a lighter complexion than any other savages he had ever seen. Their language was difficult to understand, yet it showed the nation to be of the Algonquin stock. Their food was largely of wild rice, which grew in great abundance in their country. They were adepts in fishing, and hunted, with skill, the game which abounded in the forests. They had their homes and hunting grounds upon the stream which still bears their name.

Nicolet soon resumed his journey toward the Winnebagoes, who had already been made aware of his near approach; for he had sent forward one of his Hurons to carry the news of his coming and of his mission of peace. The messenger and his message were well received. The Winnebagoes dispatched several of their young men to meet the "wonderful man." They go to him—they escort him—they carry his baggage. He was clothed in a large garment of Chinese damask, sprinkled with flowers and birds of different colors. But, why thus attired? Possibly, he had reached the far east; he was, really, in what is now the State of Wisconsin. Possibly, a party of mandarins would soon greet him and welcome him to Cathay. And this robe—this dress of ceremony—was brought all the way from Quebec, doubtless, with a view to such contingency. As soon as he came in sight, all the women and children fled, seeing a man carrying thunder in his two hands; for thus it was they called his pistols, which he discharged on his right and on his left. He was a manito! Nicolet's journey was, for the present, at an end. He and his Huron's "rested from their labors," among the Winnebagoes, who were located around the head of Green bay, contiguous to the point where it receives the waters of Fox river. Nicolet found the Winnebagoes a numerous and sedentary people, speaking a language radically different from any of the Algonquin nations, as well as from the Hurons. They were of the Dakota stock. The news of the

Frenchman's coming spread through the country. Four or five thousand people assembled of different tribes. Each of the chiefs gave a banquet. One of the sachems regaled his guests with at least one hundred and twenty beavers. The large assemblage was prolific of speeches and ceremonies. Nicolet did not fail to "speak of peace" upon that interesting occasion. He urged upon the nation the advantages of an alliance, rather than war, with the nations to the eastward of Lake Huron. They agreed to keep the peace with the Hurons, Nez Percés, and, possibly, other tribes; but, soon after Nicolet's return, they sent out war parties against the Beaver nation. Doubtless the advantages of trade with the colony upon the St. Lawrence were depicted in glowing colors by the Frenchman. But the courageous Norman was not satisfied with a visit to the Winnebagoes only. He must see the neighboring tribes. So he ascended the Fox river of Green bay to Winnebago lake—passing through which he again entered that stream, paddling his canoe up its current, until he reached the homes of the Mascoutins, the first tribe to be met with after leaving the Winnebagoes; for the Sacs and Foxes were not residents of what is now Wisconsin at that period—their migration thither, from the east, having been at a subsequent date. Nicolet had navigated the Fox river, a six-days' journey, since leaving the Winnebagoes.

The Mascoutins, as we have seen, were heard of by Champlain as early as 1615, as being engaged in a war with the Neuter nation and the Ottawas. But, up to the time of Nicolet's visit, and for a number of years subsequent (as he gave no clue himself to their locality), they were only known as living two hundred leagues or more beyond the last mentioned tribe—that is, that distance beyond the south end of the Georgian bay of Lake Huron. Their villages were in the valley of the Fox river, probably in what is now Green Lake county, Wisconsin. They had, doubtless, for their neighbors, the Miamis and Kickapoos. They were a vigorous and warlike nation, of Algonquin stock, as were also the two tribes last mentioned. Nicolet, while among the Mascoutins, heard of the Wisconsin river, which was distant only three days' journey up the tortuous channel of the Fox. But the accounts given him of that tributary of the Mississippi were evidently very confused. A reference to the parent stream (confounded with the Wisconsin) as "the great water," by the savages, caused him to believe that he was, in reality, but three days' journey from the sea; and so he reported after his return to the St. Lawrence. Strange to say, Nicolet resolved not to visit this ocean, although, as he believed, so near its shores.

He traveled no further upon the Fox river, but turned his course to the southward. And the Jesuits consoled themselves, when they heard of his shortcoming, with the hope that one day the western sea would be reached by one of their order. "In passing, I will say," wrote one of their missionaries, in 1640, "that we have strong indications that one can descend through the second lake of the Hurons . . . into this sea."

But why should Nicolet leave the Fox river and journey away from the Mascoutins to the southward? The answer is, that, at no great distance, lived the Illinois. Their country extended eastward to Lake Michigan, and westward to the Mississippi, if not beyond it. This nation was of too much importance, and their homes too easy of access, for Nicolet not to have visited them. Upon the beautiful prairies of what is now the state bearing their name, was this tribe located, with some bands, probably nearly as far northward as the southern counties of the present State of Wisconsin. It is not known in how many villages of these savages he smoked the pipe of peace. From their homes he returned to the Winnebagoes.

Before Nicolet left the country, on his return to the St. Lawrence, he obtained knowledge of the Sioux—those traders from the west who, it will be remembered, were represented as coming in canoes upon a sea to the Winnebagoes; the same "sea," doubtless, he came so near to, but did not behold—the Wisconsin and Mississippi rivers! Although without beards, and having only a tuft of hair upon their crowns, these Sioux were no longer mandarins—no longer from China or Japan! Bands of this tribe had pushed their way across the Mississippi, far above the mouth of the Wisconsin, but made no further progress eastward. They, like the Winnebagoes, as previously stated, were of the Dakota family. Whether any of them were seen by Nicolet is not known; but he, doubtless, learned something of their real character. There was yet one tribe near the Winnebagoes to be visited—the Pottawattamies. They were located upon the islands at the mouth of Green bay, and upon the main land to the southward, along the western shores of Lake Michigan. On these Algonquins—for they were of that lineage—Nicolet, upon his return trip, made a friendly call. Their homes were not on the line of his outward voyage, but to the south of it. Nicolet gave no information of them which has been preserved, except that they were neighbors of the Winnebagoes.

So Nicolet, in the spring of 1635, having previously made many friends in the far northwest for his countrymen upon the St. Lawrence, and for France, of nations of Indians, only a few of which had before been heard of, and none ever before visited by a white man; having been the first to discover Lake Michigan and "the territory northwest of the river Ohio;" having boldly struck into the wilderness for hundreds of leagues beyond the Huron villages— then the Ultima Thule of civilized discoveries; returned, with his seven dusky companions, by way of Mackinaw and along the south shores of the Great Manitoulin island to the home thereon of a band of Ottawas. He proceeded thence to the Hurons; retracing, afterward, his steps to the mouth of French river, up that stream to Lake Nipissing, and down the Mattawa and Ottawa to the St. Lawrence; journeying, upon his return, it is thought, with the savages upon their annual trading-voyage to the French settlements. And Nicolet's exploration was ended.

Mission on

Lake Superior

The high-minded Governor Champlain esteemed "the salavtion of a soul worth more than the conquest of an empire." If this was more or less than the French policy, the cross was destined to accompany the fleur-de-lis throughout the vastness of New France. To save the souls of the savages came the black-robed friars of the Society of Jesus. They were ready to carry their altars to the ends of the earth.

The first Jesuit missionaries went into the Huron country in 1634. Thirty years later they had extended their parish to the far shores of Lake Michigan and Lake Superior. They built bark chapels beside unnamed rivers and set up their altars in remote camps of the Indians. When Radisson and Groseilliers explored the southern shore of Lake Superior, gentle Father Ménard soon followed, erecting the Mission of the Holy Ghost; he lost his life in that dark country. When Sieur de St. Lusson at Sault Ste. Marie proclaimed French possession of all the lakes and the land around them, four Jesuit priests sanctified a cedar cross and sang a *Te Deum* on behalf of the tribes assembled there.

In the fall of 1665 Father Claude Allouez coasted the shore of Lake Superior (he called it Lake Tracy, after the lieutenant-general of New France) to the Huron settlement on Chequamegon Bay where he reopened Ménard's mission at La Pointe du St. Esprit. After serving that outpost for four strenuous years he went on to Lake Michigan, to found a new mission at Green Bay. At La Pointe he was succeeded by young Jacques Marquette.

During twenty-five years in the western wilds Allouez traveled all the upper lakes and many of the rivers. His callused hands baptized unnumbered savages. The journal of his years on Lake Superior was recorded in the volume of 1668 of the *Jesuit Relations*—the annual report of the labors of the Jesuit priests in America.

TOWARD THE BEGINNING of September, after coasting along the shores of the Lake of the Hurons, we reached the Sault; for such is the name given to a half-league of rapids that are encountered in a beautiful river which unites two great Lakes—that of the Hurons, and Lake Superior.

This River is pleasing, not only on account of the Islands intercepting its course and the great bays bordering it, but because of the fishing and hunting, which are excellent there. We sought a resting place for the night on one of these Islands, where our Savages thought they would find provision for supper upon their arrival; for, as soon as they had landed, they put the kettle on the fire, expecting to see the Canoe laden with fish the moment the net was cast into the water! But God chose to punish their presumption, and deferred giving any food to the starving men until the following day.

On the second of September, then, after clearing this Sault, —which is not a waterfall, but merely a very swift current impeded by numerous rocks,—we entered Lake Superior, which will henceforth bear Monsieur de Tracy's name, in recognition of indebtedness to him on the part of the people of those regions.

The form of this lake is nearly that of a bow, the Southern shore being much curved and the Northern nearly straight. Fish are abundant there, and of excellent quality; while the water is so clear and pure that objects at the bottom can be seen to the depth of six brasses.

One often finds at the bottom of the water pieces of pure copper, of ten and twenty livres' weight. I have several times seen such pieces in the Savages' hands; and since they are superstitious, they keep them as so many divinities, or as presents which the gods dwelling beneath the water have given them, and on which their welfare is to depend. For this reason they preserve these pieces of copper, wrapped up, among their most precious possessions. Some have kept them for more then fifty years; others have had them in their families from time immemorial, and cherish them as household gods.

For some time, there had been a sort of great rock, all of copper, the point of which projected from the water; this gave the passersby the opportunity to go and cut off pieces from it. When, however, I passed that spot, nothing more was seen of it; and I think that the storms—which here are very frequent, and like those at sea—have covered the rock with sand. Our Savages tried to persuade me that it was a divinity, who had disappeared for some reason they do not state.

This Lake is, furthermore, the resort of twelve or fifteen distinct nations—coming, some from the North, others from the South, and still others from the West; and they all betake themselves either to the best parts of the shore for fishing, or to the Islands, which are scattered in great numbers all over the Lake. These peoples' motive in repairing hither is partly to obtain food by fishing, and partly to transact their petty trading with one another, when they meet. But God's purpose was to facilitate the proclaiming of the Gospel to wandering and vagrant tribes—as will appear in the course of this Journal.

Having, then, entered Lake Tracy, we spent the whole month of September in coasting along its southern shore—where, finding myself alone with our Frenchmen, I had the consolation of saying holy Mass, which I had been unable to do since my departure from Three Rivers.

We then crossed the Bay named for saint Theresa by the late Father Ménard. There this brave missionary spent a winter, laboring with the same zeal which afterward made him sacrifice his life in quest for souls. I found, at no great distance thence, some remnants of his labors, in the persons of two Christian women who had always kept the faith, and who shone like two stars amid the darkness of that infidelity. I made them pray to God, after I had refreshed their memory concerning our mysteries. . . .

There is here a false and abominable religion, resembling in many respects the beliefs of some of the ancient Pagans. The Savages of the regions recognize no sovereign master of Heaven and Earth, but believe there are many spirits—some of whom are beneficent, as the Sun, the Moon, the Lake, Rivers, and Woods; others malevolent, as the adder, the dragon, cold, and storms. And, in general, whatever seems to them either helpful or hurtful they call a Manitou and pay it the worship and veneration which we render only to the true God.

These divinities they invoke whenever they go out hunting, fishing, to war, or on a journey—offering them sacrifices, with ceremonies appropriate only for Sacrificial priests.

One of the leading old men of the Village discharges the function of Priest, beginning with a carefully prepared harangue addressed to the Sun—if the eat-all feast, which bears a certain resemblance to a holocaust, is held in its honor. During this invocation, all the Guests eat even to the last morsel; after which a man appointed for the purpose takes a cake of tobacco, breaks it in two, and throws it into the fire. Everyone cries aloud as the tobacco burns and the smoke rises aloft; and with these cries the sacrifice ends.

I have seen an idol set up in the middle of a village; and to it, among other presents, ten dogs were offered in sacrifice, in order to prevail on this false god to send elsewhere the disease that was depopulating the Village.

As, moreover, these people are of gross nature, they recognize no purely spiritual divinity, believing that the Sun is a man, and the Moon his wife; that snow and ice are also a man, who goes away in the spring and comes back in the winter; that the evil spirit is in adders, dragons, and other monsters; that the crow, the kite, and some other birds are genii, and speak just as we do; and that there are even people among them who understand the language of birds, as some understand a little that of the French.

They believe, moreover, that the souls of the Departed govern the fishes in the lake; and thus, from earliest times, they have held the immortality, and even the metempsychosis, of the souls of the dead fishes, believing that they pass into other fishes' bodies. Therefore they never throw their bones into the fire, for fear that they will offend these souls, so that they will cease to come into their nets.

They hold in very special veneration a certain fabulous animal which they have never seen except in dreams, and which they call Missibizi, acknowledging it to be a great genius, and offering it sacrifices in order to obtain good sturgeon-fishing.

They also say that the little nuggets of copper which they find at the bottom of the water in the Lake, or in the Rivers emptying into it, are the riches of the Gods who dwell in the depths of the earth. . . .

This part of the lake where we have halted is between two large villages, and forms a sort of centre for all the Nations of these regions, because of its abundance of fish, which constitute the chief part of these peoples' sustenance.

Here we have erected a little Chapel of bark, where my entire occupation is to receive the Algonquin and Huron Christians, and instruct them; baptize and catechise the children; admit the Infidels, who hasten from all directions, attracted by curiosity; and make them see the truths of our faith.

CLAUDE DABLON

Marquette's

Last Journey

Jacques Marquette (1637–1675) had just six years in the western wilds, but he left a cherished and enduring name. Scholarly, chivalrous and compassionate, harried by illness but serene of spirit, this Prince of the Jesuits won the savages to himself if not to Christian doctrine while he found the way into new leagues of the American wilderness.

After serving at the Mission of Sault Ste. Marie, Marquette went on to relieve Ménard at remote La Pointe. Here, from a captured Illinois tribesman, he first learned of the great river Michisipi five days' journey to the west. When the Hurons were driven from Chequamegon Bay by enemy Sioux, Marquette fled with them to the Straits of Mackinac. There he built a new chapel of St. Ignace on the shore of Lake Michigan. And there in the fall of 1672 came Louis Jolliet with instructions that Marquette join him in a search for the Mississippi River. Passing down the Wisconsin in June, 1673, they found the Old Big Deep Strong River, followed it a thousand miles south, and returned to Lake Michigan by way of the Illinois and Chicago rivers.

The next spring Marquette returned to the Illinois country to erect a mission there. After an arduous season among the prairie tribes, illness compelled him to turn "homeward"—to the lonely mission of St. Ignace. The little party made the muddy Chicago portage and followed the eastern shore of Lake Michigan, paddling toward Michilimackinac. Marquette did not live to reach that destination. Journey's end came halfway up the Michigan shore, near the site of present Ludington.

In the *Jesuit Relations,* Volume 59, Father Dablon recorded Marquette's last voyage on the Illinois rivers and Lake Michigan.

FATHER JACQUES MARQUETTE, having promised the Ilinois on his first voyage to them, in 1673, that he would
return to them the following year, to teach them the mysteries of our religion, had much difficulty in keeping his word.
The great hardships of his first voyage had brought upon him a
bloody flux, and had so weakened him that he was giving up the
hope of undertaking a second. However, his sickness decreased;
and, as it had almost entirely abated by the close of the summer
in the following year, he obtained the permission of his superiors
to return to the Ilinois and there begin that fair mission.

He set out for that purpose, in the month of november of the
year 1674, from the bay des puants, with two men, one of whom
had made the former voyage with him. During a month of navigation on the lake of the Ilinois, he was tolerably well; but, as soon as
the snow Began to fall, he was again seized with his bloody flux,
which compelled him to halt in the river which Leads to the Ilinois.
It was there that they constructed a Cabin in which to pass the
winter, amid such inconveniences that, his malady increasing more
and more, he saw clearly that God was granting to him the favor
which he had so many times besought from him; and he even told
his two Companions very plainly that he would certainly die of that
malady, and during that voyage. Duly to prepare his soul, despite
the severe disposition of his Body, he began this so severe winter
sojourn by the retreat of st. ignatius, which he performed with
every feeling of devotion, and many Celestial Consolations; and
then he passed the whole of the remaining time in holding communion with all Heaven,—having, in these deserts, no intercourse
with the earth except, with his two Companions. He confessed
them and administered Communion to them twice in the week, and
exhorted them as much as his strength permitted him. A short time
after christmas, that he might obtain the favor of not dying without
having taken possession of his Dear mission, he invited his Companions to make a novena in honor of the immaculate conception of
the blessed virgin. His prayer was answered, against all human
probability; and his health improving, he prepared himself to go to
the village of the Ilinois as soon as navigation should open,—which
he did with much Joy, setting out for that place on the 29th of
march. He spent eleven Days on the Way, during which time he had
occasion to suffer much, both from his own Illness, from which he
had not entirely recovered, and from the very severe and unfavorable weather.

On at last arriving at the village, he was received as an angel from Heaven. After he had assembled at various times the Chiefs of the nation, with all the old men, that he might sow in their minds the first seeds of the gospel, and after having given Instruction in the Cabins, which were always filled with a great crowd of people, he resolved to address all in public, in a general assembly which he called together in the open Air, the Cabins being too small to contain all the people. It was a beautiful prairie, close to a village, which was Selected for the great Council; this was adorned, after the fashion of the country, by Covering it with mats and bearskins. Then the father, having directed them to stretch out upon Lines several pieces of chinese taffeta, attached to these four large Pictures of the blessed Virgin, which were visible on all sides. The audience was Composed of 500 chiefs and elders, seated in a circle around the father, and of all the Young men, who remained standing. They numbered more than 1,500 men, without counting the women and children, who are always numerous,—the village being Composed of 5 or 600 fires. The father addressed the whole body of people, and conveyed to them 10 messages, by means of ten presents which he gave them. He explained to them the principal mysteries of our Religion, and the purpose that had brought him to their country. Above all, he preached to them Jesus Christ, on the very eve (of that great day) on which he had died upon the Cross for them, as well as for all the rest of mankind; then he said holy mass. On the third Day after, which was easter sunday, things being prepared in the same manner as on Thursday, he celebrated the holy mysteries for the 2nd time; And by these two, the only sacrifices ever offered there to God, he took possession of that land in the name of Jesus Christ, and gave to that mission the name of the Immaculate Conception of the blessed virgin.

He was listened to by all these peoples with universal Joy; and they prayed him with most earnest Entreaty to come back to them as soon as possible, since his sickness obliged him to return. The father, on his side, expressed to them the affection which he felt for them, and the satisfaction that they had given him; and pledged them his word that he, or some other of our fathers would return to Carry on that mission so happily Inaugurated. This promise he repeated several times, while parting with them to go upon his Way; and he set out with so many tokens of regard on the part of Those good peoples that, as a mark of honor they chose to escort him for more than 30 leagues on the Road, vying with each other in taking Charge of his slender baggage.

SECTION 2ND. *The Father Is Compelled to Leave His Ilinois Mission. His Last Illness. His Precious Death in the Heart of the Forest.*

After the Ilinois, filled with great esteem for the gospel, had taken Leave of the father, he Continued his journey, and shortly after reached the lake of the Ilinois, upon whose waters he had to journey nearly a hundred leagues, by an unknown route whereon he had Never before traveled; for he was obliged to coast along the southern Shore of the lake, having come by the northern. But his strength was so rapidly diminishing that his two men despaired of being able to bring him alive to the end of their journey. Indeed, he became so feeble and exhausted that he was unable to assist or even to move himself, and had to be handled and carried about like a child.

Meanwhile, he Preserved in that condition an admirable equanimity, resignation, Joy, and gentleness, consoling his dear Companions and encouraging them to suffer patiently all the hardships of that voyage, in the assurance that God would not abandon them after his death. It was during this voyage that he began to make more special preparation for death. He held Communion, sometimes with our Lord, sometimes with his holy mother, or with his guardian angel, or with all paradise. He was often heard repeating These words: *Credo quod redemptor meus vivit;* or, *maria, mater gratiae, mater dei, memento mei.* In addition to the spiritual exercise, which was read to him every Day, he requested toward the close that they would read to him his meditation preparatory for death, which he carried about with him. He recited every Day his breviary; and although he was so low that his sight and strength were greatly enfeebled, He continued to do so to the last day of his life, despite the remonstrance of his companions.

Eight Days before his death, he was thoughtful enough to prepare the holy water for use during the rest of his illness, in his agony, and at his burial; and he Instructed his Companions how it should be used.

The evening before his death, which was a friday, he told them, very Joyously that it would take place on the morrow. He conversed with them during the whole Day as to what would need to be done for his burial; about the manner in which they should inter him; of the spot that should be chosen for his grave; how his feet, his hands, and his face should be arranged; how they should erect a

Cross over his grave. He even went so Far as to counsel them, 3 hours before he expired, that as soon as he was dead they should take the little Hand-bell of his Chapel, and sound it while he was being put under ground. He spoke of all these things with so great tranquility and presence of mind that one might have supposed that he was concerned with the death and funeral of some other person, and not with his own.

Thus did he converse with them as they made their way upon the lake,—until, having perceived a river, on the shore of which stood an eminence that he deemed well suited to be the place of his interment, he told them that That was the place of his last repose. They wished, however, to proceed farther, as the weather was favorable, and the day was not far advanced; but God raised a Contrary wind, which compelled them to return, and enter the river which the father had pointed out. They accordingly brought him to the land, lighted a little fire for him, and prepared for him a wretched Cabin of bark. They laid him down therein, in the least uncomfortable way that they could; but they were so stricken with sorrow that, as they have since said, they hardly knew what they were doing.

The father, being thus Stretched on the ground in much the same way as was St. Francis Xavier, as he had always so passionately desired, and finding himself alone in the midst of These forests, for his companions were occupied with the disembarkation, he had leisure to repeat all the last acts in which he had continued during these last Days.

His dear companions having afterward joined him, all disconsolate, he Comforted them, and inspired them with the confidence that God would take care of them after his death, in these new and unknown countries. He gave them the last Instructions, thanked them for all the charities which they had exercised in his behalf during the whole journey, and entreated pardon for the trouble that he had given them. He charged them to ask pardon for him also, from all our fathers and brethren who live in the country of the Outaouas. Then he undertook to prepare them for the sacrament of penance, which he administered to them for the last time. He gave them also a paper on which he had written all his faults since his own last Confession, that they might place it in the hands of the father superior that the latter might be enabled to pray to God for him in a more special manner. Finally, he promised not to forget them in Paradise; and, as he was very Considerate, knowing that they were much fatigued with the hardships of the preceeding Days, he bade them go and take a little repose. He assured them that his hour was not yet so very near, and that he would awaken them when the time should come—as, in fact, 2 or 3 hours afterward he did summon them, being ready to enter into the agony.

They drew near to him, and he embraced them once again, while they burst into tears at his feet. Then he asked for holy water and his reliquary; and having himself removed his Crucifix, which he carried always suspended round his neck, he placed it in the hands of one of his Companions, begging him to hold it before his eyes. Then, feeling that he had but a short time to live, he made a last effort, Clasped his hands, and, with a steady and fond look upon his Crucifix, he uttered aloud his profession of faith, and gave thanks to the divine majesty for the great favor which he accorded him of dying in the Society, of dying in it as a missionary of Jesus Christ,—and, above all, of dying in it, as he had always prayed, in a Wretched cabin in the midst of the forests and bereft of all human succor.

After that, he was silent, communing within himself with God. Nevertheless he let escape from time to time these words, *Sustinuit anima mea in verbo ejus;* or these, *Mater Dei, memento mei*— which were the last words he uttered before entering his agony, which was, however, very mild and peaceful.

He prayed his companions to put him in mind, when they should see him about to expire, to repeat frequently the names of Jesus and Mary, if he could not himself do so. They did as they were bidden; and, when they Believed him to be near his end, one of them Called aloud, "Jesus, Mary!" The dying man repeated the words distinctly, several times; and as if, at These sacred names, Something presented itself to him, he Suddenly raised his eyes above his Crucifix, holding them Riveted on that object, which he appeared to regard with pleasure. And so, with a countenance beaming and all aglow, he expired without any Struggle, and so gently that it might have been regarded as a pleasant sleep.

His two poor Companions, shedding many tears over him, composed his Body in the manner which he had prescribed to them. Then they carried him devoutly to burial, ringing the while the little Bell as he had bidden them; and planted a large Cross near his grave, as a sign to passers-by.

When it became a question of embarking, to proceed on their journey, one of the two, who for some Days had been so Heartsick with sorrow, and so greatly prostrated with an internal malady, that he could no longer eat or breathe except with difficulty, bethought himself, while the other was making all preparations for embarking, to visit the grave of his good father, and ask his intercession with the glorious virgin, as he had promised, not doubting in the least that he was in Heaven. He fell, then, upon his knees, made a Short prayer, and having reverently taken some earth from the tomb, he pressed it to his breast. Immediately his sickness Abated, and his sorrow was changed into a Joy which did not forsake him during the remainder of his journey.

SECTION 3RD. *What Occurred at the Removal of the Bones of the Late Father Marquette, Which Were Taken from His Grave on the 19th of May, 1677, the Same Day as That on Which He Died in the Year 1675. A Brief Summary of His Virtues.*

God did not permit that a deposit so precious should remain in the midst of the forest, unhonored and forgotten. The savages named Kiskakons, who have been making public profession of Christianity for nearly ten years, and who were instructed by father Marquette when he lived at the point of st. Espirit, at the extreme of lake superior, carried on their last winter's hunting in the vicinity of the lake of the Illinois. As they were returning in the spring; they were greatly pleased to pass near the grave of their good father, whom they tenderly loved; and God also put it into their hearts to remove his bones and bring them to our church at the mission of st. Ignace at missilmakinac, where those savages make their abode.

They repaired then, to the spot, and resolved among themselves to act in regard to the father as they are Wont to do toward Those for whom they profess great respect. Accordingly, they opened the grave, and uncovered the Body; and, although the Flesh and Internal organs were all Dried up, they found it entire, so that not even the skin was in any way injured. This did not prevent them from proceeding to dissect it, as is their custom. They cleansed the bones and exposed them to the sun to dry; then, carefully laying them in a box of birch-bark, they set out to bring them to our mission of st. Ignace.

There were nearly 30 Canoes which formed, in excellent order, that funeral procession. There were also a goodly number of iroquois, who United with our algonkin savages to lend more honor to the ceremonial. When they drew near our house, father nouvel, who is its superior, with father piercon, went out to meet them, accompanied by the frenchmen and savages who were there; and having halted the Procession, he put the usual questions to them, to make sure that It was really the father's body which they were bringing. Before conveying it to land, they Intoned the *de profundis* in the presence of the 30 Canoes, which were still on the water, and of the people who were on the shore. After that, the Body was carried to the church, care being taken to observe all that the ritual appoints in such ceremonies. It remained exposed under the pall, all that Day, which was whitsun-monday, the 8th of June; and on the morrow, after having rendered to it all the funeral rites, it was lowered into a small Vault in the middle of the church, where it rests as the guardian angel of our Outaouas missions. The savages often come to pray over his tomb.

Voyage

of the *Griffin*

The first commercial vessel on the Great Lakes carried three notable men to the heart of North America. When the *Griffin* sailed into Lake Erie on an August day in 1679, La Salle, Tonty and Hennepin were at the beginning of their great journeys in the wilderness.

It was La Salle's expedition, with a threefold purpose—to tap the rich fur trade on Lake Michigan, to explore the Mississippi valley, and to extend New France from Canada to the Gulf of Mexico by a chain of forts and trading stations. So the brig *Griffin*, forty-five tons, named for the leader's coat-of-arms, was built on the Niagara River near the mouth of Lake Erie. It was the first sailing vessel to steer a course on the upper lakes.

Standing at the rail, Father Louis Hennepin wore a coarse gray robe with pointed hood; his feet were sandaled and from his waist-cord swung crucifix and rosary. He was thirty-seven years old, a restless Récollet friar, a priest with the heart of an adventurer. Hennepin was Flemish and no friend of the Jesuits. A stranger to humility and sacrifice, he was hardy, courageous and headstrong, zealous for action and jealous of fame.

He had the good fortune to realize all his ambitions. Like the gentle and chivalrous Marquette, this vain friar was in the path of great undertakings. On that August day he was beginning an adventure beyond even his boldest expectations—discovery of many wonders, captivity among savage tribesmen and eventual fame in Europe as the author of *A Description of Louisiana* and *A New Discovery of a Vast Country in America*.

His first book, written in the Récollet convent at St. Germain-en-Laye in 1682, was an exciting narrative with vivid pictures of the American wilderness and its savage tribes. In 1697 he enlarged upon his adventures in *A New Discovery*, making impossible claims for himself and appropriating material from other explorers. But his book was full of absorbing interest and information.

In both volumes Hennepin narrated the voyage of the *Griffin*. The first account, in *A Description of Louisiana*, was more direct and concise than the other. Here it is, with unfamiliar names ["Lake Frontenac" for Lake Ontario, "Lake Conty" for Lake Erie, "Lake Orleans" for Lake Huron, "Lake Condé" for Lake Superior, "Lake Dauphin" for Lake Michigan] but with plainly recognizable seas, rivers, bays and islands.

WE EMBARKED to the number of thirty-two persons, with our two Recollect Fathers who had come to join me, our people having laid in a good supply of arms, merchandise, and seven small iron cannon.

At last, contrary to the pilot's opinion we succeeded in ascending Niagara river. He made his bark advance by sails when the wind was strong enough, and he had it towed in the most difficult places, and thus we happily reached the entrance of Lake Conty.

We made sail the 7th of the month of August, in the same year 1679, steering west by south. After the "Te Deum" we fired all the cannon and wall pieces, in presence of several Iroquois warriors who were bringing in prisoners from the nations on the prairies, situated more than five hundred leagues from their country, and these savages did not neglect to give a description of the size of our vessel to the Dutch of New York, with whom the Iroquois carry on a great trade in furs, which they carry to them in order to obtain fire arms and goods to clothe themselves.

Our voyage was so fortunate that on the morning of the tenth day, the feast of Saint Lawrence, we reached the entrance of the Detroit (strait) by which Lake Orleans empties into Lake Conty, and which is one hundred leagues distant from Niagara river. This strait is thirty leagues long and almost everywhere a league wide, except in the middle where it expands and forms a lake of circular form, and ten leagues in diameter, which we called Lake St. Clare, on account of our passing through it on that Saint's day.

The country on both sides of this beautiful strait is adorned with fine open plains, and you can see numbers of stags, does, deer, bears, by no means fierce and very good to eat, poules d'inde and all kinds of game, swans in abundance. Our guys were loaded and decked with several wild animals cut up, which our Indian and our Frenchmen killed. The rest of the strait is covered with forests, fruit trees like walnuts, chestnuts, plum and apple trees, wild vines loaded with grapes, of which we made some little wine. There is timber fit for building. It is the place in which deer most delight.

We found the current at the entrance of this strait as strong as the tide is before Rouen. We ascended it nevertheless, steering north and northeast, as far as Lake Orleans. There is little depth as you enter and leave Lake St. Clare, especially as you leave it. The discharge from Lake Orleans divides at this place into several small channels, almost all barred by sandbanks. We were obliged to sound them all, and at last discovered a very fine one, with a depth of at least two or three fathoms of water, and almost a league wide at all points. Our bark was detained here several days by head winds and this difficulty having been surmounted, we encountered a still greater one at the entrance of Lake Orleans, the north wind which had been blowing some time rather violently, and which drives the waters of the three great lakes into the strait, had so increased the ordinary current there, that it was as furious as the bore is before Caudebec. We could not stem it under sail, although we were then aided by a strong south wind; but as the shore was very fine, we landed twelve of our men who towed it along the beach for half a quarter of an hour, at the end of which we entered Lake Orleans on the 23d of the month of August, and for the second time we chanted a Te Deum in thanksgiving, blessing God, who here brought us in sight of a great bay in this lake, where our ancient Recollects had resided to instruct the Hurons in the faith, in the first landing of the French in Canada, and these Indians once very numerous have been for the most part destroyed by the Iroquois.

The same day the bark ran along the east coast of the lake, with a fair wind, heading north by east, till evening when the wind having shifted to southwest with great violence, we headed northwest, and the next day we found ourselves in sight of land, having crossed by night a great bay, called Sakinam, [Saginaw] which sets in more than thirty leagues.

On the 24th we continued to head northwest till evening, when we were becalmed among some islands, where here was only a fathom and a half or two fathoms of water. We kept on with the lower sails a part of the night to seek an anchorage, but finding none where there was a good bottom and the wind beginning to blow from the west, we headed north so as to gain deep water and wait for day, and we spent the night in sounding before the bark, because we had noticed that our pilot was very negligent, and we continued to watch in this way during the rest of the voyage.

On the 25th the calm continued till noon, and we pursued our course to the northwest, favored by a good southerly wind, which soon changed to southwest. At midnight we were compelled to head north on account of a great Point which jutted out into the lake; but we had scarcely doubled it, when we were surprised by a furious gale, which forced us to ply to windward with mainsail and foresail, then to lie to till daylight.

On the 26th the violence of the wind obliged us to lower the topmasts, to fasten the yards at the clew, to remain broadside to the shore. At noon the waves running too high, and the sea too rough, we were forced to seek a port in the evening, but found no anchorage or shelter. At this crisis, the Sieur de la Salle entered the cabin, and quite disheartened told us that he commended his enterprise to God. We had been accustomed all the voyage to induce all to say morning and evening prayers together on our knees, all singing some hymns of the church, but as we could not stay on the deck of the vessel, on account of the storm, all contented themselves with making an act of contrition. There was no one but our pilot alone, whom we were never able to persuade.

At this time the Sieur de la Salle adopted in union with us Saint Anthony of Padua as the protector of our enterprises and he promised God if He did us the grace to deliver us from the tempest, that the first chapel he should erect in Louisiana should be dedicated to that great Saint.

The wind having fallen a little we lay to, all the night and we drifted only a league or two at most.

On the morning of the 27th we sailed northwest with a southwest wind, which changed towards evening into a light southeast trade wind, by favor of which we arrived on the same day at Missilimakinac, where we anchored in six fathoms of water in a bay, where there was a good bottom of potter's clay. This bay is sheltered from southwest to north, a sand bank covers it a little on the northeast, but it is exposed to the south which is very violent.

Missilimakinac is a point of land at the entrance and north of the strait, by which Lake Dauphin empties into Lake Orleans. This strait is a league wide and three long, and runs west northwest. Fifteen leagues east of Missilimakinac you find another point which is at the entrance of the channel by which Lake Condé empties into Lake Orleans. This channel has an opening of five leagues, and is fifteen in length. It is interspersed with several islands, and gradually narrows in down to Sault Sainte Marie, which is a rapid full of rocks, by which the waters of Lake Condé are discharged and are precipitated in a violent manner. Nevertheless they succeed in poling canoes up one side near the land, but for greater security a portage is made of the canoe and the goods which they take to sell to the nations north of Lake Condé.

There are Indian villages in these two places; those who are settled at Missilimakinac, on the day of our arrival, which was August 26th, 1679, were all amazed to see a ship in their country, and the sound of the cannon caused an extraordinary alarm. We went to the Outtaoüactz to say mass and during the service, the Sieur de la Salle, very well dressed in his scarlet cloak trimmed with gold lace, ordered the arms to be stacked along the chapel and the sergeant left a sentry there to guard them. The chiefs of the Outtaoüactz paid us their civility in their fashion, on coming out of the church. And in this bay where the Griffin was riding at anchor, we looked with pleasure at this large well equipped vessel, amid a hundred or a hundred and twenty bark canoes coming and going from taking white fish, which these Indians catch with nets, which they stretch sometimes in fifteen or twenty fathoms of water, and without which they could not subsist.

The Hurons who have their village surrounded by palisades twenty-five feet high and situated near a great point of land opposite the island of Missilimakimac, proved the next day that they were more French then the Outtaoüactz, but it was in show, for they gave a salute by discharging all their guns, and they all have them, and renewed it three times, to do honor to our ship, and to the French, but this salute had been suggested to them by some Frenchmen, who come there, and who often carry on a very considerable trade with these nations, and who designed to gain the Sieur de la Salle by this show, as he gave umbrage to them, only in order better to play their parts subsequently by making it known that the bark was going to be the cause of destruction to individuals, in order to render the one who had built her odious to the people.

The Hurons and the Outtaoüactz form alliances with one another in order to oppose with one accord the fury of the Iroquois, their sworn enemy. They cultivate Indian corn on which they live all the year, with the fish which they take to season their sagamity. This they make of water and meal of their corn which they crush with a pestle in a trunk of a tree hollowed out by fire.

The Indians of Sainte Marie du Long Sault are called by us the Saulteurs on account of the place of their abode, which is near the Sault, and where they subsist by hunting stags, moose or elk, and some beaver, and by the fishing of white fish, which is very good, and is found there in great abundance, but this fishery is very difficult to all but these Indians who are trained to it from childhood. These latter do not plant any Indian corn as their soil is not adapted to it, and the fogs on Lake Condé which are very frequent, stifle all the corn that they might be able to plant.

Sault Ste. Marie and Missilimakinac are the two most important passes for all the Indians of the west and north who go to carry all their furs to the French settlements and to trade every year at Montreal with more than two hundred loaded canoes.

During our stay at Missilimakinac, we were extremely surprised to find there the greater part of the men whom the Sieur de la Salle had sent on ahead to the number of fifteen, and whom he believed to be long since at the Illinois. Those whom he had known as the most faithful, reported to him that they had been stopped by the statements made to them on their way at Missilimakinac; that they had been told that his enterprise was only chimerical, that the bark would never reach Missilimakinac, that he was sending them to certain destruction, and several other things of the kind, which had discouraged and seduced most of their comrades, and that they had been unable to induce them to continue their voyage; that six of them had even deserted and carried off more than 3,000 livres worth of goods, under the pretext of paying themselves, saying that they would restore the surplus over what was due them, and that the others had stupidly wasted more than twelve hundred livres worth, or spent it for their support at Missilimakinac, where they had been detained, and where provisions are very dear.

The Sieur de la Salle was all the more provoked at this conduct of his men, as he had treated them well, and made some advances to all, among the rest having paid on account of one of them 1200 livres that he owed various persons at Montreal. He had four of the most guilty arrested without giving them any harsher treatment. Having learned that two of the six deserters were at Sault Sainte Marie, he detached the Sieur de Tonty with six men who arrested them and seized all the goods which they had in their hands, but he could not obtain any justice as to the others. The high winds at this season long retarded the return of the Sieur de Tonty, who did not reach Missilimakinac till the month of November, so that we were dreading the approach of winter and resolved to set out without waiting till he arrived.

On the 2nd of the month of September, from Missilimakinac we entered Lake Dauphin, and arrived at an island situated at the entrance of the Lake or Bay of the Puants, forty leagues from Missilimakinac, and which is inhabited by Indians of the Poutouatami nation. We found some Frenchmen there, who had been sent among the Illinois in previous years, and who had brought back to the Sieur de la Salle a pretty fair amount of furs.

The chief of this nation who had all possible affection for the Count de Frontenac, who had entertained him at Montreal, received us as well as he could, had the calumet danced to the Sieur de la Salle by his warriors; and during four days' storm while our vessel was anchored thirty paces from the bay shore, this Indian chief believing that our bark was going to be stranded, came to join us in a canoe at the risk of his life and in spite of the increasing waves, we hoisted him with his canoe into our vessel. He told us in a martial tone that he was ready and wished to perish with the children of Onnontio, the Governor of the French, his good father and friend.

Contrary to our opinion, the Sieur de la Salle who never took any one's advice, resolved to send back his bark from this place and to continue his route by canoe, but as he had only four, he was obliged to leave considerable merchandise in the bark, a quantity of utensils and tools. He ordered the pilot to discharge every thing at Missilimakinac, where he could take them again on his return. He also put all the peltries in the bark with a clerk and five good sailors. Their orders were to proceed to the great fall of Niagara, where they were to leave the furs, and take on board other goods which another bark from Fort Frontenac, which awaited them near Fort Conty was to bring them, and that as soon as possible thereafter, they should sail back to Missilimakinac, where they would find instructions as to the place to which they should bring the bark to winter.

They set sail on the 18th of September, with a very favorable light west wind, making their adieu by firing a single cannon; and we were never afterwards able to learn what course they had taken, and though there is no doubt, but that she perished, we were never able to learn any other circumstances of their shipwreck than the following. The bark having anchored in the north of Lake Dauphin, the pilot against the opinion of some Indians, who assured him that there was a great storm in the middle of the lake, resolved to continue his voyage, without considering that the sheltered position where he lay, prevented his knowing the force of the wind. He had scarcely sailed a quarter of a league from the coast, when these Indians saw the bark tossing in an extraordinary manner, unable to resist the tempest, so that in a short time they lost sight of her, and they believe that she was either driven on some sandbank, or that she foundered.

The Golden Age

of the Canoe

After 1759, their year of disaster, the French had no more empire in America. But the fur trade was a French enterprise, and there were still Frenchmen and halfbreeds at the posts and depots on the Lakes. When British ships came up the St. Lawrence and Scotch merchants enlarged the warehouses at Three Rivers and Montreal, the fur trade revived and expanded. Then came the golden age of the canoe.

Historian and naturalist, Henry Beston (1888–1968), with a life-long interest in the province of Quebec and its people, has looked back at the early routes of trade and travel, and at the hardy canoemen who toiled over portages and dipped their paddles into westward-flowing water. These pages are taken from *The St. Lawrence*, 1942.

THE "CANOE" we know today, though in a general sense the gift of the Algonquin tribes of the northeast, is more particularly a Chippewa creation, a Chippewa masterpiece. Living in the heart of the old canoe-birch country, every man of the nation with his eye and mark on some great tree, the tribe united as no other a special skill in design with the finest of materials. The lovely curve of bow and stern remains for us their sign. Every Indian nation of the birch region had its own native and tenacious image of that bold symmetry. Some made of it a quasi-perpendicular, some put the depth here, others there: a stranger could be placed by the line of his canoe as easily as by the cut of his moccasins. To the Chippewas alone was reserved the sense of the curve in its perfection, in its unique and beautiful rightness. Strong, well-made, capable of carrying heavy loads yet easy to portage, the Chippewa model like the covered wagon is a part of the history of the continent.

This was the craft which was to make possible the opening and mapping of something like a fourth of North America. In celebrating the covered wagon we have forgotten a little this episode of the canoe. Enlarged by its Indian builders for the fur trade of the old Canadian northwest, it kept its Chippewa character and strength, making itself a vessel for cargoes and crews without losing one touch of its old beauty of design.

Three principal types were in use in the trade. The great Montreal canoe or *canot du maître,* intended for use on the larger lakes and more navigable streams could be anywhere between thirty and forty-five feet long. Such a vessel could carry tons of furs eastward from the posts. Fourteen men made up the crew. The north canoe, or *canot du nord,* was a smaller type; built for use in the wilderness itself, it averaged twenty-five feet in length and carried a crew of eight. Between these familiar models stood an intermediate third, the bastard, or *le bâtard,* which carried a crew of ten. Small canoes such as we know today were also everywhere in use. To judge by many old pictures and sketches, sails were sometimes rigged, being most probably raised up on occasions when it was possible to "sail before the wind" in light airs.

The canoe workshops remained in the birch country and on the Lakes. Once built, the canoes of the trade went in for that liveliness of color which is so good for the soul. It was not for nothing that the later eighteenth century had rediscovered and enlarged the bright possibilities of paint. Gunwales were festooned or spaced in green and white or in red and white, and there was almost invariably a design of some kind—an Indian head, a bear, a sun or a moon with features, clasped hands—painted bow and stern. The paddles of strong red cedar were also painted with stripes and gaieties.

A carry down the beach into the placid water of some cove and the craft was ready for its man. He was at hand. Hardy and enduring as few strains have been in history, unwashed, merry, and famously polite, short of legs and powerful of shoulder, pure French now, and now half-Indian, the canoe had already invented its own human being, the woods their man, the legendary and incomparable voyageur.

III

Westward beyond the great horizons of Superior, westward beyond the strange, jade-green waters and the tense yet empty wind, westward a thousand and even a long two thousand miles away, the forts and stations of the fur companies stood in the immense solitudes of the forest. From the dying out of the great plains north to the arctic barrens, from the Lakes west to the mountain descents to the Pacific, the wilderness spread wide over a solitude of the continent, a region of lakes and woods, rapids and rushing rivers, bogs and quaking swamps and mountains without a name. Within, there lay hidden a complexity, some valleys and forest floors teeming with life, others strangely with scarce a sign of any thing alive. Till the arrival of the fur trade, nothing which was not a part of nature disturbed a quiet of nature widespread and empty as the sky. Only the nomad Indians of the American north, the Dene, the hardy Chippewa, the Crees, and the western Montagnais were a part of its existence, crossing it with scarce the bending of a branch or a footprint in the leaves.

A great skein of waterways leading west and north out of Lake Superior was the gateway to the mystery. Indians had been the first to use the passage, tying river to lake and lake to river again, and the French had been aware of it since 1731, La Verendrye and his guides having gone in as far as the Lac des Bois.

By the end of the eighteenth century, the fur trade had chosen and made customary a great passage to the woods known as the "Great Trace." It began at Montreal with the waters above Lachine, and entering the Ottawa ascended that stream of many portages to the Mattawa, a tributary flowing from the west. This in turn led to Lake Nipissing, and from Nipissing, hailing with a cheer a westward-flowing stream, the voyageurs descended to Georgian Bay and the waters of the Lakes. The charming island of Michilimackinac, depot and administrative station of the trade upon the Lakes, next awaited the adventurers: here the "brigades" going into the deeper wilderness separated from those bound to nearer posts. So distant were many stations that it took the best of summer to arrive, and the voyageurs wintered at the forts.

All summer long the pretty island was a scene of bustle and activity. Goods were transshipped, crews sorted out and reassembled, the sick attended to, and canoes repaired. Standing on the heights at night, looking out into the vast darkness above Huron, one could see fires burning all up and down the lower beach, each glow of fire crowded close about with its own company.

For those bound north and west, the next great station was Grand Portage on the western shore of Superior. (It is today a town in Minnesota just below the Canadian frontier.) Here nine miles of rapids on the St. Francis River made necessary a long carry. In the great days of the trade homemade roads had been built at the carry, and a score of wagons and several hundred horses assisted the voyageur crews to move their goods and canoes to the navigable waters. Ahead lay the entering chain of lake and river widenings, the Lac du Bois Blanc, the Lac de la Pluie, the Lac des Bois, and, ultimately, the great lake "Ouinnipique." Beyond lay the unknown, the white streams and the forest-brown, the named and the unnamed, the peaceful and the perilous. At dangerous rapids there were always crosses to be seen against the forest wall, each with its voyageur's cap fading in the sun.

Standing near the greater portages and by the junctions of streams, the forts of the trade awaited their first arriving hail.

Each had its chief, or *bourgeois*, usually a Scot, each its tally-men, clerks, and accountants, each its population forever changing and mingling, of trappers and hunters, half-breed children and Indian wives, voyageurs, scouts, and forest adventurers. The Indians and half-breeds were usually the trappers, taking the animals in winter when the pelts were at their best. In the spring, bands would arrive with their catch, the furs hanging behind them from their shoulders. Such a population lived as it could. Now buffalo meat and deer went into the pot, now flour, grease, wild rice, and a bear's haunch all cooked together into some hearty Indian mess. (An Indian stew can last for years, seemingly recreating itself miraculously from the bottom of the pot.) With nothing but the forest about it for a thousand miles the fort lived its vigorous life of direct contacts, slept in its blankets and buckskins, drank its rum, smoked its tobacco, wrestled out its male rivalries, listened to its interminable Indian legends, and married "according to the custom of the country." Parentage could be vague. "*Que voulez-vous?* What d'ye want, laddie?" said one Scot trader to an Indian boy. "*Monsieur,*" replied the youngster with gravity, "*vous êtes mon père.*"

French was the common tongue. Wild and outlandish as such a life must have been it is clear that it did not become barbarous. The natural good manners and sociability of the French Canadian kept it all a remarkably good-tempered adventure. It was with a gesture of politeness that one was offered a little more of the bear.

With portages to make and currents to battle, with loads of supplies to carry in and heavy furs to carry out, with the wilderness for a country and elemental danger ever near, the life of a voyageur was no adventure for the weak. In good weather and when not fighting a wind or a stream a crew could paddle fantastic distances. Between earliest dawn and summer's dark, canoes often managed sixty, seventy or even eighty miles. One observer speaks of about forty strokes of the paddle to the minute—a brisk rhythm and speed. Two meals a day were eaten and after a hard carry, a third. They ate everything. Pemmican, fish, birds' eggs and almost any kind of bird, hawks among them, squirrels, porcupines, dough cakes and grease dumplings—all these were downed with relish by the evening fire.

The contemporaries of the voyageurs who accompanied them on their expeditions above all remembered the singing of the crews. Mile after mile they sang, singing together with the thrust of their swift strokes, the gay, choral sound echoing back upon them from the enclosing walls of the forest or floating off across the stillness of lakes into the north and the unknown. It was ever a cheerful sound, a sound of labor and the human spirit, a music of the body's good will and the heart's content. Old ballads and songs of France made up the substance of the singing, most of them unchanged in verse or tune, though now and then a wind from the spruces had blown across a song making it more Canadian in its language and mood. It is a man's world which is here reflected; its concerns are going courting, the formal elegancies of wooing, the pains of youth and broken hearts, and noble and ceremonious farewells. Nothing can exceed their decorum. To this pleasant and old-fashioned treasury the voyageur came in time to add new songs of his own but the old songs remained his favorites. If they were not Canadian in the beginning, he made them Canadian by adding himself.

So the cavaliers bow, sweeping off their seventeenth century hats to tunes made for harpsichords, the lover laments, and the soldier returns from the wars. And all the while the forest passes by, the white water rolls over the rock, the sides of the canoe scrape with a rasp through the pitcher plants, and the paddles dip and thrust and rise gleaming together in the sun.

IV

No adventure of the Canadian past so stirred the heart as the departure of the voyageurs from their depot at Lachine. One came upon them in the busy spring, some camping by the river in the open fields, Montreal and its church bells behind them to the east, and before them the afternoon sun and the adventure of the west. For days before the embarkation wagons had been arriving with their loads, rolling through the farming villages and deepening the ruts and puddles with their weight of trade goods, provisions and supplies. In and out of the offices and wharves, busy at a hundred tasks, yet always finding a moment to toss back a jest, swarmed the adventurers, a whole French-Canadian countryside of Gaspards,

Aurèles, Onesimes, and Hippolytes. There was much to be done. Here, on the beach, men crouched by a canoe making some last repair, here clerks scrambled over boxes and bags checking and rechecking the trading goods, the trinkets, beads, axes, knives, awls, blankets, and bolts of bright red English flannel, here an official studied the enlistment papers of some new engagé. At a counter to one side, a crowd selected the shirts, trousers, handkerchiefs, and blankets due them from the company, Iroquois Indians from Caughnawaga, famous paddlemen, reaching in and seizing with the rest. Late in the afternoon, those who were quiet over a pipe could hear the eternal murmur of the miles of rapids, and the floating, clanging summons of the Angelus.

The moment of departure waited upon weather and the wind. To prevent a last and too-thirsty festival of farewell, efforts were sometimes made to conceal the probable day, but men concerned have sixth sense in these matters, and the world was apt to share the secret, and all Montreal, finding the morning fair, came to say good-bye. Ladies with escorts watched from the shores, British officers, mounted on English horseflesh rode to good places in the fields, British soldiers even, their flaxen hair and blue Sussex eyes a new note in the throng, strolled in pairs among the Indians. Citizens and citizenesses, wives and children, parents and kin, company directors and curés—all these were at hand to see the start. It was early May, and the Montreal country had left winter behind and was taking courage in the spring; on far shores and near, under the cool wind, appeared the green.

In and out of the press, heroes of the occasion, moved the voyageurs. Old hands and new, it was their day. Even the young Scot clerks who were to go as passengers to the forts shared the importance and the glory. Custom demanding that the beginning and end of a journey should be carried off in style, every voyageur was dressed in the best he had. A woolen tunic or long shirt worn outside and belted about with a bright, home woven sash—the charming, old-fashioned ceinture flèchee—Indian leggings or even homespun trousers, a red knitted cap, and heavy-duty Indian moccasins —this was the costume. A beaded Indian pouch worn at the waist, Iroquois or Chippewa work, was a particular *sine qua non:* indeed, all veterans were engayed with Indian finery. Voyageurs belonging to the governor or chief factor's brigade had feathers in their caps. Often a small British flag was flown from each canoe. The fleet sailed by "brigades," by groups under one command, and these kept together, maneuvering with careful paddles in the current falling to the Lachine. Are all afloat, all loaded, all officers and passengers in their seats? Then go! Church bells rang, guns were fired, and on the broad river paddles dipped and thrust forward in a first strong, beautiful and rhythmic swing. At the same moment the river covered itself with singing. The fleet beginning to open, the brigades sorting out, one could see nothing but canoes for miles, hundreds upon hundreds of the laden craft all striking as one into the purplish-brown waters of the Ottawa.

At the northwestern corner of Montreal Island stood a church of Ste. Anne, patroness of sailors and of voyageurs. Here the brigades made a first halt and landing, the paddlemen and bowsmen, the steersmen, clerks and passengers all trooping up from the beach to pray for a safe voyage and a safe return. It was the custom to make some small offering, and the Scot Presbyterians it is said, made theirs in propriety with the rest. Soon they were all of them on the river again, the church hidden by some turn of the stream, some brigades falling into their measure and stroke, some out of high spirits leaping ahead with a song. "En roulant, ma boule, roulant," and out of sight they go. Thrust by thrust, by quiet waters and by furious streams, through the summer plague of the stinging flies and the blessed coming of the early cold, the paddles will swing across the half of a continent, making their way into the forest, into the land of Keewaytin, the northwest wind, the ancient land where nothing has changed since the beginning of the world.

To the Big

Sea Water

Explorer, ethnologist, and wilderness diplomat, Henry Rowe Schoolcraft (1793–1864) served for twenty years as Indian agent on the Northwestern frontiers, living first at Sault Ste. Marie and later on Mackinac Island. During the long winters in that country he was a scholar, poring over Indian lore and languages and writing his *Algic Researches* that gave Longfellow the material for *The Song of Hiawatha*. When spring unlocked the waters he was a traveler, on his way to government councils, Indian camps and remote trading stations. He knew the lakes and rivers like a *vóyageur*.

The journeys he liked best were on Lake Superior, the Big Sea Water of the Algonquins. The vast cold lake and its noble shoreline stirred his deepest feelings. Everything about the "blue profound" of Superior moved him, except its name; and he tried to replace that empty designation of the "upper lake" with something better. He liked the Ojibway *Gitchegomee*, but felt that it needed some form of elision to come into popular use. His proposal was *Algoma*, which would properly designate the "Sea of the Algonquins." But this sonorous name, like a bell ringing over tossing water, never caught on.

In the summer of 1831 Schoolcraft led an expedition to the tribes on the southern shore of Lake Superior and along the upper Mississippi. With him went his brother James L. Schoolcraft, his brother-in-law George Johnston who was in charge of the Chippewa sub-agency at La Pointe, young Dr. Douglass Houghton—to vaccinate the Indians—a Detroit printer named Melancthon Woolsey, and a detail of troops, under Lt. Robert Clary, along with guides, interpreters and *voyageurs*.

The narrative is taken from *Personal Memoirs of a Residence of Thirty Years with the Indian Tribes on the American Frontiers,* 1851.

LAKE SUPERIOR lay before us. He who, for the first time, lifts his eyes upon this expanse, is amazed and delighted at its magnitude. Vastness is the term by which it is, more than any other, described. Clouds robed in sunshine, hanging in fleecy or nebular masses above—a bright, pure illimitable plain of water—blue mountains, or dim islands in the distance—a shore of green foliage on the one hand—a waste of waters on the other. These are the prominent objects on which the eye rests. We are diverted by the flight of birds, as on the ocean. A tiny sail in the distance reveals the locality of an Indian canoe. Sometimes there is a smoke on the shore. Sometimes an Indian trader returns with the avails of his winter's traffic. A gathering storm or threatening wind arises. All at once the *voyageurs* burst out into one of their simple and melodious boat-songs, and the gazing at vastness is relieved and sympathy at once awakened in gayety. Such are the scenes that attend the navigation of this mighty but solitary body of water. That nature has created such a scene of magnificence merely to look at, is contrary to her usual economy. The sources of a busy future commerce lie concealed, and but half concealed, in its rocks. Its depths abound in fish, which will be eagerly sought, and even its forests are not without timber to swell the objects of a future commerce. If the plough is destined to add but little to its wealth, it must be recollected that the labors of the plough are most valuable where the area suitable for its dominion is the smallest. But even the prairies of the West are destined to waft their superabundance here.

We passed the lengthened shores which give outline to Taquimenon Bay. We turned the long and bleak peninsula of White Fish Point, and went on to the sandy margin of Vermilion Bay. Here we encamped at three o'clock in the afternoon, and waited all the next day for the arrival of Lieut. Robert Clary and his detachment of men, from Fort Brady, who were to form a part of the expedition. With him was expected a canoe, under the charge of James L. Schoolcraft, with some supplies left behind, and an express mail. They both arrived near evening on the 28th, and thus the whole expedition was formed and completed, and we were prepared to set out with the latest mail. Mr. Holliday came in from his wintering grounds about the same time, and we left Vermilion Bay at four o'clock on the morning of June 29th, J. L. S. in his light canoe, and chanting Canadians from Sault Ste. Marie, and we for the theatre of our destination.

We went about forty miles along a shore exclusively sandy, and encamped at five o'clock in the evening at Grand Marais. This is a striking inlet in the coast, which has much enlarged itself within late years, owing to the force of the north-west storms. It exhibits a striking proof of lake action. The next day we passed the naked and high dunes called Grand Sable, and the stormbeaten and impressive horizontal coast of the Pictured Rocks, and encamped at Grand Island, a distance of about 130 miles. I found masses of gypsum and small veins of calcareous spar imbedded in the sandstone rock of the point of Grand Sable. Ironsand exists in consolidated layers at the cliff called Doric Rock.

The men and boats were now in good traveling trim, and we went on finely but leisurely, examining such features in the natural history as Dr. Houghton, who had not been *here* before, was anxious to see. On the 1st of July, we encamped at Dead River, from whence I sent forward a canoe with a message, and wampum, and tobacco, to Gitchee Iauba, the head chief of Ancekewywenon, requesting him to send a canoe and four men to supply the place of an equal number from the Sault Ste. Marie, sent back, and to accompany me in my voyage as far as *La Pointe*.

GEOLOGY.—We spent the next day in examining the magnesian and calcareous rubblestone which appears to constitute strata resting against and upon the serpentine rock of Presque Isle. This rock is highly charged with what appears to be chromate of iron. We examined the bay behind this peninsula, which appears to be a harbor capable of admitting large vessels. We ascended a conical hill rising from the bay, which the Indians call *Totösh*, or Breast Mountain. Having been the first to ascend its apex, the party named it Schoolcraft's Mountain. Near and west of it, is a lower saddle-shaped mountain, called by the natives The Cradle Top. Granite Point exhibits trap dykes in syenite. The horizontal red sandstone, which forms the peninsula connecting this point with the main, rests against and upon portions of the granite, showing its subsidence from water at a period subsequent to the upheaval of the syenite and trap. This entire coast, reaching from Chocolate River to Huron Bay—a distance of some seventy miles—consists of granite hills, which, viewed from the top of the Totösh, has the rolling appearance of the sea in violent motion. Its chief value must result from its minerals, of which iron appears to constitute an important item.

We reached Huron River on the 4th of July about three o'clock in the afternoon, having come on with a fine wind. At this place we met Mr. Aitkin's brigade of boats, seven in number, with the year's hunts of the Fond du Lac department. I landed and wrote official notes to the Sault Ste. Marie and to Washington, acquainting the government with my progress, and giving intelligence of the state of the Indians.

TRADERS' BOATS.—Mr. Aitkin reports that a great number of the Indians died of starvation, at his distant posts, during the winter, owing to the failure of the wild rice. That he collected for his own use but eight bushels, instead of about as many hundreds. That he had visited Gov. Simpson at Pembina, and found the latter unwilling to make any arrangements on the subject of discontinuing the sale of whisky to the Indians. That I was expected by the Indians on the Upper Mississippi, in consequence of the messages sent in, last fall. That efforts continue to be made by the agent at St. Peters, to draw the Chippewas to that post, notwithstanding the bloodshed and evils resulting from such visits. That a hard opposition in trade has been manifested by the Hudson's Bay Company. That they have given out medals to strengthen and increase their influence with our Indians. And that liquor is required to oppose them at Pembina, War Road, Rainy Lake, Vermilion Lake and Grand Portage.

DOG AND PORCUPINE.—While at Huron River, we saw a lost dog left ashore, who had been goaded by hunger to attack a porcupine. The quills of the latter were stuck thickly into the sides of the nose and head of the dog. Inflammation had taken place, rendering the poor beast an object of pity and disgust.

BURROWING BIRDS.—At Point Aux Beignes (Pancake Point) one of the men caught a kingfisher by clapping his hand over an orifice in the bank. He also took from its nest six eggs. The bank was perforated by numbers of these orifices. At this point we observed the provisions of our advance canoe, put *in cache*, to lighten it for the trip down the bay. Leaving Mr. G. Johnston and Mr. Melancthon Woolsey at this point to await the return of the canoe, I proceeded to Cascade, or, as it is generally called, Little Montreal River. Johnston and Woolsey came up during the night. Next morning an Indian came from a lodge, leading a young otter by a string. The animal played about gracefully, but we had no temptation to purchase him with our faces set to the wilderness. At the latter place, which is on a part of the Sandybay of Graybeast River, the trap formation, which is the copper-bearing rock, is first seen. This rock, which forms the great peninsula of Kewywenon, rises into cliffs on this bay, which at the elevation called Mammels by the

French, deserve the name of mountains. Portions of this rock, viewed in extenso, are overlaid by amygdaloid and rubblestone—the latter of which forms a remarkable edging to the formation, in some places, on the northwest shore, that makes a canal, as at the Little Marrias.

KEWEENA PENINSULA.—We were six days in coasting around this peninsula, which is highly metalliferous. At some points we employed the blast, to ascertain the true character and contents of the soil. At others we went inland, and devoted the time in exploring its range and extent. We examined the outstanding isolated vein of carbonate of copper, called *Roche Vert* by the French. In seeking for its connection on the main shore, I discovered the black oxide in the same vein. In the range of the greenstone about two leagues south of this point, a vein of native copper, with ores and veinstones, was observed, and specimens taken.

The N. W. coast of the peninsula is greatly serrated and broken, abounding in little bays and inlets, and giving proofs of the terrible action of the storms on this rugged shore.

Notes of these examinations and of a trip inland were made, which cannot here be referred to more particularly.

UNFLEDGED DUCKS.—The men had rare and very exciting sport, in coasting around the peninsula, in catching the young of the onzig—which is the sawbill. In the early part of the month of July, the wings of the young are not sufficiently developed to enable them to fly. They will run on the water, flapping their unfledged wings, with great speed, but the gay Frenchmen, shouting at the top of their lungs, would propel their canoes so as to overtake them whenever the little fugitives could not find some nook in the rock to hide in. They chased down one day thirteen in this way, which were found a most tender and delicate dish. The excitement in these chases was extreme. At the *Grand Marrias* (now near Fort Wilkins) we obtained from the shore of the inner bay, agates, stilbite, and smoky quartz, &c.

SINGULAR VIVACITY.—In going from this bay through a rock-bound strait, the rain fell literally in sheets. There was no escape, and our only philosophy was to sit still and bear it. The shower was so great that it obscured objects at a short distance. All at once the men struck up a cheerful boat song, which they continued, paddling with renewed energy, till the shower abated. I believe no other people under the sun would have thought of such a resource.

TRAMP IN SEARCH OF THE PICTURESQUE.—The wind rising ahead, we took shelter in an inlet through the trap range, which we called Houghton's Cove. After taking a lunch and drying our things, it was proposed to visit a little lake, said to give origin to the stream falling into its head. The journey proved a toilsome one; but, after passing through woods and defiles, we at length stood on a cliff which overlooked the object sought for—a pond covered with aquatic plants. Wherever we might have gone in search of the picturesque, this seemed the last place to find it. On again reaching the lake the wind was found less fierce, and we went on to Pine River, where we encamped on coarse, loose gravel.

SEARCH FOR NATIVE COPPER.—The next day the wind blew fiercely, and we could not travel. In consequence of reports from the Indians of a large mass of copper inland, I manned a light canoe, and, leaving the baggage and camp in charge of Lesart, went back to a small bay called Mushkeeg, and went inland under their guidance. We wandered many miles, always on the point of making the discovery, but never making it; and returned with our fatigue for our pains. It was seven o'clock in the evening before we returned to our camp—at eight the wind abated, and we embarked, and, after traveling diligently all night, reached the western terminus of the Keweena portage at two o'clock next morning—having advanced in this time about twenty-four miles. Next day, July 10, the wind rose again violently ahead.

ISLE ROYAL DESCRIED.—In coming down the coast of the Keweena Peninsula, we descried the peaks of this island seen dimly in the distance, which it is not probable could have been done if the distance were over sixty miles.

INDIAN PRECAUTION, THEIR INGENUITY.—We found several Chippewa Indians encamped. They brought a trout, the large lake trout, and were, as usual, very friendly. We saw a fresh beaver's skin stretched on the drying hoop, at the Buffalo's son's lodge. But the women had secreted themselves and children in the woods, with the dried skins, supposing that a trader's canoe had landed, as we had landed in the night. This may give some idea of the demands of trade that are usually made, and the caution that is observed by them when a trader lands.

We here saw the claws of two owls, with the skin and leg feathers adhering, sewed together so closely and skilfully, by the Indian women, as to resemble a nondescript with eight claws. It was only by a close inspection that we could discover the joinings.

LAKE ACTION.—The geological action of the lake against the high banks of diluvion, at this spot, is very striking. It has torn away nearly all the ancient encamping ground, including the Indian burials. Human bones were found scattered along the declivity of fallen earth. An entire skull was picked up, with the bark wrappings of the body, tibia, &c.

At seven in the evening the tempest ceased so as to enable us to embark. We kept close in shore, as the wind was off land, a common occurrence on these lakes at night. On turning the point of red sandstone rock, which the Indians call *Pug-ge-do-wau* (Portage), the Porcupine Mountains rose to our view, directly west, presenting an azure outline of very striking lineaments—an animal couchant. As night drew on, the water became constantly smoother; it was nine before daylight could be said to leave us. We passed, in rapid succession, the *Mauzhe-ma-gwoos* or Trout, Graverod's, *Unnebish*, or Elm, and Pug-ge-do-wa, or Misery River, in Fishing Bay. Here we overtook Lieut. Clary, and encamped at one o'clock A. M. (11th). We were on the lake again at five o'clock. We turned point *a la Peche*, and stopped at River *Nebau-gum-o-win* for breakfast. While thus engaged, the wind rose and shifted ahead. This confined us to the spot.

NEBAUGUMOWIN RIVER.—Mr. Johnston, Dr. Houghton, and Mr. Woolsey, made an excursion in a canoe up the river. They went about three or four miles—found the water deep, and the banks high and dry on the right side (going up), and covered with maple, ash, birch, &c. At that distance the stream was obstructed by logs, but the depth of water continued. Dr. H. added to his botanical collection. Altogether appearances are represented more favorable than would be inferred from the sandy and swampy character of the land about its discharge into the lake.

EAGLES.—While at the *Mauzhe-ma-gwoos* River, Lieut. Clary captured a couple of young eagles, by letting his men cut down a large pine. One of the birds had a wing broken in falling. They were of the bald-headed kind, to which the Chippewas apply the term *Megizzi*, or barker. He also got a young mink from an Indian called *Wabeno*. The men also caught some trout in that river, for which it is remarkable.

At two o'clock the wind had somewhat abated, so as to allow us to take the lake, and we reached and entered the Ontonagon River at half past four o'clock. Mr. Johnston with the store canoe, and Lieut. Clary with his boat, came in successively with colors flying. *Kon-te-ka*, the chief, and his band saluted us with several rounds of musketry from the opposite shore. Afterwards they crossed to our camp, and the usual exchange of ceremonies and civilities took place. In a speech from the chief he complained much of hunger, and presented his band as objects of charitable notice. I explained to him the pacific object of my journey, and the route to be pursued, and requested the efficient co-operation of himself and his band in putting a stop to war parties, referring particularly to that by Kewaynokwut in 1824, which, although raised against the Sioux, had murdered Finley and his men at Lake Pepin. This party was raised on the sources of the Ontonagon and Chippewa. I told him how impossible it was that his Great Father should ever see their faces in peace while they countenance or connive at such dastardly war parties, who went in quest of a foe, and not finding him, fell upon a friend. He said he had not forgotten this. Even now, I continued, a chief of the Sauks was trying to enlist the Indians in a scheme of extreme hostilities. It was a delusion. They had no British allies to rally on as in former wars. The time was past—past forever for such plans. We are in profound peace. And their Great Father, the President, would, if the scheme was pursued by that chief, order his whole army to crush him. I requested him to inform me of any messages, or tobacco, or wampum they might receive, on the subject of that chief's movement, or any other government matter. And to send no answer to any such message without giving me notice.

At three o'clock on the morning of the next day (12th July), Dr. Houghton, Mr. Johnston, Lieut. Clary, and Mr. Woolsey, with nine Canadians and one soldier, set out in my canoe to visit the copper rock. Konteka sent me a fine carp in the morning. Afterwards he and the other chief came over to visit me. The chief said that his child, who had been very ill, was better, and asked me for some white rice (*waube monomin*) for it, which I gave. I also directed a dish of flour and other provisions to enable him to have a feast.

INDIAN TOMB.—One of the Indians had a son drowned a few days before our arrival; the grave was neatly picketed in. On the west side of the river is a grave or tomb above ground, resembling a lodge, containing the coffin of a chief, who desired to be thus buried, as he believed his spirit would go directly up.

Konteka has a countenance indicative of sense and benevolence. I asked him the number of his band. He replied sixty-four men and boys, women and girls. Sixteen were hunters, of whom thirteen were men grown.

KAUGWUDJU.—The Porcupine Mountains, which first loomed up after passing Puggedawa Point, were very plainly pictured before us in the landscape. I asked Konteka their Indian name. He replied

Kaug Wudju. I asked him why they were so called. He said from a resemblance to a crouching procupine. I put several questions to him to ascertain the best place of ascent. He said that the mountain properly faced the south, in a very high perpendicular cliff, having a lake at its bottom. The latter was on a level with Lake Superior. To see this lake it was necessary to go round towards the south. It was a day's journey from the lake to the top of the cliff. To the first elevation it was as far as to the Red Rocks—say three miles, but through a cedar thicket, and bad walking.

VISIT TO THE COPPER ROCK.—The party returned from this place on the 13th, late in the afternoon, bringing specimens of the native copper. They were nine hours in getting to the forks, and continued the rest of the day in getting to the rock, where they encamped. They had been four hours in descending what required nine in going up. The doctor brought several fine and large masses of the pure metal.

LAKE SHORES.—I had a final conference with the Indians of the Ontonagon on the morning of the 14th July, and at its conclusion distributed presents to all. I sent Germain with a canoe and men for St. Mary's with dispatches, and embarked for La Pointe at half past eight, A. M. After keeping the lake for two hours, we were compelled by adverse winds to put ashore near Iron River; we were detained here the rest of the day. After botanizing at this spot, Dr. Houghton remarks, that since arriving at the Ontonagon, he finds plants which belong to a more southerly climate.

The next morning (15th) we embarked at three o'clock and went on finely—stopped for breakfast at Carp River, under the Porcupine Mountains—the *Pesabie* of the Indians. On coming out into the lake again the wind was fair, and increased to blow freshly. We went on to Montreal River, where it became a side wind, and prevented our keeping the lake. I took this occasion to walk inland eleven *pauses* on the old portage path to Fountain Hill, for the purpose of enjoying the fine view of the lake, which is presented from that elevation. The rocks are puddingstone and sandstone, and belong to the Porcupine Mountain development.

Returned from this excursion at seven o'clock—took a cup of tea, and finding the wind abated, re-embarked. By ten o'clock at night we reached and entered the Mauvaise River, where we found Lieut. Clary encamped. After drying our clothes we went on to La Pointe, which we reached at one o'clock in the morning, and immediately went to Mr. Johnston's [Agency] buildings.

J A M E S   K .   J A M I S O N

By Cross

and Anchor

At remote La Pointe, following the labors of Allouez and Marquette, the mission was forgotten. The chapel weathered and wasted while water lapped the shore and the silent aurora streamed up through the stars. Then came another black-robed priest with crucifix swinging at his side. After 165 years Frederick Baraga took up the mission on Chequamegon Bay.

Slight, hardy and fearless, with a scholarly mind and tireless devotion, Father Baraga carried the cross through a wilderness parish. He voyaged in a canoe with Indian and halfbreed paddlers; in winter he went by snowshoe and dog team. Between journeys he translated the gospels into Indian dialects. Through writings in German, French and his native Slovenian he made Lake Superior known in the universities and seminaries of Europe.

Father Baraga knew hunger, cold and exhaustion, and the mercy of Providence. While crossing Lake Michigan in a leaky canoe without food or firearms, he saw the hand of God. "As we rode past a small rocky island, the Indians noticed that many large sea birds flew up from the shore, and immediately surmised that these birds have their nests there. We landed and found a benevolent gift of Providence, namely 130 eggs, which were as large and as palatable as goose eggs. Thanking God, we resumed our journey."

On Madeline Island in Chequamegon Bay Father Baraga built the church of St. Joseph, gracing it with oil paintings from Austria. At L'Anse on Keweenaw Bay he established the Assinins Mission with its school for Indian children. During the copper rush he ministered to German and Irish Catholics along with his Indian converts. Eventually he became Bishop of the Upper Peninsula. At his death in 1868 he was buried in the crypt of St. Peter's Cathedral on Baraga Avenue in Marquette.

When Father Baraga arrived at Sault Ste. Marie in 1835 there was just one trading schooner, the *John Jacob Astor*, on Lake Superior. In that pioneer vessel, with Captain Stanard, the discoverer of (misspelled) Stannard's Rock, he made the eighteen-day journey to La Pointe. The voyage is described by James K. Jamison in the early pages of *By Cross and Anchor,* 1946.

ABOARD the *John Jacob Astor,* Father Baraga regretted more than once that he had not chosen the alternative of a dispatch canoe. Adverse winds and calms followed by sudden violent summer storms combined to delay them or drive the ship out of her course. Also, she was on her maiden voyage, and though Captain Stanard was obviously a capable master, he had yet to learn her ways and whims. Now he humored her.

Nevertheless, the missionary sometimes forgot this impatience at the delay. There were hours of quiet contemplation on deck, where he often sat alone. At other times Captain Stanard joined him and the two had long talks.

Recollections of many things the Indians on the lower lakes had told him, his own perusal of the *Jesuit Relations* and his conversations with the ship's master built a background against which Father Baraga could place himself, as he journeyed westward on the single vessel plying this enormous lake.

In that summer of 1835 the Lake Superior country was as undeveloped with respect to its enormous and varied natural resources as it had been when the first white man beheld it. Except for one item. And that single item, furs, had by this time been exploited almost to the point of exhaustion. Yet in the very course of exploitation the Lake Superior country had accumulated a full, rich, and romantic history extending across two centuries.

The physical geography of the North American continent being what it is, the first trade lines of the fur industry were laid down far to the north. The French penetrated the interior from their bases on the St. Lawrence River by the easiest water routes they could find. Thus it was that of the two peninsulas that were to form the state of Michigan, that to the north—the southern shore of Lake Superior—was well known to Europeans before any white man had visited the south peninsula. Sault Ste. Marie is a century older than Detroit.

One day Father Baraga said to Captain Stanard: "Captain, I have been thinking about this lake and the country around it. Do you know that it is an *old* new country? Strange expression, but it is true. It is old in the sense that the governments that claimed it have known it for two centuries. It is new in the sense that it remains quite uninhabited and its resources, except fur, are undiscovered."

"You are right, Father. But there is one thing I think they will discover one of these days, and that is copper. The Indians have made small articles from it for as far back as their history goes, I guess. I am not a book man, you know; I learn these things from what I see and hear."

"Yes, the Jesuits speak of copper and other minerals in their *Relations*," Father Baraga told him. "Etienne Brulé was on Lake Superior in 1616 and Jean Nicolet saw it a few years afterward. That was long before the English had settled any colony except Virginia."

"Well, the Americans have got the country now for certain, and they are descended from the English settlers. But the white men who live up here are still pretty nearly all French—and most of 'em have Indian blood in 'em now. The Americans never went in for that kind of thing much, nor the English either—marrying Indian women, I mean, and getting to live more or less like Indians. The French didn't seem to care about laying claim to the land—just fell right in with the natives, come day, go day. But the Americans, why, they want the land and everything on it and in it—except the Indians. They don't want the Indians."

"No, I am afraid they don't want the Indians," the missionary agreed.

"You know, Father, I met a Frenchman this summer at the Sault —a real book-learned Frenchman he was. He spoke some English, so we could visit with each other. One day he brought me to a place along the rapids and took a piece of paper out of his pocket and read it out loud in French— waved his arms a good deal while he was doing it. When he finished I says, 'What was that?' He says, 'Captain, that was one of the great jokes of history!' And he laughed —laughed good and hard. Finally he hands me the paper and says, 'Here, Captain, take this paper and keep it. Your descendants will enjoy it.' If you will wait a minute, Father, I'll get the paper. Maybe you can tell me what it says—it's French writing."

In a moment Captain Stanard returned and handed a paper to Father Baraga. The priest glanced through the writing and smiled.

"I think, Captain, your French friend had a sense of humor," he said. Thereupon he translated for the other's benefit:

At this spot St.-Lusson, a Cavalier of France, unfurled a banner emblazoned with the lilies of the Bourbons, raised his sword in a graceful gesture, stepped forward and spoke the following words: "In the name of the Most High, Most Mighty and Redoubtable Monarch, Louis XIV, of the name, Most Christian King of France and Navarre, we take possession of said place of St. Mary's of the Falls, as well as Lakes

Huron and Superior, the Manitoulin Islands, and of all other countries, rivers, lakes and tributaries contiguous, as well discovered as to be discovered, which are bounded on the one side by the northern and western seas and on the other side by the south sea, including all its length and breadth."

Smiling, he handed the paper back to the captain.

"Well, I'll be—blest!" the latter exclaimed, looking down at the writing. "No wonder the fellow laughed!"

"Captain," Father Baraga said, "it seems to me that I can sit here now and see in one direction the retreating figures of an old regime, and in the opposite direction the onrushing vanguard of a new regime. I see both of them clearly. It has been as though these great waters and their environs have been sleeping for two hundred years. On my way here I saw those restless Americans on the Ohio River; they were crowding the wharves in Detroit just after they had come in through the Erie Canal. They were tall, stalwart men and with them were their wives and their children and their cattle and their household goods. That French cavalier made one historical gesture when he thrust the staff of the Bourbon flag into the ground at his feet, but each of these Americans will be making quite another kind of historical gesture when he thrusts his spade into the earth. God be merciful to my poor Indians!"

"Yes, things are going to change," agreed Captain Stanard.

When Father Baraga was alone once more, he thought: It has been a century and a half since Allouez and Marquette were on Lake Superior. I wonder if I shall find at that Pointe du Saint Esprit that Allouez named, any vestige of their work?

He recalled now what he had learned during his first months in America, while he waited at Cincinnati for Bishop Fenwick to take him to his mission station at Arbre Croche. Allouez had been at La Pointe for four years, beginning in his restless endeavor what Marquette was to take over for a year or two until he departed to join Joliet in the expedition that explored the Upper Mississippi River. Marquette was at La Pointe in 1669, and now Frederick Baraga was succeeding him in 1835; for no priest had been there in the interim.

How much of what Allouez and Marquette saw on this lake has changed by now? he wondered. If I am to rely upon what my Indians below here have told me, then the end of the fabulous fur trade is near. And though all the motions of that old regime are still being made, nevertheless a period is ending. Am I to inherit all the accumulated ills that it has brought these Indians?

Day followed day in seemingly endless succession. Even Captain Stanard grew fretful when he was compelled to turn and run before a storm. On that occasion only the immensity of the lake gave them the sea-room necessary to save the little schooner.

Finally, on the eighteenth day after they had left the Sault, the master announced, "Father, if all goes well we should make a landing at La Pointe some time between daybreak and noon tomorrow."

"*Deo gratias!*" murmured the priest from his heart.

II

THE FORTUNE

HUNTERS

While trafficking in beaver skins the French traders heard Indian tales of copper ledges, and sometimes they saw copper arrowtips, spearheads and ornaments. The priests as well as the traders felt the lure of that precious metal, which the Indians guarded with religious care. In 1640 Father Lallemont wrote of copper nuggets as big as a man's fist on the Lake Superior shore, and Allouez in 1667 saw lumps of copper lying on the lake bottom. Father Dablon repeated a story of Chippewa superstition: Four Indians landed on a floating island (Isle Royale) where the shore was covered with copper. Quickly they gathered up the metal and pushed off in their canoe. When an accusing voice followed them, the frightened savages returned the riches to the beach.

This would not happen when white men took the Copper Rock from Ontonagon and mined the deep lodes of the Keweenaw.

The lustrous boulder in the bed of the Ontonagon River on the south shore of Lake Superior had been known to white men since the time of Allouez. French *voyageurs* hacked off pieces of it; later the English traders tried to carry it away. While that four-ton chunk of copper remained in the river bed, legends grew around it.

In 1826 Henry Rowe Schoolcraft set out from the Soo with a party of sixty-two troops and civilians in a fleet of seven flat-bottomed, sharpbowed mackinaw boats for an Indian council at the head of Lake Superior. For eighteen days, in fine June weather, "traversing the lake by its shores and bays," they journeyed to the songs of the *voyageurs*. At Fond du Lac (site of present Duluth) they found a great gathering of Chippewas from the northern lakes and forests. In a spacious bower supported by posts and roofed with branches, Schoolcraft conducted the council. Forty silver medals were presented to the chiefs, who conceded the white man's right "to explore and take away the native copper and copper ores, and to work the mines and minerals in the country."

Before the last Indian had left the council grounds white men were working with ropes and rollers on the Ontonagon Boulder. When their apparatus failed, they piled brush over the rock and set it afire. The boulder did not melt, but when they drenched it with river water some chunks scaled off. The mass of copper, bigger than a bale of peltry, remained there for another generation. When Douglass Houghton saw it in 1840 he figured its weight at three to four tons.

Then came Jim Paul, a roving frontiersman who claimed it by discovery, and Julius Eldred, a Detroit hardware man, who paid some Chippewas $150 for the rock he had not seen. When Eldred came up the Ontonagon in the spring of 1843 with a boatload of provisions and equipment, he found Jim Paul already in possession, having spent the winter guarding his boulder. While these two wrangled, Major Walter Cunningham arrived with a War Department order to transport the rock to Washington. Jim Paul seems to have asserted prior rights; with a crude capstan and some grunting Indians he dragged the rock down to navigable water and loaded it onto a scow. Then merchant Eldred bought it again, paying Paul $1800 for his labors. That summer the boulder was shipped aboard the schooner *Algonquin* to the Soo, carted around the falls, and loaded on the schooner *William Brewster* for Detroit. When it arrived there in October, 1843, every citizen hurried to the riverfront. Eldred let no one aboard. That night he got the rock ashore, and next day it went on exhibition for twenty-five cents a head.

Soon the U.S.S. *Erie* of the Revenue Service arrived in Detroit and the government claimed the rock by right of Indian treaties. The boulder went to Buffalo aboard the *Erie*, and by rail to Washington. After three years of controversy Congress granted Julius Eldred "for time and expenses in purchasing and removing the mass of native copper, commonly called the Copper Rock," the sum of $5664.98. Today it lies in the Smithsonian Museum, where streams of visitors pass it with hardly a glance.

No more copper rocks were found in the Lake Superior wilderness, but deep in the greenstone and traprock lay vast veins of copper ore. In the middle 1840s the word went out and the fortune hunters hurried in. On the long Keweenaw cape the copper towns sprang up—Eagle River, Copper Harbor, Calumet, Hancock and Houghton. Those names were soon known in financial houses in Boston, New York, London, Paris and Amsterdam. In fifty years the Keweenaw mines yielded more than half the copper produced in North America.

In the search for copper some hopeful men discovered the first iron range on Lake Superior, and one of them believed "the time might come when it would be worth something." When the Soo Canal was opened in 1855 the brig *Columbia* carried on her deck a mound of red iron ore. In a generation that would become the predominant commerce of the lakes and the foundation of vast fortunes.

In the next forty years landlookers found the five great ranges ringing Lake Superior in an arc of iron ore. From the pioneer Marquette range prospectors went south into the old blunted hills of the Menominee, and soon the iron ore port of Escanaba developed on Lake Michigan. West of the Menominee lay the Gogebic, a belt of rich hematite stretching for fifty miles across the Michigan-Wisconsin boundary; the port of Ashland became its terminal.

Each range had its own drama, its tales of toil, frustration and heady fortune. For twenty years miners on the way to the Vermilion district, near the Canadian border, trekked through the rough Mesabi country.

In the late 1880s the first Mesabi ore beds came to light, and in ten years the Giant Range was producing more than all the rest together. West of the tip of Lake Superior the Cuyuna Range sent its production to the port of Superior, while Vermilion ore went to Two Harbors and the endless Mesabi ore flowed to both these ports and to the high trestled docks at Duluth. In this northern wilderness developed the greatest railroad traffic in the world, the long ore trains rolling down to the lake ports with their lofty loading docks.

Geography has been generous to North America, with its great forests and grasslands, its rich soil and its oil and minerals underground. In the heart of the continent were the makings of a great steel industry —vast coal deposits in the upper Ohio valley, the rich iron ranges ringing Lake Superior, and midway between them the limestone beds along Lake Huron. There were the mines and the quarries, and between them stretched the linked lakes—a spacious and shining waterway to carry the endless cargoes.

The

Mineral Veins

When Governor Cass of Michigan Territory sought a man to give some scientific lectures in frontier Detroit, he was referred to a scholar at Rensselaer Polytechnic School in Troy, New York. In 1830 the scientist landed in Detroit and Cass was astonished to find a slight, brisk, blue-eyed youth of twenty. Soon he was a leading citizen of Michigan.

Shortly after his arrival in the West, Douglass Houghton was appointed physician and botanist in Schoolcraft's expedition to the headwaters of the Mississippi. In Detroit he practiced medicine, lectured on chemistry and geology, played the flute and helped to organize the University of Michigan. In 1837 he proposed a geological survey of the state. So began his annual seasons in the field and his historic reports of geology and topography. The first extensive survey of the Upper Peninsula came in 1840, an exploration of 170 miles of wilderness from Point Detour to the Montreal River. Accompanied by three assistants and nine packers and paddlers, Houghton spent five months, "mostly without tents and blankets," in the rough Lake Superior country. Before they left the field the fall storms had come; for weeks the men lived with wet and cold.

That winter, still worn from his labors, Houghton wrote a masterful account of the Upper Peninsula geology, a scholarly report lit with a guarded excitement. "Upon the whole (while I would carefully avoid exciting any unfounded expectations among our citizens, and caution them to avoid engaging in wild schemes with a view to gain sudden wealth) the examinations and surveys which have been made would serve fully to justify the conclusion that this region of country will prove a continued source of wealth to our State." His later reports found copper ores even more extensive than the first survey indicated.

On a stormy October night in 1845 Douglass Houghton was steering a mackinaw boat toward the lights of Eagle River. Then snow blotted out the lights and a burst of wind overturned the boat. Two of his men floundered to shore. Next spring the body of Douglass Houghton was found on the rugged coast of Keweenaw, where he had mapped the traprock, conglomerate and greenstone. By that time the copper rush was on. His expedition of 1840 cost twelve thousand dollars, the greatest bargain the State of Michigan ever made.

Houghton's report of the Survey of 1840 included this summary:

WHILE I am fully satisfied that the mineral district of our state will prove a source of eventual and steadily increasing wealth to our people, I cannot fail to have before me the fear that it may prove the ruin of hundreds of adventurers, who will visit it with expectations never to be realized. The true resources have as yet been but little examined or developed, and even under the most favorable circumstances, we cannot expect to see this done but by the most judicious and economical expenditure of capital, at those points where the prospects of success are most favorable. It has been said of the Cornish district, in respect to the supposed large aggregate profits, that "a fair estimate of the expenditure and the return from all the mines that have been working for the last twenty or thirty years, if the necessary documents could be obtained from those who are interested in withholding them, would dispel the delusion which prevails on this subject, as well as check the ruinous spirit of gambling adventure which has been productive of so much misery." And if these remarks will apply to a comparatively small district, which has been explored and extensively worked for centuries, with how much more force must they apply to the mineral district of our own state. I would by no means desire to throw obstacles in the way of those who might wish to engage in the business of mining this ore, at such time as our government may see fit to permit it, but I would simply caution those persons who would engage in this business in the hope of accumulating wealth suddenly and without patient industry and capital, to look closely before the step is taken, which will most certainly end in disappointment and ruin.

The extreme length of what I have denominated the mineral district, (within the limits of Michigan,) may be estimated at a fraction over 135 miles, and it has a width varying from one to six miles; but it must not be imagined that mineral veins occur equally through all portions of it, for sometimes, for many miles together, none have been noticed, and the situation of the country is such as to render it probable they never will be. The range and course of the mineral district has been so far defined as to render it unnecessary to say more upon this subject, to enable such persons as may wish to examine, to pass directly along its complete length.

I have thus far omitted to allude particularly to the large mass of native copper, which has been so long known to exist in the bed of Ontonagon river, lest perhaps this isolated mass might be confounded with the products of the veins of the mineral district. That this mass has once occupied a place in some of these veins is quite certain, but it is now perfectly separated from its original connection, and appears simply as a loose transported bowlder.

The attention of the earliest travelers was called to this mass of metallic copper by the natives of the country, and it has been repeatedly described by those who have visited it. The mass now lies in the bed of the westerly fork of the Ontonagon river, at a distance which may be estimated at 26 miles, by the stream, from its mouth. The rugged character of the country is such, that it is but rarely visited, in proof of which I may state, that upon my visit to it, during the last year, I found broken chisels, where I had left them on a previous visit, nine years before, and even a mass of the copper, which at that time had been partially detached, but which, for the want of sufficient implements, I was compelled to abandon, was found, after that interval, in precisely the same situation in which it had been left.

The copper in this bowlder, is associated with rocky matter, which, in all respects, resembles that associated with that metal in some portions of the veins before described, the rocky matter being bound together by innumerable strings of metal; but a very considerable proportion of the whole is copper, in a state of purity. The weight of copper is estimated at from three to four tons.

While the mass of native copper upon Ontonagon river cannot fail to excite much interest, from its great size and purity, it must be borne in mind, that it is a perfectly isolated mass, having no connection whatever with any other, nor does the character of the country lead to the inference that veins of the metal occur in the immediate vicinity, though, as before stated, the mineral district crosses the country at a distance of but a few miles.

Horizon North

Thirty-four years after the historic geological survey of 1840, that field trip was recalled by Bela Hubbard, Douglass Houghton's first assistant. By then Hubbard had forgotten the mosquitoes and deer flies, the rain and wind, the cold camps on rocky shores. He remembered the bright new world of Lake Superior, the wild hills and the rugged coast, the long northern twilight and the aurora streaming through the stars.

A reflective man and a graceful writer, Bela Hubbard lived to see what Douglass Houghton had predicted—the wealth of the mineral lands and the dramatic growth of lake commerce. But in his *Memorials of Half a Century*, 1887, he looked back at Lake Superior in 1840, before the world had found it.

AMONG THE PLEASANTEST of all my reminiscences of travel is that of the exploration, in connection with the geological survey of Michigan, of the coasts of our upper peninsula in 1840.

The party of this expedition was composed of the State geologist, Dr. Douglass Houghton; his two assistants, C. C. Douglass and myself; Fredk. Hubbard, in charge of instrumental observations; and, for a part of the way, H. Thielson, a civil engineer, and Charles W. Penny, a young merchant of Detroit, supernumeraries.

We left Detroit in the steamer "Illinois," arriving at Mackinac, May 23. Here two boat crews were made up, consisting of six Canadians. These belonged to that class so famous in the palmy days of the fur trade and the French régime, now extinct, and known to history as "*coureurs de bois*." They were of mixed blood, in some, the French, in others, the Indian, predominating. Bred to the business, they would row without fatigue from daybreak until dark, —twelve or fourteen hours,—unlade the boats, pitch the tents for the *bourgeois*, pile up the baggage, prepare the evening meal, and then creep under their blankets in the open air and enjoy the sound sleep that labor bestows.

The principal dependence of these voyageurs for food—we had no leisure for hunting and little for fishing—was upon a soup of beans, with a most liberal supply of water, into which a piece of pork was dropped. A cake of hard-bread was allowed to each.

The boats for the passage of the Sault were each about twenty feet long by four broad, lightly constructed of pine and cedar, with sharp bows, and were drawn out of the water at night. At the Sault, to which provisions had been forwarded, one of these boats was exchanged for a "Mackinac barge," sufficiently large to carry two months' provisions and all our baggage.

A voyage to and upon our great lake at the time of my story was by no means the easy journey it is now. North of Mackinac, no steamers and no regular line of sail-vessels traversed the waters. The ship-canal around the waters of the Sault had not then been projected. Furs and fish constituted the only commerce, and the latter found too few customers to make the trade profitable. The American Fur Company had its headquarters at Sault Ste. Marie, where was a village of some twenty or thirty houses, mostly of logs, and the United States maintained a garrison. On the opposite shore was a small English settlement, consisting of a few white-washed cabins and Episcopal and Baptist mission establishments. Here also the Hudson's Bay Company had a post.

At L'Anse had been established for many years a factory of the American Fur Company, the only buildings being a log house, storehouse, and barn, and near by a Baptist mission, consisting of a dozen neat huts of logs and bark. Near the extreme west end of the lake this company had another factory or trading-post at La Pointe.

These were the only white settlements on the south shore of this great lake. At two or three points, transient fishing-camps might be met with. Else, all this region was wild and solitary almost as when a century earlier, it was traversed by the canoe of the Jesuit missionary or echoed to the rude songs of the wild employees of the fur traders. To a large part of the country, on the southern border, within the territory of the United States, the Indian title had not been extinguished. But the settlements of the aboriginal race were rare; probably the whole region did not number 1000 souls.

Apart from the scientific animus of the expedition, our party, in the ardor of youth, could not but look forward to the new and strange scenes which awaited us with somewhat of the enthusiasm that inspired the first explorers of this region of vast forests and inland seas. We were to voyage almost in the same mode as those travellers, to witness scenes as yet little changed, and partaking of the same character of solitude and mystery.

Though I wander from my narrative, I must linger a moment over the impression produced by the romantic island which was our starting-point, Michilimackinac.

Connected with the story of the early wanderings of the French, their perilous missions in the far wilderness, the fur trade, with its fort, its agents, its *coureurs de bois* and numerous employees, its bustle, show, and dissipation, its traffic and its enormous profits, and with the numerous native tribes which were rendezvoused, —no place in the North-west possesses greater historic and traditionary interest. The town retained, as it still does, much of its old-time character. The crescent bay in front was still a lounging-place for the American Ishmaelite, whose huts often covered the beach; and this was the last place on the frontier where the Mackinac barge might be manned and equipped, as a century ago, by a motley crew of half-breed voyageurs.

The natural beauties and wildness of the island, its situation, enthroned at the apex of the peninsula of Michigan and embracing magnificent views of water and island, its lake breezes and pure cold air, and the excellence of its white-fish and trout, have long made it one of the most attractive of watering-places. The proposal to conserve it as a national park is worthy of its character, and it is to be hoped that thus its natural beauties, and what remains of its woods, will be preserved forever to the nation.

On the morning of May 26 we took our departure from Mackinac, with a moderate breeze and a clear sky,—a thing to be noted where fogs are so frequent,—and coasting by St. Martin's Island, entered les Cheneaux.

The river, or more properly Strait of Ste. Marie, is a series of channels, winding amid innumerable islands. Some of these, as St. Joseph and Drummond, cover many square miles, but the greater number are much smaller, and often occupy only a few acres. They line the whole northern coast of Lake Huron, and are occasioned by the junction between the silurian lime rocks and the azoic or primary rocks of Canada.

These islands are but little elevated above the water, and are wooded to the edge with cedar, fir and birch. The evergreen trees are completely shrouded in a tapestry of parasitic moss. This is a true lichen, and is not allied to the great Southern epiphyte which it so strongly resembles. It hangs in long festoons, giving the woods a fantastic and gloomy appearance, but the effect is very beautiful.

What are called "les Cheneaux" are passages among islands of this description. They are seldom wide enough to admit any but the smallest craft, and so intricate as to form a perfect labyrinth, where any but the practised mariner might wander long, "in endless mazes lost."

To the north and east of St. Joseph Island the Ste. Marie parts the two systems of rocks, and an instant change takes place in the character of the scenery. Instead of low, timbered shores, the islands rise in abrupt cones, rounded and water-worn, to the height of twenty to one hundred feet, presenting bare knobs of hornblende and quartz. The surfaces are worn smooth, by the action of glaciers, and are frequently covered with a thick carpet of lichens. Among these is, in profusion, the beautiful reindeer moss. A few miles to the right, in Canada, hills of granite rise to a height of 500 to 1000 feet, and form a background to the view.

To the geologist these low hills and rounded knobs have an absorbing interest. Agassiz tells us that America has been falsely denominated the new world; that "hers was the first dry land lifted out of the waters; hers the first shore washed by the ocean that enveloped all the earth beside." The antiquary finds in this portion of America a very respectable antiquity. To its known civil history he adds evidence of the existence of a race of men familiar with this region ages before its discovery by the French, who were by no means despicable cultivators of the arts, and he infers a human history—could he but gather the full record—possibly as ancient as the pyramids. But science points to a period infinitely more remote. We had reached and stood upon what was the skeleton of our earth, when but a crust above the seething fires beneath, not only ages before man had a being upon its surface, but probably ages before what we call the "Old World" had been raised by the forces of nature above the universal ocean. Here was antiquity unmeasured by any human standard. Time itself was young then. This backbone of the earliest continent still stretches unbroken from the Atlantic to the western plains. During the unnumbered years in which the surface of the earth has been changed by successive upheavals and depressions it has stood unmoved.

Around the base of these low granite and metamorphic hills, in the bed of the river, lies a sandstone rock, which we shall find rising into cliffs along the coast of the lake above. It is the lowest of the paleozoic series, the first rock which brings to our eyes evidence of life upon this continent, and, if geologists speak truth, the first which bears witness to the dawn of life upon our earth. Of the earliest forms of organic life two only have with certainty been found in this rock, the *lingula* and the *trilobite*. And these, in the perfection and adaptation of their structure, equal the most perfect beings of their kind which exist at the present day. Thus the first record of the earliest life, upon the most ancient sea beach which the earth affords, is in apparent condemnation of the development hypothesis of Darwin. Are they then evidence of sudden and independent creation, or must we believe that these forms had their origin in some yet more remote and obscure past, and that we behold in these silurian rocks only their perfect development?

Following the northerly channel, the Ste. Marie soon expands into a broad and lovely sheet of water, twelve miles long, called Lake St. George. We have escaped from the labyrinth of rocky isles, the southern shores are again densely wooded, while the azoic rocks are seen on the Canada side, stretching off to the north-west, and terminating in a series of mountainous knobs,—the vertebrae of the world before the Flood. To this lake the Narrows succeed, and here for the first time the Ste. Marie assumes the appearance of a river, being contracted to less than 1000 feet, with a current and occasional rapids.

We passed frequent memorials of the Indian inhabitants. It is not to be wondered at that this region abounds with them, since with an eye to natural beauty this poetical race selects the loveliest spots for the resting-places, both of the living and the dead. The graves were close cabins of logs, thatched with bark, and the places selected are among the most beautiful and elevated sites, as if the souls of the departed braves could hear the echoing paddle and watch the approach of the distant canoe. The burial-place of the chief is designated by a picketed enclosure, and here it is customary for the voyaging Indian to stop, kindle his camp-fire at the head of the grave, and, on departing, to leave within the enclosure a small portion of the provisions he has cooked, for the use of the occupant. A flat cedar stake at the head exhibits in red paint the figure of some bird or brute,—the family totem of the deceased. Often is seen a small cross, erected as an emblem of his faith in Holy Catholic Church, while close by, in strange contrast, is that evidence of his unalterable attachment to the creed of his fathers,—the basket of provisions that is to support his journeying to the land of spirits.

The camping ground of the voyageur has been that of the Indian from time immemorial. The wigwam poles are recognized from a distance, in some open glade along the shore, left standing after the vagabond inmates have departed. And there is often to be found an old canoe, a camp-kettle, a cradle swinging from the poles, and invariably a litter of picked bones and dirty rags, completely covering the spot, with the burnt brands and ashes of the cabin fire in the midst. Sometimes we meet a rude altar of stones, on which are laid bits of tobacco and other petty offerings to the Manitou. Sometimes the scene is varied by the cabin of a Canadian Frenchman, who, unable to resist the charm of savage life, is bringing up his family of half-breed children in a condition little akin to civilization.

Early on the morning of May 30 we reached the Sault, and proceeded to encamp at the head of the rapids. This required a portage of several rods. The remainder of the day was spent at the village, in witnessing the novel mode of fishing, and other sights pertaining to this remote frontier post.

Preparations for our lake expedition being completed, on the first of June we took our departure from the head of the rapids. Here lay at anchor a beautiful light brig belonging to the American Fur Company, and which bore the name of its founder, John Jacob Astor. Close by its side was a schooner, which had been built by the Ohio Fishing and Mining Company, at Cleveland, and had just made the portage around the rapids. Another vessel was preparing for a similar transportation. With three such crafts floating on its bosom, our great lake seemed to have already lost something of its oldtime character, when, a wide waste of waters, it was traversed only by the canoe of the Indian and voyageur. Its importance as a great commercial highway had thus begun to be foreshadowed, but, in fact, its waters still laved a savage wilderness.

Some natural phenomena pertaining to a high northern latitude had begun to exhibit what were marvels to our unaccustomed eyes. One of these was the lengthened twilight, the sun continuing to irradiate the horizon with a bright flash, until nearly midnight. In fact, it was quite possible to tell the hour of the night at any time, by the light which indicated the sun's position. The Auroras, too, were surpassingly brilliant; often the electric rays streamed up from every point of the horizon, meeting at the zenith and waving like flame. I note these simple and common phenomena because they were novel to us, and it is only those who travel and encamp in the open air who enjoy to the full such scenes of beauty and wonder.

A summer temperature had now set in, and we witnessed another characteristic of this high latitude,—the sudden advance of the season. During the three days of our stay at this place, vegetation, which a week before had hardly commenced, sprung into active life. Trees then bare were now in full leaf. This phenomenon though common to our side of the Atlantic, we had nowhere else seen so conspicuously displayed.

Space will not permit a narrative of our journey, a two-months' coasting voyage along the whole southern side of Lake Superior. Nor can I write, except briefly, of the beauties of the scenery, most of which is now so well known; of Gros Cap and Point Iroquois, those rockbuilt pillars of Hercules that guard the entrance, and

> Like giants stand,
> To sentinel enchanted land;

of White-fish Point and its surroundings; of the grand, wild and varied rocky coast; of the many beautiful streams, flashing with cascades, and filled with the speckled trout; or of our scientific researches and observations. I will venture only to relate an occasional incident, and to delineate some features of the coast scenery which seem to me have been too little noticed or too imperfectly described by others.

Westward from White-fish Point stretch for many miles broad beaches of sand and gravel, backed by hills clothed with Norway-pines, spruce, hemlock, cedar, and birch. These beaches form extensive fishing-grounds, of which parties had already availed themselves. Every one knows the superiority of Lake Superior white-fish, in size and flavor, over those of the lower waters. Yet in relating the following experience I am aware of the risk which I run of being set down as the retailer of a "fish story."

As we were rowing along the beach, some object was descried at a distance, making out of the water. All, at once, gave vigorous chase. On our near approach, the animal, which proved to be an otter, dropped upon the sand a fish which he had just hauled out, and retreated into the lake. This fish, which was scarcely dead, was of a size so extraordinary that it might truly be called—the fish, not the story—a whopper! It measured two and a half feet in length, and one foot five inches in circumference. We had no accurate means of weighing, but its weight was fairly estimated at fifteen pounds! The flesh was delicious in proportion, and made our whole party several capital meals.

These beaches terminate at a deep harbor called the Grand Marais. Hitherto the hills or dunes of sand have been of no great elevation. But now occurs a phenomenon which, though it seems not to have been classed among the wonders of this region, nor described in any books of travel, so far as I am aware, may well be called extraordinary, and worthy a place among the scenic wonders of America. It is a miniature Sahara, several miles in extent, and in many of its peculiar features resembling those lifeless, sandy deserts which are so distinguishing phenomena in some parts of the world. It is known to the French voyageurs as "Le Grand Sable."

Steep cliffs are first observed rising from the water with a very uniform face, of about 200 feet in height, beyond which are visible barren dunes, rising still higher in the distance. On our approach the whole appeared like lofty hills enveloped in fog. This proved to be nothing less than clouds of sand which the winds are constantly sweeping toward the lake, and which formed a mist so dense as to conceal completely the real character of the coast.

On ascending these steep and wasting cliffs, a scene opens to view which has no parallel except in the great deserts. For an extent of many miles nothing is visible but a waste of sand; not under the form of a monotonous plain, but rising into lofty cones, sweeping in graceful curves, hurled into hollows and spread into long-extended valleys. A few grass roots and small shrubs in some places find a feeble subsistence, and are the only vegetation. But thrusting through the sand are several tops of half-buried pines, barkless, and worn dry and craggy by the drifting soil while below the surface their bodies appear to be in perfect preservation. To our imagination they seem the time-worn columns of an antique temple, whose main structure has long ago tumbled into dust, or been buried, like the ruins of Egypt, beneath the drift of many centuries.

The surface sand is mostly packed quite hard, and may be trod as a solid floor. This, in many places, is strewed thickly with pebbles; the deep hollows present vast beds of them. Among these are a great variety of precious stones common to the rocks of the country; agates, chalcedony, jasper, quartz of every shade of color and transparency, with hornstone, trap, and other minerals. All are worn smooth, and often beautifully polished by the sharp, drifting sands, and many rich specimens were obtained. We were reminded of the valley of diamonds in the Arabian tales, which it was the fortune of Sinbad to discover, in a scarcely less singular depository.

In the rear of this desert, about two miles from the coast, timber is again met with. Here, just at the edge of the wood, a small and beautiful lake lies embosomed; on the one side a rich tract of maple forest; on the other, barren and shifting sand. It broke on our view, from amidst the realm of desolation, as did the unexpected fountain to which Saladin led the weary cavalier, Sir Kenneth, over the sandy plains of Palestine, as told in the magic pages of Scott. We named it not inaptly, I think, "the diamond of the desert." Around this sheet of water we found snow, on the tenth of June, in large quantities, buried beneath a few inches of sand.

From the diamond lake, issues a small stream, which, after making its way through the sand, reaches the clay that constitutes the base of these dunes, and tumbles a perfect cascade into the greater lake. This rivulet separates the dense maple forest which lies on the east from cliffs of driven sand, which rise abruptly to a height that far overlooks the woodland, and are the commencement of the grand and leafless sables.

The view on ascending these is most entrancing. On the one side stretches beneath, and far away, the verdant forest; while, by a transition as sudden as it is opposite in character, on the other side every feature of the landscape seems as if buried beneath hills of snow. The desert surface might be likened to that of an angry ocean, only that the undulations are far more vast, and the wave crests more lofty than the billows of the sea in its wildest commotion. Looking upward from one of these immense basins, where only the sand-wave meets the sky the beholder is impressed with a sublimity of a novel kind, unmixed with the terror which attends a storm upon the Alps or on the ocean. The scene, wild and unique, may well claim this brief praise, though hitherto unsung, and lacking the charm of historical association—"the consecration and the poet's dream."

Twelve miles beyond this singular region the beaches terminate, and the sand-rock makes its appearance on the coast, in a range of abrupt cliffs. These are "The Pictured Rocks." They have been often described, but no description that I have seen conveys to my mind a satisfactory impression of their bold, wild, and curious features. . . .

Thirty miles west from the Pictured Rocks, at Chocolate and Carp rivers, we first met, in their approach to the shore, the axoic or primary rocks, which from here onward constitute so interesting and important a feature in the geology of the country. Of their scientific or their economical character it is not my purpose to speak, further than to say that to them belong the iron beds, which are such a mine of wealth to our State. Here, a few years after our visit, sprang into life the busy and thriving city of Marquette. But at the time of which I speak, all was a solitude.

From hence to Keweenaw Bay ranges of granite knobs rise into considerable hills, and around them lie a series of quartzites, slates, and metamorphosed sandstones. The granites are pierced by dykes of trap, which in some cases form straight, narrow, and often lofty walls, in others have overflowed in irregular masses. Here Pluto, not Neptune, has been the controlling spirit, and has left the witness of his rule upon the face of the country. Ascending the knobs of granite and quartz, the change is most striking. To the east the eye embraces a tract lying in immense broad steppes of the sandstone, extending beyond the Pictured Rocks; while to the west are seen only rolling hills and knobs, terminating in the Huron Mountains.

I can add nothing to what is so well known of the mineral riches of this part of the country. But there is in its building stones a wealth that is hardly yet begun to be realized. No more beautiful and serviceable material than the easily-worked and variously-tinted sandstone is found in the West; and her granites, already broken by natural forces into convenient blocks, and as yet untried, will command a market in the time coming, when the solid and durable shall be regarded as chief requisites to good architecture.

Following our westerly direction to Point Keweenaw, we find the dominion of Pluto established on a most magnificent scale. Not only is his energy displayed in the stern and rockbound coast, but in the lofty ranges of trap, which rise into rugged hills of from 400 to 900 feet above the lake. Within these are secreted, but scarcely concealed, those wonderful veins of native copper, here quarried rather than mined, in masses such as the world has nowhere else produced.

But of all this wealth nothing was then known, except that traces of copper were visible at a few places along the coast, and that a large mass of the native metal lay in the bed of Ontonagon River, long revered by the Indians as a Manitou, and mentioned in the relations of the early French historians.

I will but add, as the result of this season's explorations, that the report of the State geologist, published the ensuing winter, unravelled the whole subject of the mode of occurrence of the copper and its associated minerals, in the most complete and scientific manner. It first made known the immense value which Michigan possessed in its hitherto despised Upper Peninsula; and its immediate effect was to arouse an interest in this then wild and uninhabited Indian territory, which has led to the opening up of its mines, and its present teeming prosperity.

On the third of July we encamped at Copper Harbor, and spent several days in exploration of the surrounding country, and in blasting for ores. Several blasts were got ready for the great national jubilee, which we commemorated in the noisy manner usual with Americans, by a grand discharge from the rocks. We succeeded in producing a tremendous report, and the echo, resounding from the placid water as from a sounding-board, pealed forth in corresponding reverberations for several minutes. Later in the day we retired to our camp and partook of an equally grand dinner. It consisted of pigeons, fried and stewed, corn and bean soup, short-cake and hardtack, pork, and—last but not least—a can of fine oysters, which had been brought along for the occasion. Truly a sumptuous repast for a party of wilderness vagrants, even on a Fourth of July anniversary!

At the Ontonagon, an adventure befel, which it becomes a true knight-errant to relate. It was our purpose to pass up this river to the large mass of copper already alluded to. As we landed at the mouth there were noticed, on the opposite side of the river, several Indian lodges. As soon as we had dined, a few of the occupants crossed over in canoes, shook hands with us, giving the usual greeting of "Bo jou," and received a small gift of tobacco and bread. Accompanying were half a dozen young boys, some of whom had remarkably fine features. We could not but notice, as an unusual circumstance, that several of the men were painted black. One athletic fellow in particular, in this grimy coloring, and naked except the clout, made a very grotesque though savage appearance. The devil himself, however, is said not to be so black as he is painted, and this fellow seemed rather to act the buffoon than the noble warrior.

The party proved to belong to the Buffalos, whose chief we had met at River Tequamenon, near the eastern end of the lake, and were under the command of the son of their chief. The latter was a resolute-looking fellow, of about 26 or 30 years of age. His face was painted red, and he wore a medal bearing the likeness of John Quincy Adams. We paid little attention to the Indians, although aware that on several occasions exploring parties had been stopped at the mouth of this river and turned back.

We had made but two or three miles progress up the stream when the rapid stroke of paddles was heard, and a canoe, manned with Indians, shot quickly around a bend below and came into sight. The savages were seated, as their custom is, in the bottom of their bark so that only heads and shoulders were visible. As each applied his whole strength the canoe skimmed over the surface like a young duck, while the dashing of so many paddles caused her to seem propelled by a waterwheel.

Our leader's boat, which was ahead, immediately lay to and raised her American flag. "If they want to fight," said the Doctor, "we'll give them a chance." Our two boats moved into line, and the doctor's assistants armed themselves, one with a revolver, the other with a rusty shot-gun, our entire military resource. The canoe was soon alongside, and the heads and shoulders proved to belong to the bodies of eight stout natives, headed by the young chief. Dr. Houghton held out his hand to be shaken as before. He then asked, through an interpreter, if they recollected the man who had put something into their arms when they were sick, a number of years ago. This something was vaccine for the small-pox, Doctor H. having accompanied the Schoolcraft expedition, in the capacity of physician and botanist. To this the chief, who doubtless well knew, made no reply, but demanded our errand up the river, and said that he and his men had been stationed at the mouth by his father, the head of the tribe, with orders to allow no boat to pass up without that chief's permission. He added further, that we had not paid him, the son, the respect that was his due, by calling at his lodge and leaving a present. Our leader replied that he was sent hither by their great Father, whose instructions he should obey; that he should ascend the river as far as suited him, and that he did not recognize in them any authority to stop him.

CHIEF. You must wait at the mouth until the Buffalo comes up. Else I and my band shall go with you, and see that you take nothing.

DOCTOR. I have been here before, and shall go now, as I am ordered by your great Father. I know the country and do not need a guide.

CHIEF. This country belongs to us.

DOCTOR. I know that this country is Indian territory, but the treaty of 1826 allows citizens of the United States to visit it. Neither shall I ask consent of the chief to take what I please. But, being acquainted with the Buffalo, I have no objection to showing him what I bring away.

At this stage of the altercation another canoe came in sight, which proved to contain the boys. But this time two of the Indians had made free to step into our small boat, where they seated themselves with great appearance of familiarity. The affair would have had enough of the ludicrous mingled with its serious aspect to warrant us in making light of it, and holding no further parley, but for two considerations, which we could not afford to overlook. Owing to the numerous rapids, the barge which contained our whole stock, could be got up only ten miles, while we had to proceed to the forks, twenty miles further, in our smaller boat, and thence five miles by foot. And in case of a trial of strength with the Indians, no dependence could be placed upon our hired voyageurs, most of whom were allied to the opposite party, both in blood and training.

Pointing to a bend in the river, our detainers now said, "We are determined that you shall not go beyond that point tonight." This audacious order determined us to at once break off all conference, so asserting our intention to be no longer hindered or delayed, we prepared for immediate departure. After some consultation among themselves the chief answered, that if we would then and there make them a present of a keg of pork and a barrel of flour we would be allowed to proceed, but should be expected to bestow a further present to the head chief on our return.

To this bold demand, which plainly appeared to be a levy of blackmail, an act of piracy, Dr. Houghton replied that he would give them *as a present* such things as they stood in immediate need of, but nothing more. Nor should he recognize the shadow of a right to demand even that. Accordingly, a bag filled with flour, and some pork and tobacco were offered and the leader agreed to accept his present in powder, lead, and provisions at La Pointe, whither we were bound.

The parley being at an end, we drew off and pushed up the stream. The hostiles remained awhile in consultation, and then withdrew in the opposite direction. A few miles above we encamped for the night.

It was a necessity, as I have stated, to leave our barge behind with all our stores, while the exploring party were absent for two days and a night. Of course this dilemma was known to the enemy. Holding a council of war the next morning, it was resolved to leave with our goods four of the men, together with the gun. They received most positive orders to fire upon the first Indian who touched the baggage, in case any of them should return, as we had reason to expect. And our captain added with solemn emphasis, that if any man failed in fidelity, his own life should pay the forfeit. Having thus played upon their fears, we pursued our laborious journey, reached the Copper Rock at nightfall, and, tired with the day's toils, laid down beneath the cover of the forest and slept soundly.

The next morning we proceeded to the difficult task of detaching portions of the metallic mass, which was successfully accomplished, and we brought away about twenty-five pounds of it. I will here add, that this copper boulder was, a few years afterwards, removed through the agency of Mr. Eldred, of Detroit, and taken to Washington, where it enriches the museum of the Smithsonian Institution. It is now no novelty to see very much larger masses brought down and landed on the dock at our smelting works.

But to conclude the narrative: on reaching camp, on our return, we learned that the chief, with several of his band, had been there, but had touched nothing, and according to his own account, had taken the trail for Lake Flambeau, in order to join a war-party, then organizing, of the Chippewas against the Sioux. Notwithstanding this story we fully expected to meet these fellows again at the mouth, and to whip them there if we could. But when we reached the place all was silent, and the lodges deserted.

I will only add to this long story, that our captain's order was never presented. We learned further, on reaching La Pointe, that the party which waylaid us had known of our journey from the first; that they had "smoked over it," had dogged us the whole way up the lake, subsisting themselves by fishing, and that when we met they were nearly starved.

A few days brought us to the islands called by Carver "The Apostles." On one of the largest of these, Madeline, at La Pointe, is located a general depot of the American Fur Company, for all the western parts of the lake, and the chain of lakes and rivers leading into it. It had become, in consequence, an asylum for all the old traders of that part of the country, and the temporary abode of great numbers of Indians. After pitching our tents on the beach, in front of the fort, amid a crowd of Indians and equally idle half-breeds, we were welcomed by the company's factor, Dr. Borup, Mr. Oakes, the factor from Fond-du-lac, and Mr. Bushnell, the Indian agent, and invited to all the hospitalities of the place.

During our whole voyage from the Sault we had not seen the face of a white man, except at the mission of L'Anse, and a casual fishing party. But here, at the end of our wandering, far from what we had been accustomed to consider the limits of civilization, we were greeted in the families of these gentlemen, not only by features to which we had been so long strangers, but all the attendant civilized refinements. The dress and manners of the East, the free converse with friendly voices of our own and the gentle sex, the music of a piano, the sound of the church-going bell and Christian services, seemed to us rather like a return to our homes than the extreme of a two-months' journey in the wilderness.

It may interest my hearers to know in more detail what composed a post so remote, and which was to me so much a surprise.

La Pointe at that period was one of those peculiar growths known only to an era which has long passed away, or been banished to regions still more remote. What is called the company's "fort" consisted of two large stores painted red, a long storehouse for fish, at the wharf, and a row of neat frame buildings painted white. The latter were occupied by the half dozen families in the company's employ. These dwellings, with the two stores, formed opposite sides of a broad street, in the centre square of which was planted a large flag-pole. Upon this street also clustered sundry smaller and unpainted log tenements of the French and half-breeds. Half a mile from the fort were the Protestant and Catholic missions. The former boasted a good frame mansion of two stories, attached to which was a school, numbering thirty scholars. The Catholic mission had a large number of followers, including the French and Indians. In all, the settlement contained about fifty permanent tenements. Besides these were perhaps an equal number of Indian lodges, irregularly disposed in vacant spaces, and adding to the size and picturesque character of the village. Several hundred Indians usually found constant employ in the fisheries at this place.

This was the oldest, as well as most remote, of the Jesuit missions in the North-west, having been established by Father Allouez, in 1665. It was then a gathering place of many Indian nations, and was hundreds of miles from the nearest French settlement.

It has additional interest from the fact that it witnessed the youthful and zealous labors of Pere Marquette, who came, in 1669, to take the place of Father Allouez, among the Ottawas, Hurons, and other tribes of the neighborhood. It was at La Pointe that Marquette planned that voyage of first discovery, exploration and missionary enterprise down the Mississippi which has rendered his name illustrious.

In the families I have mentioned might be detected an intermixture of Indian blood, which detracts little even from the fairness of the daughters, and the ladies as well as the gentlemen are intelligent and highly educated. Their lives, when not occupied in business, are spent in reading and music; and during the long, cold winter, frequent rides are taken on the ice, upon which they pass from island to island in sledges drawn by dogs.

I could not but picture to my mind, outside of this intelligent circle, the festivities which marked this distant post, at that season, in the more palmy days of the fur trade; when it would be crowded with the hangers-on of such an establishment, returned from their sojourn in the trapping grounds, or their toilsome voyages to and from Montreal and Quebec, bent on lavishing away their season's earnings in days of idleness or debauch, and in "long nights of revelry and ease."

Much of this old-time character still remained. The motley population, the unique village, the fisheries and furs, the Indian dances and pow-wows, the mixture of civilization and barbarism, the isolation, broken only by occasional and irregular arrivals from the world below—made up a scene for which we were little prepared, which will not be easily forgotten, but of which I can give only this meagre description.

Death at

Eagle River

On a winter day in 1892 in a bare, weathered house on Kimball Street death came to the oldest settler at Sault Ste. Marie. He was half Scotch and half Chippewa, but wholly *voyageur*.

Born in 1799 on the site of future Superior, Wisconsin, Peter Mc-Farland followed his father in the service of the Hudson Bay Company; he made many journeys over Lake Superior and through the wilds to Hudson Bay. When Douglass Houghton began his geological surveys he chose Peter McFarland as his chief boatman. He became a trusted companion and friend.

When their mackinaw boat capsized off Eagle River in 1845, Douglass Houghton and two men, Tousin Piquette and Oliver Larimer, were lost, along with Houghton's black and white spaniel Meemee, and all his field notes, specimens and instruments. Two other men, Peter McFarland and Baptiste Bodrie, reached shore and struggled through the snowstorm to Eagle River.

The story they told was recalled by the *Sault Ste. Marie News* at the time of McFarland's death and was recorded in volume 22 of the *Michigan Pioneer Collections*.

D R. HOUGHTON camped out the night of the 12th of October at Eagle Harbor; on the morning of the 13th he started in his boat with the undersigned acting as voyageurs, with three barrels of flour, a bag of peas, some pork, tent and bedding and a traveling portfolio, for Eagle river, a distance of eight miles, to the westward. On arriving at Eagle river they there took in some additional clothing for the surveying party and proceeded five miles still farther west to the storehouse of Hassey & Avery; they arrived there at noon and immediately commenced unloading the boat;

after waiting some time the miners at work on the location of Hassey & Avery came in to their dinner and from some of them Dr. Houghton procured the key of the storehouse and deposited his provisions. We all took dinner here, after which we started for Mr. Hill's surveying party, a distance of three miles on the shore. Dr. Houghton and Peter McFarland then started into the woods on the line and not finding Mr. Hill he returned to the boat and found by the arrival of Tousin Piquette and Oliver Larimer that Mr. Hill and his men were two miles still further up the lake. Dr. Houghton then started in his boat in pursuit of Mr. Hill, with McFarland, Bodrie, Piquette and Larimer; we met Mr. Hill and his party about sundown and after remaining nearly an hour and transacting some business we then put back with the same persons for the purpose of reaching Eagle river that night. We had nothing in the boat but some bedding and the portfolio; at the time of leaving there was a gentle land breeze and a heavy sea from the outside. Dr. Houghton took his usual seat in the stern as steersman, while four of us rowed the boat. On arriving opposite the Hassey location Peter McFarland asked Dr. Houghton if he was going to stop. Dr. Houghton replied, "No, for if I do not get to Eagle river tonight Oliver Larimer will lose his passage down the lake." McFarland them stated to Dr. Houghton that he was afraid it was going to blow. Dr. Houghton replied, "No, I guess not; a land breeze can't hurt us." By this time we were opposite the storehouse of Hassey & Avery. McFarland then told Dr. Houghton that he must go ashore at the warehouse, as Larimer's baggage was at that place. At this we put into the landing and after getting the baggage we then started for Eagle river. The wind was about the same as when we left Mr. Hill except that it commenced snowing a little and to grow dark; after rowing nearly three miles we found ourselves opposite a place called the sand beach. At this place the wind changed and commenced blowing from the northeast and the snow came faster. In a short time we encountered a heavy sea, caused by a reef projecting into the lake about a mile and a half. McFarland then asked Dr. Houghton to go ashore at the sand beach. Dr. Houghton replied: "We had better keep on—we are not far from Eagle river, pull away boys, pull hard." At this, Bodrie spoke in the French language to McFarland, and said, "We had better go ashore." Dr. Houghton immediately inquired of McFarland, "What did Bodrie say?" McFarland told him, when Dr. Houghton replied, "We had better go to Eagle river tonight, as we shall there have a new log house to dry us in." The wind and snow kept increasing and after rowing some time, Dr. Houghton remarked, once or twice, "Pull away, my boys, we shall soon be in, pull away," and encouraged us by similar expressions. We commenced shipping water and made but little progress. After knocking and rolling about among the breakers for over an hour and it storming all the time, McFarland bailed the boat out and advised Dr. Houghton to put on his life preserver. The bag containing it was handed to him and he placed it at his side; instantly a heavy sea struck the boat and filled it. Dr. Houghton then proposed going ashore. McFarland told him he could not land; that the coast opposite there was all rocks. Dr. Houghton immediately put the boat about saying, "We must go ashore; we can do nothing here." Within 200 yards of the shore we shipped another sea, which was followed by a larger billow, and the boat capsized with all hands under her. McFarland was the first person from beneath, and upon rising to the top of the water, caught hold of the keel of the boat at the stern. Upon looking around, he saw a man's arm about half way out of the water. He instantly lowered himself and caught the man by the coat collar, and upon bringing him up, it was Dr. Houghton, who recognized him. McFarland told him to take off his gloves and hold on to the keel of the boat. The advice was followed; McFarland still preserved his hold. Dr. Houghton then remarked, "Peter, never mind me, try to go ashore if you can; I will go ashore well enough." Instantly a heavy sea struck the boat, throwing it perpendicularly into the air. It fell over backwards, and Dr. Houghton disappeared forever. McFarland regained the boat and upon getting in, discovered for the first time one of his companions, Bodrie, in the water and clinging to the bow. In this position they both remained some fifteen minutes, but saw nothing more of their companions. The sea washed them out again. McFarland drifted towards the rocks and got a loose hold. In a moment he was washed off and was carried to and fro against the rocks some three times. The fourth wave landed him on the top of a ledge of rocks, and by clinging to a crack in the rocks, and getting hold of a small bush, he succeeded in saving himself. After landing he looked around him and could see nothing but the boat filled with water and the bedding floating. Soon he heard a voice among the rocks, asking in French, "Who is that?" McFarland replied, "It is me, Peter." The man was Bodrie. We commenced looking about in every direction and hallooed at the top of our voices, but heard no answer. We continued examining, until we found ourselves growing chilly and stiff, when Bodrie remarked, "Well, we have lost our brothers; it may be that one of us will get to Eagle river to tell their fate." We started and on the way down McFarland fell several times from exhaustion and cold. Bodrie roused his companion up and they finally succeeded in reaching Eagle river between the hours of 11 and 12 at night. We told what had happened and within an hour the entire coast was lined, in search for the bodies, by miners and others, who were near at hand.

Signed,
PETER McFARLAND,
BAPTISTE BODRIE.

ANGUS MURDOCH

Land, Luck
and Money

One of the lasting stories of the north country tells how a famous copper mine was discovered by a pig. A solitary settler on the Keweenaw peninsula, out looking for his pig, heard a squealing from between the roots of a tree. He pulled the pig out of the hole—and with it the first chunk of copper from the Calumet and Hecla location, which became the richest copper mine on earth.

While some strikes were as accidental as that, others came after stubborn search and toil. The story of the Cliff Mine, the first big copper find on Lake Superior, has been told many times—and never more graphically than by Angus Murdoch in his *Boom Copper,* 1943.

JOHN HAYS was a Pittsburgh pharmacist bedeviled by his own pills and prescriptions. He frankly detested "pill-doctoring" and spent as much time as he could in the woods with his hunting dog and muzzle loader. When the news of copper up north reached Pittsburgh, it awakened a twofold interest in the restless druggist. He saw a chance of making a fortune in copper, and his adventurous soul stirred with the thought of a new wilderness to explore. But even in those days, no businessman could lock the front door, hang out a sign, "Have Gone to the Keweenaw—Back Later," and with no further ado, set off to hunt copper. Like any modern businessman who yearns to get away from it all, Hays paid his personal physician a call.

Dr. C. G. Hussey listened with a sympathetic ear—the two were old friends and for years had hunted and fished together—and, after going through the motions of a physical examination, gave his diagnosis.

"John," he said, "You are in an extremely run-down condition. My advice is that you take an immediate trip to Lake Superior. Probably the region in which they've just discovered copper would be the most beneficial. I'll pay half of your expenses, and if you should happen—just happen, mind you—to see anything that looks good, why—"

That very afternoon John Hays left Pittsburgh with a haste unbecoming a sick man. In the succeeding weeks his impatience gave great annoyance to schooner captains who sailed him north and then west. He finally reached Copper Harbor, some time during July, 1843, among the first arrivals suffering from the copper fever. He made friends energetically and within a week was calling everyone in town by his first name. Prospectors, thirsty from searching the range, found him always willing to stand treat, provided they returned his hospitality by talking about their prospects.

One morning when he was holding court and buying drinks a sad-eyed stranger undertook to entertain the drinkers with an almost Shakespearean account of his special misfortune. Hays, listening idly, pricked up his ears when the stranger pounded on the bar and declaimed:

"I got three of the best god-damned claims on the Keweenaw— pure copper sticking right out of the greenstone on one of them— and I can't raise a cent to take the stuff out. What I need is a partner."

Hays reached for the bottle, poured the stranger another drink and began asking questions. The prospector was a Bostonian named Jim Raymond who held the rather useless distinction of being the first man to register a claim at the mineral agency at Copper Harbor. It seemed he *did* hold three claims, and before long the persuasive Hays had borrowed a pencil from the bartender and was scribbling an agreement on the back of an old letter. This paper gave Hays and his friend, Dr. Hussey, the option to purchase one-sixth interest in all three claims for the sum of $1,000.

Hays immediately set off for Pittsburgh to bring home the glad tidings. Dr. Hussey listened, fascinated, to his glowing description of the Keweenaw. The two soon worked themselves into a fever of enthusiasm and agreed at once that a mere one-sixth interest in three guaranteed bonanzas would never do. The eventual result was the formation of the Pittsburgh & Boston Mining Company. Boston was represented by Raymond and several friends who had grubstaked him, and they contributed the three claims for their shares in the corporation. Pittsburgh contributed the capital, through Hays, Dr. Hussey, and several others—notably another physician who later wagered his entire stack of chips on a single bet.

With the earliest whisper of spring, 1844, Hays again set off for the Keweenaw. With him were a geologist, nine husky Pennsylvania coal miners, and an amazing assortment of boxes, crates, and barrels containing supplies and mining equipment. Clearly, Hays, Hussey, *et al.*, meant business. But this was the second year of the copper boom, when the rush to the Copper Country was reaching its full momentum. Many other hopefuls stood on the docks at Cleveland waiting their turn for passage to the Sault. The few schooners then plying Huron were far overtaxed by the unprecedented demands of passengers and freight. For a moment, though no more, Hays was stymied. Then, crowding past the others, John strode up to the master of the schooner *Swan*. "What'll you take to charter your boat?" he asked. It was a sellers' market, and Captain Ben Stannard's price was stiff. Nevertheless, when they heard about it, the Pittsburgh & Boston shareholders approved Hays' expensive impetuosity, as they did his subsequent charter of the *Algonquin* for the last leg of the journey to the Copper Country.

All through the spring and summer of 1844, Hays and his party searched the first of Raymond's claims. The land was located close to Copper Harbor and was probably chosen as the scene of initial exploration because Douglass Houghton had blasted out his provocative "forty pound boulder of solid copper" in this area. The party grubbed here and there all summer long with little or nothing to show for their efforts. Then, just as autumn was beginning to tint the maples, a soldier from near-by Fort Wilkins showed Hays specimens of ore he had found while repairing the stockade around the fort. The soldier was rewarded with $50 for his perspicacity. Hays and his geologist searched for and soon found the vein from which the ore had come. During early December, the first shaft in the Copper Country was put down.

Soon Copper Harbor was ringing with the news: "They've found a rich vein of black copper oxide on the Pittsburgh & Boston location!"

It was a proud day for John Hays. He brought the triumphant news to Pittsburgh himself, together with a sackful of ore samples. Dr. Hussey and his fellow shareholders in P. & B. were jubilant and regaled all who would listen with accounts of wealth to come. The Boston shareholders had an even more concrete reason for rejoicing. A firm of assayers in the Hub found that the ore contained 86 per cent fine copper.

The dreams of the P. & B. shareholders, however, were still only dreams. The miners had sunk the shaft just fifteen feet when the vein pinched out entirely. Like the Lake Superior Company, Hays' forces were working nothing but a shallow pocket. Undaunted, Hays ordered his men to continue the shaft downward. The hammer and drill men toiled mightily, for the miners liked the little druggist and hated to see him fail. But by the time the shaft reached one hundred and twenty feet it was evident, beyond any doubt, that there was no more black copper oxide. Thirty to forty tons of ore had been taken from the first shaft put down on the Keweenaw Peninsula, and from the mineral the Roxbury Chemical Works near Boston smelted ingot worth $2,968.70. That sum was all Hays could show the shareholders for their investment of $25,000.

But the Pittsburgh & Boston's board of directors were still game. They voted unanimously to forget this initial failure and levied an assessment upon the stockholders. With fresh funds at his disposal, John Hays began explorations on the second of Jim Raymond's claims. This property was located about twenty-five miles down the Peninsula from the first diggings. In the course of his prospecting, Raymond had clambered up the greenstone bluffs common to this area, and at one point on the clifflike face he had seen outcroppings of native copper. As he had told Hays, somewhere within the heart of the bluff should be a rich ore body.

On the advice of geologists, Hays set his men to driving a tunnel or adit into the base of the bluff. The miners had worked inward only about seventy feet when they came upon a mass of solid native copper so large it took days of blasting to bring out the huge chunk so that the tunneling could continue. Back of the immense mass was more native metal in chunks of various sizes—so much copper that it was certain this was not another deceptive pocket. Now, for sure, Hays and the Pittsburgh & Boston had struck it rich!

But there was no time for rejoicing—the druggist and his men were too busy getting out metal. John did take time off to climb to the top of the bluff and christen his location the Cliff Mine. It's good to think of the wiry little pharmacist, silhouetted against the deep blue of a Lake Superior sky, freed forever from his mortar and pestle.

The discovery of the Cliff mass by systematic mining deep beneath the hard rock bluff had a reviving effect on the Copper Country. Those who had said the Keweenaw was a mineralogical freak and the first copper finds were nothing more than hopelessly deceitful pockets had to eat their words. Men and money flowed north and west again. In fact the Cliff Mine, as much as the issuance of title to mining lands, was responsible for turning the Copper Country from a prospectors' camp into a genuine mining district.

Soon great copper masses were a daily occurrence at the Cliff. Many were so immense they required days of cutting before they could be divided into sections small enough to transport to the dock at Eagle River. An old-timer, still living, recalls the latter days of the mine and remembers the picture of the Eagle River dock, piled high with huge masses awaiting shipment.

"Most all of them," he'll tell you, "were bigger than my out-house back there."

Three-quarters of all the metal taken from the Cliff came out in the form of masses weighing anywhere from a ton to a hundred tons. The rock surrounding the masses was so richly mineralized that a primitive method could be used to free the "barrel work." Vein rock and cordwood were piled on top of each other in layers until as much as sixty tons of rock were heaped up. The pyre was then lighted off. After it had burned for days, cold water was dashed over the blistering-hot mineral. The rock was shattered, and the metal could then be freed in a rude stamp mill.

All this was easy and profitable, but it didn't last forever. A time came when the Cliff's adit met only barren rock. The geologists believed that the main ore body was yet to be found. That, they thought, lay somewhere farther underground, and advised Hays to sink a vertical shaft from the top of the bluff. Hays agreed, for it was certain that underground exploration couldn't continue until the mine was equipped with a practicable hoisting system. The job of sinking this shaft was directed by Edwin J. Hulbert, who later was to find the greatest bonanza of the Copper Country—the great Calumet conglomerate bed.

The Cliff stockholders soon learned how expensive hard-rock shafting can be, and what heavy demands it could make on the company treasury. In fact, by the time the shaft had reached seven hundred feet working funds were entirely exhausted. This in spite of early successes. The Company's operations had already involved a stock investment of $150,000 as well as assessments levied on shareholders of an additional $110,000. Yet there was no more copper in sight.

By this time, Pittsburgh & Boston had divided itself into two factions. The Pennsylvania contingent called a meeting in Pittsburgh, only formally inviting the Bostonians to attend. A most discouraging report was given to the assembly. Nevertheless, the ever optimistic Pennsylvanians voted for another assessment to pay for continuing the shaft downward. The Boston shareholders, who came anyway, had had enough of copper mining and voted unanimously, "Not another penny."

At this point, Dr. Charles Avery arose and asked the assembled directors, "What about copper mining in Europe—how deep do they sink shafts over there—does anyone know?"

No one did know, but all realized that the answer was important. Captain Edward Jennings, superintendent of the Cliff, who had come to Pittsburgh for instructions was summoned before the meeting and then plied with questions. Jennings, a Cousin Jack who had left Cornwall with several generations of copper mining experience behind him, spoke right up.

"No, sir," said he. "Seven hundred feet is no fair test for a shaft. Why, in Cornwall we hardly ever find any copper above eight hundred feet. Of course the gentlemen's money is not my money, but—"

This was enough for Dr. Avery, who held one-sixth of the Pittsburgh & Boston stock. "I'll lend the company $60,000. Let's sink that shaft a few hundred feet more."

The Doctor wagered the savings of a lifetime, but fortunately the gamble turned out to be a lucky one. Eighteen months later the Cliff forces struck rich vein rock again. Shortly afterward, the company repaid Dr. Avery in full and was able to declare the handsome dividend of another $60,000 as well. This was paid to shareholders in 1849—the first dividend ever paid in the Copper Country.

Unfortunately, during that crucial year and a half, many of the stockholders had lost hope and either forfeited their stock or sold it below the subscription price of $25 per share. They soon regretted their lack of faith. The Cliff began clearing $20,000 net profit every thirty days and the Boston Stock Exchange was quoting Pittsburgh & Boston at $300 per share. During one happy period every pound of copper stoped out of the Cliff's in'ards put six and one-half cents into shareholders' pockets. Nowhere in the world had so much copper ever been taken from so small an area of mineral land.

Now that he was wealthy, John Hays' early subterfuge caught up with him, so to speak. He became genuinely ill from overwork, and Dr. Hussey was then completely serious when he advised Hays to travel for his health. John and his wife toured Europe; but all the while he couldn't forget his beloved Cliff. American smelters were having trouble with the hundred-ton masses, and Hays conceived a special furnace able to handle these awkward lumps with ease. He journeyed to Swansea, Wales—then the greatest smelting center in the world—expecting to study the Welsh methods before completing his own ideas. Hays had assorted specimens ranging in size from a few pounds to a show piece of a ton and a half shipped to Swansea. These astounded British scientists but apparently produced only jealousy among the Welsh smelting magnates. They carefully avoided giving him any cooperation. Not in the least nonplused, Hays returned to Pittsburgh and built the sort of furnace he had had in mind in the first place. Its entire top could be lifted off, so that the huge masses of lake copper could easily be lowered inside. The furnace proved a great success, doubtless to the chagrin of the Swansea magnates.

Pittsburgh & Boston, satisfied with a return of over 200 per cent in dividends on paid-up capital, sold the property in 1871 as the lower levels grew meager. A Cliff Mining Company was formed, the old levels were unwatered, and the property buzzed with activity again. Nearly 6,000,000 more pounds of copper were produced before this second chapter of the mine was concluded nine years later. Then the Tamarack Mining Company, flush with profits from its shafts on the Calumet conglomerate, tried its corporate hand at working the Cliff location. It, however, was unsuccessful and was the last to mine the property. As this is being written, diamond drill crews are making test borings in the vicinity of the original shafts. Geologists examine the drill cores with patient care, hoping to find indications of extensions or continuations of the Cliff fissure vein.

For the most part, however, the Cliff is a ruin, its shafts filled with water and its once populous village a disheveled, crumbling ghost town—important only as a tourist attraction. A few tottering buildings and a weed-grown cemetery are the only remaining monuments to *forty million pounds of copper*. Today, few remember the Cliff was the first mine in the district to prove that fortunes could be made in Michigan copper. Provided, of course, your efforts were backed by the proper combination of Land, Luck, and Money.

CHARLES LANMAN

Copper Fever

Writer, artist and traveler—"the picturesque explorer of our country," Washington Irving called him—Charles Lanman (1819–1895) was born in Monroe, Mich., with a trace of Algonquin blood from his French-and-Indian mother. While pursuing a journalistic career in Cincinnati and New York he managed to spend long seasons of writing and sketching in Canada and the Northwest. He later became private secretary to Daniel Webster and an official in the Department of the Interior. Handsome, genial, urbane, with an endless fund of stories from his youthful wanderings, he was a social favorite in Washington.

In 1846 Lanman made a canoe trip with Indians and *voyageurs* along the shore of Lake Superior. It was an idyllic season. "Delightful indeed were those summer days on the bosom of the great northern lake . . . but the nights I spent on the lonely shores have made a deeper impression upon me." After the campfires had winked out he walked alone on the midnight beach, with the ghostly banners of the aurora streaming over the dark sea.

In the copper country Lanman looked at men and nature with realistic eyes. He saw bright prospects for industrious miners and none at all for the more numerous riffraff of the copper rush. This sketch is taken from *Adventures in the Wilds of the United States*, 1856.

I AM the owner of a few shares of copper stock, but exceedingly anxious to dispose of my interest, at the earliest possible moment, and on the most reasonable terms. This remark defines my position with regard to copper in general, and may be looked upon as the text from which I shall proceed to make a few general observations on the copper region of Lake Superior. I am curious to find out how it will seem, for the public at large, to read something which is not a purchased puff. Those, therefore, who are unaccustomed to simple matters of fact, will please pass on to another chapter of my book, or lay it down as the most insipid volume that was ever published.

It is undoubtedly true, that all the hills and mountains surrounding this immense lake, abound in valuable minerals, of which the copper, in every form, is the most abundant. The lamented Douglass Houghton has published the opinion, that this region contains the most extensive copper mines in the known world. The discoveries which have been made during the last three years would lead one to suppose this opinion to be founded in truth.

Not to mention the ship loads of rich ore that I have seen at different times, I would, merely to give my reader an idea of what is doing here, give the weight of a few distinguished discoveries that I have actually seen.

The native copper boulder, discovered by the traveller Henry, in the bed of the Ontonagon river, and now in Washington, originally weighed thirty-eight hundred pounds; a copper mass of the same material lately found near Copper Harbor, weighed twelve hundred pounds; at Copper Falls, the miners are now at work (1846) upon a vein of solid ore, which already measures twenty feet in length, nine in depth, and seven and a half inches in thickness, which must weigh a number of tons; and at Eagle River another boulder has lately been brought to light, weighing seventeen hundred pounds.

As to native silver, the Eagle River valley has yielded the largest specimen yet found about this lake, the weight of which was six pounds ten ounces. These are mineral statistics from which may be drawn as great a variety of conclusions as there are minds.

The number of mining companies which purport to be in operation on the American shore of Lake Superior and on our islands, is said to be one hundred; and the number of stock shares is not far from three hundred thousand. But notwithstanding all the fuss that has been, and is still made, about the mining operations here, a smelting furnace has not yet been erected, and only three companies, up to the present time, have made any shipments of ore. The oldest of these is the Lake Superior Company; the most successful, the Pittsburgh and Boston Company; and the other is the Copper Falls Company, all of which are confined in their operations to Point Keweenaw.

This point is at present the centre of attraction to those who are worshipping the copper Mammon of the age. It is a mountainous district, covered with a comparatively useless pine forest, exceedingly rocky and not distinguished for its beautiful scenery. As to the great majority of the mining companies alluded to, they will undoubtedly sink a good deal more money than they can possibly make; and for the reason, that they are not possessed of sufficient capital to carry on the mining business properly, and are managed by inexperienced and visionary men—a goodly number of whom have failed in every business in which they ever figured, and who are generally adventurers, determined to live by speculation instead of honest labor. The two principal log cabin cities of Point Keweenaw are Copper Harbor and Eagle River. The former is quite a good harbor, and supports a vacated garrison, a newspaper, a very good boarding-house, and several intemperance establishments. The latter has a fine beach for a harbor, a boarding-house, a saw-mill, and a store, where drinking is the principal business transacted. The number of resident inhabitants in the two towns I was unable to learn, but the sum total I suppose would amount to fifty souls.

Altogether perhaps five hundred miners and clerks may be engaged on the whole Point, while about as many more, during the summer, are hanging about the general stopping places on the shore, or the working places in the interior. This brotherhood is principally composed of upstart geologists, explorers, and location speculators. From all that I can learn, about the same state of things exists on the Canada side of the lake. Twenty companies are already organized for that section of country, the most promising of which is the Montreal Mining Company; but not a pound of ore has yet been smelted or taken to market, so that the "subject theme," for the present, is as barren of real interest there, as in our own territory. Rationally speaking, the conclusion of the whole matter is just this: the Lake Superior region undoubtedly abounds in valuable minerals, but as yet a sufficient length of time has not elapsed to develop its resources; three quarters of the people (the remaining quarter are among the most worthy of the land) now engaged in mining operations, are what might be termed dishonest speculators and inexperienced adventurers: but there is no doubt that if a new order of things should be brought into existence here, all those who are prudent and industrious would accumulate fortunes.

I ought not to leave this brazen theme, without alluding to the science of geology as patronized in the mineral region. Not only does the nabob stockholder write pamphlets about the mines of the *Ural* mountains, and other *neighboring* regions, but even the broken-down New York merchant, who now sells whisky to the poor miner, strokes his huge whiskers, and descants upon the black oxyd, the native ore, and the peculiar formation of every hillside in the country. Without exception, I believe, all the men, women and children residing in the copper cities, have been crystalized into finished geologists. It matters not how limited their knowledge of the English language may be, for they look only to the surface of things; it matters not how empty of common sense their brain-chambers may be, they are wholly absorbed in sheeting their minds and hearts with the bright red copper, and are all loudly eloquent on their favorite theme.

But the grand lever which they use to advance their interests, is the word "conglomerate," which answers as a general description of the surrounding country. You stand upon a commanding hill-top, and whilst lost in the enjoyment of a fine landscape, a Copper Harbor "bear" or "bull," recently from Wall street, will slap you on the shoulder, and startle the surrounding air with the following yell: "That whole region, sir, is *conglomerate,* and exceedingly rich in copper and silver." You ask your landlady for a drop of milk to flavor your coffee, and she will tell you "that her husband has exchanged the old red cow for a conglomerate location somewhere in the interior," thereby proving that a comfortable living is a secondary consideration in this life. You happen to see a little girl arranging some rocky specimens in her baby-house, and on your asking her name, she will probably answer—"Conglomerate the man, my name, sir, is Jane." But enough. It will not do for me to continue in this strain, for fear that my readers will, like my mining friends, be made crazy by a remarkable conglomerate literary specimen from the mineral region.

The

Compass Needle

While Douglass Houghton was making his geological survey of 1844, U.S. deputy surveyor William A. Burt was running township lines in future Marquette County. Burt was a self-taught man from New England. As a youth he had learned astronomy by tracing the stars above his father's pasture; since then he had invented a solar compass in which he took great pride. That compass served him well in the iron lands of Upper Michigan.

On September 19, 1844, running a section line between future Negaunee and Ishpeming, Burt noted extraordinary fluctuations of the compass needle. He wrote:

EAST BOUNDARY of Township 47 North, Range 27 West. The line is very extraordinary, on account of the great variations of the needle, and the circumstances attending the survey of it. Commenced in the morning, the 19th of September; weather clear, the variation high and fluctuating, on the first mile, section one. On sections 12 and 13, variations of all kinds, from south 87 degrees east, to north 87 degrees west. In some places the north end of the needle would dip to the bottom of the box, and would not settle anywhere. In other places it would have variations 40, 50, and 60 degrees east, then west variation alternating in the distance of a few chains. Camped on a small stream in section 13.

During this season the barometer man in Burt's party was Jacob Houghton, a younger brother of Douglass Houghton. He kept a diary more expressive than Burt's bare field notes. Of that first discovery of Lake Superior iron ore he wrote a more memorable account:

On the morning of the 19th of September, 1844, we started to run the line south between ranges 26 and 27. As soon as we reached the hill to the south of the lake, the compassman began to notice the fluctuation in the variation of the magnetic needle. We were of course using the solar compass, of which Mr. Burt was the inventor, and I shall never forget the excitement of the old gentleman when viewing the changes of the variation, the needle not actually traversing alike in any two places. He kept changing his position to take observations, all the time saying, "How could they survey this country without my compass? What could be done here without my compass?" It was the full and complete realization of what he had foreseen when struggling through the first stages of his invention. At length the compassman called for us all to "come and see a variation which would beat them all." As we looked at the instrument, to our astonishment the north end of the needle was traversing a few degrees to the south of west. Mr. Burt called out, "Boys, look around and see what you can find." We all left the line, some going to the east, some going to the west, and all of us returned with specimens of iron ore, mostly gathered from outcrops. This was along the first mile from Teal Lake. We carried out all the specimens we could conveniently.

In 1885, forty-one years later, Peter White quoted this passage from Jacob Houghton's diary. "These ores," he added, "today make nearly one third of all the iron produced in the United States."

Finding the

Iron Mountains

The spring of 1845 brought the first rush of fortune-hunters to the North. Lured by the scientist's reports and by wild rumors of awaiting riches, hundreds of men sought the mineral lands. Among them was Philo M. Everett, a Connecticut Yankee who had settled in Jackson, Michigan.

Upon news of the discoveries of 1844 Everett organized a dozen of his neighbors into the Jackson Mining Company; they meant to mine silver and copper. At Detroit, in June of 1845, Everett loaded supplies onto a steamer for Sault Ste. Marie. At the Soo he bought a two-masted mackinaw boat and paid ten dollars to get it hauled around the falls. He hired halfbreed Louis Nolan, a veteran of the Lake Superior country, to sail the boat to the mineral locations.

Everett was in search of copper, but when Nolan told of a rusty purplish ore near Teal Lake he decided to look at it. Landing on the site of future Marquette, the party packed in to Teal Lake, fifteen miles through the hardwood forests. There they found Chief Majji-Gesick who showed them a black and glinting hill that was superstitiously shunned by the Indians. At the roots of a big pine tree lay chunks of heavy rock "as bright as a bar of iron just broken."

Everett packed some samples back to his boat. He returned to lower Michigan in October, having been four months away. Though it would be years before their riches came to light, he had found the iron mountains.

His narrative is recorded in volume 11 of the *Michigan Pioneer Collections*.

IN 1844 the copper interest of Lake Superior got to fever heat, especially in Boston, by the reports of Professor Jackson, of Boston. A friend of his in Detroit, whom I was then doing business with, gave me the history of Jackson's work in exploring on the shores of Lake Superior, and in the spring of 1845 I determined to visit Lake Superior and see for myself, if possible, what all that talk amounted to. I proposed to some of my friends to join me in a speculation of that nature, and I soon collected thirteen members. The association papers were made out and signed by all the members, and our company was called the Jackson Mining Company of Jackson, Michigan. I then sent to our Senator at Washington, Mr. Norvel, asking him to procure a number of permits from the Secretary of War, giving permission to locate a mile square each any where on the south shore of Lake Superior, for mining purposes, and as the season was advancing I made ready at once to leave for Lake Superior on receipt of my permits. Our permits were issued on the 16th of June, 1845, and I believe that was the last day permits were ever issued, the transaction of the Secretary of War being declared illegal; but Congress legalized the act and gave permission for any person to locate a mile square on the south shore of Lake Superior by leaving a person in charge of the location. I received our permits on the 19th of June, and on the 20th of June, 1845, I left my home in Jackson for Lake Superior, bought my supplies in Detroit, and took a steamer for Mackinaw, as there was no boat then running direct to the Sault as now. I purchased a coasting boat at Mackinaw and put it on board the *General Scott*, a small side wheel steamer, making three trips a week from Mackinaw to the Sault. It was said no boat could go up the Sault river then, drawing over nine feet of water.

I was somewhat surprised on arriving at the Sault to find such an immense warehouse for traffic with the Indians of the northwest. My first duty was to transport my coasting boat over the portage of three quarters of a mile and ship the most of my supplies to Copper Harbor, that being copper headquarters. We struck our tent at the head of the portage preparing for a start. The next thing in order was to procure a coaster, one that was familiar with the lake. The thought of coasting along the rocky and desolate shores of Lake Superior, not knowing at any time what we were to meet with next, was not a pleasing one, especially in passing the pictured rocks. It was well known that there were long stretches of coast there where no boat could land and that Lake Superior often got very angry in a

few minutes. Louis Nolan was recommended to me as the best man
for that purpose in the Sault. He was a large, stout man, well acquainted with the lake and all the northwest. I found him engaged
with a trader gathering in fish. He was a little over six feet high,
well proportioned, a Frenchman with a slight mixture of Indian
blood, with an intelligent countenance and pleasant address, and
very polite. I made my business known and inquired if he was well
acquainted with the lake. He replied that he had coasted the length
of the lake many times, on both sides, and also had traveled many
times to Hudson's Bay and had been employed by the fur company
for many years as a clerk. Now we think of a clerk as one sitting in
an easy chair in a warm office, writing at a desk; but a fur company's clerk is quite a different thing. He must be able to write a
fair hand, be a good accountant, and be able to take a ninety pound
pack on his back and travel all day from one Indian camp to another, collecting furs and living entirely on wild meat, mostly rabbits, for the fur companies only supplied bread food enough to last
their clerks to headquarters. The ninety pound pack consists of
Indian goods, and that is the standard weight of all fur companies'
packs. Knowing these facts before, I was at once satisfied he was the
man for us. He made a proposition for the season to pilot, pack and
cook for us. The bargain was then concluded, but he wanted two
days in which to prepare for the summer trip. It was granted. He
now remarked: "You say you are going to Copper Harbor for copper ore; you don't want to go to Copper Harbor for ore, there is
plenty at Carp River. There is more ore back of Carp River (now
Marquette) up at Teal Lake than you can ever get away—two
mountains of it—only two or three miles apart." I inquired what
kind of ore it was. "Don't know much about ore;" and having a few
specimens of ore with me, I spread them out and requested him to
point out the ore like the ore at Teal Lake. He shook his head,
putting his finger on a piece of Galena lead ore saying that was the
most like it, but that wasn't it. "It looks like rock, but it wasn't rock,
several bowlders lay beside the trail, worn smooth, and shined
brightly." "When did you see this ore last?" I inquired. "Thirty six
years ago I went from Carp River to Menominee with some Indians, and never having seen anything like it, I distinctly remember
it." "How old are you?" "Most sixty." His description of the ore two
or three miles further on was equally surprising. The trail ran along
the north side of a bluff, fifty feet high, of solid ore. This description greatly surprised me, for I learned he was a Christian man of
the Roman Catholic faith, was perfectly truthful and reliable, never
used profane language and never got drunk. What could it be? It

was not copper, that was evident, for I showed him copper specimens, and that was not it, as he termed it. I had never heard of iron in this district, and therefore thought nothing of its being iron.

Now, as I had two days to wait, I took a stroll about the town. Passing down the portage, I noticed several canoes in the rapids, two Indians in each canoe, standing erect as steadily as if on land. I watched them for several hours, for I had never seen or heard of such a way of taking fish. The man in front soon dipped in his scoop net and took out a large whitefish. It was strange to see how that frail bark canoe could be shot into the foaming rapids, as white as milk, and could be managed by that Indian. The forward one, when he saw a fish, would lay down his setting pole, take up his scoop net, dip up his fish, and again take up his setting pole with surprising ease, and the canoe would again be shot into the foaming rapids still further. Few white men could stand erect in this canoe a single moment. I sat on the shore for a long time, scarcely thinking of the passing hours.

I next visited the fort, a beautiful site for a city—such a handsome plat of ground on every side. Not far from the fort was the Baptist mission, under the charge of Rev. Mr. Bingham, a very pleasant gentleman. He told me he went on board of a schooner at Buffalo, with his family, bound for the Sault, if I remember rightly, in 1833, to take charge of the mission. He had a lovely family—his girls were like roses in a wilderness. He told me much of his labors with the Indians; he thought he had done them much good, and I had no doubt of it. He had taught them to read and write, and from my long acquaintance with the Indians in Oneida county, New York, where they had every facility for school and church, I knew that was about all that could be made of them. They seem to lack a capacity for anything further. After they get that far, as soon as they are out of school they will join a dog feast, according to the old Indian custom.

But the two days were now wearing away. Louis reported at our tent for duty with his pack of blankets and tent cloth, together with a shot gun, having the appearance of being manufactured in Queen Anne's time, but it was a deadly weapon, dangerous at both ends, as one of our party could testify a few days afterwards. He ventured to fire it at some game, was knocked sprawling on the ground, and went with a lame shoulder for many days. He said it kicked like a mule. No one of our company had the courage to fire it afterwards during the whole summer.

We were not long in finding out that we had made a wise choice in our coaster. He knew every point and every stream that entered the lake. When it came time to camp, he would run the boat ashore at the mouth of a stream where we could catch all the speckled trout we wanted for supper and breakfast. He never left his seat on the stern of the boat. When we sailed, he steered, and when we rowed he paddled and steered. He was supplied with trolling line, as well as gun. The first day I said to him, "Can't you catch some trout by trolling?" "No trout here; too much sand beach," he said; but one day as we were passing a rocky point he took out his trolling line, saying, "May be we can catch trout here." He threw out his line and a big trout took it before the hook was twenty feet from the stern of the boat, and I saw several others after it. He took in several fine ones in a few minutes and went to winding up his line. I asked him to let me take it and catch a lot. I shall never forget the look he gave me, saying; "What you want of them? you have now more than we can eat; do you wish to waste the Indians' food?" That was a break-down argument. I admitted he was right, and said no more.

On arriving at Teal Lake, we found the ore just as he had described it. There lay the boulders of the trail, made smooth by the atmosphere, bright and shining, but dark colored, and a perpendicular bluff fifty feet in height, of pure solid ore, looking like rock, but not rock, and on climbing a steep elevation of about seventy feet, the ore cropping out in different places all the way, we came, at the top, to a precipice many feet deep. Hundreds of tons of ore that had been thrown down by the frost lay at the bottom. It was solid ore, but much leaner than that on the other side. From all that could be seen, it seemed that the whole elevation for half a mile or more was one solid mass of iron ore. No rock could be seen, and all that visited it came to the same conclusion, until the mine was fairly opened. By measurement, the outcrop was found to be three quarters of a mile southwest of the southeast corner of Teal Lake.

The other outcrop, two miles further on, was a beautiful sight. On the north side of the hill it was a perpendicular bluff of about fifty feet of pure iron ore and jasper in alternate streaks, but more jasper than iron.

Another small outcrop appeared a mile further on, for several years known as the little location (now known as Lake Superior mine). With all its beauty, that high bluff proved worthless; but the Cleveland mine, near by, only a few rods from its base, was soon discovered, and proved one of the best mines in the country.

On arriving at Copper Harbor, I found the government mineral office on the island opposite the harbor, which in fact formed the harbor. The white tents on the island appeared like an army encampment. Presenting my permit and description, the officer looked it over, saying, "Where is Teal lake? It is not on my map." I told him the Indians called it twenty five miles southwest of Carp river, and it took us a day and a half to go there. That was all I knew about it. He said to me: "Mark the lake on the map." I refused to do so, saying that it might work us an injury, as it was pretty certain to be wrong. He measured off twenty five miles on his map and marked out Teal lake with our permit on the south side, as given in the description. I did not lay a permit on what is now known as the Cleveland, believing, as Louis said, we had all the ore we could ever get away, of the very best quality and nearer the lake, preferring to let some other party take it and help to open the country. I had only seen this kind of rock ore once before. That was twenty miles from Black river in Oneida county, New York, between that place and Lake Champlain. That ore was precisely the same as the specular ore of Lake Superior. At Copper Harbor I met Professor Shepard, of New Haven, Connecticut, and I showed him the iron. He said it was as fine ore as he had ever seen, but thought it nearly worthless as it was so far away; it would be like lifting a weight at the end of a ten foot pole. But when I parted with him in the fall he said he had thought much about that iron, and believed I had better take care of it; the time might come when it would be worth something.

The

Stained Rock

A century ago Americans took strenuous measures to overcome ill health: Richard Henry Dana sailed in a square-rigger around Cape Horn, Francis Parkman traveled on horseback across the plains, and Raphael Pumpelly took his invalid wife on a prospecting trip to the wilds of Lake Superior.

In 1869 at Harvard, young Raphael Pumpelly began teaching the first mining course in North America. He had just three students, but he kept them fascinated with his huge frame draped over the lecture stand, his golden beard and sea-blue eyes, and his accounts of field trips in far places.

Pumpelly was just thirty-one but he had explored and prospected around the world. Back in America in 1867 he was hired by the Lake Superior Ship Canal Company to make a selection of two hundred thousand acres of federal lands in northern Michigan. The company wanted a search for gold and copper, but Pumpelly persuaded them that their best prospects lay in white pine and iron ore. In the spring of 1868, with an assistant geologist and four Indians, he started inland from Marquette.

Far up the Michigamme River they met another canoe. Out of it stepped a veteran explorer who for a thousand dollars offered to lead them to a large outcrop of specular and magnetic ore. Toiling through hardwood forest and cedar swamp, they found the outcrop with evidence of an extensive ore body. Following magnetic attraction they selected a belt of land running for twenty miles along the ore formation. Like any geologist Pumpelly was seeing two landscapes, the one he hacked his way through and another, a million years earlier, when the Menominee cliffs were the coast of a heaving Cambrian sea that slowly laid its sandstones over great blocks of limestone and iron ore.

The next spring Pumpelly was there again, with Duke William of Württemberg who wanted to see the American frontier. The seventy-year-old duke proved to be a good man in the woods, accepting without complaint wet camps and hard travel. Now Pumpelly had an audience more responsive than halfbreed canoe-men. Drying his long legs beside a campfire, he talked about geology, astronomy, archaeology, his life with shepherds and bandits in Corsica, his journey through the Gobi Desert in midwinter, his love of vast and lonely places. This season he chose lands west of Gogebic Lake in a region that showed little iron outcrop but frequent dippings of the compass needle. It was to become the Gogebic Range, about half of which (the land grant being limited to odd-numbered sections) he selected for the canal company.

In Boston at the end of the summer Pumpelly was married, and that fall he began teaching. How a prank on the part of some Harvard boys led to the discovery of the Gogebic iron range is told in these pages from Raphael Pumpelly's *Reminiscences*, 1918.

D URING THE WINTER of 1870–71 we boarded in Cambridge. Toward the end of the college year something happened that changed the course of our life. Some students who had a grudge against the two very estimable ladies who kept the house exploded a key of powder on the veranda. It blew in the window of the room where these ladies were sitting. My wife was in the room above, and the shock was so severe that it affected her health, and proved fatal to the child we were expecting. This, and the fact that the Boston climate disagreed with me, made me decide to discontinue lecturing. Pending the expected increase of the fund for the Sturgis-Hooper professorship, my salary was almost nominal, and it had become necessary to do outside work. So I turned to Lake Superior to capitalize the experience I had gained there.

Mr. Quincy Shaw and Mr. Alexander Agassiz agreed to my proposition that they should supply the money to buy lands, and that I should have the right to buy a quarter interest in these lands at cost. The purchases were to be confined to lands carrying pine, the iron formation, hardwood, and sandstone. Hardwood was then very valuable for furnaces making charcoal iron, and the Lake Superior brown sandstone was in great demand.

My wife wanted to go with me, and I felt that out-of-door life might hasten her recovery. So as soon as she was able to travel we went to Marquette. I bought a bark canoe and hired a large sailboat and skipper and two Canadian voyageurs, one of them, Henri Ledouceur, with his educated Indian wife, Priscilla. These, with two tents, supplies, guns, fishing tackle, and abundant township maps, formed the outfit. As guests, we had Mrs. Calvert Vaux and her daughter.

On a beautiful summer day we sailed out of Marquette harbor. As far as Portage Lake the south shore is formed by cliffs of the brown sandstone, some of which I hoped to find worth taking. Two weeks or more were spent in exploring this shore, and canoeing up the streams. The scenery was of unending charm. The many-colored cliffs of the indented coastline were overhung by a luxuriant growth of primeval forest, and the entering streams were outlets of chains of lakes nestling in wild scenery, and abounding in trout or pickerel and ducks. There were beavers, partridges, and porcupines; and now and then a deer. However, we took of these only for food fish, ducks, and partridges. The spruce-partridge is a stupid bird. He would wait patiently while we made a pole with a noose to pull him down. Those were delightful camping experiences in that bracing air under the northern stars. The flickering light of the campfire penetrated mysterious recesses in the dark forest. The silence was broken only by the hooting of an owl or the long, uncanny cry of a loon.

Late on one afternoon the sky showed menace of a sudden storm that left us barely time to reach the lee side of a nearby island and to get ashore, when the elements broke loose. The island was a mass of flat-lying strata of quartzite. Large broken masses of this rock forming the surface were covered by a thick growth of moss, out of which grew a dense forest of spruce. Everywhere the moss-covered pitfalls threatened broken legs or worse. Our fire ignited the moss hanging from a spruce. Instantly the flames shot upward. Only the drenching rain saved us from the terrors of a burning forest.

The wind god of the lake celebrates when the sun god leaves the Northern house. On the wings of the storm he lays low the forest. Catching up a spark, he turns to ashes whole townships— woods, villages, people. Burning treetops fly ahead through the air to cut off escape.

Two days long the clouds flew by above us, and the wind howled through the forest, but we were safe except for falling trees and the pitfalls.

I think it was in this storm that the steamer *Huron* went down with all on board. Some of our friends were on it, including Professor Hodges.

Mrs. Calvert Vaux and her daughter turned homeward at Houghton.

Sometime in October we reached Bayfield in Wisconsin, where

there was a U. S. Land Office. I had two reasons for going there. One was to look for pine lands, the other was to outfit for a visit to the lands I had taken for the Canal Company when we were made to shift a part of the first grant. I wanted to see whether my assumed iron range really existed and whether the even numbered sections were promising.

As it was important to keep the object of the exploration secret, I drew a line on the map for a trail parallel to the supposed iron range, but about a mile distant. It extended about thirty miles to Lake Gogebic. Along this I sent a party of Indians under a head packer to make *caches* of provisions at specified points, and make a quick return. Major Brooks was to meet me at the Montreal River, and we were to study the route together, with only two packers who could keep us supplied from the *caches*.

In the meantime there appeared a man offering to sell the notes of several thousand acres of pine land. An examination of the land office records showed the lands to be open for entry. These I bought after some random test examinations.

A sail across the bay brought us to the mouth of the Montreal River. It was my intention to take my wife to the point where we should meet Major Brooks, and begin our exploration, and to leave her there in a stationary camp with the Indian woman Priscilla and her husband. As she was not yet strong enough to make the journey through the woods on foot, Indians were engaged to carry her in a hammock sung on a pole.

Around their campfire, that lighted up the dark recesses of the forest, these Indians were a picturesque group. Their leader wore a decorative name. We liked the sound of it so much that it caused him more than his share of work. It was *Jin-go-ben-e-sic*—War Eagle.

Henri and Priscilla made a delightful stationary camp in a stately forest and near the river. In a large tent, with one side open to the air, they made a thick, soft bed of carefully thatched hemlock boughs, and arranged all the possible conveniences for a prolonged stay. Their own tent was put up close by the large one. There were abundant provisions, and Henri was an expert in getting game and trout. As both Henri and Priscilla were devotedly attached to my wife, I felt that I was leaving her under health-bringing and happy conditions, for she loved the primeval forest in all its aspects.

During the previous winter I had read Whittlesey's account of the occurrence of magnetic ores in northern Wisconsin, which seemed to be possibly a continuation of the formation we were to look for in Michigan. So we had agreed that Brooks should begin on the Wisconsin side and try to trace the formation to our meeting point near the state line.

We decided first to try to trace the iron formation through to Lake Gogebic, about thirty miles distant, and then to examine it more carefully on the way back. It took us more than two weeks to trace it to the point where we lost it west of Lake Gogebic. What we saw was very discouraging. There really was a continuous iron formation resting on quartzite, and this on granite, but it was totally unlike any that we had seen. The few outcroppings showed only ferruginous slates or in places bands of highly siliceous magnetic ore.

By the time we were ready to return a foot of snow had fallen, making hopeless any further examination. So we parted, Major Brooks intending to go eastward after studying the relation of the Cambrian sandstone to the Keweenaw trap rocks, while I started back on the trail made for the *caches.*

One morning, as we reached the top of a high hill, Jingobenesic startled me. He pointed to the southeast. Far away above the forest there stood a wall of dense smoke. It rose high in the sky, and stretched along many degrees of the horizon. It clearly meant an overwhelming conflagration—one that threatened destruction to everything in its course. We could not judge of its distance, but I thought of my dear wife in the heart of that vast forest, and twenty miles from the lake and safety, and it would take us nearly two days to reach her camp!

While I was hurrying forward in this anxiety, we met a messenger bringing a telegram and letters. He had been sent on from the stationary camp, and brought news of the great forest fire in Oconto County, Wisconsin, that was destroying whole villages and their inhabitants. The fact that it was more than 200 miles off and to leeward relieved my anxiety. Early in the morning, before reaching the Montreal River, I left the blazed trail, and climbed a high hill to look towards the wall of smoke. The hill was on the quartzite of the iron formation. It commanded a grand view over the great forest that, extending around Lake Superior, stretched away to the north, to gradually dwindle to the stunted vegetation of the Arctic zone.

I sat long trying to solve a problem of duty. The telegram I had received the day before was from Messrs. Lee, Higginson and Company. My large purchase of pine land was not approved; they did not want to accept my draft. I had wired back, by the messenger, that objections came too late, but I was left in a dilemma; for, notwithstanding the unfavorable appearance of the iron formation, I was intending to take up the even numbered sections in accordance with the policy I had followed in locating tracts on iron formation for the Canal Company. I now felt that I should be criticized for buying a large amount of iron land of which I could not speak with more confidence than I could show in the case of a formation so different from any known on Lake Superior.

While thus thinking I noticed numerous yellow stains of limonite in the rock. What is luck? Those yellow spots! They determined my fortune. I knew they probably had no important significance, but there was a remote possibility that they meant concentration of iron oxides in the overlying formation. I decided to take, for the pool at least, this tract, about two miles long.

I found the stationary camp abandoned. It had been left at least two days or more.

We followed a well-marked trail made in the snow by the party in moving towards the mouth of the Montreal River. It was after midnight when we reached the lake and found the camp.

In the bracing air, and under the devoted care of her attendants, my dear wife had recovered her strength. Priscilla had enlivened the time by telling Indian legends and tales of the wars between her people and the Eskimos, for she came from the North, and she had taught her mistress how to make and embroider moccasins. A hammock-stretcher was no longer needed; in spite of the snow, the trip out was made on foot.

At Bayfield I found a letter from Agassiz objecting strongly to the purchase of iron lands.

We took passage on a propellor to Marquette. It was the last trip for the season, and the boat was crowded with quarrymen, nearly all of them drunk.

Soon after leaving these men became so uncontrollable as to produce a serious situation, for they were overcoming the crew. The captain got out the hose and was beginning to play it on them when, on emerging from among the Apostle Islands, we came into a choppy sea. This quickly settled matters by leaving the floors covered with very unsettled victims.

And now came on a furious storm that placed us in danger of adding to the list of wrecks on that rocky coast. We even could not enter Eagle Harbor—the only place of refuge. No sea-craft could equal the old-time propellor for a training in seasickness.

At the land office in Marquette I again faced the problem that had sorely troubled me on the quartzite ridge in the woods. On the books the even numbered sections were all open for entry. From my notes I could cover all the iron formation along twenty miles of even sections. Under ordinary circumstances I would, without hesitation, have taken the risk. However, since that telegram about pine lands, and Agassiz's letter, seemed to show lack of confidence in my judgment, I preferred not to invest in lands on an iron range of which I could not speak with some confidence. As I shall show, I missed the opportunity of a lifetime. I was, of course, debarred from buying with my own money. Still I bought, on the joint account, two miles of the range adjoining the quartzite ridge. Those two miles now form the Newport and Geneva mining properties. They have produced till now (1915) 12,000,000 tons of ore.

Two or three years later a miner by the name of Moore, thrown out of work by the panic of 1873, was employed in looking for pine. There wasn't any pine land in the region. He sat down to smoke and curse his luck on a hill several miles east of the land I had taken. At his side rose the upturned roots of a great tree that had been felled by a recent storm. Where its roots had been there was exposed a smooth surface of black rock. Lifting a piece, Moore found it very heavy, and, being a miner, he knew it was not ordinary rock, though he had never seen anything like it, so he put it in his pocket as a curiosity. An assayer found that it was a very pure bessemer iron ore. Moore raised money to buy the tract, which became the Colby mine, and long before I heard of the find all the even sections, excepting my purchase, were taken up. Thus was started the great Gogebic iron range. Every section along it is dotted with mines which, together, have produced, up to 1915, over eighty million tons of bessemer ore.

Landlooker

When young John Longyear of Lansing, Michigan, went to Lake Superior in 1873, he expected to spend a season or two in the North country. But he remained for many years as surveyor, timber cruiser and iron hunter in the Lake Superior wilderness. As a government surveyor he explored the Wagon Road Grant near Lake Gogebic. A few years later, as agent for the Lake Superior Ship Canal, Railway and Iron Company, he made land grant selections along the future Gogebic range; by taking up adjoining tracts he laid the foundation for his own great fortune. He played a leading part in opening the Menominee and Gogebic iron ranges, and he was a pioneer prospector in the Mesabi.

Longyear had gone North for his health. With an eighty-pound pack on his shoulders and a dip compass in hand he found both health and fortune. After his great Norrie mine near Ironwood began production in 1885, John Longyear was a capitalist. But he never forgot his first seasons in the woods. Shortly before his death in 1922 he wrote down his memories of the wilderness years. They were published by the Marquette Historical Society in 1960.

I WAS twenty-three years old when, in May, 1873, I boarded the steamer "Rocket" at Detroit and made my first trip to Lake Superior. On the night of May 31st we lay in the ice near Grand Island in Lake Superior until daylight, when the steamer began moving slowly through the broken ice cakes. In all, we passed through a field of ice forty miles in extent and reached Marquette about noon on June 1st. At that time Marquette was a thriving little city of three thousand people and the only port on Lake Superior from which iron ore was shipped. Marquette County was the Lake Superior Iron Ore District; all the developed mines but one were there. The exception was the Spurr Mine, just over the line in Houghton (now Baraga) County.

In 1873 the Upper Peninsula of Michigan was practically an undeveloped wilderness, nearly covered with a heavy growth of standing timber. There were a few towns scattered around the edges of the lake shore, and the manufacture of pine lumber had been begun at several points. For some years railways had been in operation from Marquette westward to the Champion Mine, with a short branch going south to the Republic Mine. Another road, now part of the Chicago and Northwestern, had been in operation between Escanaba and Ishpeming for several years. In 1872 the Northwestern extended its road from Green Bay to Menominee and Escanaba. This made a through line from Marquette and Ishpeming to Chicago. Also in 1872 the Marquette, Houghton & Ontonagon Railway had been completed to L'Anse, at the head of Keweenaw Bay, a distance of sixty-two miles. There was also a narrow-gauge road, twelve miles in length, running from Hancock northeasterly to the Calumet & Hecla copper mine. These, I believe, were the only railroads in operation at that time.

The forest spread almost unbroken throughout the extent of the territory. Copper mines had been operated at various points on the Copper Range in Keweenaw, Houghton, and Ontonagon counties since 1845, but many of these had been abandoned, and in 1873 only a few copper mines were in operation.

Iron ore shipments from Marquette County had first been made in 1856, on the completion of the first "Soo" canal. The mining of iron ore had slowly increased, and in 1873, 1,250,000 tons of ore were shipped from the Lake Superior district. This was a record production, and calamity-howlers predicted that such overproduction would surely destroy the market. Thirty-four years later a season's output of the Lake Superior iron districts was more than 42,000,000 tons of ore.

In 1873 the schooner "Pelican" loaded and left the Marquette docks with 1,050 tons of iron ore, a record cargo. The calamity-howlers also protested against the use of such big ships, as they were sure that large vessels could not be made to pay on the lakes. The usual ships now being built (in 1920) on the lakes carry ten thousand and twelve thousand tons, and some fifteen-thousand-ton boats are now being constructed. Ships which carry five thousand tons or less are unprofitable because they cannot carry enough to pay expenses.

In regard to the extent of timberland, the great forest fires of 1871, which had destroyed Peshtigo in Wisconsin, as well as other towns, had crossed the Menominee River into Michigan and burned over the southern part of Menominee County. Near Republic a cyclone in 1868 had blown down the timber over an area of several square miles. A series of pine plains bordered the Chicago and Northwestern Railroad between Escanaba and Negaunee, and some small areas of pine could be found at various points near the mouths of streams on the shores of Lake Superior and Lake Michigan. There were also some open wet savannas in the eastern half of the Upper Peninsula. With these exceptions, the entire area was covered with a heavy, original forest, consisting of large stands of mixed timber, such as sugar or rock maple, yellow birch, basswood or linden, white pine, hemlock, spruce, etc. In the swamps was a dense growth of white cedar, while the bottom lands were timbered with elm, black ash, etc.

The impression prevailed outside the peninsula that it was a bleak, inhospitable, semipolar region, in which agriculture would be impossible, and the country was supposed to be of no value except for timber and minerals. Fertile farms and fruit orchards now flourishing in various parts of the Upper Peninsula prove how mistaken this notion was.

In 1873, a fairly passable wagon road ran from near the outer end of Keweenaw Point to Rockland and Ontonagon. The excellence of this road was mainly due to the natural material over which it was laid, for very little work had been done on it or, in fact, on any Upper Peninsula wagon road at that time. Such roads as there were reached back only short distances from the towns along the lake shore. They were nothing but surface tracks, commonly known as "tote-roads," such as were built by lumbermen for hauling supplies to their camps. These roads were usually about as rough as it is possible for horses to travel over.

On this government survey trip, I had with me a man named R. S. Thomas, an old woodsman and landlooker. After one or two days spent in Marquette getting maps, plats of government lands, etc., we traveled to L'Anse, sixty-two miles by rail. Then, with two Indians and one white man, packers hired in Marquette, we went on foot southwesterly by way of the old L'Anse and Lac Vieux Desert Trail for a distance of about fifteen miles. Leaving the trail, we then walked westerly and southwesterly through the woods, following section lines of the old government linear survey of 1846. . . .

About noon of the first day out from L'Anse we stopped for lunch at a small stream which crossed the trail. As we were eating, a party of three men came up the trail, having left L'Anse only a short time after we did. Woodsmen looking at vacant government lands were always very suspicious of each other; I have even heard tales of races from the woods to the land office to secure valuable tracts of timber. The three men also stopped to eat, and we began the usual series of cautious questions to ascertain where they were going, etc. Their outfit filled us with amusement. Two of the men carried double-barreled shotguns, and each of the three carried a heavy oilcloth valise and a blanket. They had no tent and no dishes, except for a tin cup apiece. The valises, when opened, were full of soda crackers about four inches square.

A few minutes talk with them showed that they were utterly ignorant of the wilderness and innocent of any sort of woodcraft. After considerable talk, Thomas said to them, "If you leave this trail, you will never come out of these woods alive." He finally suggested that they had better come with us, which they did. I have forgotten their names, but I do remember that they came from Oshkosh, Wisconsin. One was a blacksmith, another a wheelwright, and Randall, the leader of the group, was a man-of-all-work who had been in various parts of the United States. He said he had been shown in Oshkosh a nugget of gold by a man who told him he found it on the headwaters of the Ontonagon River. As the headwaters of the Ontonagon drain a territory about twenty-five by fifty miles in extent, and the entire region was then covered by a dense forest with no settlements or roads, the task these men had set themselves, of finding the place where the gold came from, was a large one. It developed that Randall had once chopped wood in California for three months in a gold-mining camp, and that was the extent of his experience in prospecting for gold. The other men were friends of his and had joined his expedition for a holiday frolic. Randall was unable to run a straight course in the woods even with the aid of a pocket compass.

After we had been cruising in the unbroken forest for about two weeks, the day before we reached the military wagon road, Bill, one of the men, remarked to Thomas and me: "If we had not met you our bones would have remained in these woods a long time. We never could have got out by ourselves," and he probably was right. The oldest man remarked, "Oh, we would have come out somewhere." To which Bill replied, "Yes, at the little end of the horn."

At every camp and every stream crossing where we stopped long enough, Randall, the gold seeker, would pan the sand. One rainy day when we stayed in camp, I was lying on the blankets when he came into the tent and lay down beside me to whisper, "I have found it!!" "Found what?" I asked, and he answered, "Gold!" "Where is it?" I said. He replied, "I lost it in the sand." "Find some more then," I suggested, but he never did.

Those three men had provided themselves with moccasins, supposed to be the appropriate thing for the woods, which were made of lightweight buckskin of a type usually sold to tourists. They had fitted them like ordinary shoes and were wearing only one light sock inside. In a few days their feet, being accustomed to the support of thick-soled shoes, soon swelled to at least double their usual size, and the moccasins wore to shreds. We were able to fit two of them out with extra footgear belonging to our party, but Bill's feet had swelled so much that he was obliged to use some empty provision bags which were wrapped around and then tied over his feet.

When we reached Rockland they bought some carpet slippers, but Bill could not find any large enough. Although he ordinarily wore a number seven shoe, he bought size ten slippers, split them in order to get his feet in, and then tied them on his feet with strings around the slippers and over the insteps. This was the only time I ever met anyone utterly ignorant of woodcraft undertaking an excursion in the woods, and Thomas was probably the instrument of Providence in preventing their destruction.

After about two weeks in the woods, with supplies nearly exhausted, we reached the military wagon road. It was then being built south from Rockland through the center of Range 39 to the Wisconsin state line. The construction camp at that time lay some twenty miles south of Rockland. Thomas was something of a bluffer and, though we had had a heavy day of tramping, after supper at the camp he suggested that he would like to walk on to Rockland that night, all of twenty miles, and asked me in a loud voice what I thought about it. I replied that I would go if he would. He then asked each one of the party in turn and received the same answer. I think he was somewhat surprised at this, for he had expected us to demur. He then said, "All right, we'll go," and we started.

After we traveled about six miles, the night became very dark. We were then in a part of the road built one or two years before. We could see the notch in the outline of the treetops, caused by trees removed in clearing the road, and thus we kept in the roadway. Thomas stopped, and again took a vote as to what we should do. We all voted to go on, but after walking a few rods further, Thomas stopped and said, "It is too hard on the boys," meaning the Indians, who had made no objection. None of us required much urging to stop, and spreading tents and blankets on the grass in the roadway, we lay down to sleep.

At once we were attacked by swarms of gnats, called by the Indians "no-see-ums." These little pests are almost invisible but burn like fire when they bite. Clothing and blankets seemed to be no protection against them. As soon as daylight was strong enough to see our way, we got up and started off for Rockland.

We had taken no food from the construction camp and expected no breakfast. After going about two miles we found a small camp occupied by three men who were chopping timber by the roadside to widen the clearing to fifty feet. We inquired as to chances for breakfast. They said they had eaten almost the last of their provisions, as they expected a supply wagon in a few hours. They made us welcome to anything they had, which we found to consist of a somewhat rancid shank of ham about four inches long. We cut this up into eight pieces, which we fried, and ate the lean meat, the fat being too sour. After this breakfast we proceeded to Rockland, where we arrived about noon.

At four o'clock that same afternoon we started with a team and wagon for Houghton, forty-eight miles to the northeast. The road passed along or near the crest of the copper-bearing Trap Range. The wagon was a dilapidated affair, and about eighteen miles from Rockland one wheel gave out. The young man driving the wagon said the Halfway House was only a mile farther and that we would have to walk there, which we undertook to do while he drove off ahead, leaving us to follow.

Bill's feet were so swollen and painful that it was impossible for him to walk, so he remained in the wagon. My feet also were very sore, but I felt able to walk a mile rather than ride in a wagon which had a wheel ready to collapse at any moment. The body of the wagon rested on high springs, and if the wheel did collapse, anybody in the cart was almost certain to be thrown out with considerable violence.

That Halfway House was several miles down the road, and we limpingly walked that distance through the thickest swarms of mosquitoes I have ever seen. We tied handkerchiefs over our necks and with a handful of brush constantly switched the insects away from our faces and ears. I also kept the hand not occupied with the brush swinging quickly back and forth in order to prevent the mosquitoes from lighting on it. My hand encountered so many mosquitoes in swinging that I looked down several times to see if I was walking in redtop grass, as the insects brushing against my hand created that impression.

Arriving at the Halfway House, which we found was all of six miles from the point where the wagon left us, we discovered a clearing of some five acres in which stood a group of log buildings belonging to the stage company. The people keeping the house had

instructions to feed no one except those who came on the conveyances of the stage company. However, with the three men who
had joined us on our first day out from L'Anse, we made a party of
eight, and there were only two men at the Halfway House. We
assured them that we would not leave without supper, that we were
willing to pay for it, but that supper must be forthcoming. After
perfunctorily pleading their orders, they acknowledged that we
were strong enough to get supper if we wanted it, and proceeded to
furnish us with an excellent meal.

At the Halfway House some idle wagons were standing near the
barn, and fortunately one of them was of the same size and make as
ours. We borrowed one of its wheels and placed our own broken
wheel in the wagon to be repaired after we reached Houghton. Our
driver said he knew the owner of the other wagon and it would be
all right. We probably would have taken the wheel anyway, as it
was a case of necessity.

After supper we went on with the wagon and arrived in
Houghton at four o'clock in the morning, having had two days of
hard work and two nights without sleep. At eight o'clcok that morning we took the little steamer *Ivanhoe*, which ran between
Houghton and L'Anse in connection with the railway, and the train
took us to Marquette that same evening. Next morning Thomas
wakened me at ten-thirty wanting to know if I was going to sleep
all day. It was Sunday, and we could not go to the land office until
nine o'clock Monday morning, so I slept right through till breakfast
time Monday.

After a few days' rest in Marquette, we started off on another
trip. Thomas, a Scotchman named McQuarrie, and I, with two Indian packers went southwesterly from Champion along the iron
formation running north and south in the west side of Township 46
North, Range 30 West. On this trip I saw my first outcrop of iron
ore on undeveloped properties and had my first experience with a
dip needle and with local magnetic variations of the compass.

Thomas went to L'Anse to get packmen and I was to meet him
and McQuarrie at Champion the following day. I arrived at Champion at the time agreed upon, but Thomas and McQuarrie did not
get there until the next day. There was no hotel and I had to hunt
for board and lodging. The Champion mine and a charcoal iron
furnace were the only enterprises at the "location," as all isolated
mining camps or other human habitations were called. After some
inquiry, I found a French boardinghouse where I could stay. It was
occupied mainly by Canadian-French wood choppers and charcoal
burners. I was assigned one of the six beds in the loft under the roof

of the one-story log house. This loft was reached by a vertical ladder nailed to the wall in the corner of the building.

They held a wild and boisterous dance in the house that night. I went to bed quite early, but not to sleep. There was too much noise. During the night the remaining beds in the loft were filled by men who were hoisted up the ladder by others not quite so drunk. Two men above and as many as necessary below pulled and pushed the "paralyzed" merrymaker into the loft, where he was tumbled into any bed that was vacant. Towards morning drunkenness seemed to have overcome the party and, as quiet came on, I went to sleep. Much to my surprise, when I descended in the morning, I found no sign of the night's revelry. The neat-looking landlady and her daughter had the house in order and a good breakfast was served. Had it not been for the disheveled men left in the loft overhead, I should have been inclined to attribute the scenes of the past night to bad dreams. After breakfast the landlady left to attend a wedding, and I was astonished to see her walk out arrayed in a silk dress and a beautiful lace shawl. She looked like a product of high civilization rather than a "grub-slinger" for a lot of booze-guzzling roustabouts. Thomas, McQuarrie, and the packers arrived before noon, and I departed from the boardinghouse, never to see it again.

Another time while waiting to hear from Thomas, I made a short trip into the woods north of Humboldt. On my return I camped beside the river in an old burning near the station. In the morning, about daylight, a violent thunderstorm descended upon us. The wind tore the tent pegs out, and the rain fell in such sheets that nothing was visible more than twenty feet away. The Indian packer hung onto the tent inside and covered our supplies with blankets as well as he was able, while I was outside trying to replace the tent pegs as fast as the wind pulled them up. Fortunately the storm lasted only a few minutes. In less than half an hour the sun was shining. We built a fire and spent the next four hours drying our outfit so that we could pack it for transportation on the train to Marquette.

After this trip Thomas left me in order to purchase some of the iron lands we had seen. He said he would be back in a few weeks, but I never saw him again, except once, and that was some ten or fifteen years later when I ran across him in Chicago. We had some correspondence after he left Marquette, but he did not succeed in buying any of the iron lands he wanted.

The

Iron Hills

As a youth of twenty-one Peter White wrote the bill of lading for the first shipment of iron ore—six barrels consigned from Marquette to Detroit—on July 7, 1852. He lived to see his name on a six-hundred-foot freighter carrying ten-thousand-ton cargoes down the Lakes. He led a charmed life and left a legendary name.

Born in Rome, N.Y. on the Erie Canal, he was taken west to Green Bay in his boyhood. Years later people would call Upper Michigan "Peter White's country." Even in youth his eyes turned northward. At fifteen he worked his way to the Soo, where he applied for a job on the schooner *Merchant,* sailing to the mineral lands. The *Merchant* had no place for him, and on that voyage it sank, with all hands, near Grand Island and the Pictured Rocks.

From the Soo Peter White shipped as deckhand on the schooner *Bela Hubbard* for Detroit. The *Hubbard* capsized off Thunder Bay, but the crew were taken off by the steamer *Chicago.* At Bay City, jumping from a pile of lumber on the docks, the young seaman broke his arm. When they arrived at Detroit the arm was so swollen that a doctor prepared to amputate it. At the last minute another doctor intervened; he reduced the swelling with applications of whisky and scalding water, then he set the bones.

From Detroit Peter White sailed north with a construction crew to build a lighthouse crib on Waugoshance Reef near Mackinaw. After two years on Mackinac Island he joined a party under Robert J. Graveraet of Massachusetts bound for the iron lands on Lake Superior.

At this point the following narrative begins. It is taken from a paper read by Peter White at the annual meeting of the Pioneer Association of Michigan in 1885.

I HAD made one ineffectual attempt, shortly after the first excitement over the discoveries of copper in 1845, to go up to Lake Superior, which had gained a great hold on the imagination of the boys of that day. I got as far as the Sault, and endeavored, without success, to get passage by the little schooner *Merchant,* which was the only craft just then going up the lake. I had no money, and they would not let me work my way. Had I got passage, it is safe to say, some one else would be giving you this narrative to-day. The schooner was never heard of afterwards; she went to the bottom, with all on board. The second time I had better luck. I joined a party, under the lead of the late Robert J. Graveraet, which set out from Mackinac in April, 1849, on the old steamer, *Tecumseh,* with the intention of claiming and developing all the iron mountains which had then been, or should subsequently be, discovered in that region. At Sault Ste. Marie, we succeeded in crowding our large Mackinac barge up the rapids, and after eight days' rowing, towing, poling and sailing, we landed at what was then called Indian town, near the present site of the freight station of the Detroit, Mackinac & Marquette Railroad in the city of Marquette. The next morning we started for the much-talked-of iron hills. At the Cleveland mountain we found Capt. Samuel Moody and John H. Mann, who had spent the previous summer and winter there. I well remember how astonished I was the next morning, when Captain Moody asked me to go with him to dig some potatoes for breakfast. He had half an acre on the summit of the hill, since known as the Marquette Company's Mountain, partially cleared and planted with potatoes. This was in the month of May, and the winter's snow had preserved them. He opened one or two hills and filled his pail with large and perfectly sound potatoes. He then said: "I may as well pull up a few parsnips and carrots for dinner, to save coming up again;" and sure enough he had them in abundance. From this time till the 10th of July we kept possession of all the iron mountains then known west of the Jackson, fighting mosquitoes at night and black flies through the day. On the 10th of July we returned to the lake shore.

Mr. Harlow had arrived with mechanics, goods, lots of money, and what was better than all, we got a glimpse of some female faces. At one o'clock of that day we commenced clearing the site of the present city of Marquette. We began by chopping off the trees and brush at the point of the rocks just south of the Cleveland ore docks. We cut the trees close to the ground and threw them bodily over the bank onto the lake shore; then, under the direction of Captain Moody, we began the construction of a dock, which we thought would stand like the pyramids. We did this by carrying these whole trees into the water and piling them in tiers crosswise, until the pile was even with the surface of the water. Then we wheeled sand and gravel upon it, and by the end of the second day had completed the structure upon which we looked with no little pride. The eastward, or outer, end was solid rock and all inside that was solid dirt, brush and leaves. We thought it would last as long as the adjacent beach itself. On the third day we continued to improve it by corduroying the surface, and by night of that day it was, in our eyes, a thing of beauty to behold. Our chagrin may be imagined when, on rising the next morning, we found that a gentle sea had come in during the night and wafted our dock to parts unknown. The sand of the beach was as clean and smooth as if it had never been disturbed by the hand of man. It was a long time before anyone had the hardihood to attempt the building of another dock. The propellers would come to anchor sometimes as far as two miles from shore, and freight and passengers were landed in small boats. Cattle and horses were pitched overboard and made to swim ashore.

The boiler for the Marquette forge was plugged, heaved overboard three miles out, and towed ashore. Your narrator has a vivid recollection of that boiler, which he took a contract to fill, after it was placed, for a dollar and a half. It required nearly four days' hard work with two pails and a yoke. This was the first steam boiler introduced into Marquette county. During the ensuing winter and spring (of 1850) the original Jackson Company had exhausted both its capital and credit, the Marquette Company's forge was now finished, and the Marquette Company entered upon the process of exhausting theirs. Their forge was burned early in 1853. These early developments in Marquette county were never stimulated or encouraged, by any return upon any capital invested, in any single instance until 1863. It was all a work of faith and perseverance, founded upon intuitions which were sound and sure, but which it took twenty years to realize. Meanwhile man after man and company after company cast all they had into the gulf which time only could fill. Those days were days of hardships to the early settlers.

Marquette, in 1851–3, consisted of a few houses, a stumpy road winding along the lake shore; a forge which burned up after impoverishing its first owners; a trail westward, just passable for wagons, leading to another forge (still more unfortunate in that it did not burn), and to the developed iron hills beyond, with two or three hundred people uncertain of the future—they had fallen into the march of the century and were building better than they knew.

Among the privations of those days which did not involve actual suffering was the great uncertainty and infrequency of the mails. During the earlier years of the settlement of Lake Superior copper and iron regions, the government provided no mail transportation except a monthly mail to such military posts as Copper Harbor and Sault Ste. Marie. During the season of navigation the steamers and sail vessels usually carried a mail to such parts as they entered. But this was without compensation, and it was often the case that the postmaster at Sault Ste. Marie forgot, or for some other reason, failed to put it on; then great was the disappointment at all the lake ports on the arrival of a mail-less craft. You who have always lived in a country provided with frequent and regular mails can but feebly appreciate what it is to live for months in a distant part of the country where few or no mail facilities are enjoyed. It is a subject almost as important to most people as food and raiment. The most ignorant or the illiterate, and the poorest of the poor have letters written for them, and to themselves, and enjoy receiving letters from far-off friends with intense delight. From 1848 to 1854 Marquette county was one of the isolated places that the government did not think it worth while to provide with winter mail facilities, and keenly was this deprivation felt by the people then living there. By hook or by crook the people managed to get a mail once in a while—but I have known intervals of three or four months at a time when no mail, or letter, paper or news of any kind was received by anyone in the county. Then when a mail did arrive all work was suspended—even the cooking and the washing—until the letters could be read or devoured. In those years I had more or less (personally) to do with the getting or the carrying of the mails —sometimes with dogs, sometimes with Indians, and sometimes on my own back I brought in the mail-bags. Often traveling through the woods, and over deep snow on snow-shoes, hundreds—I might almost say thousands of miles, and I would not like to do it again. Neither would I like to have another person so punished. In this connection I will tell you of an incident that happened to me some years later.

In all counties where wood-chopping or charcoal burning is carried on, you will find the Canadian Frenchman. So they came to Marquette in great numbers; many of them could not read and write, but still the sweet consolation they derived from receiving letters from friends in Canada or New York State was unmistakable. Many of them actually thought that I went to Montreal or Quebec or New York State to get their letters; they couldn't see how else I could appear with them there. Thus it was that I was made the subject of many a legend, among the Frenchmen and their families, during the years that followed, wherein dogs, sledges, snow-shoes, woods, wolves and other animals of the forest went to make up the hodge-podge. Even in later years, when the government did provide for a mail, there would always be certain months when its transporation would be impossible, owing to the depth and softness of the snow. This would occur in March and April, and sometimes, the first half of May. It was during one of those years that I was postmaster at Marquette. One night a steamer arrived (the first boat of the season), bringing the accumulated mail of two months or more, and it was very large. I had taken it to my office and was distributing it as expeditiously as possible, by lamp or candlelight. My postoffice was very small, in the rear end of a store, with only room enough for a small table, a chair and a place for a mail bag, twenty-four alphabetical mail boxes on my right, and forty-eight 8x10 boxes to rent. I was standing, emptying the mail from the bags, onto the table, then distributing the letters and papers into the proper boxes, so as to be ready for the eager crowd that would come for mail after six o'clock in the morning. Then it was that I heard steps approaching through the store towards the postoffice. I looked, to behold Michael Belloin, a tall and very powerful Frenchman. It was apparent that he had been buying some of the wet goods on the steamer, for he staggered towards me, saying: "You got any lette for Micho, Monsieur Pete?" I answered, "The mail is not yet open, you will have to come in the morning," whereupon, he said, "I guess I will come into your little poss offis and sit on dat little chair, and see you put dose paper and dose lette in that box." Suiting the action to the word, he undertook to enter the narrow door, when I exclaimed, "There isn't room for you, it is against the law, you cannot come in!" "Oh, ho, what you spose I care for de law or you neder. I will come in anyhow. You can't stop me." As he lifted one foot to step over a mail bag at the door I gave him a quick push which caused him to fall backwards to the floor, and very much enraged him. Arising he paced backward and forward across the store floor, outside of my office, grating his teeth and clenching his fists, calling me all manner of names in French, and uttering all sorts of imprecations and epithets. At last, finding that I did not pay any attention to him, he stopped in front of the little door and delivered himself about thus:

"You want to preten you don stan French. Mon dieu, you can't talk good Linguish; you're jus a half a breed, half French and half Injin. I know wat you want; you want me to strike you, then you bring me on de justis offis to-morrow morning and make me pay five dollar! Aha! you can't fool Frenchman lika dat. You come on to de street if you want me to strike you. If I strike you I won't leave two greas spot on you. If I strike you, you'll tink it is a French horse kick you! You see dat spit down dere? The sun he come, he dry it up, dat's jus like you. If I strike you you can't fine yourself no more. You wouldn't know where you gone to. I come to your poss offis to quire for some lette, and I hax you jus so polite I can, if you got any lette for Micho, and you say get out. Ain't you shame yourself; don't you sorry you treat me dat way? I'll goin to tell you something make you sorry you say so cross to me. I tink I'll make you face come red. Some Frenchmen been come here good many year ago, he ben tole me dat you use to carry de mail on your back, and a pack on your back, a hax in your hand, snow-shoe on your feet, and sometime tree poor little dog on a train, draw de mail tru de woods, and your tree little dog was so poor you could see right true him, coz you was so dam poor you didn have money to buy provision for dat dog. Now you got to be the poss offis master, and you tink you are de biggest big bug on dis town. And when I come to your poss offis, jus so polite I can, and hax you you got any lette for Micho? you say 'get out dar' like one dam dog! I like to know if dats de way to treat a gentleman. I gues you didn't tot dat I know I could tell you all dat! You tink now you're biggest big bug on this whole town."

But better times were in store for us. A ship canal at Sault Ste. Marie and a railroad to the mines were in the near future. The shipping or exportation of iron ore in either large or small quantities had not entered into the ideas or plans of the earliest settlers in the country; their only thought was to manufacture either bar or bloom iron which could bear the cost of many handlings—particularly the very costly transportation over the portage at Sault Ste. Marie. The realization of the ship canal project at the Sault transformed the existing dream of a railroad from Marquette to the iron mountains into a certainty. In August, 1852, Congress passed an act granting to the State of Michigan 750,000 acres of land, to be located within the State, for the purpose of aiding in the construction and completion of a ship canal around the falls of Ste. Marie. This was largely due to the persevering efforts of Mr. John Burt, of Detroit. At this juncture Mr. Charles T. Harvey rendered valuable service in inducing the right men to go in and furnish the capital to carry out what was universally considered to be a work of enormous magnitude, surrounded by unfavorable circumstances, and in the way of whose successful termination and inauguration almost insuperable obstacles lay. The names of the men who backed Mr. Harvey with capital and encouragement in the construction of the canal deserve to be enrolled in the archives of this association, and I am proud to mention them here for that purpose. They were: John F. Seymour, Erastus Corning, James F. Joy, J. W. Brooks, J. V. L. Pruyn, Joseph P. Fairbanks, and John M. Forbes. These names are well known and have been recognized in very many large and honest enterprises in different quarters of the United States during the past forty years. The land was selected about one-third in the upper and two-thirds in the lower peninsula. The total cost of the construction of the canal was $1,000,000. Mr. John Burt, of Detroit, who had rendered important services in various ways during the construction of the canal, was, at its completion, appointed its first superintendent.

Many other persons, all of whose names I cannot recall, were personally instrumental in promoting the building of the canal, among these should be mentioned: Judge Wm. A. Burt, the father of Mr. John Burt; Captain Canfield, of the United States Topographical Corps; Mr. J. W. Brooks, Dr. Morgan L. Hewitt, and the late Heman B. Ely. The canal proved equal to all expectations in its workings for several years, but later on the vast increase of commerce made it necessary to use larger lake craft, drawing a greater depth of water than this canal would accommodate, and the State of Michigan was induced to spend some part of the earnings of the canal on its enlargement, but all that was done in this way was so manifestly inadequate that Congress was again successfully appealed to and asked to make a cash appropriation on the score of its being a great national work on the national frontier. The general government has made repeated appropriations which have been expended under the skillful direction of General Weitzel and General O. M. Poe, until the locks are now the largest and most perfect and durable structures of the kind in the world. I might say in closing my reference to the canal that the State of Michigan, under the advice of Governor Jerome, very wisely transferred its title and interest, with the care and management of the canal, to the United States. Congress has by public act accepted the trust and has since made this great national highway free to the commerce of the world.

Seven

Iron Men

The Mesabi story is a drama in itself, a tale of dreams and despairs, of honesty and deceit, of fruitless search, heartbreaking toil and chance discoveries. Its iron has influenced the course of history.

Before 1890 hundreds of iron miners had passed over the Mesabi hills on the rough way to the Vermilion district. Under their trails lay the banded iron formation, red, blue, yellow, brown and purple, like a huge layer cake. Unknowing, they trudged on, slapping mosquitoes and cursing the muskeg.

In 1870 in Duluth, timber cruiser Lewis Merritt told his growing sons about that rough country. His eyes burned and his voice rose when he said there was iron waiting to be uncovered all along the Mesabi hills—untold iron, he insisted, worth more than all the gold in California.

Mesabi means "giant." The first explorer of the giant range was solitary Peter Mitchell; in 1881 he dug a six-foot pit and took out rich red ore. For ten years nothing happened, except that mining experts hacked their way through the bush and brought back negative reports. And the Merritt brothers began searching.

Among the stubborn men of history are the seven sons of Lewis Merritt. Remembering their father's prophecy they crossed and crisscrossed the Mesabi. Trekking over the ice-locked winter land and the sinking ground of summer they explored the back country. They bought up land from homesteaders, woodsmen and lumber companies. They packed in supplies and dug test pits. Other men toiled and dreamed for a season, and put their gear away. The Merritts kept on. At last, in November 1890, they found rich ore at Mountain Iron, and a few months later slouching John McCaskill led them to a mass of iron ore tangled in the roots of a blowdown near Embarrass Lake. These discoveries, fourteen miles apart, became the famous Mountain Iron and Biwabik mines, and a new iron rush began.

The story of the Merritts is vividly told in Paul de Kruif's *Seven Iron Men*, 1929, from which these pages are taken.

A WISE MAN has worked it out, and proved, I believe, that time is the fourth dimension of everything; of this discovery your present story-teller understands neither the mathematics nor the philosophy. But surely, to produce the present clanging, hammering, high-reaching, proud and comfortable age of steel, *successions of events* have been of enormous importance. It is fantastic to remember how the immense rocky northern platform, that backbone of the American Continent on which Lon [Merritt] and his band were now playing out their proud and pitiful little drama, should have been born in fire so many aeons ago—bringing iron up into the boiling waters. Then, before there were any intelligent creatures at all to feel the lack of iron ore, came primitive life, came immensely ancient microbes to prepare it. Surely there's a kindly God, who created those absurd little *Gallionella*—though nobody knows now what He called the iron-eating microbes—but anyway here were these sub-visible beings, planted there to toil for numberless millenniums laying down the iron. . . .

This iron, it's almost certain, was afterward covered by sediments, which congealed into enormous masses of rock, so thick a hundred Lon Merritts could never have sniffed the iron out from under them. But no matter: convenient myriads of centuries passed —before there were men—so that wind, so that water, could wear these protecting rocks away, and enrich the deposits of iron. Yet it was maybe still not exposed, or ready to use, when fishes and oysters were the proud owners of America, nor when successions of lizards, dinosaurs, mastodons, and saber-toothed tigers, had their geologic day in dominating what's now for a moment *our* country. But what did that matter, because what would those slimy, ferocious, and unenlightened creatures have done with iron, anyway?

Then for a long time, and maybe several times, the crunching white masses and the vast cold doom of the continental ice-cap hid Lake Superior's rim, but it was of absolutely no consequence: if there were men to the south—*if* there were—they were slant-browed savages with no notion of how iron might be forged into suspension bridges, motor cars, plows, bathrooms, and baby buggies. But how marvelous was this glacier, and how wise the Great Hand that melted it, for while this epic thaw almost uncovered a strange tremendous deposit of iron, it left blue water that would be the one proper, cheap, convenient way to carry that iron to men who would later need it. From this melt, so perfectly timed in our succession of events, it was only a geological hour till hybrid millions of men, modern, clever—call them *Homo sapiens* if you will—swarmed over the Alleghenies and on to the prairies; and they were full of a tilling and building energy generated—maybe—by this very fact of their first generation hybridity. They stretched out their hands, called for iron, wanted inexhaustible millions of tons of red ore to smelt into pig iron to convert into steel. They were ably led, and their leaders—capitalists, iron-masters—bawled and roared for ore that must be cheaper, cheaper, to cut the costs in the newly-begun standardized production of—everything.

Now we come, suddenly, out of the murky ruck of ancient time, to the middle eighties of the nineteenth century. At this point in the long and logical march of happenings, there is a tiny occurrence, a seemingly insignificant concatenation of events at the Head of the Lakes. In its own way it is as lucky, as happy for all of us, as necessary for America's arrogant age of steel, as any of the more remote, more grandiose, more spectacular acts of God. The damp north country around Lake Superior's rim is aswarm with iron hunters now. Prospectors, geologists, professors of the science of minerals, practical mining men—are drilling, theorizing, exploring, test-pitting, for the ore that's now being sucked down the lakes into Carnegie's blast furnaces; into a hundred other flaring, roaring midwestern stoves the ore goes in an endless stream of long lean boats. But where's cheaper ore, endlessly abundant iron to be had for a song? In the scientific reports of that day, not a geologist would have risked his name to say there was more ore, cheaper ore, than that already found on the Marquette, the Menominee, the Gogebic, and the Vermilion Iron Ranges.

But at this very moment there exist Leonidas Merritt and his band of brothers. Leonidas is absolutely uneducated, in the formal and accepted sense, in the science of rock-reading; what is worse, in the few of his writings that remain, now yellowed by time—for these were the defiant writings of his heyday in the nineties—you will find all experts lumped together under the scornful designation of "scientific squirts!" Not only must such sarcastic disrespect be held as a black mark against Leonidas, but he might, in those early days, have been very properly denounced as a fool and a visionary for not sticking to his timber cruising.

Professor Chester had come, and George Stuntz—who certainly could command even the contemptuous Leonidas's respect—had shown Chester real iron mines by Vermilion Lake. But, having been chaperoned by Stuntz pretty thoroughly over the eastern end of the Mis-sa-be Heights, the professor had very properly condemned this desolate region. Lon himself would have had to admit the professor's accuracy; for to this day no respectable iron deposit has been uncovered on the Mis-sa-be east of the Embarrass River—which was where Stuntz and Chester went. The brilliant geological family of the Winchells, of whom the head was the sagacious old Alexander, had ranged these hills, had made close studies of its rocks, had found never an ounce of iron fit to sell or to smelt. The noted rock-reader, Irving, had cruised as far away from water as you'd expect a geologist to do; he'd dubbed the iron-bearing Mis-sa-be rocks "Animikie," discovered a lot about their enormous age, and found no hint of real iron. Yet our bull-headed chief of what he liked to call the Ne-con-dis—the band of brothers—came near breaking the backs of his brothers, Alfred, Cassius, and his nephews, John E. and Wilbur, sending them back, and back up there. His was an unheard-of, an extravagant, an idiotic persistence.

Even if he was so intensely parochial, so narrow-minded as to turn up his nose at geologists, scientists, Lon might have taken a hint from the failures of men of his own craft, bushwhackers, landlookers. Peter Mitchell of Ontonagon had made diggings and they'd come to no good. When the Duluth and Iron Range Railroad was cut across the Mis-sa-be to Stuntz's mines on Lake Vermilion, the cruisers Mallman and Geggie had seen suspicious red streaks, that were said by the historian Van Brunt "to have shouted iron." But they followed these streaks—and came back to Duluth with empty pack-sacks. Gil Goff, looking land west from Grand Rapids for the Saginaw pine-dukes, did report: "In '83 I done land-looking—and seen iron," but his alleged observations came to nothing. Even the able David Adams came back from the western Mis-sa-be in the middle eighties with empty hands. To the complete hopelessness of all these ventures the official Monograph No. 43 of the United States Geological Survey testifies:

"Since the late sixties . . . not a single deposit of iron ore of such size and character as to warrant exploration had been shown up. In fact the range had been turned down by many mining men who examined it."

Yet Leonidas strained his own back, and his bank-book too, plodding back up in there, again, again.

Established iron companies, like the Minnesota Iron Company, not headed by visionaries, but by men like Charlemagne Tower, sent the best men they could hire to Mis-sa-be. The geologist H. V. Winchell wrote of these wild-goose chases: "Iron experts of good repute were sent to examine the outcrops of ore known at that time . . . The journey was an arduous one into a dense wilderness, and there is no wonder they did no test-pitting or drilling. They were sent to examine outcrops, which they properly enough condemned, for the only iron to be seen was in thin strata of magnetite banded with jaspery quartz."

Lon Merritt kept following his conscience. . . .

In the high summer of what was probably '88, though the exact year is in dispute, Cassius Merritt found real iron, excellent hematite, merchantable ore on the Mis-sa-be Heights. He ran across a chunk of it in Section 31 of Town 58 North, Range 18 West of the Fourth Principal Meridian of Minnesota. He wasn't on a cruise looking for iron—excepting that, obedient to Leonidas, he forever had an eye open for it; his job just now was that of head explorer for a corps of engineers. He was showing these engineers where to locate their road, because they were making a preliminary survey for what they hoped was going to be a railroad from Duluth all the way northwest to Winnipeg. It turned out to be an imaginary railroad, an air-castle of a line that has never come to exist in reality to this day. But for this story that doesn't matter at all. What matters is that just at the geographical Height of Land on the Central Mis-sa-be, Cassius Merritt picked up a heavy hunk of pure iron. It was at that significant, mysterious spot where all the little springs to the north of him headed for bleak Hudson Bay, where all the creeks to the south of him did their bit to help fill the Gulf of Mexico and the Atlantic Ocean. Cassius had come to this spot simply and purely because this was the easiest grade over the Mis-sa-be on the line from Duluth to Winnipeg.

He put the chunk of iron in his pack-sack and shut his mouth about it. He expertly led the survey of experts all the way to the wild country at the crossing of the Big Fork River; from there on Cashie completed a topographical survey all the way north to the Canadian line, to the nine-mile-post, west of the Lake of the Woods. On September 3d he got back to Duluth; honestly he told of his iron find to his boss, Mr. Rogers, who with M. B. Harrison was duly impressed by it. He then went to Leonidas—with permission—and said:

"Lon, you're right. There's real iron on the Mis-sa-be."

—Though all Cassius had seen was one bowlder of it, and not at all a mine or any extensive outcrops. But this was enough for Leonidas Merritt. The place where Cashie had found it was, with his entirely characteristic accuracy, marked down to the dot. It was, so Lon pointed out triumphantly, only two looks and a holler from the other place, where Cassius had spotted that great mound of lean ore, on the day, three years before, when young John E. had got himself so foolishly lost. In their long, visionary, hide-and-go-seek game for iron, there is no doubt that Lon and Alf were now getting warm, getting hot.

It was a great piece of luck for the Merritts that they were just now on the up; their fifteen fly-bitten, break-boned years of pine-looking were at last bringing cash, real money. "Why, we were that flush we could actually hire a packer, to tote our grub in for us," said John E., long after. And when they ran out of money, Lon and Alf would sell off another rich pine location, and soak the cash that came from it into new exploring parties. In '89, the year after Cassius had found that fine chunk of pure ore, the Merritts literally swarmed over the Mis-sa-be hills; Leonidas, Cassius, the stolid, shrewd Alfred, Wilbur, and his lean-jawed young brother Bert, Lewis J. and John E.—whom by now you couldn't lose anywhere— began a gigantic and foolish search of Lon's devising. I say foolish, because almost all of the wise heads, the old-timers of the head of the lakes, thought it was not only foolish, but downright crazy—

Why try what not only scientific geniuses, but practical, sensible prospectors had given up long ago? Everybody knew the only place there was iron in the whole north country was up toward Lake Vermilion. Now it's perfectly true that Leonidas had sent off John E. and Cassius to that water-infested country, to make their first magnetic surveys—and this shakes somewhat the legend that Lon had primary faith in the profitless Mis-sa-be hills from the start. But Lon's luck was with him; in a way he was *forced* southwest toward the Mis-sa-be Heights—because the rich and powerful Minnesota Iron Company had picked up nearly all of the "good stuff"—as Lon called it—round Lake Vermilion. These wealthy, successful operators wanted no part of Mis-sa-be, had been told it was worthless, by mine captains and professors. So here are Lon and his crew, plodding back and forth through the woods of the Grandmother Hills, willy-nilly. From this it must not be understood that Lon hadn't followed his conscience, hadn't kept faith in his father's strange prophecy. But it's well to remember that events, and human motives leading up to triumphs, to tragedies, are not simple, but are, on the other hand, full of chances, improvisations, whimsies of fate, complexities....

While John E. and Uncle Cashie were doing their mapping for magnetic attraction—and being laughed at by old-timers down in Duluth, for everybody knew that the magnetic iron in that country was too lean, no good—Alfred had started digging holes in the Mis-sa-be crest above them. In March of '89 this plodding citizen had started into the bush from Tower—the town where in winter a six-foot thermometer with zero at the top was wanted, to tell men how cold it really got. "With six men and three dog trains—toboggans—we went by way of Pike River and across Rice Lake, and we were the dogs," muttered Alfred. Of the Merritt boys, Alf was at this time the only one you might call a practical miner. Back in the early seventies he had, in the intervals between a dozen other more or less profitless activities, cracked rock, and dug underground in a vain hunt for fabled copper on Isle Royale in Lake Superior.

Close by where Cashie had found his hunk of fine ore the year before, they stopped, after days of toil through the snow when on some days eight hours of pulling, pushing, hacking, cursing and grunting had carried them forward three-quarters of a mile, no more. They cut down pines with their cross-cut saws, and built a camp from the fallen trees. Alf at the head of them, working slowly, steadily, and as hard as any, these six men began digging holes on the Mis-sa-be crest—till, after weeks, they struck the banded taconite, with a little iron in it, till, after months, they struck ancient firestone, granite with next to no iron at all. "It must be deeper," said Alfred to Lon. And Leonidas, grotesque in his white coat, smoked glasses, and pith helmet, hurried back to Duluth, sold more pine land, bought diamond drills and engines, hired gangs of men and cut a tote road twenty-seven miles west through the woods all the way from Mesaba Station of the D. and I. R. railroad, to get in the drills and the engines to run them.

Alf and his men drilled, through lean-iron taconite, and into the granite, and found no iron. The summer was passing; the sumac and the wild cherry were getting ready to set the country aflare with yellow and red. "There's nothing here, Lon," said Alfred. And for want of something better they agreed to dig, next spring, down the slope farther south. During the winter southward they cut their trails. Spring of 1890 was here now, with its melting snow, to the tune of a harshly musical, ecstatically hopeful twittering of song-sparrows, and with a low mysterious gurgling of a thousand rills of snow water trickling south beneath the pine needles. Once more Alf, Leonidas, and their men began digging, farther south, always a little farther; and the ground was strangely soft and reddish, and they abandoned their diamond drills. They were past the line where Cashie and Johnnie's compass had shown its maximum dip. Wasn't it here they should have turned up ore? Together they peered over the maps on their minits. Still they found no iron, but only taconite, only worthless, jaspery rock. "Let's try it a bit farther south," agreed Alf and Lon.

Now strange things began to happen: the wheels of their lumber wagons sank through the carpet of pine needles, got bogged in deep ruts, red ruts of a peculiar, powdery red soil—heavy. Alfred picked up handfuls of it, hefted it, handed it to his men, to Lon. "That's iron," he said, and was enormously puzzled, and tugged at his magnificent mustache. "It can't be nothing else than float ore. Don't believe a mine could lay this way—close to the top like this. And it's fine, too fine, like dirt. What we want is a *vein* of ore—" Nearby in the bush, too, they saw strange signs, and didn't particularly heed them. Here was a spot where a deer had scuffed up the pine needles, laid bare the ground, red ground and heavy. . . .

They ran out of money once more. At their wit's end, both of them returned to Duluth, leaving their test-pit crew in the bush, and tried to raise the cash to go on. "We were then rushing around town to get money to pay these expenses," testified Leonidas, long after, before Congressman Stanley and his solemn Congressional Committee. "We had spent then $20,000 on the Mountain Iron, I remember . . . We had a miner in there, a German, who was a good miner, as miners go, you know. He was a good man, an honest, straightforward man."

This good, honest, and straightforward man was Captain J. A. Nicols, at the head of the Merritt test-pit crew. To Captain Nicols, Lon and Alf had given orders to keep going south, to dig down at the foot of the hill. By these orders the good Captain was offended, and who blames him, for he was a man experienced in the lay of land where you might expect, on the grounds of both theory and practice, to find iron. So the Captain and his men climbed back toward the crest, and started work again—where Alfred had already failed for a hopeful, dismal, year and a half.

It looked as if the money might be raised, from more pine land sold, or mortgaged, and the brothers came, in the middle of November of 1890, back to the clearing on the hillside. They came back to find that the good, honest and straightforward German had disobeyed their orders; and doom for all straightforward Germans flared in Leonidas Merritt's eyes.

"Here, now, we've worked long enough on this rim, let's go down in the basin and sink a pit," shouted Lon.

Nicols was disgusted, and nobody should blame him, and nobody did blame him, excepting maybe the indomitable Leonidas and the silent but shrewd Alfred. "He said he had some reputation as a mining man, which he had," said Leonidas, "and he did not propose to be called, with the rest of us, farmers. They used to call us farmers and lumberjacks and all that sort of thing, in derision. . . . We told him to come to Duluth, and we would send up men that did not have any reputation as miners!"

Then, while Lon exhorted, Alfred grabbed a shovel, drove it through the pine needles into the soft earth—shovel after shovelful he turned up. . . . Nicols looked, then gaped. While Lon argued, Alf said it—with shovels.

So Leonidas won his discussion. Nicols gave in, and agreed to dig where Lon told him to dig. Alfred and Leonidas went back to Duluth, being, alas, not yet quite sure about getting their money. The next morning—this was the 16th of November of 1890—the honest Nicols started digging again, not quite where Lon had ordered him to nor yet where Alf had shown him real iron, but, being a stubborn as well as a straightforward man, a little way back up the hill. What happened that day is history, and should be recorded solemnly, and without excitement. Let it be transcribed from the Twentieth Annual Report, Minnesota Geological Survey, Part IV, entitled "The Mesabi Iron Range," by Horace V. Winchell, F.G.S.A.:

"On the sixteenth day of November, 1890, workmen under the direction of Capt. J. A. Nicols, of Duluth, Minnesota, encountered soft hematite in a test-pit on the northwest quarter of section three, township fifty-eight, range eighteen, west of the fourth principal meridian. This mine, now called the Mountain Iron, was the first body of soft ore discovered on the Mesabi iron range."

The next day the good Captain Nicols came back to Duluth, to Alfred and Leonidas, with fifty pounds of rich, marvelous, 64 per cent iron in his pack-sack. He came back, converted, asking the elated Leonidas and the never-excited Alfred:

"What are we going to do? People have been attracted here and they have already come . . . There are trails here and they are looking this country over. What shall we do, cover this up and leave it?"

It is their day of days. It is the beginning of the vindication of old Lewis Howell Merritt's outlandish prophecy, made twenty-five years before to his rising and lusty young band of buckos, to Leonidas, to Alfred in the log house by the bay in Oneota. It is the real start of the proof of George Stuntz's prediction that here, in this Godforsaken northwest land, is the commercial heart of the continent.

"Cover it up!" says Leonidas, with a snort, to Captain Nicols. "You go on there and dig. We want ore. We want to build a railroad to it. You go on there and dig, and find the bottom of that ore. You open it up."

So the Merritts and their men began to dig, toward wonders they themselves nor their dead father had ever dreamed of. Not a

year, not a month were these bushwhackers ahead of their time—
for the furnaces down below must have iron ore, limitless millions
of tons of red, blue, black and purple ore, for the age of steel, for
America the iron-hungry Gargantua. They wouldn't, like George
Stuntz, have to be content with eight dollars a day, and a destitute
death in the Red Cross Hospital. No rich men had helped them to
their discovery: they'd grubstaked themselves. They owned the
iron—and what power now didn't lie before them? So they started
to dig.

III

WIND FROM THE
WEST

The lakes were French until 1760, when abruptly they became British. The British rule lasted a scant generation, but they were still the "English Seas" after the Treaty of 1783. Nominal control by the new American nation did not alter the life of the northern posts where British troops and traders stayed on. In 1792 in the stone barracks on Mackinac Island, Captain William Doyle of the twenty-fourth British Regiment, in the presence of Lieutenant Edward Charleton of His Majesty's Fifth Infantry, generously wrote out for trader John Johnston a grant of land—three hundred feet on the south side of the river at St. Mary's, running back forty acres in depth, bounded on the northeast by a lot belonging to Antoine Landry and on the southwest by the old Jesuit burying ground. None of them thought about the quaintness of an English officer in the King's name bestowing to an Irish trader territory ceded a decade past to the United States. The English would continue in possession a while longer. Not until the arrival of the Cass expedition in 1820 was the flag of the United States seen at the Soo.

But the lakes were the way to the Northwest, and in the War of 1812 Americans won in fact what had been awarded to them after the Revolution. They yielded it briefly—being driven from Detroit, Chicago and Michilimackinac—and then, gathering the frontier forces, they come into control in 1815. What followed was a surge of migration, one of the great impulses of American history, flowing to Detroit, then through the Mackinac Straits to frontier Wisconsin and Illinois.

In mid-America the prevailing wind is from the west. In the 1820s the west wind brought a sense of space and distance, of new inviting lands, of a luring, glowing future. It stirred restlessness in Vermont and Massachusetts, and in Scotland, Holland and Scandinavia. At Buffalo the emigrants crowded onto lake vessels; some of those travelers knew no English except the magic word "Wisconsin."

In 1833 there were eleven steamships on the lakes, and they carried forty-three thousand people west from Buffalo. Two vessels voyaged all the way to Chicago and Green Bay. Returning from Lake Michigan they wore evergreen branches at their topmasts, a souvenir from remote country.

Into the woods went surveyors to map the country that would soon be claimed and occupied. The lower shores of Lake Michigan bordered fertile lands where the Dutch and the Danes, the Scotch and the Germans, along with Yankee settlers, would bring the fields to harvest. North of Saginaw and Green Bay stretched the dark pine forests. Into their silence would come the thud of the axe and the cry of the sawmill, and down the lakes would go deckloads of lumber to build the spreading cities. Along the northern shores the lakemen steered past the first coastal lights at Waugoshance Reef and Ile au Galets (sailors have always called them Wobbleshanks and Shillagalee). According to legend some of the surveyors, losing themselves in the maze of ponds and pines and sandhills, never came out of that dense country. From the ghostly gleam of a campfire and voices on the wind it is supposed that they are in there somewhere, still sighting transits and running section lines.

Lake Superior was remote, even after the canal opened it to the inland commerce. Until the 1890s post offices beyond the Soo were addressed L.S. (Lake Superior), the newspapers were dated that way, and a man going from Duluth or Marquette to Chicago, Detroit or Cleveland spoke of "returning to the United States." The North was a back-of-beyond country, and a luring one, like Alaska in the twentieth century.

It was a lake of legends. Travelers wrote of the Indian superstitions and the Pictured Rocks, of floating islands, mysterious fog banks, and capes hung upside down on the horizon. Constance Fenimore Woolson described a wandering boatman, driven back and forth over the great lake, who could not find a harbor until the explorer priests brought the Christian cross to that dark land. Then the old sailor died in peace, and the Great Spirit turned his boat to stone.

> You see it there among the Rocky Pictures,
>   The mainsail and the jib just as they were;
> We never passed it with a song or laughter
>   In the gay days when we were voyagers;
> The best among us doffed our caps in silence;
>   The gayest of us never dared to mock
> At the strange tale that came down from our fathers,—
> The pictured legend of the old Sail Rock.

While its commerce grew, legends persisted on the Big Sea Water.

USHER PARSONS

With Perry
at Put-in-Bay

Above South Bass Island, commonly called Put-in-Bay, the Perry Monument rises into the sky. On stormy nights waves boom and thunder in the coves, recalling a distant battle. For three hundred centuries, ever since the glacier left its mark on the limestone ledges, Lake Erie has laved the island shores. They have been peaceful islands, these thirty thousand years, except for one violent day in the summer of 1813.

Commodore Perry had nine vessels, mounting fifty-five guns; the British had six ships of superior tonnage and firepower. At noon Perry sailed out of Put-in-Bay, and for three hours the cannon thundered. When the smoke blew off and the guns fell silent, Perry's flagship counted 83 casualties among a company of 132 men. Of many accounts of the Battle of Lake Erie the most dramatic is the story of a young surgeon on the flagship *Lawrence*.

On that tenth day of September, 1813, Dr. Usher Parsons, though wasted with lake fever, was on his feet "with all the amputating to perform." During the action five cannon balls passed through the surgical room. Some of his patients were dispatched before he could attend them; others were killed a few minutes after his ministration.

Ten days after the battle Dr. Parsons wrote to his parents in Rhode Island: "I have enjoyed very bad health during this cruise and am reduced to a skeleton, and will never cross this or any other lake again."

His account of the Battle of Lake Erie was not written until 1852, but after thirty-nine years that day was still seared upon his memory. This excerpt begins with the departure of Perry's fleet from the Presque Isle harbor (now Erie, Pennsylvania) to contest the British control of the lake.

THE FLEET was manned by sailors partly from Newport, and partly from Lake Ontario. The two larger vessels, Lawrence and Niagara, were built and rigged precisely alike, and carried 132 officers and men each. By the 10th of July, the guns were mounted on board all the vessels, and the men were exercised at them several times a day.

On Sunday the 18th of July, two respectable missionaries who were passing through Erie, were invited by the Commodore on board one of the large ships, where as many officers and men as could be spared from all the vessels were assembled to hear prayers that were offered up for the success of the expedition. I shall never forget their fervent pleadings in our behalf, that we might subdue the hostile fleet, and thereby wrest from savage hands the toma-hawk and scalping-knife, that had been so cruelly wielded against the defenceless settlers on the frontiers, and that in the event of a victory, mercy and kindness might be shown to the vanquished.

The bar of Erie had thus far served as a fortification to prevent the enemy from entering the harbor where our fleet was preparing, but it now presented a serious obstacle to our egress. The two large brigs drew three feet of water more than there was on the bar. On Sunday evening, the 1st of August, the work began of clearing the Lawrence of cannon and balls, to lighten her; and immense scows called camels were placed under her sides, and being sunk to the water's edge, timbers were passed through from side to side of the ship, the ends of which were blocked up, resting on these float-ing foundations. Plugs were now put into the scows, and the water bailed out, and as they rose they lifted the ship two feet, and this not being enough, the ballast and other heavy articles were taken out, till she was raised another foot, when she was able to pass over the bar.—The Niagara was served in like manner, but the smaller vessels had previously passed over without the aid of camels. Be-fore the large vessels were fairly over, the enemy hove in sight, and fired a few balls which did not reach us. The Pennyslvania regiment paraded, and the small vessels that were out returned the enemy's fire. Had they come near enough to do execution while we were struggling over the bar, they might have destroyed our fleet with little difficulty.

On the 6th of August we sailed, with the fleet not more than half officered and manned, across the lake, wishing to encounter the enemy before the large new ship joined his squadron, but they had sailed for Malden, and we returned to Erie the next day, where we found Captain Elliot just arrived from Lake Ontario, with nearly 100 officers and men. A new arrangement was now made of officers throughout the fleet, and we soon sailed up the lake in pursuit of the enemy, and anchored on the 15th in Put-in-Bay, in a cluster of islands near the head of the lake. On the 17th we sailed to the mouth of Sandusky bay, and on anchoring fired three guns, waited ten minutes and fired three more. This was a signal previously agreed upon by letters that passed between Perry and Harrison. In the evening, Colonel Gaines with a number of officers and Indians arrived on board, and reported General Harrison to be twenty-seven miles distant, with an army of 8000 militia, regulars and Indians.—Our boats were sent to bring the General and his suite on board, where they arrived on the 19th, late in a rainy evening. The General brought his two aides, Colonel McArthur, afterwards Governor of Ohio, and Colonel Cass, now Senator in Congress, with many of his principal officers, two hundred soldiers and fifty Indians, including the chiefs of several nations. They remained on board with us two days, to settle the plans of their future operations. The General learned that our crews were weakened by sickness, and on returning to the army sent us some thirty or forty volunteers to serve with our sailors. Our crews became still more unhealthy, the Commodore and half of the officers were on the sick list with lake-fever. The two senior medical officers were confined to their berths, and the junior one [Usher Parsons] was so reduced by the disease, that in visiting the sick on board the different vessels, he was unable to climb up the ship's sides, and he was hoisted in and out like a barrel of flour or cask of water.

We now looked into the harbor of Malden, by way of returning the civilities the enemy had shown us at Erie. This kind of polite attention was repeated two or three times, until the evening of the 9th of September, when we anchored in Put-in-Bay. On the following morning at sunrise, there was a cry from the mast-head, sail ho! all hands sprang from their berths, and ere we could dress and reach the decks the cry was repeated again and again, until six sail were thus announced. Signal was made to the fleet, "Enemy in sight! get under way!" and the hoarse voice and shrill pipe of the boatswain resounded through all the ships, all hands up anchor!

The wind at this time was from the Southwest, light and baffling, which prevented our weathering the island in our way, and it continued so until ten o'clock, when it veered to the Southeast, which enabled us to clear the island, and stand out upon the lake. We now discovered the English squadron, five or six miles to the leeward, hove to in a line, and equidistant about half a cable's length. The vessels were freshly painted, and with the morning sun shining upon their broadsides, and their red ensigns gently unfolding to the breeze, they made a very gallant appearance. Our squadron bore down to engage them, with the wind on our larboard quarter. They were arranged with the Chippewa, of one long eighteen pounder on a pivot ahead; the Detroit of nineteen guns, bearing the broad pendant of the Commodore, next; the Hunter of ten guns, the third; the Queen Charlotte of seventeen guns, fourth; Lady Prevost of thirteen guns, fifth, and the Little Belt of three guns, sixth. Captain Perry immediately arranged his line of battle, with his own ship to fight the Detroit, broad pendant against broad pendant, Commodore against Commodore. Two gun-boats, the Ariel and Scorpion, ranged ahead on our larboard bow, a little out of a straight line. The Caledonia, of three long twenty-four pounders, came next, after the Lawrence, to encounter the Hunter; the Niagara next, to fight the Queen Charlotte, and the Somers, Porcupine, Tigris and Tripp, to encounter the Lady Prevost and Little Belt. Thus arranged, our fleet moved on to attack the enemy, distant at ten o'clock about four or five miles. The Commodore next produced the burgee, or fighting flag, hitherto concealed in the ship. It was inscribed with large white letters on a blue ground, that could be read throughout the fleet, "DON'T GIVE UP THE SHIP," the last words of the expiring Lawrence, and now to be hoisted at the mast-head of the flag-ship bearing his name. A spirited appeal was made to the crew assembled upon the quarter-deck, who returned three hearty cheers that were repeated along the whole line of our vessels, and up went the flag to the top of the fore-royal. The Commodore brought me a package of papers, having a piece of lead attached to them, and gave orders in the event of his falling, to throw the papers overboard; they were instructions from Government, and letters from Mrs. Perry.—The grog ration being served out, drums and fifes struck up the thrilling air, "all hands, all hands, all hands to quarters," calling all to their respective stations. The Commodore was on the quarter deck with two young officers, Thomas Breese and his own brother, Alexander Perry, whose duty it was to run with his orders to every part of the ship, for in the din and uproar of battle no officer can be heard ten feet off. The hatches were now closed excepting a small aperture ten inches square, through which powder-cartridges were to be passed up from the magazine by boys nimble of foot during the battle, and through which light was admitted into the surgeon's room, where the wounded were to be brought. The floor of this apartment was on a level with the surface of the water outside, and consequently the wounded were as much exposed to the enemy's cannon balls as if they were on deck. Six men were directed to bring the wounded below, and to assist the surgeon in moving them.

Every preparation being made, and every man at his post, a profound silence reigned for more than one hour, the most trying part of the whole scene. It was like the stillness of the atmosphere that precedes the hurricane, while the fleet moved on steadily till a quarter before meridian, when the awful suspense was relieved by a cannon-shot aimed at us from the flag-ship Detroit, one mile distant. It was like an electric shock, and was soon followed by another. The two gun-boats ahead of us now fired one or two long guns. At this time the Ariel, Scorpion, Lawrence, Caledonia and Niagara were all in their respective stations in the order they are named, distant from each other about half a cable's length. The other vessels not sailing quite so well were a little out of their stations astern. At ten minutes before twelve, fire was opened from all the long guns of the enemy. At five minutes before meridian, the Lawrence beginning to suffer, returned the fire from her long bow gun, a twelve pounder, when the two gun-boats ahead were ordered by trumpet, to commence the action, and the Caledonia and Niagara astern, opened their fire with their long guns. The sternmost vessels soon after opened also, but at too great a distance to do much injury. Perry finding himself not sufficiently near to do execution with his carronades, made all sail again, and ordered the word to be passed by trumpet to the vessels astern. The order was responded to and transmitted along the line by Captain Elliot of the Niagara, whose vessel was stationed next but one astern of the Lawrence. But the Niagara did not make sail with the Lawrence, and accompany her down into close action as ordered, but continued her long shot with two bow guns, (having shifted the left one over to the starboard side.) Perry pressed on, and supposing himself near enough, fired his forward carronades, but finding they did not tell, he pressed on still nearer, suffering terribly, and getting near enough for execution he opened a rapid and most destructive fire upon the Detroit. The Scorpion and Ariel ahead were not deemed worthy of the enemy's aim, yet those small vessels having heavy cannon fought nobly and with great effect. The Caledonia astern followed the Lawrence into close action against her antagonist the Hunter. But the Niagara, which, when the battle began was within hail of the Lawrence, did not follow her down toward the enemy's line, so as to encounter her antagonist the Queen Charlotte. The Niagara, I say, did not make sail when the Lawrence did, but hung back for two hours, when she should have followed the example of the Lawrence, and grappled with the Queen Charlotte at the same time that vessel did the Detroit. The Queen was expecting it, but as her antagonist did not come up, she shot ahead to fire upon the Lawrence, and in so doing she passed the Hunter, that had been ahead between her and the Detroit. After a lapse of two hours Elliot filled his sails and came up, the Caledonia moved on towards the Hunter, which had now dropped astern and to the leeward of the Queen. Elliot in order to approach the Queen must pass the Caledonia, which he did to the windward or outside of her, and was approaching the Lawrence, which however was crippled and was dropping astern a perfect wreck. Elliot then, instead of passing directly to engage the Queen, luffed to the windward to go round and outside of the Lawrence, and while abreast of her larboard beam, and nearly half a mile distant, Perry left the Lawrence for the Niagara in a boat, and boarded her when she had reached a little ahead of the Lawrence on her larboard bow. The Lawrence now hauled down her flag and ceased firing. Perry sent Elliot to the small vessels astern to bring them up, and turning his ship's head eight points towards the enemy's line, making a right angle in her course, he went within pistol-shot of the Detroit's bow, and took a raking position. The Detroit in attempting to wear to bring her broadside to her, fell on board the Queen Charlotte, and gave Perry a chance to rake both ships, which he did so effectually that in five minutes they hauled down their colors. Perry now shot further ahead, near the Lady Prevost, which from being crippled in her rudder, had drifted out of her place to the leeward, and was pressing forward toward the head of the line to support the two ships. Perry gave her a broad-side which silenced her battery. The Hunter next struck, and the two smaller vessels attempted to escape, but were overhauled by the Scorpion and Tripp, and thus ended the action at near four o'clock, P.M.

Let us now advert for a moment to the scenes exhibited in the flag-ship Lawrence. The wounded began to come down before the Lawrence opened her battery, and for one I felt impatient at the delay. In proper time however as it proved, the dogs of war were let loose from their leash, and it seemed as though heaven and earth were at logger-heads. For more than two long hours, little could be heard but the deafening thunders of our own broad-sides, the crash of balls dashing through our timbers, and the shrieks of the wounded. These were brought down faster than I could attend to them, farther than to stay the bleeding, or support the shattered limbs with splints, and pass them forward upon the berth deck. Two or three were killed near me, after being wounded. I well remember the complaints that the Niagara did not come up. "Why does she hang back so, out of the battle?" Among those early brought down was Lieutenant Brooks, son of the late Governor Brooks, of Massachusetts, a most accomplished gentleman and officer; and renowned for personal beauty. A cannon-ball had struck him in the hip, he knew his doom, and inquired how long he should live; I told him a few hours. He inquired two or three times how the day was going, and expressed a hope that the Commodore would be spared. But new-comers from deck brought more and more dismal reports, until finally it was announced that we had struck. In the lamentations of despair among the wounded, I lost sight of poor Brooks for a few minutes, but when the electrifying cry was heard that the enemy's two ships had struck, I rushed on deck to see if it were true, and then to poor Brooks to cheer him, but he was no more,—he was too much exhausted by his wounds to survive the confusion that preceded this happy transition.

When the battle had raged an hour and a half, I heard a call for me at the small sky-light, and stepping toward it I saw it was the Commodore, whose countenance was as calm and placid as if on ordinary duty. "Doctor," said he, "send me one of your men," meaning one of the six that were to assist me, which was done instantly. In five minutes the call was repeated and obeyed, and at the seventh call I told him he had them all. He asked if any could pull a rope, when two or three of the wounded crawled upon deck to lend a feeble hand in pulling at the last guns.

When the battle was raging most severely, Midshipman Lamb came down with his arm badly fractured; I applied a splint and requested him to go forward and lie down; as he was leaving me, and while my hand was on him, a cannon-ball struck him in the side, and dashed him against the other side of the room, which instantly terminated his sufferings. Charles Pohig, a Narragansett Indian, who was badly wounded, suffered in like manner.

There were other incidents that were less painful to witness. The Commodore's dog had secreted himself in the bottom of the closet containing all our crockery. A cannon-ball passed through the closet, and smashed crockery and door, covering the floor with fragments. The dog set up a barking protest against the right of such an invasion of his chosen retirement.

Lieutenant Yarnel had his scalp badly torn, and came below with the blood streaming over his face; some lint was hastily applied and confined with a large bandanna, with directions to report himself for better dressing after the battle, and he insisted on returning to the deck. The cannon-balls had knocked to pieces the hammocks stowed away on deck, and let loose their contents, which were reed or flag tops, that floated in the air like feathers and gave the appearance of a snow-storm. These lighted upon Yarnel's head covered with blood, and on coming below with another injury, his bloody face covered with the cat tails made his head resemble that of a huge owl. Some of the wounded roared out with laughter that the devil had come for us.

The hard fighting terminated about three o'clock. As the smoke cleared away the two fleets were found completely mingled, the small vessels astern having come up to the others.—The shattered Lawrence lying to the windward was once more able to hoist her flag, which was cheered by a few feeble voices on board, making a melancholy sound compared with the boisterous cheers that preceded the battle.

The proud though painful duty of taking possession of the conquered ships was now performed. The Detroit was nearly dismantled, and the destruction and carnage had been dreadful. The Queen was in a condition little better. The whole number killed in the British fleet was forty-one, and of wounded ninety-four. Every commander and second in command, says Barclay in his official report, was either killed or wounded. In our fleet were twenty-seven killed, and ninety-six wounded; of the twenty-seven killed, twenty-two were on board the Lawrence, and of the ninety-six wounded, sixty-one were on board this same ship, making eighty-three killed and wounded out of one hundred and one reported fit for duty in the Lawrence on the morning of the battle. On board the Niagara were two killed and twenty-three wounded, making twenty-five; and out of these twenty-five, twenty-two were killed or wounded after Perry took command of her.

After four o'clock, a boat was discovered approaching the Lawrence. Soon the Commodore was recognized in her, who was returning to resume the command of his tattered ship, determined that the remnant of her crew should have the satisfaction of witnessing the formal surrender of the British officers. It was a time of conflicting emotions when he stepped upon deck; the battle was won and he was safe, but the deck was slippery with blood, and strewn with the bodies of twenty officers and men, some of whom had set at table with us at our last meal, and the ship resounded everywhere with the groans of the wounded. Those of us who were spared and able to walk, met him at the gangway to welcome him on board, but the salutation was a silent one on both sides; not a word could find utterance.

And now the British officers arrived, one from each vessel, to tender their submission and with it their swords. "When they had approached, picking their way among the wreck and carnage of the deck, they held their swords with the hilts towards Perry, and tendered them to his acceptance. With a dignified and solemn air, the most remote possible from any betrayal of exultation, and in a low tone of voice, he requested them to retain their side-arms, inquired with deep concern for Commodore Barclay and the wounded officers, tendering to them every comfort his ship afforded," and expressing his regret that he had not a spare medical officer to send them, adding that he had only one on duty for the fleet, who had his hands full.

Among the ninety-six wounded there occurred three deaths; a result so favorable was attributable to the plentiful supply of provisions brought off from the Ohio shore, to fresh air, the wounded being ranged under an awning on the deck until we arrived at Erie ten days after the action, and also to the devoted attention of Commodore Perry to every want.

Those who were killed in the battle were committed to the deep at night-fall, the Episcopal service being read over them. On the following morning, the two fleets sailed into Put-in-Bay, where the slain officers were buried on shore. The scene was a solemn one. Equal respect was paid to the slain of the two fleets. Minute-guns were fired from the fleet, a martial band preceded performing a funeral dirge, and the corpses were ranged in alternate order of American and British, and the procession followed in like order to the graves, where the funeral service was read. A striking contrast this to the scene presented two days before, when both the living and the dead now forming this solemn and fraternal train were engaged in fierce and bloody strife, hurling at each other the thunder-bolts of war.

H . M A S S E Y

By Steamer
to the West, 1828

The first Great Lakes steamboats carried rival flags—the American *Ontario* and the Canadian *Frontenac;* in 1817 they splashed up and down Lake Ontario with passengers and horses along the rail and mixed cargo below deck. Beyond the Niagara barrier the pioneer *Walk-in-the-Water* began the Buffalo-Detroit run in 1818. For three years this startling vessel, with a tall black stack between her rigged foremast and mainmast, was the sole steamboat on Lake Erie. But others came in the 1820s—the *Superior, Henry Clay, Niagara, Cuyahoga, William Penn, Pioneer, Chippewa* and *Enterprise.*

Occasionally in the 1820s one of these vessels ventured up Lake Huron and beyond, but their regular destination was Detroit, the jumping-off place for the far West. The Detroit River was lined with ribbon farms, each with its windmill and apple orchard, and the village of Detroit numbered some two thousand French and Indians. When a steamer approached, the boom of its signal cannon drew the whole town to the landing.

In these years Lake Erie's few ports had no harbor works, and landings could not be made during rough weather. Sometimes passengers for Cleveland, Huron or Black River were carried on to Detroit, hoping to debark at their proper destination on the return trip. That was the case on a voyage in 1828, recalled years later in a letter to the *Detroit Free Press.*

MICHIGAN WAS REGARDED at the East as being as much Indian territory as any portions of the country in the more remote West have since become. Detroit was the extreme limit of regular steamboat navigation westward upon the lakes; indeed, but few sailing vessels found inducements to proceed further. If there are few who are interested in the recital of events in the past, similar to those here named, there are fewer still whose personal knowledge dates back so far, and who are both able and willing to furnish the same for publication.

On Monday, the last day of August, 1828, the writer set out from his home in central New York in company with some friends who had decided to make their future home in Detroit, this new and beautiful city of the West. We left by stage at an early hour in the morning and, after a long and tiresome day's ride, reached what was then called "Salt Point," afterwards Syracuse. We here embarked the next morning on the canal for Buffalo, a method of travel but recently introduced but exceedingly popular on account of its freedom from fatigue and because of the greater social advantages, as well as being cheaper than by stage, the only other method of public conveyance in the direction we were going.

After journeying in this manner for three days and nights we reached Buffalo, then only a good-sized village, in time to take passage Friday morning on the good steamer *Niagara,* whereof Pease was master, bound for Detroit. We counted ourselves fortunate in having secured passage on this vessel, though the smallest on the line, yet first on account of her reliability as to time and ability to complete the round trip, Buffalo to Detroit and return, within a week. Of the six vessels comprising the line are remembered (and the same number of Captains) as those mentioned in the article referred to: The *Henry Clay, Cuyahoga, William Penn,* and *Niagara.* The captains were Norton, Blake, Milas, and Pease, the latter in the *Niagara.*

The second steamboat on Lake Erie was the *Superior,* built in 1822. This vessel, at the time of my journey, the fall of 1828, was lying partly sunk in Buffalo Creek, her engine removed, and otherwise thoroughly dismantled. I do not think she was ever in commission afterward, at least as a steamer.

It should be remarked that there were few, if any, harbors on Lake Erie where a landing could be made from a steamer except by means of a small boat, and this only when wind and weather would permit. Passengers were thus landed from the *Niagara* at Dunkirk, Erie, and Ashtabula; but when we arrived off the mouth of the Cuyahoga River—there was no Cleveland then—the sea had become too rough to make the attempt; the same occurred at Huron and Black River. The consequence was that passengers were obliged to remain on board, trusting to have better luck on the downward voyage. We reached Detroit on Sunday at noon. A gun was fired from on board the steamer, as was customary on all the boats of the line, when about a mile from the city. This usually brought to the landing a large portion of the population, composed at that time very largely of French with a free scattering of Indians.

I think all the other boats of the line made their landing at the up-town docks, mostly Newberry's, but the *Niagara* came to at a new wharf which had recently been built about a mile further down the river, where extensive improvements were being made, among them a hotel more spacious and elegant than any previously existing in the city, known as the Mansion House, kept by a New York landlord by the name of Alman. A short distance below, fronting the river, was the pretty, home-like and unpretentious residence of Gov. Cass.

Later in the autumn* Gov. Cass chartered the steamer *Henry Clay* for a month, going in her with his suite and Territorial officers to Green Bay, where he had arranged to meet the tribe of the Winnebago Indians, who were the owners and occupants of a large portion of the adjacent territory. The desire of the Governor was to treat with them for their possessions in exchange for lands farther west, and for other valuable considerations. After a session of two weeks he was successful in negotiating one of the most important and valuable treaties ever made between our government and the Indian tribes.

The steamer and party on their return ran down Lake Michigan to Fort Dearborn, an ancient stockade fort, which was all that existed in the way of improvement where the city of Chicago is now.

Some weeks after the return to Detroit of the Governor and party, on the afternoon of a beautiful, balmy Indian summer's day, there appeared on the broad river above the city, stretching away as far as the eye could reach toward Lake St. Clair, a vast flotilla of canoes, bringing as voyagers in this manner, all the way from Green Bay, many hundreds of the Governor's friends, the Winnebagoes. The trip was taken according to a promise that they would repay the visit he had made to them. Before evening all had arrived and landed upon the river's bank above the city, where they were welcomed by the Governor—and in fact by nearly the entire population of the city. There were about as many of one sex as of the other, and of all ages, dressed in their best apparel—doubtless to a large extent consisting of the blankets and other articles given or paid to them at the time the treaty was made.

* Traveler Massey has the wrong season. It was in June, 1827, that Governor Cass took over the *Henry Clay* for his trip to the Buttes des Morts treaty council.

The visit lasted two or three weeks, during which time they were the guests of the Governor, and were well provided for. The military and police force of the city were made particularly subservient to their protection and care.

This was to most of them their first introduction to civilized life, and it must be said that to their manners and deportment there was not at first any exceptions to be noted; but it must, also, with equal truth, be said that toward the last it became evident that they were not improving as a result of their intercourse with the whites.

Hundreds of them frequently assembled on the green in front of the Governor's residence, where they engaged for an hour or more at evening in the violent contortions called dances, peculiar to the race, all of them sufficiently exciting, but the war dance most of all.

They finally embarked in the same manner in which they came, for a passage through the solitary lakes, several hundred miles to their homes.

Immigrant Boat
to Detroit

The lake country was news in the 1830s—as California would be news a generation later—and the Eastern press filled many columns with reports of lake travel. In 1833 the *New York American* sent Charles Fenno Hoffman on a western tour. He traveled by stage coach and steamboat, and—though he had lost a leg in a childhood accident—rode horseback over the prairies. Back to New York he sent letters full of local color and human interest.

Late in November, 1833, Hoffman rode a stage from Pittsburgh to Cleveland. After two hundred miles of forest-framed roads he looked at Lake Erie "like one who has come out of a pent-up chamber into the full and free air of heaven." On his third evening there he heard a clangor of bells from the lakefront: the last steamboat of the year was calling at Cleveland. Hurrying down to the harbor he joined a swarm of immigrants on the steamer *New York*. The report of that trip makes one of the vivid chapters of his *A Winter in the West*, 1835.

DETROIT, MICHIGAN, November 25 [1833]. I had just left the reading-room of the Franklin Hotel, in Cleaveland, and was making myself at home for the rest of the evening, in my own neat chamber, when the sound of a steamboat-bell, about nine o'clock, gave note that one of these vessels, which at this stormy season cannot navigate the lake with any regularity, had touched at Cleaveland on her way to this place. No time was to be lost, and huddling my clothes, &c. into my trunk as quickly as possible, I jumped into a vehicle, waiting at the tavern door, and in a few minutes was upon the quay. Here I witnessed a scene of indescribable confusion. The night was dark and somewhat gusty, and the boat and the wharf were both crowded with boxes, bales, and the effects of emigrants, who were screaming to each other in half as many languages as were spoken at Babel. Lanterns were flashing to and fro along the docks, and hoarse orders and countermands, mingled with the harsh hissing of the steam on every side. At length we pushed from the shore, and escaping in a moment from the head of the mole, stood fairly out into the lake, while the bright beacon of the Cleaveland lighthouse soon waned in the distance, and was at last lost entirely. I found myself, upon looking around, on board of the fine steamboat *New-York*, Captain Fisher, to whose politeness I was much indebted for showing me about the boat before turning in for the night. Taking a lantern in his hand, and tucking my arm under his, he groped about among his motley ship's company like Diogenes looking for an honest man.

Our course first led us through a group of emigrants collected around a stove, mid-ships, where an English mother nursing her infant, a child lying asleep upon a mastiff, and a long-bearded German smoking his meerchaum on the top of a pile of candleboxes, were the only complete figures I could make out from an indefinite number of heads, arms, and legs lying about in the most whimsical confusion. Passing farther on, we came to two tolerable cabins on either side of the boat just forward of the wheels, both pretty well filled with emigrants, who were here more comfortably bestowed. We next passed the forward barroom (there being another abaft for cabin-passengers), and finally came to the bow, of which a horse and several dogs had already been the occupants for so many days,—the *New-York* having been twice driven into port and delayed by stress of weather,—that it might have been mistaken for either stable or kennel. A noble English blood-hound, the second dog only of that rare breed that I have ever seen, here attracted my attention, and delayed me until I made his acquaintance; which was but a moment, however, for every dog of a generous strain can tell instinctively when a friend of his kind approaches him.

Among others of the canine crew, too, there was a fine spaniel, whose deplorable fate, subsequently, I may as well mention here as elsewhere. The master of poor Dash, it seems, went ashore during the night at Huron, where the boat put in to land way-passengers; and the animal, springing eagerly along a plank at his call, was kicked from his narrow foothold, by some brute of a fellow, into the lake. The night was dark, and the shadow of the high wharf shut out the few lights on shore from the view of the poor animal, while those on board of the boat led him away from the land. He swam after us, yelling most piteously, until his suffocating cries were lost in the freshening sea, which probably the next morning tossed him a carrion on the shore. Had I witnessed the act of throwing him overboard, I could scarcely have restrained myself from pitching the dastardly perpetrator of the cruelty after the victim of his brutality: for if there be one trait in men which awakens in me indignation amounting almost to loathing of my kind, it is to see human things treating those parts of the animal creation beneath them as if this earth was meant for none of God's creatures but man.

But to return to our travels through this floating castle: We next ascended a steep stairway to the upper deck of all, and I here spent some moments rather amusingly in surveying the furniture of the emigrants with which it was crowded. They differed according to the origin of their owner. The effects of the Yankee were generally limited to a Dearborn wagon, a feather-bed, a saddle and bridle, and some knickknack in the way of a machine for shelling corn, hatchelling flax, or, for aught I know, manufacturing wooden nutmegs for family use. Those of the Englishman are far more numerous; for John Bull, when he wanders from home, would not only, like the roving Trojan, carry his household gods with him into strange lands, but even the fast-anchored isle itself, could he but cut it from its moorings. Whenever, therefore, you see an antique-fashioned looking-glass, a decrepit bureau, and some tenderly-preserved old china, you will probably, upon looking further, have the whole house-keeping array of an honest Briton exposed to your view.

But still further do the Swiss and Germans carry their love of family relics. Mark that quaint-looking wagon which lumbers up a dozen square feet of the deck. You may see a portrait of it among the illuminated letters of a vellum-bound edition of Virgil's Bucolics. It was taken from an Helvetian ancestor that transported Cæsar's baggage into winter-quarters. It might be worth something in a museum, but it has cost five times its value in freight to transport it over the Atlantic. What an indignity it is to overwhelm the triumphal chariot with the beds and ploughs, shovels, saddles, and sideboards, chairs, clocks, and carpets that fill its interior, and to hang those rusty pots and kettles, bakepans, fryingpans, and saucepans, iron candlesticks, old horseshoes, and broken tobacco-pipes, like trophies of conquest over Time, along its racked and wheezing sides. That short man yonder, with square shoulders and a crooked pipe in his mouth, is the owner; he, with the woollen cap, that is just raising his blue cotton frock to thrust his hand into the fob of his sherrivalleys. That man had probably not the slightest idea of the kind of country he was coming to. His eyes are but now just opening to his new condition; nor will he sacrifice a particle of his useless and expensive trumpery until they are completely open. That man has not yet a thought in common with the people of his new abode around him. He looks, indeed, as if he came from another planet. Visit him on his thriving farm ten years hence, and, except in the single point of language, you will find him (unless he has settled among a nest of his countrymen) at home among his neighbours, and happily conforming to their usages; while that clean-looking Englishman next to him will still be a stranger in the land.

I subsequently looked into the different cabins and compartments of the boat not yet visited, and had reason to be gratified with the appearance of all; though the steamboat *Michigan*, which I have since visited at the docks here, puts me completely out of conceit of every part of the *New-York*, except her captain. The *Michigan*, machinery and all, was built at Detroit; and without entering into a minute description of it, I may say, that fine as our Atlantic boats are, I do not recollect any on the Atlantic waters, for strength and beauty united, equal to this. A great mistake, however, I think, exists here in building the boats for these waters with cabins on deck, like the river boats. In consequence of such a large part of the hull being above water, they are rendered dangerous during the tremendous gales which sweep Lake Erie, and are often compelled to make a port of safety several times during a passage. The English steamers which ply between Dover and Calais are built like other sea-vessels; and having their machinery below, can consequently keep on their course in a sea where one of ours would live but a few minutes. I was fortunate, considering the stormy season of the year, in having a tolerably smooth passage across the lake, there being but few persons sea-sick on board of the boat, and I happily not included in the number. But it must be very unpleasant, during a heavy blow, to be tossed on the short cobble sea which the light fresh water of these lakes always breaks into beneath the wind.

We passed a number of islands in the morning soon after breakfast; some of them mere rocks, and others several miles in circumference. On one of these, of a few acres in extent, a row-boat, in which a man undertook to transport himself and one or two members of his family to the shore, was wrecked some years since. The father and brother, with a daughter of about twelve years, managed to subsist upon the snakes and snails they found among the rocks, until a passing vessel took them off, after some ten days of suffering.

It was during a shower, shortly after noon, when some low

wooded islands on the American side of the lake, with a tall flag-staff peering above the haze from the little town of Amherstburg on the British shore, indicated that we had entered the mouth of the Detroit River. The wind, which was now beginning to rise into a threatening tempest, compelled us to hug the Canadian shore so closely that the red-coated sentinel pacing along the barracks above Fort Malden was plainly seen from the boat. The river soon after narrows sufficiently for one to mark with ease the general appearance of its banks, and the different settlements upon their course. Their appearance must be pretty in summer, when fields and woods show to the most advantage. But now, though slightly undulating, with a sudden rise from the river of some fifty or sixty feet, the adjacent country is too low to be strikingly beautiful. Those, however, who admire the Delaware below Trenton, if they can dispense with the handsome seats which ornament its not very clear waters, may find a charm in the gentle banks and transparent tide of the Detroit River.

The city of Detroit itself stands upon an elevated piece of table-land, extending probably for some twenty miles back from the river, and being perfectly unbroken for at least two miles along its margin. Beneath the bluff—for the plain is so high as almost to deserve the name—is a narrow bustling street of about half a mile in length, with the wharves just beyond it; and fifty yards inboard runs a spacious street called Jefferson Avenue, parallel with the lower street and the river; the chief part of the town extends for a mile or two along the latter. The dwelling-houses are generally of wood, but there are a great many stores now building, or already erected, of brick, with stone basements. The brick is generally of an indifferent quality; but the stone, which is brought from Cleaveland, Ohio, is a remarkably fine material for building purposes. It is a kind of yellow freestone, which is easily worked when first taken from the quarry, and hardens subsequently upon exposure to the air. There are at this moment many four-story stores erecting, as well as other substantial buildings, which speak for the flourishing condition of the place.

The want of mechanics is so great, however, that it is difficult as yet to carry on these operations upon the scale common in our Atlantic cities, although the demand for houses in Detroit, it is said, would fully warrant similar outlays of capital. The public buildings are the territorial council-house, situated upon an open piece of ground, designated on an engraved plan of the city as "The Campus Martius," a court-house, academy, and two banks. There are also five churches, a Catholic, an Episcopal, a Presbyterian, Baptist, and

Methodist. The Catholic congregation is the largest; their stone church, after remaining several years in an unfinished state, is soon, it is said, to be completed with funds derived from Rome; it will make an imposing appearance when finished. The population of Detroit is, I believe, between three and four thousand—it increases so rapidly, however, that it is difficult to form an estimate. The historical associations, the safety, and commodiousness of the harbour, with its extensive inland commercial advantages, must ever constitute this one of the most interesting and important points in the Union.

RALPH KEELER

Stowaway

In the 1830s, after years in the schooner trade, Captain Gilman Appleby of Conneaut became master of the steamer *North American*, carrying travelers and immigrants from Buffalo to western Lake Erie. In the 1840s he took command of the *Indiana*, with a brass band on deck and an iron Indian astride her smokestack. One of his passengers on an eastbound trip was a nine-year-old boy on the way from Toledo to an orphan school in Buffalo. Long afterward young Ralph Keeler dreamed of the iron warrior pointing a bowed arrow through a cloud of coal smoke and brass music.

Two years later Ralph Keeler ran away with five pennies in his pocket, hiding himself in the foc'sle of the steamer *Diamond*. The five coppers were a talisman, and they carried him through some chancy fortunes as scullion, cabin boy and stowaway.

From these boyhood travels Ralph Keeler (1840-1873) developed a lasting wanderlust that took him to distant lands. He became a roving writer and lecturer, sometimes appearing with Mark Twain on the lecture platform.

The story of his youth is told in *Vagabond Adventures*, 1870.

THE CAPTAIN of the steamer *Diamond*, never in the habit of looking pleased at anything, did not depart from his habit, but rather carried it to an unwonted degree of frowning and darkling excess, when he saw me at work again about the table, at the next meal after leaving Conneaut. He said nothing to me, however, but, calling up the steward, had a long, stormy talk with him.

The steward in self-defence was, of course, obliged to tell how I had stowed myself away in the forecastle, which, I need not say, did not enhance the commander's opinion of me. What that irate gentleman would have done with me—whether he would not have thrown me bodily into the lake if it had not been for the earnest deprecation of the steward—is even yet, in quiet, reflective moments, an interesting problem to my mind.

At last the captain's unwilling consent was obtained to take me to Buffalo, where, as my intercessor said, I had friends. It happened that the steamer was bound up the lake to Toledo, where, also, I had relatives,—a fact which I did not make known to the steward. I was now compassed about, it will be seen, by prospects of capture on every hand. I had my reasons, nevertheless, for wishing to be left at Buffalo instead of Toledo. The latter city was so small that my relatives would easily lay hold of me there; and the former, being not only a larger city, but so much farther away, I should stand a much better chance of concealment, and, what was of almost equal importance, I should be sure of an additional week's board before the steamer reached there.

At Toledo, therefore, I scarcely went ashore at all. During the return trip to Buffalo my mind was exceeding busy with daring and mighty schemes of escape from the steward, whom circumstances had now metamorphosed into a walking terror to me. That honest fellow had confided to me that he considered it his duty, and for my interests, to have an interview with the people from whom I had fled, and to do I know not what other appalling things toward providing me with a suitable, permanent home.

I did not, however, think it prudent to express my demurrer at his prospective proceedings, choosing secretly to trust the hope of sustaining it rather to my legs than to my eloquence. Accordingly, when we had arrived at Buffalo, I watched my opportunities, and, seizing the right moment, fled precipitately up the docks, unobserved by my well-meaning, self-imposed guardian.

Two hours subsequently, deeming myself safe, I walked boldly on board of the old steamer *Baltic*. Here, by a wonderful freak of fortune, it was not ten minutes till I had "shipped" as cabin-boy, at the marvellous salary of ten dollars a month. Surely, I have never felt so rich or independent since. I went to work with a will, inspired to undertake anything, in any weather, by a calm sense of security, and by the princely guerdon which loomed high in my imagination at the end of the month. In the course of time, too, I am happy to say here incidentally, I overcame completely my remarkable tendency to seasickness.

The *Baltic*, then having seen her best days, did not belong to any regular line, but went rolling and creaking about on roaming commissions for freight and passengers all over the lakes. Up to the time of the inglorious *dénouement* in which my life as one of her crew ended, I can remember nothing of moment which happened, except that the sense of my own importance and of my accumulating wealth grew daily in strict proportion; and that her captain was a perpetual mountain to me, bearing down very hard on my expansive spirit, but never quite crushing it.

With a few exceptions, indeed, my experiences with captains were strikingly disagreeable, but not, I think, peculiar. From actual brutality, or a mistaken sense of duty,—applying especially to boys and common sailors,—your ordinary captain, on lake or ocean, has often seemed to me, in some respects, less human than the ship over which he tyrannizes. With regard to this cold autocrat of the venerable steamer *Baltic* I recollect a queer, boyish fancy I entertained, I forget whether in earnest or in sportive retribution; namely, that the Nor'westers had not only piled up the breakers which threatened continually in the hard, wrinkled folds and lines of his face, but had also blown the warmth, and, in a word, all the heart out of his voice and manner.

As the month drew near its close, however, and the ten dollars earned by my own hands were soon to be mine, the contumely of my commander had little weight against the buoyancy and growing independence of my spirit. I had been in the *Baltic* just three weeks and four days on the eventful morning when she was to leave Toledo. It had been my habit, once a week, to wash my only shirt in the pantry and to wait about the kitchen till it dried, with my coat buttoned up to my chin. Now, on this same morning, I had just issued from the latter place with my clean shirt in my hand, when the captain told me to do something,—I forget what. I assured him I would as soon as I could put on my shirt. He told me to do it right away, at the same time coupling me and my garment blasphemously together, and consigning us, figuratively, to a port where, for aught I know, there may be many collectors but no custom-houses.

I gave the captain to understand, still more bluntly, that I would do nothing till I had made my toilet; and, inspired by a memory of former wrongs, as well as a consciousness of prospective opulence, I used to my superior officer other language of a saucy and independent kind. Whereupon the captain, in sailor phrase, "tacked" for me, and I "tacked" for the shore. Here, then, I demanded my pay, but the enraged commander solemnly averred that he would see me first in that tropical port just alluded to, and *then* I should never have a cent.

Shortly after, the boat pushed off into the stream. A sympathizing friend threw me a paper of crackers from the pantry on the upper deck; and, as the *Baltic* got under way, there I stood on the wharf, with my paper of crackers in one hand, and my only shirt in the other, clamoring for my wages.

I stood leaning against the splintered pile, which had been one of her hitching-posts, and watched the *Baltic* as she faded slowly out of sight. My courage seemed to fade with her. It was not the loss of my place and probably of my dinner that crushed me, but— after so many wealthy dreams—this utter financial ruin! What were my five coppers, still jingling loosely in my pocket, to the dollars I had lost, or to the combined capital of my relatives in that very city? The contest was plainly hopeless. For as much as a half-hour I considered myself delivered bound into the hands of my pursuers. Indeed, the dock on which I was making this mental soliloquy happened to be but a short distance from the warehouse of an uncle of mine, then a commission-merchant and ship-owner in Toledo.

At last, I betook myself despondently to a neighboring shed and donned my shirt, and then, as under some desperate spell, walked straight toward my uncle's office. I crossed the threshold and saw him in conversation with some gentlemen. While waiting till he should notice me, I beheld, through the office window, the little steamer *Arrow*, almost ready to start for Detroit. I knew that the *Baltic* was also going to Detroit, and thought that I might possibly get my money if I followed her thither. Only those unfortunate persons who have been suddenly prevented from committing suicide when in the very act will thoroughly understand, I think, the feeling with which I hailed this thought. Instantly my comprehensive vow to have nothing more to do with relatives flashed across my mind.

Seeing that my uncle had not yet observed me, I turned quickly on my heel, and made hastily for the dock of the steamer *Arrow*. I concealed myself on board of her till she was under way, when, making my case known to the steward, I was allowed to work my passage in the cabin to Detroit.

It was that season when, as many dwellers by the Western lakes will remember, the *Arrow* was the fastest boat on those waters. We passed the other steamer somewhere off Monroe lighthouse; and on the same afternoon, therefore, as the old *Baltic* came up to the wharf at Detroit, there I stood before the astonished eyes of her captain, again clamoring for my wages,—with this difference only, that my shirt was now on my back, and my crackers carefully stowed away in my pocket with my five coppers.

HENRY HOWE

Salmon Sweatland's

Funeral

The first settlers in Connecticut's Western Reserve, which bordered Lake Erie for 120 miles, took up land on the lake shore. Near the Pennsylvania-Ohio boundary, in the northeast corner of Ashtabula County, lay the little farm of Salmon Sweatland, who spent more time hunting and fishing than hacking at his half-cleared field. With the help of his hounds he sometimes drove a herd of deer into the lake, putting out after them in a canoe. When he had used up his powder and bullets he towed the game ashore.

The story of a lake "hunt," on an unexpectedly windy morning, was recorded by Henry Howe in his *Historical Collections of Ohio,* 1847.

IT WAS a lovely morning in early autumn, and Sweatland, in anticipation of his favorite sport, had risen at the first dawn of light, and without putting on his coat or waistcoat left his cabin, listening in the meantime in expectation of the approach of the dogs. His patience was not put to a severe trial ere his ears were saluted by the deep baying of the hounds, and on arriving at the beach he perceived that the deer had already taken to the lake, and was moving at some distance from the shore. In the enthusiasm of the moment he threw his hat upon the beach, his canoe was put in requisition, and shoving from the shore he was soon engaged in a rapid and animated pursuit. The wind, which had been fresh from the south during the night and gradually increasing, was now blowing nearly a gale, but intent on securing his prize, Sweatland was not in a situation to yield to the dictates of prudence. The deer, which was a vigorous animal of its kind, hoisted its flag of defiance, and breasting the waves stoutly showed that in a race with a log canoe and a single paddle, he was not easily outdone.

Sweatland had attained a considerable distance from the shore and encountered a heavy sea before overtaking the animal, but was not apprized of the eminent peril of his situation until shooting past him the deer turned towards the shore. He was however brought to a full appreciation of his danger when, on tacking his frail vessel and heading towards the land, he found that with his utmost exertions he could make no progress in the desired direction, but was continually drifting farther to sea. He had been observed in his outward progress by Mr. Cousins, who had arrived immediately after the hounds, and by his own family, and as he disappeared from sight, considerable apprehensions were entertained for his safety.

The alarm was soon given in the neighborhood, and it was decided by those competent to judge that his return would be impossible, and that unless help could be afforded he was doomed to perish at sea. Actuated by those generous impulses that often induce men to peril their own lives to preserve those of others, Messrs. Gilbert, Cousins and Belden took a light boat at the mouth of the creek and proceeded in search of the wanderer, with the determination to make every effort for his relief. They met the deer returning towards the shore nearly exhausted, but the man who was the object of their solicitude was nowhere to be seen. They made stretches off shore within probable range of the fugitive for some hours, until they had gained a distance of five or six miles from land, when meeting with a sea in which they judged it impossible for a canoe to live, they abandoned the search, returned with difficulty to the shore, and Sweatland was given up for lost.

The canoe in which he was embarked was dug from a large whitewood log, by Major James Brookes, for a fishing boat: it was about fourteen feet in length and rather wide in proportion, and was considered a superior one of the kind. Sweatland still continued to lie off, still heading towards the land, with the faint hope that the wind might abate, or that aid might reach him from the shore. One or two schooners were in sight in course of the day, and he made every signal in his power to attract their attention, but without success. The shore continued in sight, and in tracing its distant outline he could distinguish the spot where his cabin stood, within whose holy precincts were contained the cherished objects of his affections, now doubly endeared from the prospect of losing them forever. As these familiar objects receded from view, and the shores appeared to sink beneath the troubled waters, the last tie which united him in companionship to his fellowmen seemed dissolved, and the busy world, with all its interests, forever hidden from his sight.

Fortunately Sweatland possessed a cool head and a stout heart, which, united with a tolerable share of physical strength and power of endurance, eminently qualified him for the part he was to act in this emergency. He was a good sailor, and as such would not yield to despondency until the last expedient had been exhausted. One only expedient remained, that of putting before the wind and endeavoring to reach the Canada shore, a distance of about fifty miles. This he resolved to embrace as his forlorn hope.

It was now blowing a gale, and the sea was evidently increasing as he proceeded from the shore, and yet he was borne onwards over the dizzy waters by a power that no human agency could control. He was obliged to stand erect, moving cautiously from one extremity to the other, in order to trim his vessel to the waves, well aware that a single lost stroke of the paddle, or a tottering movement, would swamp his frail bark and bring his adventure to a final close. Much of his attention was likewise required in bailing his canoe from the water, an operation which he was obliged to perform by making use of his *shoes*, a substantial pair of *stoggies*, that happened fortunately to be upon his feet.

Hitherto he had been blessed with the cheerful light of heaven, and amidst all his perils could say, "The light is sweet, and it is a pleasant thing for the eyes to behold the sun," but to add to his distress, the shades of night were now gathering around him, and he was soon enveloped in darkness. The sky was overcast, and the light of a few stars that twinkled through the haze alone remained to guide his path over the dark and troubled waters. In this fearful condition, destitute of food and the necessary clothing, his log canoe was rocked upon the billows during that long and terrible night. When morning appeared he was in sight of land, and found he had made Long Point, on the Canada shore. Here he was met by an adverse wind and a cross sea, but the same providential aid which had guided him thus far still sustained and protected him; and after being buffeted by the winds and waves for nearly thirty hours, he succeeded in reaching the land in safety.

What were the emotions he experienced on treading once more "the green and solid earth," we shall not attempt to inquire, but his trials were not yet ended. He found himself faint with hunger and exhausted with fatigue, at the distance of forty miles from any human habitation, whilst the country that intervened was a desert filled with marshes and tangled thickets, from which nothing could be obtained to supply his wants. These difficulties, together with the reduced state of his strength, rendered his progress towards the settlements slow and toilsome. On his way he found a quantity of goods, supposed to have been driven on shore from the wreck of some vessel, which, although they afforded him no immediate relief, were afterwards of material service.

He ultimately arrived at the settlement, and was received and treated with great kindness and hospitality by the people. After his strength was sufficiently recruited, he returned with a boat, accompanied by some of the inhabitants, and brought off the goods. From this place he proceeded by land to Buffalo, where, with the avails of his treasure, he furnished himself in the garb of a gentleman, and finding the *Traveler,* Capt. Chas. Brown, from Conneaut, in the harbor, he shipped on board and was soon on his way to rejoin his family. When the packet arrived off his dwelling, they fired guns from the deck and the crew gave three loud cheers. On landing, he found his funeral sermon had been preached, and had the rare privilege of seeing his own *widow* clothed in the habiliments of mourning.

By Ice

to Cross Village

One of the strangest episodes of Great Lakes history is the Mormon settlement on Beaver Island in the northern waters of Lake Michigan. In 1847 the eastern branch of the Mormons, then living in southern Wisconsin, sought a remote habitation. Big Beaver Island, with its scattering of Indians and fishermen, was the chosen refuge. On the island the Saints built a tabernacle, laid out the town of St. James, established a newspaper and crowned their leader James Jesse Strang as monarch of the Mormon Kingdom.

In a few years the colony grew to two thousand simple and submissive people. But their neighbors, on the other islands and the mainland, resented the Mormons. Dark tales were told—of their polygamy and counterfeiting, of stealing government timber and robbing the U.S. mails, of luring ships ashore and plundering the cargoes. Eventually the United States sent the gunboat *Michigan* to arrest the leader, but he was shot by his own followers before the government could sieze him. Then invading gentiles burned the tabernacle, sacked the "Royal Press," and drove the Mormons off the island. Strang's name was forgotten, except by lake sailors who for many years told stories of King Strang and his Mormon pirates.

Against this background Brand Whitlock wrote a novel of a French fisherman who, after a violence on the mainland, fled to the Beaver Islands with his dog Boule. On Big Beaver he found a trusting woman and lived with her quietly while King Strang's troubles grew. At last the king (named Gorel in this tale) sent Lenoir with a message to a political friend in Cheboygan. Before daybreak on a winter morning Lenoir said goodbye to his woman, called his dog, and set out over the frozen lake. His grim journey is one of the final chapters of the novel.

Ohio-born Brand Whitlock (1869-1934) jurist, reformer, diplomat and author, wrote *The Stranger on the Island* just two years before his death.

THE SUN WAS BARELY UP when Lenoir and Boule passed Loaney's Point and found themselves out on the ice of Lake Michigan. The light that was spreading solemnly through the world seemed to be rather a reflection of the cold, grey expanse of the sun, whose luminous ball glowed palely in the thick frosty haze to the east. The lake lay all about in the arctic desolation of a lunar landscape with great windrows of snow and frozen waves ridging the surface of the ice in a rhythm that had been caught by the frost and petrified in this scene of death. Here and there were hillocks of jagged ice that made the going difficult, but Lenoir strode on, the frost pinching his nose, and Boule trotted on beside him as though happy to be on his travels once more, even in such hard conditions. From time to time he would glance up at Lenoir in an effort to understand the meaning of this strange expedition, or perhaps to assure himself that he was doing what was expected of him, content, no matter how or where or why they were going, so long as he could be with his master. For Boule, in spite of all that he had been called upon to suffer and endure in life, had one advantage, at any rate, over those other sports of circumstance and laughing-stocks of fate known as mortals; he knew but one loyalty, he had but one leader to follow.

Lenoir, with a compass to guide him over the frozen waves of this immobile and ghostly sea, had only one thought for the moment, and that was to get on to Cross Village before that ball of light should describe its short arc above the lake to the south and, going down behind him, let darkness lower on the grey desolation. But around this central purpose were gathered a multitude of cares and perplexities and fears; his heart would go back to the cabin in the woods; he saw the white face of Martha, with its last strained look of anguish, as he had seen it that morning before she shut the door. . . . The main point now was that he was on his way, and a job well begun was half done. Considering the journey as one whole and entire thing he was already, now that he was started, on his way back to Martha. He began to picture to himself just how it would be when he returned; he would go up the little garden path; she would be standing in the doorway smiling, and no longer sad. And he should be back home, triumphant and in high favour with Gorel, and a great man on the island.

"Hey, Boule?"

And Boule leapt upon him and tried to lick his face, so that he had to rebuke Boule. It was no time to be wasting energy in foolish gambols with that long trudge to Cross Village before them.

The sun was getting up now and shedding its light in a sickly fashion over the ice. The brumous wintry haze was lifting; perhaps the day would be fine. And indeed, as the sun rose in the sky, the air grew clearer, the mists were gathered up in white clouds, there were widening expanses of blue sky. Lenoir felt an exhilaration in the keen air and went faster.

They were getting well out into the middle of the channel between the Beavers and the mainland, and there, where the winter winds had made a clean sweep of the snow, the ice was green and, except for the corrugations made by frozen ripples, smooth. They hastened on; the sun was now strong enough to cast shadows, and Lenoir watched Boule's shadow gradually shorten and gain on him as he trotted courageously along, until it was right under his body. It was noon then, and Lenoir drew from his pack the lunch that Martha had put up for him, and he and Boule ate it.

The sun had grown warm enough to make tiny pools on the surface of the ice—Boule would lap up the water now and then as they went along—but the ice had been firm and hard. However, as they drew near the other side of the lake—they must, by midday, have got more than halfway across, having been six hours on the way—they came upon a long crack in the ice, a lateral rift running north and south, produced, no doubt, by the uncertain currents in that part of the lake. They leapt the crack easily and went on, but as they went they came upon other cracks, seams and fissures, and Lenoir began to wonder, had the ice begun to break up?

But there was only one thing to do, and that was to push on. Off to the north he could now see Skilagalee—as the Americans in those parts called the little Ile aux Galets—a tiny island where in summer the blue lake poured its foam on the white pebbles along the beach; now, with navigation closed, it was dead, and the low, white tower of its lighthouse stood cold and lonely against the sky, unlighted at night, and but a part of the wintry desolation. But to reach Cross Village Lenoir must bear south by east, leaving the island as it were on his port side, and he still had some eight miles to go before he could reach the mainland. Some changed quality, a perceptible dimness in the air, caused him to glance back and there in the southwest he saw the dark gathering thickness of a storm; a sudden gust of cold air struck him.

"*Allons, Boule, mon vieux!*" he said, and hurried on with longer strides. And Boule, pricking his ears forward, a look of concern gathering on his brows, trotted on more rapidly and more resolutely.

Five minutes later the squall was upon them, a cold, biting wind swirling the great snow-flakes about them in a mass that darkened the sky, filled all the air, and made it impossible to see before them. Boule was whining uneasily, and keeping close to his master's feet as Lenoir, bending before the storm, pressed on. Then, suddenly, Boule made a great leap forward, and in that same instant, before he knew what had happened, Lenoir felt himself immersed in the icy water of the lake. After the first cold shock of surprise, he struck out, almost automatically beginning to swim; it was hard work, heavily clad as he was and with a pack on his back, and he felt a sense of relief when, after a lunge or two, his mittened hands touched the edge of the ice before him. He held to it, trying to scramble out of the water, and then, all at once, there was the friendly muzzle of Boule thrust into his face, and in another moment Boule had him by the collar of his coat. Boule braced himself on his four feet and tugged and hauled until finally Lenoir managed to climb on the ice. Standing there, wet to the skin, in that whirlwind of snow, he was aware from a sudden giddiness that the ice was not firm under his feet; and then he realized that he was on a floe. He was afraid to go forward now, afraid to move, and he and Boule huddled there. He had no notion of the size of the floe, or whether it was floating in any considerable space of open water, but it was moving, slowly. There was nothing to be done; he could only drift on this raft of ice at the mercy of wind and current.

Boule was seized with a fit of shivering, and Lenoir put his arms about him and held him tight. And thus they waited. . . . The squall passed; the whirlwind of snow was dancing away in the twilight over the jagged ice towards the Michigan shore. Only a few flakes were left to float in the cold air. The wind was hauling somewhat to the south, and the floe was moving now towards the north-east. And night was coming down upon the lake. . . . After a while they felt a shock and heard the noise of grinding ice. And in what remained of the light they moved cautiously forward to find that the floe had grounded on the pebbly beach of Skilagalee.

The lighthouse, out of service during the winter months, was closed and uninhabited, but it was no great task to force the door of the kitchen at its back. Lenoir found a tinder-box and lighted a fire at which he dried his clothes and warmed himself, and then, after a pull at his flask, he and Boule settled down for the night, hugging each other closely to keep warm, and waited for the dawn.

As soon as its grey light spread over the lake, Lenoir made observations to the east of the island. The ice stretched away in an unbroken, if rough and jagged, expanse as far as he could see; the frost of the night must have tightened it, and now that it was daylight, he would venture forth and make a dash for it. They had eight miles to cover, and Lenoir's hands and feet were acting very strangely that morning; they were numb and tingling and stiff, and their movements hard to control. But he scrambled on, climbing over hillocks of jagged ice, making headway somehow until at last he saw the yellow bluffs along the Michigan shore, and high upon them the great wooden cross that had been lifted up there by Père Marquette. An hour later he and Boule were crawling up the icy bluff into Cross Village.

U. P. HEDRICK

Arrival at

L'Arbre Croche

Three centuries ago explorers paddling past the wild shores of Little Traverse Bay took bearings from a twisted pine on a bold bluff above Lake Michigan. This was L'Arbre Croche—the Crooked Tree. The name survived long after the landmark was gone.

In 1874 the district was opened to homesteading, and a small land rush began. Among the newcomers was the Hedrick family from Iowa. Young U. P. Hedrick, who would become a famous horticulturalist, grew up in that beguiling world of woods and waters. Years later he looked back at the north country in his reminiscent narrative, *Land of the Crooked Tree*, 1948.

T HE WATERS THAT TOUCH the shores of the Land of the Crooked Tree have as their seaward boundary a line drawn from the point of one to that of the other of two well-marked capes, Waugoshance and Charlevoix. From point to point it was some forty miles. The boundary line on the water can be seen as a bright thread of blue, the *ba-esk-ko-be* of the Indians, the horizon of the whites. The shore itself measures more than twice forty miles, because it is broken by bays and coves. The southern boundary is marked by a nearly circular bay some five or six miles in diameter, called La Petite Traverse to distinguish it from La Grande Traverse, a larger bay a half-day's sail southward.

Sometimes this shore is bordered and bottomed with glistening boulders, rocks, and pebbles of many colors. The forest, always of several species of evergreens and white birches, comes down to the water. Sometimes the shore and bottom are of glistening yellow sand, of which there is a windblown waste of drifting dunes supporting a curious dune-land flora. Always the lake is kept in its basin by a high bluff, which in places is lapped by the water; but mostly bluff and water are separated by dunes or swamps. Every mile or two, brooks or little rivers ripple and gurgle through the sands or roar down the bluffs and over the rocks from the tangles of the forest.

Until long after the beginning of the nineteenth century, these waters and the great lake of which they are a part had been a solitary sea on which were seen only the canoes of traders, trappers, and Indians. Jesuit missionaries first saw the country three centuries ago and gave it the name L'Arbre Croche, as St. Leger had told us, from a large crooked tree standing prominently on a high bluff overlooking Lake Michigan. Priests, explorers, trappers, fishermen, and Indians long knew this land as the home of the Ottawa and Chippewa before whites were allowed to own any piece of it.

When, in 1874, Washington permitted whites to "take up" land from the government as homesteads and to buy it from Indian owners, there was a rush of farmers, lumbermen, fishermen, pigeon trappers, and summer resorters to settle the new country. Now the horizon marked one of the world's great travel routes. Men from the Atlantic seaboard had discovered the Middle West and now were building western states and cities. Steamships crowded with passengers were hourly passing to and fro. Fleets of sailing ships, rich with wealth from western farms or eastern factories, sailed across the sea between our capes. Steam, as yet, could not compete with wind.

Travel by land had but recently reached the forests of the Land of the Crooked Tree. A trail led north and south from the old town to which we had come, but it was almost impassable in summer, and in winter only travelers on snowshoes could make use of it. To the people of the town, the world beyond was "outside"; its people, "outsiders."

This was the land to which my father was bringing his family.

* * *

Named after the bay, Little Traverse, the harbor town to which we had come, was the capital and metropolis of the Land of the Crooked Tree. The name and the description given by Father to his open-eared children had carried our interest to a high pitch. Now, at sight of the primitive little trading-post, we were all eyes.

From the deck of the *Menominee* we had seen that the habitations were small and shabby, but the three or four trading houses and a golden-steepled church looked large and fine. Close at hand, however, we saw that these great buildings, and the lesser ones as well, were about to tumble down. There was not a patch of paint, a new board, or a bright shingle on any one of them.

The hotel to which Joutel took us was the weather-beaten remains of an old government warehouse. Swinging and creaking over the front entrance was a signboard with a huge golden star painted on a brilliant blue background. At the bottom of the board we read "The Star Hotel." Sun, wind, and rain had warped the walls and roof, warped the shingles, and painted the building an ashy gray, which in the morning sun seemed luminous. The glare of the shining walls was relieved by splashes of green moss in joints between shingles and cornices.

Yet to me, the Star Hotel was a palace, and, despite its disreputable exterior, had a homelike atmosphere when compared with the *Menominee*, which had no semblance of a home, whatsoever. The words "landlord" and "landlady" had a strange fascination for me. They seemed to suggest very superior human beings. Now, at last, I was to see what these lords of creation were like.

How disappointed I was! The mistress of the Star was a tall, lean, withered, stoop-shouldered woman in a plain gray, worn, soiled garment. She welcomed my mother in a high-pitched, tremulous voice, so nearly a sob that I wondered what she was crying about and wished Mother would say something to comfort her.

At night the landlady's face and figure troubled me in a strange way. I would waken with the fear that the old woman was approaching her end. This was the period of my life when I had a dread of facing the fact of death. The landlady dead, however, would have been little different from the landlady living, so worn, thin, and pale she was.

As the hostess of the Star and my mother went about the business of getting acquainted inside the house, we children were attracted by a commotion outside. We heard derisive hoots and calls: "*B'jou, Cochon! 'allo, Cochon!*" from the throats of a pack of red-skinned urchins.

The cause of the excitement was an enormous, unwieldy man. Never before had I seen a man so rolling in fat. Folds of flesh filled out his bagging clothes and padded the bones of his legs and arms. The knuckles of his hands were completely lost. His feet were hidden from his own sight, so that he could not see where to place them and must shuffle and stumble along, feeling his way. You would expect a man of his bulk to have a booming bass voice; but as he stopped to chide his tormentors, it turned out that he spoke in a shrill falsetto, with a tremor in his voice that gave it a strangely pathetic note like the mournful cry of some bird.

Father had told us about this fat man, and we knew him at once as the landlord of the Star, *Le Cochon* to the Indians, "Hog Smith" to the whites. Later, I learned that the introduction of the pig by the French in this part of the world had furnished the aborigines with several words to describe human beings.

After what seemed ages, the landlady took us to our rooms in the second story. This part of the building, once a storeroom, had been divided by unpapered partitions into a dozen bedrooms, with rough boards and uncarpeted floors creaking at every step. The ramshackle stairs possessed the one note of beauty in the building. The railing was curly bird's-eye maple, beautifully polished by hands that had slid down it. Father said we had many maples on our farm, and that some day we should live in a home finished in curly maple.

Without his airy hopes, how could my father have lived?

The two rooms in the hotel for our family looked out on a rough, weedy yard, pastured by the domestic animals of the village; beyond was a road deep in sand, from which a cloud of dust arose. Up and down the street were Indian habitations, mostly log cabins. Through our open windows came the noise of drowsy insect voices, and now in the heat of the day there was a rank odor from fish litter, mingled with the more pleasant smell of tarred nets. My mother looked out of the window to see the blue waters of the harbor, drew a long breath, and began unpacking.

Our night in this hostelry was anything but pleasant. Fleas swarmed in the beds. They at once scented fresh, young blood, and soon there were dozens on my body. Long afterwards I read of a monk who for some sin was punished by being made to sleep in a bed where fleas abounded. If he suffered as did I in the Star, the penance should have secured him pardon for his most damning sins. Even Father, who enjoyed a good bed, was upset by this scourge of fleas, but to Mother's denunciations of a human habitation overrun with this pest of dogs he could only say: "It might be worse!"

There were other troubles in the night. A thunderstorm with a gale of wind came up, and the Star creaked and swayed like a boat at sea. The howling of dogs made the night unearthly. Little Traverse, we soon came to know, was a dog's paradise.

The daylight hours for the next few weeks in the land of our adoption were spent in exploration. The old town is now so changed that ghosts of those old days, returning, would recognize only two landmarks, both of which will endure to the end of time. One of these is the harbor into which we came. A hundred ocean ships could safely anchor here. In the summer, few craft made use of this anchorage, but in the storms of autumn, sailing vessels of all descriptions, from little schooners to great six-masters, and side- and stern-wheel steamers anchored in the harbor. Always the sight of a storm-driven boat heading our way brought a thrill of excitement to old and young. This shipping brought business to the traders, but left work for Father Zorn, the village priest, in mending the morals of his people.

Most of the life of the town was along the water front, and here, where there was much to see and do, was our playground. Besides the sailing craft of commerce, there were fishing smacks pulled up alongside fish houses, about which were all the gear of the industry: nets, barrels, anchors, sails, and kettles of tar. On the shore and the long wharf were tiers of pungent hemlock bark and lumber awaiting ships. Through the town ran a brook in which minnows were netted for bait to catch larger fish off the wharf.

The point of land that separated the waters of the harbor from those of the lake was sand, tortured into monstrous shapes by wind and water. The sand, the wind, and a climate slightly different because of the temperature of water on its three sides made a home for plants unlike those of the mainland. These peculiarities set "the Point," as all called it, apart as a special place. To the Indians it was a home of ghosts and spirits, hallowed by legend and story. This long-pointed, tree-covered, arrowhead of land was to white children, in the days before summer colonists took it over to the last square inch, a fairyland, all the more delightful for being a sanctuary from the superstitious young Indians.

The other of the two landmarks was a high perpendicular bluff back of the town. The face of the bluff was cut with paths on which adventures with the roving domestic animals of the town could be undertaken by boys with a slingshot or a bow and arrow. From the top, we could see the harbor and far out over the lake.

The largest trees on the face of the bluff were aspens, junipers, scrub oaks, and thorns. In June, violets, hepaticas, and yellow dog-tooth violets filled the open spaces between the clumps of small trees; in July, the slope was covered with a cloak of wild-rose blooms; in August, the bluff was a piece of porcelain, enameled with daisies, milfoils, and red grasses; September found the high bank hung with a shaggy Persian rug splashed with the yellow and purple of goldenrods and asters on a background of red sumac, scarlet scrub oak, the yellows of aspens, and the greens of junipers.

My father had a rare eye for natural beauty. On Sunday afternoons he often took the family up the bluff for "a view." On the transparent crystalline days of the northern summer, the outlines of distant objects were sharpened as from alpine heights. We saw from the top of the bluff every detail of the shabby Indian village beneath, the harbor and its shipping, the curiosities in land formation of the long point, the deep-curving bay surrounded by undulating wooded hills, and far to the west in the lake the blue *ba-esk-ko-be* of the Indians. Bending over all was the clear blue sky— no purer blue this side of Paradise.

IV

THE STORIED

STRAITS

Michilimackinac has been spelled sixty-eight ways, but it always means the Great Turtle. A strategic place between blue Lake Huron and gray Lake Michigan, its story is older than history.

The turtle-shaped island was revered by the tribes, who believed it had risen miraculously from the straits. From all directions the Indians came; they made it a gathering place, a scene of intertribal meeting and exchange, a ceremonial ground. In 1670 the Jesuits built a mission on the island, but when Marquette arrived in 1671 he moved it to the northern mainland at Point St. Ignace, where a fort and a trading post grew up beside it. When Cadillac transferred the garrison to Detroit the fires went out. But the straits were too strategic to be abandoned. Soon Canadian traders built a new post on the south point of the narrows. A French fort was erected there, the missionaries raised a new chapel and Indian camps spread along the shore.

To this settlement of traders, soldiers and tribesmen, the riotous *voyageurs* came, spring and fall. French was the language of the place until 1760, when a British triumph on the St. Lawrence forced an evacuation of the rich fur station. A British garrison took it over in 1761, and was soon massacred by the Indians. When Indian resistance was crushed, the British reoccupied the fort in 1764. Sixteen years later the garrison was moved to Mackinac Island, which Governor Patrick Sinclair bought from the tribes for £5,000; after two removals the settlement at the straits had returned to the site of the original mission, a hundred years before. Here the English built their fortress between two empires—the white man's empire to the east, the red man's to the west.

Of this northern Gibraltar, Lord Bathurst wrote: "Its influence is felt among the Indian tribes at New Orleans and the Pacific Ocean; vast tracts of country look to it for protection and supplies, and it gives security to the great establishments of the North West and Hudson's Bay companies by supplying the Indians on the Mississippi."

At the end of the Revolution, Mackinac became American, though the English remained there until the Jay Treaty sixteen years later. The British seized the island in the War of 1812, but it was restored to the United States by the Treaty of Ghent. Then began the American era; in 1817 Mackinac Island became the capital of Astor's far-reaching American Fur Company.

The American fur trade lasted but a generation, until the peltry was depleted and white settlement invaded the ancestral Indian lands. But these were the palmy days of Mackinac when the Indians came in canoe caravans laden with furs, fish, rush mats and maple sugar. Fleets of Mackinaw boats brought hides and buffalo robes from distant traders, and a stream of commerce enlivened the silver straits. Every visitor was enchanted with the place. Travelers wrote about the sheer island cliffs, wigwams and campfires along the shore, the waterfront street buzzing with a dozen Indian and European languages, and the white-walled fort gleaming above the town.

From this island (*always* pronounced "Mackinaw") came the sturdy Mackinaw boat and the brightly colored Mackinaw coat. The craft evolved slowly, as the commerce grew, but the garment came all at once. In 1812 the garrison commander found winter coming and no warm clothing for his men. November passed and the last supply boat unloaded and departed. From his Indian storekeeper the captain requisitioned a pile of Hudson Bay blankets; soon a dozen white and Indian women were sewing them into coats for the soldiers. The resulting short warm coat of plaid blanket cloth became a favorite garb of woodsmen far and wide.

After the Civil War, when railroads and steamships served the straits, Mackinac Island became a pleasure resort and a favorite scene of fiction writers. With the charm of natural beauty, of water-encircled serenity, and of a storied past, it touches the imagination.

The straits have always been a dividing line between the land below and the remote north country, but now the two are joined by an arching highway. Six miles from the island the airy bridge towers stand against the sky. Day and night, summer and winter the traffic moves above the water where Nicolet passed, the first white man to breast the straits, 330 years ago.

Morning

at Mackinac

The strategic Straits of Mackinac was a place of myth and of rendezvous for the Indians. "It is the key and the door for the people of the South," wrote Claude Dablon, "as the Sault is the key for the people of the North." With Father Dablon history came to the straits; he established a mission on Mackinac Island in 1670. A year later came Father Marquette.

Jacques Marquette had been living with the Hurons and Ottawas at La Pointe on western Lake Superior. When they were driven east by their Sioux enemies Marquette went with them, paddling along Lake Superior with what goods and gear they could take in their canoes. Arrived at Mackinac, Marquette moved the mission to the north side of the strait, where now a marble monument memorializes his bark chapel. In 1825 Henry Rowe Schoolcraft, camping at St. Ignace after a canoe trip from Green Bay, found in the sand the stumps of cedar posts which he took for the remains of the mission.

When Governor Cadillac forced the Jesuits out of the mission field in 1705, the priests burned their buildings and covered over the place where Marquette's bones were buried. Nearly two centuries later parts of a skeleton were found on the mission site; they were preserved as the remains of Father Marquette who during his last hard journeys called St. Ignace his home.

Reuben Gold Thwaites (1853–1913), long-time superintendent of the State Historical Society of Wisconsin, was editor of *The Jesuit Relations and Allied Documents* and a biographer of Marquette. In these pages he tells of Marquette's journey to the straits in 1671.

POINT KEWEENAW, which projects nearly a hundred miles into the waters of Lake Superior from the southern shore, would have greatly increased the distance between La Pointe and the Sault had early navigators been obliged to paddle around it; but this bulky peninsula is almost bisected by a chain of lakes and rivers, thus making the crossing a light task for canoemen. This short-cut route had been followed by Radisson and Groseilliers, Ménard, and Allouez, and by the Western Indians who came to the Sault to trade; and now it was used by the fugitives from La Pointe. Past the Pictured Rocks, fantastic in form and color, they wended their way as wind and weather permitted. Each night, or while storms raged upon the deep, they camped upon open stony beaches or nestled in deep ravines; occasionally fishing and hunting, to replenish their slender stores. The Indians, after their custom, frequently offered sacrifice to the storm manitou by casting clothing or food into the waves, amid wild shrieks and the beating of rude drums by juggling medicine-men. On such occasions Father Marquette, hastily setting up a rude altar and gathering the faithful about him, offered prayers to the Christian's God—confident, in his simple faith, that the fantastic, bigoted medicine-men were but sorcerers and the agents of the evil one. Following slowly the curving beach of Whitefish Bay, they crept cautiously until the narrowing shores contracted into St. Marys River, down which sweeps the deep, dark flood of Superior's overflow, to be dashed into foam over the rapids of the Sault.

Here they tarried for a time, for this was Marquette's old mission home. Father Gabriel Drüillettes, one of the oldest of the Jesuit missionaries, and Marquette's instructor at Three Rivers, was now in charge of the work at the Sault. For over twenty years had Drüillettes been engaged in ministering to savages all the way from the Abenakis in Maine to the Ottawas and Hurons on Lake Superior. He is a familiar character in New England history, because in 1650 he went as an agent of the French to visit the Puritans of Eastern Massachusetts, and suggest to them a union between New France and New England against the Iroquois. The Puritans were kind to him, for he succeeded in making an agreeable impression upon these stanch haters of Catholics; but the proposed union was not effected.

It strikingly illustrates the daring enterprise of the French, in the exploration of the interior of our continent, when we find the very Jesuit missionary who had been the guest of the Pilgrim Fathers at Plymouth, now manfully laboring among strange tribes of savages over a thousand miles westward, while the English missionaries had not yet ventured more than a hundred miles from the sea.

At the Sault, Drüillettes had been quite successful; he was a good physician, and had wrought many cures among the Indians, who accordingly respected his powers. All save the scheming medicine-men, who were ever the enemies of the black robes; for if their people lost faith in witchcraft, or no longer worshiped manitous in the olden way, and preferred white men's remedies to the fooleries of magic, then was the trade of the medicine-man gone, and his power in the village departed. But the improvement was seldom for long. If some one died under the missionary's treatment, or some disaster swept over the band, the black robe was in his turn discredited, and the medicine-man again in favor, with his nostrums and his noisy incantations to the spirits of earth and sky and water.

Finally leaving the Sault, the La Pointe Indians and their teacher with his French assistants descended the winding, island-studded River of St. Marys. At its mouth the little fleet divided into two sections, the Ottawas proceeding eastward to Manitoulin Island, where Father Louis André was awaiting them; the Hurons paddling westward to their old haunts upon the island of Michillimackinac, upon which, as stated in the preceding chapter, St. Ignace mission had already been established.

It has been held by most historians that St. Ignace mission was always located upon the mainland, to the north of the island, where is now the little city of St. Ignace, Mich., which contains a monument erected on the supposed site of the old chapel. The Jesuit fathers, in writing their letters from the heart of the American wilderness, were more particular to record conversions and other spiritual experiences than to state the exact localities of their missions. They did not foresee that their often vague geographical allusions would cause dispute two centuries later, when antiquarians came to discuss historic sites.

It is with difficulty that some of the sites of the early Jesuit missions in New France can now be established even approximately. The location of St. Ignace has been among these puzzles, although not so difficult as some of them. That the mission was first upon the island, and probably within the present village of Mackinac, a careful reading of the *Relations* should convince any one. That it was afterward moved to the mainland, to the St. Ignace of to-day, there can be no reasonable doubt; but when and under what circumstances we do not know.

It is reasonable to suppose that this removal took place in the year after Marquette's arrival; and there is abundant ground for belief that the St. Ignace monument, which is visited each summer by several thousands of tourists, represents the place where stood his little mainland chapel. Quite likely the island, at first resorted to because of its safety from attack by foes, was found too small for the villages and fields of the Indians who now centered here in large numbers; and moreover was found difficult of approach in time of summer storm, or when the ice was weak in spring and early winter. The long continuance of peace with the Iroquois removed for the time all danger from that quarter, and events proved that they had made their last attack upon the tribesmen of these far western waters.

It was probably midsummer when Marquette and his Hurons, after slowly threading their way between the forest-clad islets which stud the northwest shore of Lake Huron, finally arrived at the island of Michillimackinac. The scene which greeted them is one of the most interesting in North America.

The two sharp-pointed peninsulas of Michigan approach each other from north and south to within somewhat less than four miles. Between them lie the straits of Mackinac—the waters of Lake Michigan rushing through this narrow, island-cleft passage to join Lake Huron, being increased about forty miles to the eastward by the outflow from Lake Superior. In the center of the strait, toward its eastern end, rises Michillimackinac—a word in our day shortened to Mackinac—in shape much like a high-backed turtle, in allusion to which some scholars suppose that the Indians named the island. Its southern shore is fringed by grassy bluffs enclosing a mile or more of pebbly beach, backed by a level, fertile strand upon which Indians had camped and planted from very early times, and upon which today rests the tourist-resort village of Mackinac. From the bluffs above is obtainable a commanding view of land and water. It is a strategic point of much importance, at the junction of three great lakes—for the possession of which, in the olden days of the fur trade which centered here at Mackinac, England and America came more than once to blows. Northward the bluffs gradually descend in graceful undulations and with curious rock protuberances to the water's edge—the rocky beach now known as "British Landing."

Across the intervening four miles of water the cape of St. Ignace rises, a wide beach of sand hemmed in by dreary bluffs, which sometimes are pointed by jagged pillars of stone; while southward across the strait may be seen the sandy stretch where is now the village of Mackinaw City, in whose neighborhood the English built their first fort of logs, a hundred years after Marquette's arrival.

Mackinac Island is a beauty-spot to-day, even when its bluffs are crowned by rambling hotels and the multifarious summer homes of wealthy citizens of Chicago, St. Louis, and Detroit; when the island is traversed by dusty macadamized drives; when, in summer, the wharves are lined with noisy, bulky steam-craft from ports all the way from Buffalo to Duluth; when, in winter, ice-crushing ferry-boats transfer railway trains between St. Ignace and Mackinaw City, and garish souvenir shops and bawling guides and cabmen ply their trade among thousands of summer tourists who "do" the island sights while their steamers replenish stores.

But in the days of good Father Marquette, Michillimackinac was indeed an earthly paradise. The sky hereabout was unusually clear; light breezes, wafting over the wide waters, brought relief in the warmest days; the air was freighted with the odor of the balsam; the island was heavily wooded, chiefly with cedars, beeches, oaks, and maples, presenting a pleasing variety of form and color when seen from the highest bluffs, which, rising over three hundred feet above the straits, gave to the missionary a far-reaching view of land and water, almost incomparable.

ALEXANDER HENRY

The

King's Birthday

In 1760 Alexander Henry, age twenty-one, left his home in New Jersey to join Lord Jeffrey Amherst's expedition against Montreal. His adventures began immediately. From a wrecked boat in the St. Lawrence he was "kindly taken off" by an aide-de-camp of General Amherst. Soon afterwards he survived an attack by a drunken savage and a river journey through a blizzard in a leaky canoe. When he heard of the rich fur trade at Michilimackinac, which the victorious British would now take over from the French, he went there to seek a share in it for himself.

Henry was the first British trader at the Straits of Mackinac. In fact he got there ahead of the English garrison and had to disguise himself as a French *voyageur* until the troops arrived. Mackinac Island was occupied by a band of Chippewas. The fort stood on the mainland, directly across the strait. There in September, 1761, British troops were landed. Under the sullen eyes of the Indians they marched into the fort and ran up the English colors.

Henry quickly became an established trader, making trips by canoe and snowshoe all around the straits. He learned the Indian languages and struck up a special friendship with the Chippewa Wawatam. He knew that the Indians still regarded the British as enemies, but he did not see how deeply their hatred smoldered. This he learned on a June day in 1763 when the garrison was slaughtered while celebrating the king's birthday.

Henry survived the massacre to go prospecting for copper on Lake Superior and to carry on far-ranging trade and exploration in the Northwest. Late in life, a merchant in Montreal, he wrote his *Travels and Adventures*, which includes his famous narrative of the Indian uprising at Old Mackinaw.

IN THE COURSE of the same day I observed that the Indians came in great numbers into the fort, purchasing tomahawks (small axes of one pound weight) and frequently desiring to see silver arm bands and other valuable ornaments, of which I had a large quantity for sale. These ornaments, however, they in no instance purchased; but after turning them over, left them, saying they would call again the next day. Their motive, as it afterward appeared, was no other than the very artful one of discovering, by requesting to see them, the particular places of their deposit so that they might lay their hands on them in the moment of pillage with the greater certainty and dispatch.

At night I turned in my mind the visits of Wawatam; but though they were calculated to excite uneasiness nothing induced me to believe that serious mischief was at hand. The next day being the fourth of June was the King's birthday.

The morning was sultry. A Chippewa came to tell me that his nation was going to play at baggatiway with the Sacs or Saakies, another Indian nation, for a high wager. He invited me to witness the sport, adding that the commandant was to be there, and would bet on the side of the Chippewa. In consequence of this information I went to the commandant and expostulated with him a little, representing that the Indians might possibly have some sinister end in view; but the commandant only smiled at my suspicions.

Baggatiway, called by the Canadians *le jeu de la crosse*, is played with a bat and ball. The bat is about four feet in length, curved, and terminating in a sort of racket. Two posts are planted in the ground at a considerable distance from each other, at a mile or more. Each party has its post, and the game consists in throwing the ball up to the post of the adversary. The ball, at the beginning, is placed in the middle of the course and each party endeavors as well to throw the ball out of the direction of its own post as into that of the adversary's.

I did not go myself to see the match which was now to be played without the fort, because there being a canoe prepared to depart on the following day for Montreal I employed myself in writing letters to my friends; and even when a fellow trader, Mr. Tracy, happened to call upon me, saying that another canoe had just arrived from Detroit, and proposing that I should go with him to the beach to inquire the news, it so happened that I still remained to finish my letters, promising to follow Mr. Tracy in the course of a few minutes. Mr. Tracy had not gone more than twenty paces from my door when I heard an Indian war cry and a noise of general confusion.

Going instantly to my window I saw a crowd of Indians within the fort furiously cutting down and scalping every Englishman they found. In particular I witnessed the fate of Lieutenant Jemette.

I had in the room in which I was a fowling piece, loaded with swan-shot. This I immediately seized and held it for a few minutes, waiting to hear the drum beat to arms. In this dreadful interval I saw several of my countrymen fall, and more than one struggling between the knees of an Indian, who, holding him in this manner, scalped him while yet living.

At length, disappointed in the hope of seeing resistance made to the enemy, and sensible, of course, that no effort of my own unassisted arm could avail against four hundred Indians, I thought only of seeking shelter. Amid the slaughter which was raging I observed many of the Canadian inhabitants of the fort calmly looking on, neither opposing the Indians, nor suffering injury; and from this circumstance I conceived a hope of finding security in their houses.

Between the yard door of my own house and that of M. Langlade, my next neighbor, there was only a low fence, over which I easily climbed. At my entrance I found the whole family at the window, gazing at the scene of blood before them. I addressed myself immediately to M. Langlade, begging that he would put me into some place of safety until the heat of the affair should be over; an act of charity by which he might perhaps preserve me from the general massacre; but while I uttered my petition M. Langlade, who had looked for a moment at me, turned again to the window, shrugging his shoulders and intimating that he could do nothing for me:— "Que voudriez-vous que j'en ferais?"

This was a moment for despair; but the next a Pani woman, a slave of M. Langlade's, beckoned me to follow her. She brought me to a door which she opened, desiring me to enter, and telling me that it led to the garret, where I must go and conceal myself. I joyfully obeyed her directions; and she, having followed me up to the garret door, locked it after me and with great presence of mind took away the key.

This shelter obtained, if shelter I could hope to find it, I was naturally anxious to know what might still be passing without. Through an aperture which afforded me a view of the area of the fort I beheld, in shapes the foulest and most terrible, the ferocious triumphs of barbarian conquerors. The dead were scalped and mangled; the dying were writhing and shrieking under the unsatiated knife and tomahawk; and from the bodies of some, ripped open, their butchers were drinking the blood, scooped up in the hollow of joined hands and quaffed amid shouts of rage and victory. I was shaken not only with horror, but with fear. The sufferings which I witnessed I seemed on the point of experiencing. No long time elapsed before every one being destroyed who could be found, there was a general cry of "All is finished!" At the same instant I heard some of the Indians enter the house in which I was.

The garret was separated from the room below only by a layer of single boards, at once the flooring of the one and the ceiling of the other. I could therefore hear everything that passed; and the Indians no sooner came in than they inquired whether or not any Englishman were in the house. M. Langlade replied that he could not say—he did not know of any—answers in which he did not exceed the truth, for the Pani woman had not only hidden me by stealth, but kept my secret and her own. M. Langlade was therefore, as I presume, as far from a wish to destroy me as he was careless about saving me, when he added to these answers that they might examine for themselves, and would soon be satisfied as to the object of their question. Saying this, he brought them to the garret door.

The state of my mind will be imagined. Arrived at the door some delay was occasioned by the absence of the key and a few moments were thus allowed me in which to look around for a hiding place. In one corner of the garret was a heap of those vessels of birch bark used in maple sugar making as I have recently described.

The door was unlocked, and opening, and the Indians ascending the stairs, before I had completely crept into a small opening, which presented itself at one end of the heap. An instant later four Indians entered the room, all armed with tomahawks, and all besmeared with blood upon every part of their bodies.

The die appeared to be cast. I could scarcely breathe; but I thought that the throbbing of my heart occasioned a noise loud enough to betray me. The Indians walked in every direction about the garret, and one of them approached me so closely that at a particular moment, had he put forth his hand, he must have touched me. Still I remained undiscovered, a circumstance to which the dark color of my clothes and the want of light in a room which had no window, and in the corner in which I was, must have contributed. In a word, after taking several turns in the room, during which they told M. Langlade how many they had killed and how many scalps they had taken, they returned down stairs, and I with sensations not to be expressed, heard the door, which was the barrier between me and my fate, locked for the second time.

There was a feather bed on the floor, and on this, exhausted as I was by the agitation of my mind, I threw myself down and fell asleep. In this state I remained till the dusk of the evening, when I was awakened by a second opening of the door. The person that now entered was M. Langlade's wife, who was much surprised at finding me, but advised me not to be uneasy, observing that the Indians had killed most of the English, but that she hoped I might myself escape. A shower of rain having begun to fall, she had come to stop a hole in the roof. On her going away, I begged her to send me a little water to drink, which she did.

As night was now advancing I continued to lie on the bed, ruminating on my condition, but unable to discover a resource from which I could hope for life. A flight to Detroit had no probable chance of success. The distance from Michilimackinac was four hundred miles; I was without provisions; and the whole length of the road lay through Indian countries, countries of an enemy in arms, where the first man whom I should meet would kill me. To stay where I was threatened nearly the same issue. As before, fatigue of mind, and not tranquillity, suspended my cares and procured me further sleep.

The game of baggatiway, as from the description above will have been perceived, is necessarily attended with much violence and noise. In the ardor of contest the ball, as has been suggested, if it cannot be thrown to the goal desired, is struck in any direction by which it can be diverted from that designed by the adversary. At such a moment, therefore, nothing could be less liable to excite premature alarm than that the ball should be tossed over the pickets of the fort, nor that having fallen there, it should be followed on the instant by all engaged in the game, as well the one party as the other, all eager, all struggling, all shouting, all in the unrestrained pursuit of a rude athletic exercise. Nothing could be less fitted to excite premature alarm—nothing, therefore, could be more happily devised, under the circumstances, than a stratagem like this; and this was in fact the stratagem which the Indians had employed, by which they had obtained possession of the fort, and by which they had been enabled to slaughter and subdue its garrison and such of its other inhabitants as they pleased. To be still more certain of success they had prevailed upon as many as they could by a pretext the least liable to suspicion to come voluntarily without the pickets, and particularly the commandant and garrison themselves.

The respite which sleep afforded me during the night was put an end to by the return of morning. I was again on the rack of apprehension. At sunrise I heard the family stirring, and presently after, Indian voices informing M. Langlade they had not found my hapless self among the dead, and that they supposed me to be somewhere concealed. M. Langlade appeared from what followed to be by this time acquainted with the place of my retreat, of which no doubt he had been informed by his wife. The poor woman, as soon as the Indians mentioned me, declared to her husband in the French tongue that he should no longer keep me in his house, but deliver me up to my pursuers, giving as a reason for this measure that should the Indians discover his instrumentality in my concealment, they might revenge it on her children, and that it was better that I should die than they. M. Langlade resisted at first this sentence of his wife's; but soon suffered her to prevail, informing the Indians that he had been told I was in his house, that I had come there without his knowledge, and that he would put me into their hands. This was no sooner expressed than he began to ascend the stairs, the Indians following upon his heels.

I now resigned myself to the fate with which I was menaced; and regarding every attempt at concealment as vain, I arose from the bed and presented myself full in view to the Indians who were entering the room. They were all in a state of intoxication, and entirely naked, except about the middle. One of them, named Wenniway, whom I had previously known, and who was upward of six feet in height, had his entire face and body covered with charcoal and grease, only that a white spot of two inches in diameter encircled either eye. This man, walking up to me, seized me with one hand by the collar of the coat, while in the other he held a large carving knife, as if to plunge it into my breast; his eyes, meanwhile, were fixed steadfastly on mine. At length, after some seconds of the most anxious suspense, he dropped his arm, saying, "I won't kill you!" To this he added that he had been frequently engaged in wars against the English, and had brought away many scalps; that on a certain occasion he had lost a brother whose name was Musinigon, and that I should be called after him.

A reprieve upon any terms placed me among the living, and gave me back the sustaining voice of hope; but Wenniway ordered me downstairs, and there informing me that I was to be taken to his cabin, where, and indeed everywhere else, the Indians were all mad with liquor, death again was threatened, and not as possible only, but as certain. I mentioned my fears on this subject to M. Langlade, begging him to represent the danger to my master. M. Langlade in this instance did not withhold his compassion, and Wenniway immediately consented that I should remain where I was until he found another opportunity to take me away.

Thus far secure I reascended my garret stairs in order to place myself the furthest possible out of the reach of insult from drunken Indians; but I had not remained there more than an hour, when I was called to the room below in which was an Indian who said that I must go with him out of the fort, Wenniway having sent him to fetch me. This man, as well as Wenniway himself, I had seen before. In the preceding year I had allowed him to take goods on credit, for which he was still in my debt; and some short time previous to the surprise of the fort he had said upon my upbraiding him with want of honesty that he would pay me before long. This speech now came fresh into my memory and led me to suspect that the fellow had formed a design against my life. I communicated the suspicion to M. Langlade; but he gave for answer that I was not now my own master, and must do as I was ordered.

The Indian on his part directed that before I left the house I should undress myself, declaring that my coat and shirt would become him better than they did me. His pleasure in this respect being complied with, no other alternative was left me than either to go out naked, or put on the clothes of the Indian, which he freely gave me in exchange. His motive for thus stripping me of my own apparel was no other as I afterward learned than this, that it might not be stained with blood when he should kill me.

I was now told to proceed; and my driver followed me close until I had passed the gate of the fort, when I turned toward the spot where I knew the Indians to be encamped. This, however, did not suit the purpose of my enemy, who seized me by the arm and drew me violently in the opposite direction to the distance of fifty yards above the fort. Here, finding that I was approaching the bushes and sand hills, I determined to proceed no farther, but told the Indian that I believed he meant to murder me, and that if so he might as well strike where I was as at any greater distance. He replied with coolness that my suspicions were just, and that he meant to pay me in this manner for my goods. At the same time he produced a knife and held me in a position to receive the intended blow. Both this and that which followed were necessarily the affair of a moment. By some effort, too sudden and too little dependent on thought to be explained or remembered, I was enabled to arrest his arm and give him a sudden push by which I turned him from me and released myself from his grasp. This was no sooner done than I ran toward the fort with all the swiftness in my power, the Indian following me, and I expecting every moment to feel his knife. I succeeded in my flight; and on entering the fort I saw Wenniway standing in the midst of the area, and to him I hastened for protection. Wenniway desired the Indian to desist; but the latter pursued me round him, making several strokes at me with his knife, and foaming at the mouth with rage at the repeated failure of his purpose. At length Wenniway drew near to M. Langlade's house; and, the door being open, I ran into it. The Indian followed me; but on my entering the house he voluntarily abandoned the pursuit.

Preserved so often and so unexpectedly as it had now been my lot to be, I returned to my garret with a strong inclination to believe that through the will of an overruling power no Indian enemy could do me hurt; but new trials, as I believed, were at hand when at ten o'clock in the evening I was roused from sleep and once more desired to descend the stairs. Not less, however, to my satisfaction than surprise, I was summoned only to meet Major Etherington, Mr. Bostwick, and Lieutenant Lesslie, who were in the room below.

These gentlemen had been taken prisoners while looking at the game without the fort and immediately stripped of all their clothes. They were now sent into the fort under the charge of Canadians, because, the Indians having resolved on getting drunk, the chiefs were apprehensive that they would be murdered if they continued in the camp. Lieutenant Jemette and seventy soldiers had been killed; and but twenty Englishmen, including soldiers, were still alive. These were all within the fort, together with nearly three hundred Canadians.

These being our numbers, myself and others proposed to Major Etherington to make an effort for regaining possession of the fort and maintaining it against the Indians. The Jesuit missionary was consulted on the project; but he discouraged us by his representations, not only of the merciless treatment which we must expect from the Indians should they regain their superiority, but of the little dependence which was to be placed upon our Canadian auxiliaries. Thus the fort and prisoners remained in the hands of the Indians, though through the whole night the prisoners and whites were in actual possession, and they were without the gates.

That whole night, or the greater part of it, was passed in mutual condolence, and my fellow prisoners shared my garret. In the morning, being again called down, I found my master, Wenniway, and was desired to follow him. He led me to a small house within the fort, where in a narrow room and almost dark I found Mr. Ezekiel Solomon, an Englishman from Detroit, and a soldier, all prisoners. With these I remained in painful suspense as to the scene that was next to present itself till ten o'clock in the forenoon, when an Indian arrived, and presently marched us to the lakeside where a canoe appeared ready for departure, and in which we found that we were to embark.

Our voyage, full of doubt as it was, would have commenced immediately, but that one of the Indians who was to be of the party was absent. His arrival was to be waited for; and this occasioned a very long delay during which we were exposed to a keen northeast wind. An old shirt was all that covered me; I suffered much from the cold; and in this extremity M. Langlade coming down the beach, I asked him for a blanket, promising if I lived to pay him for it at any price he pleased; but the answer I received was this, that he could let me have no blanket unless there were some one to be security for the payment. For myself, he observed, I had no longer any property in that country. I had no more to say to M. Langlade; but presently seeing another Canadian, named John Cuchoise, I addressed to him a similar request and was not refused. Naked as I was, and rigorous as was the weather, but for the blanket I must have perished. At noon our party was all collected, the prisoners all embarked, and we steered for the Isles du Castor [Beaver Islands] in Lake Michigan.

To the

Westward

At Mackinaw, soon after the rebuilding of the British fort, Captain William Howard was succeeded by Major Robert Rogers, who was already a legendary figure on the Adirondack frontier. A big, burly, rough-hewn man, he knew the woods like an Indian, and with his hardy Rangers he had survived harsh contests with both the savages and the wilderness. A master of forest warfare, he was also vain, grasping and more bent on serving himself than the British cause.

Rogers arrived at Mackinaw in August 1765, with dual authority as commandant and Indian agent, and he soon saw promise of personal gain in the frontier commerce. Disregarding instructions he relaxed the regulation of the fur traders and gave bounteous presents to the Indians. To support his own riotous living he borrowed money from the fur merchants. He proposed to the Board of Trade in London that he become governor of Mackinaw, responsible only to the King's ministers.

To Mackinaw also came Jonathan Carver, whom Rogers had known in the Adirondack campaign. Now the two men shared the airy dream of finding the long-rumored Northwest Passage to the Orient. At Mackinaw Rogers made Carver leader of an expedition to explore the West and Northwest. Though Carver made no great discoveries, he wrote a book of *Travels* that was read in every country of Europe.

In 1768 a great Indian congress gathered at Mackinaw, with canoes dotting the straits and campfires gleaming for miles along the shore. Many presents went to the tribesmen, who were also treated to rum and cheated of their peltry. Upon complaints of Rogers' high-handed rule the authorities at Montreal ordered his arrest. The commander was put in irons and "thrown into the hold of the vessel upon a ballast of stones," as he later testified, for the long voyage to Niagara. So after three years of command at the straits the vainglorious Rogers left in ignominy.

These pages from Kenneth Roberts' novel *Northwest Passage* picture the arrival of Rogers and his wife at Mackinaw in the summer of 1765 and the departure of Carver's expedition for the fabled West.

A SLOOP carried us over Lake Ontario to the Niagara River, where carts from Fort Niagara hauled our belongings around the falls and to the *Gladwyn* schooner on the upper river. The *Gladwyn* took us the full length of Lake Erie to Detroit, across Lake St. Clair, up the broad St. Clair River into Lake Huron: then sailed northward toward the Straits of Michilimackinac. In the brilliant golden sunlight of an August noon, the approach to those straits was a pleasant one. To our left was the broad opening of the waterway connecting Huron and Michigan: to the right were the high white sides of Mackinac Island, cleanly cut against the sky in the clear air and pure light of the Northern summer; and all around the horizon, beyond the straits and beyond Mackinac Island, was an endless blue rampart behind which, almost within reach at last, lay the winding channels to Lake Superior, to the Indians of the West, to the great River Oregon, to the Northwest Passage.

When we turned into the straits, the fort and the settlement of Michilimackinac unrolled before us on the left bank; and so dwarfed were they by the long, low stretch of dunes among which they nestled that they might have been, as Ann whispered to me, a fort and settlement on the coast of Lilliput. There was nothing about the place, as we saw it from the sloop—nothing—to bear out the glowing description Rogers had given us two months before in the Brownes' back parlor.

The fort was little more than a stockaded yard, close to the water's edge. Outside the stockade were groups of long barns that I took to be traders' storehouses. At a considerable distance from the stockade a ring of small white dwellings surrounded a patch of farm land. Still farther away were three straggling Indian encampments. Even to me, who expected to see little of it, the place looked depressing. I looked at Elizabeth; she stood rigid, staring unbelievingly at the shore.

The Major, however, seemed as merry as Punchinello; he slapped his hand together and laughed explosively when a jet of smoke gushed from the stockade walls and the thump of a cannon came flatly to us across the water.

The report of the heavy gun seemed to release a spring in that distant toy settlement, for little figures moved like ants within the stockade and at the water's edge. What I had taken for rocks on the shore moved and fell apart. They were canoes and bateaux, and they came slipping out toward us like a shoal of frightened water bugs escaping from a quiet resting place. As they drew closer, we saw they were full of traders, of French voyageurs, of Indians of various tribes. They circled around us, firing muskets and shouting a tumultuous welcome. Then they closed in on the vessel to fasten like leeches against her side. Continuing to ply their oars and paddles, they hustled the sloop to the wharf, which extended outward from the fort's water-gate.

The closer we came to the place, the more populous it appeared. All the canoes in the world seemed concentrated on the shore, overturned and stacked in rows. Two companies of redcoated soldiers marched smartly from the fort, drums thumping, and lined up abreast of the wharf. People appeared in surprising numbers to see us land, but where they came from, unless they had popped up out of the ground, it was hard to see.

When the sloop was fast, Rogers jumped to the wharf to shake hands with the two young officers who commanded the two companies of soldiers. At sight of that careless figure in green coat and bucksins, the whole assemblage burst into cheers and howls of welcome. Rogers smiled and flirted his hand at them, made a hurried inspection of the two companies by walking quickly along the front of the lines, spoke pleasantly to the men, and told the lieutenants to dismiss them. With that the scores of traders, who had been waiting, went for him pell-mell as if intending to mob him. They crowded around him in a circle, all talking and gesticulating, so that they seemed people out of Bedlam.

"Here, here, gentlemen!" Rogers said good-naturedly, "give me a chance! You're holding up my wife."

Their shouts and expostulations grew louder. Those in the rear of the circle, in their eagerness to make themselves heard, jostled those in front against Rogers. From the tumult of shouting came such phrases as, "Been here a month!" "Caught by cold weather!" "Damned outrage!" "Have to feed the voyageurs!"

Rogers seized the most importunate of the traders by the front of his coat and used him as a sort of broom to sweep back the others. "You'll give me a chance to get into the fort and settle myself," he roared jovially, "or I'll push you back with bayonets!"

The traders fell away from him, muttering and staring. Rogers pulled at his little hat with both hands, straightened his coat with an angry shrug of his shoulders. "Lieutenant Christie!" he shouted. "Mr. Johnson!"

The two young officers pushed through the ring of traders.

"Who's your commanding officer?" Rogers demanded. "Why isn't he here? Where is he? Why hasn't he put these traders under control?"

"Captain Spiesmaker, sir," the lieutenant said. "He's delayed in Montreal. We expect him any day. We haven't taken any steps because we haven't had any orders. We don't know what steps to take. We've been waiting for you—or for him."

"You've heard, haven't you," Rogers asked, "that no traders are supposed to go beyond this post this year?"

The lieutenant's reply was lost in the storm of groans and objurgations that rose from the traders.

Rogers laughed. "Well, now, gentlemen, you've got to let us go to the fort, settle ourselves and get some food in us. Give me two hours: then I'll meet all of you and hear what you've got to say for yourselves. If you've got a case, you won't find me unreasonable. I hope to conduct affairs at this post in the best interests of His Majesty's Government."

Signalling to the rest of us, he started for the fort's water-gate. Around the gate-post peered a head with pop-eyes and pouting lips: from behind the gate-post came the heavy, ponderous figure of Jonathan Carver.

"Well, by God!" Rogers cried. "I thought you hadn't got here! Where you been keeping yourself?"

Carver showed his teeth in a grin, and his voice was oily. "I didn't want to intrude. I thought you might have forgotten you told me to report here. . . ."

I remember that night as a bedlam of roistering, rejoicing traders, all bent on crowding into the hot front room of the Major's house to force upon him tokens of their gratitude and esteem.

They brought kegs of brandy, rum, undiluted alcohol and wine; rare skins of all sorts—sables, mink, otter; squirrel-skin blankets; glassware, chinaware, jewelry, rifles, bolts of cloth, boxes of cigars, bundles of tobacco, fur caps, fur coats, bear skins and buffalo rugs; saddles; kitchen utensils. One even brought him a Pawnee slave—a pleasant-looking woman who, at a movement of her master's hand, crouched beside a chair or crawled beneath a table, as would a dog, and remained there until her owner snapped a finger.

A keg of rum was broached to make a punch that the traders called calibogus; and an hour later the house was crammed; scores were wandering over the parade, singing, arguing, fighting; and a dozen, among them Natty Potter, were stretched unconscious among the weeds beside the house. . . .

The breeze came in from the north on the following morning, fresh from the icy waters of Lake Superior; and it almost seemed to me, when I drew that wine-like air into my lungs and looked out at the opalescent water of the strait and the sculptured white cliffs of the island guarding its eastern end, that the events of the night before had been a fevered dream, brought on by heat, our long journey and our troubled arrival at this fort in the wilderness.

Everything and everybody in Michilimackinac seemed to have been changed by that cool breath from the enormous inland sea just beyond us. The parade was dusty no longer, but almost verdant in the golden rays of the early morning sun. The Major's house had been scoured until it shone by the Major's soldier servant, assisted by a detail of men from Lieutenant Christie's company. The Pawnee slave, installed in the kitchen, chopped wood, peeled potatoes, brought water from the well, and made herself useful to a wrinkled Frenchwoman who had materialized, witchlike, to be the Major's cook.

The Major himself, his eyes pinkly a-swim and the pouches beneath them swollen as if by bee-stings, had poured a pail of water over his head soon after sun-up, gulped down a large part of another pail, and gone striding off to the warehouses, where hundreds of spindle-shanked voyageurs in red woolen caps, gaudy sashes and deerskin leggins were piling bales of goods in heaps, preparatory to loading their canoes.

And early as it was, Elizabeth had already received four invitations to drink tea with the wives of those traders who were so fortunate as not to be married to Indian women. She was pleased with herself, and as gracious as though she had never spoken sharply to me in her life.

"You must tell me, Langdon," she said. "Shall I wear my green striped Cambray or my lavender? The lavender is the very latest, a little extreme perhaps, but wouldn't it be a greater treat for these poor wretches here to see something in the latest mode? Fancy what starved lives they lead! La, it makes me shudder!" She shivered prettily, but when I spoke highly of her lavender, she went upstairs in such high good humor that I boldly called to Ann to take my box of crayons, and set off with her to make sketches at the water-gate.

I saw when we reached the shore that the Major's enthusiasm for Michilimackinac had not been wholly exaggerated. The water was clear as the clearest glass, the islands floating in the distance were emeralds rimmed with silver; and on the beach, fishing, shouting and loading canoes, was a gay throng of Indians, voyageurs and traders.

Just off shore canoe brigades were forming. A voyageur stood at the bow and stern of each canoe, holding it fast so that its delicate skin mightn't be split by rubbing on bottom; and other voyageurs, spurred on by their trader employers, piled ninety-pound bales of goods into these craft until I marvelled they didn't sink. They were *canots du maître*—master canoes—bigger than any I had ever seen. They must have been forty-five feet long, with places for crews of fourteen; and on the high prow and stern of each canoe was painted a bright device—a beaver, a flag, a galloping horse, a bear, an Indian's head.

I could have sat sketching voyageurs all day. They were stunted and swarthy, tremendously developed above the waist and shrivelled away to nothing below. In their caps they wore red feathers, a mark of long service in canoe brigades; their leggins were bound below the knee with colored garters; and from their bright sashes hung pouches embroidered with glittering beads. Their manners were gay, too: they smiled continuously, as though they found life an enormous jest; they capered and sang songs; bragged and gesticulated.

I was hard at work, with Ann passing crayons to me as I called for them and keeping inquisitive onlookers from my elbow and easel, when Rogers, Potter and Jonathan Carver hurried from the water-gate and went to where the brigades were forming.

Rogers spoke to Mr. Bruce, and a moment later voyageurs took Carver and Bruce astride their shoulders, waded to the canoes, and deposited them among the bales in the bottom.

I stood up, dropping my crayons. "Why," I said, "I do believe Carver's going already—he's starting! If he's going, why shouldn't I?"

I hurried toward the Major, but he ignored me. Bruce signalled to his steersman, who slapped the water with his paddle and in a quavering voice sang the words, *"Ha, ha, ha, frit à l'huile."*

The crews of Bruce's five canoes broke into the song; and in time with its lilting measure their red paddle-blades darted in and out of the water with the rapidity of tongues of flame; the compact line of canoes moved off to the westward like a gigantic water-insect, paddles swinging with the regularity of machines, sixty strokes to the minute.

From all sides rose the mournful wailing of Indian women—temporary wives left behind by Bruce's voyageurs. To me their discordant howling was an echo of my own disappointment at remaining behind while others set off gaily singing:

> *"C'est un pâté de trois pigeons,*
> *Ha, ha, ha, frit à l'huile,*

Assieds-toi et le mangeons,
Fritaine, friton, firtou, poilon,
Ha, ha, ha, frit à l'huile,
Frit au beurre et à l'ognon."

I turned gloomily to the easel. Ann, on her knees beside it, was slowly picking up the dropped crayons. At my approach she rose to her feet.

"Where's Mr. Carver going?" she asked.

"To the westward."

"When's he coming back?"

I shook my head. "I don't know. In two years, perhaps, or three."

"Did you want to go, too, Langdon?"

"Of course," I said. "That's way I came here—to go to the westward. Didn't you know that? I thought I'd told you."

When she didn't answer, I looked up to find her smiling a strange, tight-lipped smile that made me think of the first time I'd seen her, when Mrs. Garvin had roughly snatched and held her so that I could sketch her starved body and her grimy face.

She offered me the box of crayons. "You haven't finished the picture."

"I know," I said. "I guess I won't do any more today."

She continued to hold the crayons before me. "It's almost done, Langdon. It only needs red chalk and scarlet for the feathers and paddles. You wont ever see so many brigades starting out at one time: I heard someone say so." She took a piece of red chalk from the box and put it in my fingers. "Look at the canoes, Langdon. Don't they look like arrows?"

I looked at the beach and the strait. There were two hundred canoes loading in the shallows; and already a score of brigades were slanting off to east and west, bound for Superior or Michigan.

As Ann had said, the flashing scarlet paddles gave each canoe the appearance of a vast arrow-head of luminous blue—an arrow-head that would pierce the wilderness for perhaps a thousand miles before it came to rest. Stirred by the thought, I hurriedly finished the first sketch and went eagerly to work on the second; and in the labor of getting my colors on paper, I forgot Rogers, Carver, Ann, and my own disappointment.

The

Old Agency

In 1833 the Indian agencies of Sault Ste. Marie and Michilimack-inac were combined, under the direction of Henry Rowe Schoolcraft. Leaving a sub-agent at the Sault, Schoolcraft moved his family into the roomy old Agency, beneath the white walls of the fort on Mackinac Island. From the Agency windows he watched the procession of lake commerce from Buffalo to Chicago. "Emigrants of every class," he wrote, "eager merchants prudently looking to their interests in the great area of migration, domestic and foreign visitors with note-book in hand, and some valetudinarians hoping in the benefit of pure air and whitefish—these constantly filled the harbor and constituted the ever-moving panorama of our enlarged landscape."

Schoolcraft remained at the Agency for eight years, continuing his study of Algonquin languages and lore and trying to protect the Indians from the rapacity of the traders. He was succeeded by Robert Stuart in 1841, who saw the end of the fur trade and the beginning of resort business on the island. Then the Agency was removed, but the rambling old house, haunted with memories, remained a Mackinac landmark until New Year's eve, 1871, when it burned to the ground.

A descendant of James Fenimore Cooper, Constance Fenimore Woolson grew up in Cleveland, with summers on Mackinac Island and Lake Superior. She wrote of miners, priests and soldiers in that country. In her novel *Anne*, a story of Old Mackinac "between blue Lake Huron with its clear air and gray Lake Michigan with its silver fogs" she pictured the fort on the hill, Indian campfires on the shore, and black forests framing the snowbound straits. After the burning of the Old Agency house, she wrote this tale, which was included in her volume of lake-country sketches, *Castle Nowhere*, in 1875.

THE OLD HOUSE is gone then! But it shall not depart into oblivion unchronicled. One who has sat under its roof-tree, one who remembers well its rambling rooms and wild garden, will take the pen to write down a page of its story. It is only an episode, one of many; but the others are fading away, or already buried in dead memories under the sod. It was a quaint, picturesque old place, stretching back from the white limestone road that bordered the little port, its overgrown garden surrounded by an ancient stockade ten feet in height, with a massive, slow-swinging gate in front, defended by loopholes. This stockade bulged out in some places and leaned in at others; but the veteran posts, each a tree sharpened to a point, did not break their ranks, in spite of decrepitude; and the Indian warriors, could they have returned from their happy hunting-grounds, would have found the brave old fence of the Agency a sturdy barrier still. But the Indian warriors could not return. The United States agent had long ago moved to Lake Superior, and the deserted residence, having only a mythical owner, left without repairs year after year, and under a cloud of confusion as regarded taxes, titles and boundaries, became a sort of flotsam property, used by various persons, but belonging legally to no one. Some tenant, tired of swinging the great gate back and forth, had made a little sally port alongside, but otherwise the place remained unaltered; a broad garden with a central avenue of cherry-trees, on each side dilapidated arbors, overgrown paths, and heart-shaped beds, where the first agents had tried to cultivate flowers, and behind the limestone cliffs crowned with cedars. The house was large on the ground, with wings and various additions built out as if at random; on each side and behind were rough outside chimneys clamped to the wall; in the roof over the central part dormer-windows showed a low second story; and here and there at irregular intervals were outside doors, in some cases opening out into space, since the high steps which once led up to them had fallen down, and remained as they fell, heaps of stones on the ground below. Within were suites of rooms, large and small, showing traces of workmanship elaborate for such a remote locality; the ceilings, patched with rough mortar, had been originally decorated with moulding, the doors were ornamented with scroll-work, and the two large apartments on each side of the entrance-hall possessed chimney-pieces and central hooks for chandeliers. Beyond and behind stretched out the wings; coming to what appeared to be the end of the house on the west, there unexpectedly began a new series of rooms turning toward the north, each with its outside door; looking for a corresponding labyrinth on the eastern side, there was nothing but a blank wall. The blind stairway went up in a kind of dark well, and once up it was a difficult matter to get down without a plunge from top to bottom, since the undefended opening was just where no one would expect to find it. Sometimes an angle was so arbitrarily walled up that you felt sure there must be a secret chamber there, and furtively rapped on the wall to catch the hollow echo within. Then again you opened a door, expecting to step out into the wilderness of a garden, and found yourself in a set of little rooms running off on a tangent, one after the other, and ending in a windowless closet and an open cistern. But the Agency gloried in its irregularities, and defied criticism. The original idea of its architect—if there was any—had vanished; but his work remained, a not unpleasing variety to summer visitors accustomed to city houses, all built with a definite purpose, and one front door.

After some years of wandering in foreign lands, I returned to my own country, and took up the burden of old associations whose sadness time had mercifully softened. The summer was over; September had begun, but there came to me a great wish to see Mackinac once more; to look again upon the little white fort where I had lived with Archie, my soldier nephew, killed at Shiloh. The steamer took me safely across Erie, up the brimming Detroit River, through the enchanted region of the St. Clair flats, and out into broad Lake Huron; there, off Thunder Bay, a gale met us, and for hours we swayed between life and death. The season for pleasure travelling was over; my fellow-passengers, with one exception, were of that class of Americans who, dressed in cheap imitations of fine clothes, are forever travelling, travelling—taking the steamers not from preference, but because they are less costly than an all-rail route. The thin, listless men, in ill-fitting black clothes and shining tall hats, sat on the deck in tilted chairs, hour after hour, silent and dreary; the thin, listless women, clad in raiment of many colors, remained upon the fixed sofas in the cabin hour after hour, silent and weary. At meals they ate indiscriminately everything within range, but continued the same, a weary, dreary, silent band. The one exception was an old man, tall and majestic, with silvery hair and bright, dark eyes, dressed in the garb of a Roman Catholic priest, albeit slightly tinged with frontier innovations. He came on board at Detroit, and as soon as we were under way he exchanged his hat for a cloth cap embroidered with Indian bead-work; and when the cold air, precursor of the gale, struck us on Huron, he wrapped himself in a large capote made of skins, with the fur inward.

In times of danger formality drops from us. During those long hours, when the next moment might have brought death, this old man and I were together; and when at last the cold dawn came, and the disabled steamer slowly ploughed through the angry water around the point, and showed us Mackinac in the distance, we discovered that the island was a mutual friend, and that we knew each other, at least by name; for the silver-haired priest was Father Piret, the hermit of the Chenaux. In the old days, when I was living at the little white fort, I had known Father Piret by reputation, and he had heard of me from the French half-breeds around the point. We landed. The summer hotels were closed, and I was directed to the old Agency, where occasionally a boarder was received by the family then in possession. The air was chilly, and a fine rain was falling, the afterpiece of the equinoctial; the wet storm-flag hung heavily down over the fort on the height, and the waves came in sullenly. All was in sad accordance with my feelings as I thought of the past and its dead, while the slow tears of age moistened my eyes. But the next morning Mackinac awoke, robed in autumn splendor; the sunshine poured down, the straits sparkled back, the forest glowed in scarlet, the larches waved their wild, green hands, the fair-weather flag floated over the little fort, and all was as joyous as though no one had ever died; and indeed it is in glorious days like these that we best realize immortality.

I wandered abroad through the gay forest to the Arch, the Lovers' Leap, and old Fort Holmes, whose British walls had been battered down for pastime, so that only a caved-in British cellar remained to mark the spot. Returning to the Agency, I learned that Father Piret had called to see me.

"I am sorry that I missed him," I said; "he is a remarkable old man."

The circle at the dinner-table glanced up with one accord. The little Methodist minister with the surprised eyes looked at me more surprised than ever; his large wife groaned audibly. The Baptist colporteur peppered his potatoes until they and the plate were black; the Presbyterian doctor, who was the champion of the Protestant party on the island, wished to know if I was acquainted with the latest devices of the Scarlet Woman in relation to the county school-fund.

"But, my friends," I replied, "Father Piret and I both belong to the past. We discuss not religion, but Mackinac; not the school-fund, but the old associations of the island, which is dear to both of us."

The four looked at me with distrust; they saw nothing dear about the island, unless it was the price of fresh meat; and as to old associations, they held themselves above such nonsense. So, one and all, they took beef and enjoyed a season of well-regulated conversation, leaving me to silence and my broiled white-fish; as it was Friday, no doubt they thought the latter a rag of popery.

Very good rags.

But my hostess, a gentle little woman, stole away from these bulwarks of Protestantism in the late afternoon, and sought me in my room, or rather series of rooms, since there were five opening one out of the other, the last three unfurnished, and all the doorless doorways staring at me like so many fixed eyes, until, oppressed by their silent watchfulness, I hung a shawl over the first opening and shut out the whole gazing suite.

"You must not think, Mrs. Corlyne, that we islanders do not appreciate Father Piret," said the little woman, who belonged to one of the old island families, descendants of a chief factor of the fur trade. "There has been some feeling lately against the Catholics—"

"Roman Catholics, my dear," I said with Anglican particularity.

"But we all love and respect the dear old man as a father."

"When I was living at the fort, fifteen years ago, I heard occasionally of Father Piret," I said, "but he seemed to be almost a mythic personage. What is his history?"

"No one knows. He came here fifty years ago, and after officiating on the island a few years, he retired to a little Indian farm in the Chenaux, where he has lived ever since. Occasionally he holds a service for the half-breeds at Point St. Ignace, but the parish of Mackinac proper has its regular priest, and Father Piret apparently does not hold even the appointment of missionary. Why he remains here—a man educated, refined, and even aristocratic—is a mystery. He seems to be well provided with money; his little house in the Chenaux contains foreign books and pictures, and he is very charitable to the poor Indians. But he keeps himself aloof, and seems to desire no intercourse with the world beyond his letters and papers, which come regularly, some of them from France. He seldom leaves the Straits; he never speaks of himself; always he appears as you saw him, carefully dressed and stately. Each summer when he is seen on the street, there is more or less curiosity about him among the summer visitors, for he is quite unlike the rest of us Mackinac people. But no one can discover anything more than I have told you, and those who have persisted so far as to sail over to the Chenaux either lose their way among the channels, or if they find the house, they never find him; the door is locked and no one answers."

"Fountain of the Great Lakes," bronze monument by Lorado Taft (1860–1936).

BUFFALO, FROM LAKE ERIE.

Buffalo harbor in the 1850's.

DETROIT IN 1820,

In 1820 the pioneer steamboat WALK-IN-THE-WATER brought scientists and explorers to Detroit to join the Cass expedition in search of the source of the Mississippi.

Milwaukee harbor. Lithograph, 1874

Chicago commerce in the 1850's.

CITY OF SUPERIOR,
Wisconsin Nov. 1856.

The LADY ELGIN at Superior, Wisconsin, in 1856, four years before she was lost, with 300 excursionists, in Lake Michigan.

The steamer JAPAN, with figurehead atop her wheelhouse.

One of Alexander McDougall's whalebacks carried his own name.

(Overleaf) Passengers leaving Duluth in 1908.

One of the lake-built ocean
freighters of World War I.

St. Marys Falls Canal celebration in 1905.

The steamer CLIFFS VICTORY, with superstructure leveled, towing through the Chicago River.

Courtesy Cleveland-Cliffs Iron Compar

Ore fleet in the ice of Whitefish Bay, above the Soo, at opening of navigation.

Sault Ste. Marie on July 4, 1963, showing the new international bridge and coffer dams enclosing the site of the new lock under construction.

(Overleaf) Mackinac Straits Bridge.

Navy Pier, Chicago, with five foreign freighters discharging cargo.

"Singular," I said. "He has nothing of the hermit about him. He has what I should call a courtly manner."

"That is it," replied my hostess, taking up the word; "some say he came from the French court—a nobleman exiled for political offences; others think he is a priest under the ban; and there is still a third story, to the effect that he is a French count, who, owing to a disappointment in love, took orders and came to this far-away island, so that he might seclude himself forever from the world."

"But no one really knows?"

"Absolutely nothing. He is beloved by all the real old island families, whether they are of his faith or not; and when he dies the whole Strait, from Bois Blanc light to far Waugoschance, will mourn for him."

At sunset the Father came again to see me; the front door of my room was open, and we seated ourselves on the piazza outside. The roof of bark thatch had fallen away, leaving the bare beams overhead twined with brier-roses; the floor and house side were frescoed with those lichen-colored spots which show that the gray planks have lacked paint for many long years; the windows had wooden shutters fastened back with irons shaped like the letter S, and on the central door was a brass knocker, and a plate bearing the words UNITED STATES AGENCY.

"When I first came to the island," said Father Piret, "this was the residence par excellence. The old house was brave with green and white paint then; it had candelabra on its high mantles, brass andirons on its many hearthstones, curtains for all its little windows, and carpets for all its uneven floors. Much cooking went on, and smoke curled up from all these outside chimneys. Those were the days of the fur trade, and Mackinac was a central mart. Hither twice a year came the bateaux from the Northwest, loaded with furs; and in those old, decaying warehouses on the back street of the village were stored the goods sent out from New York, with which the bateaux were loaded again, and after a few days of revelry, during which the improvident voyagers squandered all their hard-earned gains, the train returned westward into 'the countries,' as they called the wilderness beyond the lakes, for another six months of toil. The officers of the little fort on the height, the chief factors of the fur company, and the United States Indian agent, formed the feudal aristocracy of the island; but the agent had the most imposing mansion, and often have I seen the old house shining with lights across its whole broadside of windows, and gay with the sound of a dozen French violins. The garden, now a wilderness, was the pride of the island. Its prim arbors, its spring and spring-house, its flower-beds, where, with infinite pains, a few hardy plants were induced to blossom; its cherry-tree avenue, whose early red fruit the short summer could scarcely ripen; its annual attempts at vegetables, which never came to maturity—formed topics for conversation in court circles. Potatoes then as now were left to the mainland Indians, who came over with their canoes heaped with the fine, large thin-jacketed fellows, bartering them all for a loaf or two of bread and a little whiskey.

"The stockade which surrounds the place was at that day a not unnecessary defence. At the time of the payments the island swarmed with Indians, who came from Lake Superior and the Northwest, to receive the government pittance. Camped on the beach as far as the eye could reach, these wild warriors, dressed in all their savage finery, watched the Agency with greedy eyes, as they waited for their turn. The great gate was barred, and sentinels stood at the loopholes with loaded muskets; one by one the chiefs were admitted, stalked up to the office—that wing on the right—received the allotted sum, silently selected something from the displayed goods, and as silently departed, watched by quick eyes, until the great gate closed behind them. The guns of the fort were placed so as to command the Agency during payment time; and when, after several anxious, watchful days and nights, the last brave had received his portion, and the last canoe started away toward the north, leaving only the comparatively peaceful mainland Indians behind, the island drew a long breath of relief."

"Was there any real danger?" I asked.

"The Indians are ever treacherous," replied the Father. Then he was silent, and seemed lost in revery. The pure, ever-present breeze of Mackinac played in his long silvery hair, and his bright eyes roved along the wall of the old house; he had a broad forehead, noble features, and commanding presence, and as he sat there, recluse as he was—aged, alone, without a history, with scarcely a name or place in the world—he looked, in the power of his native-born dignity, worthy of a royal coronet.

"I was thinking of old Jacques," he said, after a long pause. "He once lived in these rooms of yours, and died on that bench at the end of the piazza, sitting in the sunshine, with his staff in his hand."

"Who was he?" I asked. "Tell me the story, Father."

"There is not much to tell, madame; but in my mind he is so associated with this old house, that I always think of him when I come here, and fancy I see him on that bench.

"When the United States agent removed to the Apostle Islands, at the western end of Lake Superior, this place remained for some time uninhabited. But one winter morning smoke was seen coming out of that great chimney on the side; and in the course of the day several curious persons endeavored to open the main gate, at that time the only entrance. But the gate was barred within, and as the high stockade was slippery with ice, for some days the mystery remained unsolved. The islanders, always slow, grow torpid in the winter like bears; they watched the smoke in the daytime and the little twinkling light by night; they talked of spirits both French and Indian as they went their rounds, but they were too indolent to do more. At length the fort commandant heard of the smoke, and saw the light from his quarters on the height. As government property, he considered the Agency under his charge, and he was preparing to send a detail of men to examine the deserted mansion in its ice-bound garden, when its mysterious occupant appeared in the village; it was an old man, silent, gentle, apparently French. He carried a canvas bag, and bought a few supplies of the coarsest description, as though he was very poor. Unconscious of observation, he made his purchases and returned slowly homeward, barring the great gate behind him. Who was he? No one knew. Whence and when came he? No one could tell.

"The detail of soldiers from the fort battered at the gate, and when the silent old man opened it they followed him through the garden, where his feet had made a lonely trail over the deep snow, round to the side door. They entered, and found some blankets on the floor, a fire of old knots on the hearth, a long narrow box tied with a rope; his poor little supplies stood in one corner—bread, salted fish, and a few potatoes—and over the fire hung a rusty teakettle, its many holes carefully plugged with bits of rag. It was a desolate scene; the old man in the great rambling empty house in the heart of an arctic winter. He said little, and the soldiers could not understand his language; but they left him unmolested, and going back to the fort, they told what they had seen. Then the major went in person to the Agency, and gathered from the stranger's words that he had come to the island over the ice in the track of the mail-carrier; that he was an emigrant from France on his way to the Red River of the North, but his strength failing, owing to the intense cold, he had stopped at the island, and seeing the uninhabited house, he had crept into it, as he had not enough money to pay for a lodging elsewhere. He seemed a quiet, inoffensive old man, and after all the islanders had had a good long slow stare at him, he was left in peace, with his little curling smoke by day and his little twinkling light by night, although no one thought of assisting him; there is a strange coldness of heart in these northern latitudes.

"I was then living at the Chenaux; there was a German priest on the island; I sent over two half-breeds every ten days for the mail, and through them I heard of the stranger at the Agency. He was French, they said, and it was rumored in the saloons along the frozen docks that he had seen Paris. This warmed my heart; for, madame, I spent my youth in Paris—the dear, the beautiful city! So I came over to the island in my dog-sledge; a little thing is an event in our long, long winter. I reached the village in the afternoon twilight, and made my way alone to the Agency; the old man no longer barred his gate, and swinging it open with difficulty, I followed the trail through the snowy silent garden round to the side door of this wing—the wing you occupy. I knocked; he opened; I greeted him, and entered. He had tried to furnish his little room with the broken relics of the deserted dwelling; a mended chair, a stool, a propped-up table, a shelf with two or three battered tin dishes, and some straw in one corner comprised the whole equipment, but the floor was clean, the old dishes polished, and the blankets neatly spread over the straw which formed the bed. On the table the supplies were ranged in order; there was a careful pile of knots on one side of the hearth, and the fire was evidently husbanded to last as long as possible. He gave me the mended chair, lighted a candle-end stuck in a bottle, and then seating himself on the stool, he gazed at me in his silent way until I felt like an uncourteous intruder. I spoke to him in French, offered my services; in short, I did my best to break down the barrier of his reserve; there was something pathetic in the little room and its lonely occupant, and, besides, I knew by his accent that we were both from the banks of the Seine.

"Well, I heard his story—not then, but afterward; it came out gradually during the eleven months of our acquaintance; for he became my friend—almost the only friend of fifty years. I am an isolated man, madame. It must be so. God's will be done!"

The Father paused, and looked off over the darkening water; he did not sigh, neither was his calm brow clouded, but there was in his face what seemed to me a noble resignation, and I have ever since felt sure that the secret of his exile held in it a self-sacrifice; for only self-sacrifice can produce that divine expression.

Out in the straits shone the low-down green light of a schooner; beyond glimmered the mast-head star of a steamer, with the line of cabin lights below, and away on the point of Bois Blanc gleamed the steady radiance of the lighthouse showing the way into Lake Huron; the broad overgrown garden cut us off from the village, but above on the height we could see the lighted windows of the fort, although still the evening sky retained that clear hue that seems so much like daylight when one looks aloft, although the earth lies in dark shadows below. The Agency was growing indistinct even to our near eyes; its white chimneys loomed up like ghosts, the shutters sighed in the breeze, and the planks of the piazza creaked causelessly. The old house was full of the spirits of memories, and at twilight they came abroad and bewailed themselves. "The place is haunted," I said, as a distant door groaned drearily.

"Yes," replied Father Piret, coming out of his abstraction, "and this wing is haunted by my old French friend. As time passed and the spring came, he fitted up in his fashion the whole suite of five rooms. He had his parlor, sleeping-room, kitchen, and store-room, the whole furnished only with the articles I have already described, save that the bed was of fresh green boughs instead of straw. Jacques occupied all the rooms with ceremonious exactness; he sat in the parlor, and I too must sit there when I came; in the second room he slept and made his careful toilet, with his shabby old clothes; the third was his kitchen and dining-room; and the fourth, that little closet on the right, was his store-room. His one indulgence was coffee; coffee he must and would have, though he slept on straw and went without meat. But he cooked to perfection in his odd way, and I have often eaten a dainty meal in that little kitchen, sitting at the propped-up table, using the battered tin dishes, and the clumsy wooden spoons fashioned with a jack-knife. After we had become friends Jacques would accept occasional aid from me, and it gave me a warm pleasure to think that I had added something to his comfort, were it only a little sugar, butter, or a pint of milk. No one disturbed the old man; no orders came from Washington respecting the Agency property, and the major had not the heart to order him away. There were more than houses enough for the scanty population of the island, and only a magnate could furnish these large rambling rooms. So the soldiers were sent down to pick the red cherries for the use of the garrison, but otherwise Jacques had the whole place to himself, with all its wings, outbuildings, arbors, and garden beds. . . .

"Jacques had been a soldier of the Empire, as it is called—a grenadier under Napoleon; he had loved his General and Emperor in life, and adored him in death with the affectionate pertinacity of a faithful dog. . . .

"When Napoleon retired to Elba, he fell sick from grief, nor did he recover until the Emperor returned, when, with thousands of other soldiers, our Jacques hastened to his standard, and the hundred days began. Then came Waterloo. Then came St. Helena. But the grenadier lived on in hope, year after year, until the Emperor died—died in exile, in the hands of the hated English. Broken-hearted, weary of the sight of his native land, he packed his few possessions, and fled away over the ocean, with a vague idea of joining a French settlement on the Red River; I have always supposed it must be the Red River of the South; there are French there. But the poor soldier was very ignorant; some one directed him to these frozen regions, and he set out; all places were alike to him now that the Emperor had gone from earth. Wandering as far as Mackinac on his blind pilgrimage, Jacques found his strength failing, and crept into this deserted house to die. Recovering, he made for himself a habitation from a kind of instinct, as a beaver might have done. He gathered together the wrecks of furniture, he hung up his treasures, he had his habits for every hour of the day; soldier-like, everything was done by rule. At a particular hour it was his custom to sit on that bench in the sunshine, wrapped in his blankets in the winter, in summer in his shirt-sleeves with his one old coat carefully hung on that peg; I can see him before me now. On certain days, he would wash his few poor clothes, and hang them out on the bushes to dry; then he would patiently mend them with his great brass thimble and coarse thread. Poor old garments! they were covered with awkward patches. . . .

"We were comrades, he and I; he would not come over to the Chenaux; he was unhappy if the routine of his day was disturbed, but I often stayed a day with him at the Agency, for I too liked the silent house. It has its relics, by the way. Have you noticed a carved door in the back part of the main building? That was brought from the old chapel on the mainland, built as early as 1700. The whole of this locality is sacred ground in the history of our Church. It was first visited by our missionaries in 1670, and over at Point St. Ignace the dust which was once the mortal body of Father Marquette lies buried. The exact site of the grave is lost; but we know that in 1677 his Indian converts brought back his body, wrapped in birch-bark, from the eastern shore of Lake Michigan, where he died, to his beloved mission of St. Ignace. There he was buried in a vault under the little log-church. Some years later the spot was abandoned, and the resident priests returned to Montreal. We have another little Indian church there now, and the point is forever consecrated by its unknown grave. At various times I told Jacques the history of this strait—its islands, and points; but he evinced little interest. He listened with some attention to my account of the battle which took place on Dousman's farm, not far from the British Landing; but when he found that the English were victorious, he muttered a great oath and refused to hear more. To him the English were fiends incarnate. Had they not slowly murdered his Emperor on their barren rock in the sea? . . .

"So the summer passed. The vague intention of going on to the

Red River of the North had faded away, and Jacques lived along on the island as though he had never lived anywhere else. He grew wonted to the Agency, like some old family cat, until he seemed to belong to the house, and all thought of disturbing him was forgotten. 'There is Jacques out washing his clothes,' 'There is Jacques going to buy his coffee,' 'There is Jacques sitting on the piazza,' said the islanders; the old man served them instead of a clock.

"One dark autumn day I came over from the Chenaux to get the mail. The water was rough, and my boat, tilted far over on one side, skimmed the crests of the waves in the daring fashion peculiar to the Mackinac craft; the mail-steamer had not come in, owing to the storm outside, and I went on to the Agency to see Jacques. He seemed as usual, and we had dinner over the little fire, for the day was chilly; the meal over, my host put everything in order again in his methodical way, and then retired to his sanctuary for prayers. . . .

"The storm increased, and I spent the night at the Agency, lying on the bed of boughs, covered with a blanket. The house shook in the gale, the shutters rattled, and all the floors near and far creaked as though feet were walking over them. I was wakeful and restless, but Jacques slept quietly, and did not stir until daylight broke over the stormy water, showing the ships scudding by under bare poles, and the distant mail-boat laboring up toward the island through the heavy sea. My host made his toilet, washing and shaving himself carefully, and putting on his old clothes as though going on parade. Then came breakfast, with a stew added in honor of my presence; and as by this time the steamer was not far from Round Island, I started down toward the little post-office, anxious to receive some expected letters. The steamer came in slowly, the mail was distributed slowly, and I stopped to read my letters before returning. I had a picture-paper for Jacques, and as I looked out across the straits, I saw that the storm was over, and decided to return to the Chenaux in the afternoon, leaving word with my half-breeds to have the sail-boat in readiness at three o'clock. The sun was throwing out a watery gleam as, after the lapse of an hour or two, I walked up the limestone road and entered the great gate of the Agency. As I came through the garden along the cherry-tree avenue I saw Jacques sitting on that bench in the sun, for this was his hour for sunshine; his staff was in his hand, and he was leaning back against the side of the house with his eyes closed, as if in revery. 'Jacques, here is a picture-paper for you,' I said, laying my hand on his shoulder. He did not answer. He was dead.

"Alone, sitting in the sunshine, apparently without a struggle or a pang, the soul of the old soldier had departed. Whither? We know not. But—smile if you will, madame—I trust he is with his Emperor."

I did not smile; my eyes were too full of tears.

"I buried him, as he wished," continued Father Piret, "in his old uniform, with the picture of Napoleon laid on his breast, the sabre by his side, and the withered sprig in his lifeless hand. He lies in our little cemetery on the height, near the shadow of the great cross; the low white board tablet at the head of the mound once bore the words 'Grenadier Jacques,' but the rains and the snows have washed away the painted letters. It is as well."

The priest paused, and we both looked toward the empty bench, as though we saw a figure seated there, staff in hand. After a time my little hostess came out on to the piazza, and we all talked together of the island and its past. "My boat is waiting," said Father Piret at length; "the wind is fair, and I must return to the Chenaux to-night. This near departure is my excuse for coming twice in one day to see you, madame."

"Stay over, my dear sir," I urged. "I too shall leave in another day. We may not meet again."

"Not on earth; but in another world we may," answered the priest, rising as he spoke.

"Father, your blessing," said the little hostess in a low tone, after a quick glance toward the many windows through which the bulwarks of Protestantism might be gazing. But all was dark, both without and within, and the Father gave his blessing to both of us, fervently, but with an apostolic simplicity. Then he left us, and I watched his tall form, crowned with silvery hair, as he passed down the cherry-tree avenue. Later in the evening the moon came out, and I saw a Mackinac boat skimming by the house, its white sails swelling full in the fresh breeze.

"That is Father Piret's boat," said my hostess. "The wind is fair; he will reach the Chenaux before midnight."

A day later, and I too sailed away. As the steamer bore me southward, I looked back toward the island with a sigh. Half hidden in its wild green garden I saw the old Agency; first I could distinguish its whole rambling length; then I lost the roofless piazza, then the dormer-windows, and finally I could only discern the white chimneys, with their crumbling crooked tops. The sun sank into the Strait off Waugoshance, the evening gun flashed from the little fort on the height, the shadows grew dark and darker, the island turned into green foliage, then a blue outline, and finally there was nothing but the dusky water.

The Skeleton on
Round Island

To the Indians the straits were haunted with old legend and superstition, and that ancient folklore lingers on in the Mackinac literature. Half a century ago William MacHarg and Edwin Balmer wrote a spectral tale, *The Indian Drum*, around the legend of a muffled sound, like a savage drum beat, that on stormy days reverberates along the windswept coast. Whatever the cause—waves booming in a rocky cove, wind moaning in a hollow tree—it comes in times of shipwreck, counting the toll of dead that the lake has taken.

Other legends were retold by Mary Hartwell Catherwood in her *Mackinac and Lake Stories*, 1899, tales commended by Francis Parkman for their fidelity to history. In "The Skeleton on Round Island," her halfbreed narrator is "full of stories"—as are the straits islands with their three hundred years of memory.

On the 15th day of March, 1897 Ignace Pelott died at Mackinac Island, aged ninety-three years.

The old quarter-breed, son of a half-breed Chippewa mother and French father, took with him into silence much wilderness lore of the Northwest. He was full of stories when warmed to recital, though at the beginning of a talk his gentle eyes dwelt on the listener with anxiety, and he tapped his forehead—"So many things gone from there!" His habit of saying "Oh God, yes," or "Oh God, no," was not in the least irreverent, but simply his mild way of using island English.

While water lapped the beach before his door and the sun smote sparkles on the strait, he told about this adventure across the ice, and his hearer has taken but few liberties with the recital.

I AM TO CARRY Mamselle Rosalin of Green Bay from Mackinac to Cheboygan that time, and it is the end of March, and the wind have turn from east to west in the morning. A man will go out with the wind in the east, to haul wood from Boblo, or cut a hole to fish, and by night he cannot get home—ice, it is rotten; it goes to pieces quick when the March wind turns.

I am not afraid for me—long, tall fellow then; eye that can see to Point aux Pins; I can lift more than any other man that goes in the boats to Green Bay or the Soo; can swim, run on snow-shoes, go without eating two, three days, and draw my belt in. Sometimes the ice-floes carry me miles, for they all go east down the lakes when they start, and I have landed the other side of Drummond. But when you have a woman with you—Oh God, yes, that is different.

The way of it is this: I have brought the mail from St. Ignace with my traino—you know the train-au-galise—the birch sledge with dogs. It is flat, and turn up at the front like a toboggan. And I have take the traino because it is not safe for a horse; the wind is in the west, and the strait bends and looks too sleek. Ice a couple of inches thick will bear up a man and dogs. But this old ice a foot thick, it is turning rotten. I have come from St. Ignace early in the afternoon, and the people crowd about to get their letters, and there is Mamselle Rosalin crying to go to Cheboygan, because her lady has arrive there sick, and has sent the letter a week ago. Her friends say:

"It is too late to go to-day, and the strait is dangerous."

She say: "I make a bundle and walk. I must go when my lady is sick and her husband the lieutenant is away, and she has need of me."

Mamselle's friends talk and she cry. She runs and makes a little bundle in the house and comes out ready to walk to Cheboygan. There is nobody can prevent her. Some island people are descend from noblesse of France. But none of them have travel like Mamselle Rosalin with the officer's wife to Indiana, to Chicago, to Detroit. She is like me, French.* The girls use to turn their heads to see me walk in to mass; but I never look grand as Mamselle Rosalin when she step out to that ice.

I have not a bit of sense; I forget maman and my brothers and sisters that depend on me. I run to Mamselle Rosalin, take off my cap, and bow from my head to my heel, like you do in the dance. I will take her to Cheboygan with my traino—Oh God, yes! And I

* The old fellow would not own the Chippewa.

laugh at the wet track the sledge make, and pat my dogs and tell them they are not tired. I wrap her up in the fur, and she thank me and tremble, and look me through with her big black eyes so that I am ready to go down in the strait.

The people on the shore hurrah, though some of them cry out to warn us.

"The ice is cracked from Mission Point to the hook of Round Island, Ignace Pelott!"

"I know that," I say. "Good-day, messieurs!"

The crack from Mission Point—under what you call Robinson's Folly—to the hook of Round Island always comes first in a breaking up; and I hold my breath in my teeth as I skurry the dogs across it. The ice grinds, the water follows the sledge. But the sun is so far down in the southwest, I think "The wind will grow colder. The real thaw will not come before to-morrow."

I am to steer betwixt the east side of Round Island and Boblo. When we come into the shadow of Boblo we are chill with damp, far worse than the clear sharp air that blows from Canada. I lope beside the traino, and not take my eyes off the course to Cheboy-gan, except that I see the islands look blue, and darkness stretching before its time. The sweat drop off my face, yet I feel that wind through my wool clothes, and am glad of the shelter between Boblo and Round Island, for the strait outside will be the worst.

There is an Indian burying-ground on open land above the beach on that side of Round Island. I look up when the thick woods are pass, for the sunset ought to show there. But what I see is a skeleton like it is sliding down hill from the graveyard to the beach. It does not move. The earth is wash from it, and it hangs staring at me.

I cannot tell how that make me feel! I laugh, for it is funny; but I am ashame, like my father is expose and Mamselle Rosalin can see him. If I do not cover him again I am disgrace. I think I will wait till some other day when I can get back from Cheboygan; for what will she say if I stop the traino when we have such a long journey, and it is so near night, and the strait almost ready to move? So I crack the whip, but something pull, pull! I cannot go on! I say to myself, "The ground is froze; how can I cover up that skeleton without any shovel, or even a hatchet to break the earth?"

But something pull, pull, so I am oblige to stop, and the dogs turn in without one word and drag the sledge up the beach of Round Island.

"What is the matter?" says Mamselle Rosalin. She is out of the sledge as soon as it stops.

I not know what to answer, but tell her I have to cut a stick to mend my whip-handle. I think I will cut a stick and rake some earth over the skeleton to cover it, and come another day with a shovel and dig a new grave. The dogs lie down and pant, and she looks through me with her big eyes like she begs me to hurry.

But there is no danger she will see the skeleton. We both look back to Mackinac. The island have its hump up against the north, and the village in its lap around the bay, and the Mission eastward near the cliff; but all seem to be moving! We run along the beach of Round Island, and then we see the channel between that and Boblo is moving too, and the ice is like wet loaf-sugar, grinding as it floats.

We hear some roars away off, like cannon when the Americans come to the island. My head swims. I cross myself and know why something pull, pull, to make me bring the traino to the beach, and I am oblige to that skeleton who slide down hill to warn me.

When we have seen Mackinac, we walk to the other side and look south and southeast towards Cheboygan. All is the same. The ice is moving out of the strait.

"We are strand on this island!" says Mamselle Rosalin. "Oh, what shall we do?"

I tell her it is better to be prisoners on Round Island than on a cake of ice in the strait, for I have tried the cake of ice and know.

"We will camp and build a fire in the cove opposite Mackinac," I say. "Maman and the children will see the light and feel sure we are safe."

"I have done wrong," says she. "If you lose your life on this journey, it is my fault."

Oh God, no! I tell her. She is not to blame for anything, and there is no danger. I have float many a time when the strait breaks up, and not save my hide so dry as it is now. We only have to stay on Round Island till we can get off.

"And how long will that be?" she ask.

I shrug my shoulders. There is no telling. Sometimes the strait clears very soon, sometimes not. Maybe two, three days.

Rosalin sit down on a stone.

I tell her we can make camp, and show signals to Mackinac, and when the ice permit, a boat will be sent.

She is crying, and I say her lady will be well. No use to go to Cheboygan anyhow, for it is a week since her lady sent for her. But she cry on, and I think she wish I leave her alone, so I say I will get wood. And I unharness the dogs, and run along the beach to cover that skeleton before dark. I look and cannot find him at all. Then I go up to the graveyard and look down. There is no skeleton anywhere. I have seen his skull and his ribs and his arms and legs, all sliding down hill. But he is gone!

The dusk close in upon the islands, and I not know what to think—cross myself, two, three times; and wish we had land on Boblo instead of Round Island, though there are wild beasts on both.

But there is no time to be scare at skeletons that slide down and disappear, for Mamselle Rosalin must have her camp and her place to sleep. Every man use to the bateaux have always his tinder-box, his knife, his tobacco, but I have more than that; I have leave Mackinac so quick I forget to take out the storekeeper's bacon that line the bottom of the sledge, and Mamselle Rosalin sit on it in the furs! We have plenty meat, and I sing like a voyageur while I build the fire. Drift, so dry in summer you can light it with a coal from your pipe, lay on the beach, but is now winter-soaked, and I make a fireplace of logs, and cut pine branches to help it.

It is all thick woods on Round Island, so close it tear you to pieces if you try to break through; only four-footed things can crawl there. When the fire is blazing up I take my knife and cut a tunnel like a little room, and pile plenty evergreen branches. This is to shelter Mamselle Rosalin, for the night is so raw she shiver. Our tent is the sky, darkness, and clouds. But I am happy. I unload the sledge. The bacon is wet. On long sticks the slices sizzle and sing while I toast them, and the dogs come close and blink by the fire, and lick their chops. Rosalin laugh and I laugh, for it smell like a good kitchen; and we sit and eat nothing but toasted meat—better than lye corn and tallow that you have when you go out with the boats. Then I feed the dogs, and she walk with me to the water edge, and we drink with our hands.

It is my house, when we sit on the fur by the fire. I am so light I want my fiddle. I wish it last like a dream that Mamselle Rosalin and me keep house together on Round Island. You not want to go to heaven when the one you think about all the time stays close by you.

But pretty soon I want to go to heaven quick. I think I jump in the lake if maman and the children had anybody but me. When I light my pipe she smile. Then her great big eyes look off towards Mackinac, and I turn and see the little far-away lights.

"They know we are on Round Island together," I say to cheer her, and she move to the edge of the fur. Then she say "Goodnight," and get up and go to her tunnel-house in the bushes, and I jump up too, and spread the fur there for her. And I not get back to the fire before she make a door of all the branches I have cut, and is hid like a squirrel. I feel I dance for joy because she is in my camp for me to guard. But what is that? It is a woman that cry out loud by herself! I understand now why she sit down so hopeless when we first land. I have not know much about women, but I understand how she feel. It is not her lady, or the dark, or the ice break up, or the cold. It is not Ignace Pelott. It is the name of being prison on Round Island with a man till the ice is out of the straits. She is so shame she want to die. I think I will kill myself. If Mamselle Rosalin cry out loud once more, I plunge in the lake—and then what become of maman and the children?

She is quieter; and I sit down and cannot smoke, and the dogs pity me. Old Sauvage lay his nose on my knee. I do not say a word to him, but I pat him, and we talk with our eyes, and the bright campfire shows each what the other is say.

"Old Sauvage," I tell him, "I am not good man like the priest. I have been out with the boats, and in Indian camps, and I not had in my life a chance to marry, because there are maman and the children. But you know, old Sauvage, how I have feel about Mamselle Rosalin, it is three years."

Old Sauvage hit his tail on the ground and answer he know.

"I have love her like a dog that not dare to lick her hand. And now she hate me because I am shut on Round Island with her while the ice goes out. I not good man, but it pretty tough to stand that."

Old Sauvage hit his tail on the ground and say, "That so." I hear the water on the gravel like it sound when we find a place to drink, then it is plenty company, but now it is lonesome. The water say to people on Mackinac, "Rosalin and Ignace Pelott, they are on Round Island." What make you proud, maybe, when you turn it and look at it the other way, make you sick. But I cannot walk the broken ice, and if I could, she would be lef alone with the dogs. I think I will build another camp.

But soon there is a shaking in the bushes, and Sauvage and his sledgemates bristle and stand up and show their teeth. Out comes Mamselle Rosalin with a scream to the other side of the fire.

I have nothing except my knife, and I take a chunk of burning wood and go into her house. Maybe I see some green eyes. I have handle vild-cat skin too much not to know that smell in the dark.

I take all the branches from Rosalin's house and pile them by the fire, and spread the fur robe on them. And I pull out red coals and put more logs on before I sit down away off between her and the spot where she hear that noise. If the graveyard was over us, I would expect to see that skeleton once more.

"What was it?" she whisper.

I tell her maybe a stray wolf.

"Wolves not eat people, mamselle, unless they hunt in a pack; and they run from fire. You know what M'sieu' Cable tell about wolves that chase him on the ice when he skate to Cheboygan? He come to great wide crack in ice, he so scare he jump it and skate right on! Then he look back, and see the wolves go in, head down, every wolf caught and drown in the crack. It is two days before he come home, and the east wind have blow to freeze that crack over —and there are all the wolf tails, stick up, froze stiff in a row! He bring them home with him—but los them on the way, though he show the knife that cut them off!"

"I have hear that," says Rosalin. "I think he lie."

"He say he take his oat on a book," I tell her, but we both laugh, and she is curl down so close to the fire her cheeks turn rosy. For a camp-fire will heat the air all around until the world is like a big dark room; and we are shelter from the wind. I am glad she is begin to enjoy herself. And all the time I have a hand on my knife, and the cold chills down my back where that hungry vild-cat will set his claws if he jump on me; and I cannot turn around to face him because Rosalin thinks it is nothing but a cowardly wolf that sneak away. Old Sauvage is uneasy and come to me, his fangs all expose, but I drive him back and listen to the bushes behind me.

"Sing, M'sieu' Pelott," says Rosalin.

Oh God, yes! It is easy to sing with a vild-cat watch you on one side and a woman on the other!

"But I not know anything except boat songs."

"Sing boat songs."

So I sing like a bateau full of voyageurs, and the dark echo, and that vild-cat must be astonish. When you not care what become of you, and your head is light and your heart like a stone on the beach, you not mind vild-cats, but sing and laugh.

I cast my eye behin sometimes, and feel my knife. It make me smile to think what kind of creature come to my house in the wilderness, and I say to myself: "Hear my cat purr! This is the only time I will ever have a home of my own, and the only time the woman I want sit beside my fire."

Then I ask Rosalin to sing to me, and she sing "Malbrouck," like her father learn it in Kebec. She watch me, and I know her eyes have more danger for me than the vild-cat's. It ought to tear me to pieces if I forget maman and the children. It ought to be scare out the bushes to jump on a poor fool like me. But I not stop entertain it—Oh God, no! I say things that I never intend to say, like they are pull out of my mouth. When your heart has ache, sometimes it break up quick like the ice.

"There is Paul Pepin," I tell her. "He is a happy man; he not trouble himself with anybody at all. His father die; he let his mother take care of herself. He marry a wife, and get tired of her and turn her off with two children. The priest not able to scare him; he smoke and take his dram and enjoy life. If I was Paul Pepin I would not be torment."

"But you are not torment," says Rosalin. "Everybody speak well of you."

"Oh God, yes," I tell her; "but a man not live on the breath of his neighbors. I am thirty years old, and I have take care of my mother and brothers and sisters since I am fifteen. I not made so I can leave them, like Paul Pepin. He marry when he please. I not able to marry at all. It is not far I can go from the island. I cannot get rich. My work must be always the same."

"But why you want to marry?" says Rosalin, as if that surprise her. And I tell her it is because I have seen Rosalin of Green Bay; and she laugh. Then I think it is time for the vild-cat to jump. I am thirty years old, and have nothing but what I can make with the boats or my traino; the children are not grown; my mother depend on me; and I have propose to a woman, and she laugh at me!

But I not see, while we sing and talk, that the fire is burn lower, and old Sauvage has crept around the camp into the bushes.

That end all my courtship. I not use to it, and not have any business to court, anyhow. I drop my head on my breast, and it is like when I am little and the measle go in. Paul Pepin he take a woman by the chin and smack her on the lips. The women not laugh at him, he is so rough. I am as strong as he is, but I am afraid to hurt; I am oblige to take care of what need me. And I am tie to things I love—even the island—so that I cannot get away.

"I not want to marry," says Rosalin, and I see her shake her head at me. "I not think about it at all."

"Mamselle," I say to her, "you have not any inducement like I have, that torment you three years."

"How you know that?" she ask me. And then her face change from laughter, and she spring up from the blanket couch, and I think the camp go around and around me—all fur and eyes and claws and teeth—and I not know what I am doing, for the dogs are all over me—yell—yell—yell; and then I am stop stabbing, because the vild-cat has let go of Sauvage, and Sauvage has let go of the vild-cat, and I am looking at them and know they are both dead, and I cannot help him any more.

You are confuse by such things where there is noise, and howling creatures sit up and put their noses in the air, like they call their mate back out of the dark. I am sick for my old dog. Then I am proud he has kill it, and wipe my knife on its fur, but feel ashame that I have not check him driving it into camp. And then Rosalin throw her arms around my neck and kiss me.

It is many years I have tell Rosalin she did that. But a woman will deny what she know to be the trut. I have tell her the courtship had end, and she begin it again herself, and keep it up till the boats take us off Round Island. The ice not run out so quick any more now like it did then. My wife say it is a long time we waited, but when I look back it seem the shortest time I ever live—only two days.

Oh God, yes, it is three years before I marry the woman that not want to marry at all; then my brothers and sisters can take care of themselves, and she help me take care of maman.

It is when my boy Gabriel come home from the war to die that I see the skeleton on Round Island again. I am again sure it is wash out, and I go ashore to bury it, and it disappear. Nobody but me see it. Then before Rosalin die I am out on the ice-boat, and it give me warning. I know what it mean; but you cannot always escape misfortune. I cross myself when I see it; but I find good luck that first time I land; and maybe I find good luck every time, after I have land.

Bridging

the Straits

In 1836 upper Michigan was an unknown region which the state reluctantly accepted in place of the disputed "Toledo strip." But it proved to be a realm of riches. Even so, it was remote, accessible only by water, a sundered land across a four-mile strait. When highways and railroads served the North, with big steam ferries plying the windy narrows, the upper peninsula was still cut off from the world below.

For a hundred years men talked of joining the divided state. One dreamer proposed a floating tunnel; another pictured a system of causeways and bridge spans from Cheboygan to Bois Blanc and Round Island, then to Mackinac Island and across to St. Ignace. While many said it was impossible, the dream of a bridge persisted.

In 1950 the Mackinac Bridge Authority convinced the Michigan legislature that a bridge could be built, and that its traffic would pay the immense cost of construction. Engineer David B. Steinman, who had built three hundred bridges on five continents, designed the span, and investors bought 100 million dollars worth of bonds. Construction began in May, 1954; the first traffic crossed the bridge in November, 1957. At last the two Michigans were linked together.

In his *Straits of Mackinac*, 1957, William Ratigan pictured a watchman on the windy bridge towers. High above the northern woods and waters, he saw the past, present and future of the straits.

WITH THE WHITE-CAPPED Straits of Mackinac hundreds of feet below, the Watchman went along the narrow catwalk that followed the path of the thick suspension span cables of the bridge. He moved as if he had eyes in his feet. In the unsettled spring weather, the wind was roaring around the clock, now hammering straight down at him from Lake Superior, now lashing sideways at him from Lake Huron or Lake Michigan to threaten his balance. . . .

As he reached the first crest of the catwalk atop South Tower, he paused, leaning with the wind, to take a long look at what he had climbed steel beams and teetered along scant footholds to see —the ageless Empire of Michilimackinac. A sea gull's wings caught the morning sun as he unbuttoned his Mackinaw to draw a deep breath at the panorama outspread below, and to get his bearings.

In his adventure across concrete-paved superstructure, steel beams, and the looping catwalk, the Watchman had come from the Mackinaw City side of the bridge, across the sixteen spans of the southern approach. The first and easiest part of his journey had reached an end at Pier 17, the South Anchorage. Here, after crossing more water than most bridges ever saw, after stretching a roadway more than a mile out into the Straits, the main feature of the Mackinac Project began.

From the South Anchorage, high as a ten-story building above the water, he had traversed the backstay span, well over a football field and a half in length, to Pier 18 where the side suspension span began. Here, if the four-lane highway for traffic and the sidewalks for maintenance and emergency use had been completed, he could have pushed forward with little effort for exactly six football fields laid end to end, until he reached Pier 19 where the South Tower of the main suspension span rose from the surface of the Straits almost twice as high as the Statue of Liberty on its pedestal.

But the four-lane highway would not be ready for regular traffic until the deer hunters came along in the Watchman's birth-month, and so he started his climb up the suspension cables that rose and fell like a giant's roller-coaster in two enormous leaps across the water, to make the Mackinac Bridge the longest suspension bridge in the world, from anchorage to anchorage, and second only to the Golden Gate Bridge in the length of its main suspension span.

It was on his way up the first loop of the cables that the Watchman took the catwalk, which gave him a narrow pathway with chain link fencing for a decking underfoot. As he toiled up the slope toward the top of the South Tower, he thanked the wooden cleats in the decking that gave him a firmer grip on the steeper slopes when the winds from three Great Lakes seemed bent on hurling him overboard. When he made his last step to the top of the tower, he felt as proud as the men who had, at long last, conquered Mount Everest.

Then, for the moment that would live forever in his memory, he stopped at South Tower. . . . Down the sag of the suspension cables and across more than a mile and a half of spans and piers, lay Mackinaw City, the jumping-off place from Michigan's Lower Peninsula. Dead ahead lay St. Ignace, the welcome mat to the Upper Peninsula, but it was still a breath-taking three and a half miles away. Off the starboard bow, so to speak, lay storied Mackinac Island. More abeam to starboard were tiny Round Island and sprawling Bois Blanc. Around the bend in the Straits on the Lake Huron mainland, but lost in atmospheric haze, lay the town of Cheboygan.

On the port side of the bridge, abaft the beam in the hazy distance, lay Waugoshance Point and Ile Aux Galets lighthouse, never called by Lake men anything but Wobbleshanks and Skillygalee. The latter stood straight off Cross Village, which held the same position around the Lake Michigan bend of the Straits as Cheboygan held on the Huron side. In this same general direction, but appearing like low clouds or smudges of smoke on the horizon, were the unbelievable Beaver Islands with their history of two monarchs—King Strang and King Ben.

Down in the water there was the usual bustle of traffic in the Straits. Observed from this height the boats seemed more toy than real, but the Watchman could identify the business and state the destination of every craft in sight. More than that, he could read the success story of America as he surveyed the scene below.

Not counting the sailboats and cruisers pleasure-bound around Mackinac Island or the hard-working tugs on the move up and down the bridge line, more than forty passenger and cargo vessels —patrolled by the magnificent snow-white Coast Guard icebreaker *Mackinaw*—could be seen either navigating or approaching the Straits. And more coming over the horizon every turn of the clock from every port on the Lakes, as well as from overseas.

There were lumber barges, iron ore carriers, oil tankers, grain carriers, passenger liners, coal carriers, limestone haulers, and assorted bulk carriers. A boat laden with taconite pellets from Silver Bay, Minnesota, hooted for passage to an excursion vessel bound up from Chicago to Mackinac with a convention crowd for the Grand Hotel. A puff of smoke from the freighter's stack told the Watchman that she had signaled, "I am directing my course to starboard," before the blast, thin with distance, could reach him. An answering puff of smoke, followed by a faint but deep-throated blast came from the excursion boat.

Tricks of the wind carried other nautical sounds to the bridge tower: four short blasts from a Lake Huron cement carrier warning a Lake Michigan fish tug, "Danger! I do not understand your course!"—the muted jingle of four bells ordering an engineer, "Full speed ahead!" A friendly salute exchanged across the water by two freighter captains as they blew three long blasts and two short ones of greeting. The impatient whistles of a Mackinac Island passenger ferry preparing to depart for the mainland. A clamor of bells as one of the car ferries docked at Mackinaw City, and a clang as the huge mouth opened to disgorge automobiles.

The predominant colors of the bulk carriers drew the nodding approval of the Watchman on Mackinac Bridge. They were mostly reds and blacks, rusts and browns, sober and steady colors that matched the importance of their jobs. A grain carrier, bound down through the Soo Canal from Fort William or Port Arthur in Canada with half a million bushels of wheat that took perhaps thirty long freight trains to deliver to the docks, needed no fancy paint to call attention to herself. Neither did an ore carrier seven hundred feet long, longer than all but a count-on-the-fingers number of ocean-going luxury liners, and laden with twenty-four thousand tons of iron ore from Lake Superior's ranges, need any loud colors to shout her value.

In the partisan mood that never left him, the Watchman wrinkled his nose at a circus-yellow Norwegian tramp steaming into the final thirty hours of her haul from Oslo to Milwaukee. She looked squat and strange in the company of the long American freighters with their conservative trim, but she was a sign of the times, a token of the many ocean vessels soon to come in ever-increasing numbers.

V

UNLOCKING
THE NORTH

In May of 1820 the busiest place in Detroit was the river landing in front of the old French farmhouse where Governor Lewis Cass administered the affairs of Michigan Territory. Three big canoes lay there—*canots du maître* thirty-six feet long and seven feet wide, fitted with mast and sail. Into them went all kinds of goods and gear, Indian presents, scientific instruments, and military supplies for an expedition to Lake Superior and the headwaters of the Mississippi. In 1820 Detroit, with its timbered fort and log stockade, and its ribbon farms lining the river, was the outfitting place for the interior wilderness.

On May 24 the canoes were loaded. Ten Canadian boatmen and ten Indian guides and hunters (at sixty cents a day) paddled up the river. Twenty soldiers and scientists followed in carriages, accompanied by half the townspeople, past Windmill Point to Lake St. Clair. At the Grosse Pointe landing they embarked. To the shouts of the villagers the canoes pushed into Lake St. Clair—"as if a new world was about to be discovered."

After that fine send-off a gale lashed Lake St. Clair and the canoes were forced ashore. Two days later they were under way again, through the St. Clair flats, past Fort Gratiot and into vast Lake Huron. Paddling from dawn to starlight they made seventy miles a day along the wild lake shore. At each new camp the world lay farther behind them.

On a June evening in that summer of 1820 a band of swarthy children was playing beside the St. Marys River, their shrill voices almost lost in the roar of the rapids. Suddenly a boy pointed down the river and the voices ceased. In silence they watched the approach of three canoes. Sunset gleamed on rifle barrels and a strange flag blew in the wind. When the craft came in to the landing the whole village had gathered.

The Cass expedition had arrived, to plant the first American flag at the strategic Sault. While the Indians watched (wearing their British coats and medals) the Americans made camp on the green riverbank.

Next morning, while the Indians ringed the camp in a somber silence, Cass announced that the United States planned to build a fort there, on land ceded at the Treaty of Greenville in 1795. Chief Sassaba, wearing eagle feathers and a red coat given him by the commandant at nearby Fort Drummond, kicked away the American presents and raised a British flag. Cass drew up his soldiers and pulled down the Union Jack.

Through his interpreter he told the chief that no foreign flag could fly on United States soil; the Indians must understand that the United States was in control here; if they resisted, a strong foot would be placed upon their necks and they would be crushed.

After a day of smoldering hostility, Sassaba paddled down the river and the tension relaxed. The other chiefs accepted the Americans, acknowledging their claim to a tract of land beside the river. In a changed atmosphere the Indians swarmed around the American presents, and the expedition moved on to Lake Superior.

The commerce of Lake Superior might be said to have begun in 1765. In that year, wrote Alexander Henry, "the exclusive trade of Lake Superior was given to myself by the commandant of Fort Michilimackinac. . . . I engaged twelve men and stocked four canoes." But it would remain "the closed lake" for nearly a century. In the summer of 1825, while his Indian paddlers pushed a *canot du nord* over the vast and empty lake, Henry Rowe Schoolcraft (who had first come north with the Cass expedition five years before) jotted in his journal: "The sources of a busy commerce lie concealed . . . in its rocks." Now, every spring, the powerful ice-breaker *Alexander Henry* cuts through the frozen narrows, escorting the big freighters to open water.

Though Alexander Henry's exclusive permit was never officially terminated, other trade came to the closed lake. The fur brigades, bringing baled peltry from Grand Portage on the northern shore, steered their canoes through a narrow canal and lock on the Canadian side of the St. Mary's. Destroyed by American troops in the War of 1812, this small lock was not rebuilt. The traffic of surveyors and prospectors a generation later was portaged around the rapids, at first in creaking carts, then on a crude tramway. Superior remained the closed lake during the feverish copper rush of the 1840s.

In those years Sault Ste. Marie was the outfitting place for the mining country, the little town busy with portage trade and swarming with men of many garbs and colors. In 1848 the eminent Louis Agassiz of Harvard College found a floating population of a thousand *voyageurs*, miners, traders and Indians. "The most striking feature," wrote his companion J. Elliot Cabot, "is the number of dram shops and bowling alleys. Standing in front of one of the hotels I counted seven buildings where liquor was sold, beside the larger stores where this was only one article among others. The roar of bowling alleys and the click of billiard balls are heard from morning till late at night. . . . All are out on a spree, or going a-fishing or bowling. Nobody is busy but the barkeepers."

This last was untrue, for the portage crews were working, even in winter when they hauled entire vessels, sail and steam, over the snowy road to Lake Superior. A few years later the place teemed with construction. While dynamite blasted above the clamor of men and mules, the canal was carved beside the rushing river.

In 1855 there were festive days when the first vessels steamed past the barrier rapids. Then Sault Ste. Marie became a quiet village while the commerce passed through. Said Disturnell's guidebook in 1863: "Lake Superior, the *ultima Thule* of many travelers, can be reached by lines of steamers from Cleveland and Detroit, or Chicago and Milwaukee." The closed lake was open to the world.

CLAUDE DABLON

Ceremony at

the Sault

The long history of Sault Ste. Marie began on a radiant June day in 1670. Before the chiefs and warriors of fourteen tribes Sieur de St. Lusson, emissary of Louis XIV, proclaimed French possession of all the Lakes and the waters that flowed to them. It was one of those stately pageants that the French enjoyed and that delighted the ceremony-loving Indians.

For six weeks the tribesmen had gathered, pitching their camps beside the rapids and feasting on trout and whitefish. Among them were merchant Nicholas Perrot, explorer Louis Jolliet, soldiers, traders, *voyageurs, coureurs de bois*, and four black-robed priests.

On the fourteenth of June the procession formed at the mission and marched to a knoll above the river, near the ancient Chippewa burial ground. Here a cedar cross was sanctified, a post was raised bearing the arms of Louis XIV on a leaden plate, the Frenchmen sang *Vexilla Regis* and St. Lusson proclaimed possession. After a volley of musketry Father Allouez spoke of the grace of the cross and the magnificence of the French monarch. A bonfire leaped up in the evening shadows and the priests sang *Te Deum*.

That night the stars shone down, the river roared in darkness, and drums throbbed around the Indian fires—as they had done before the first Frenchman came to that wild country.

The ceremony was described by Father Dablon in the *Jesuit Relation* for 1671–2.

I T IS well to afford a general view of all these Outaouac territories, not only for the purpose of designating the places where the Faith has been proclaimed by the planting of Missions, but also because the King, by very recently taking possession of them with a ceremony worthy of the eldest son of the Church, put all these tribes under the protection of the Cross before receiving them under his own—as will be set forth in the account to be given of that act of taking possession.

By glancing, as one can, at the Map of the lakes, and of the territories on which are settled most of the tribes of these regions, one will gain more light upon all these Missions than by long descriptions that might be given of them.

The reader may first turn his eyes to the Mission of Sainte Marie du Sault, three leagues below the mouth of Lake Superior. He will find it situated on the banks of the river by which this great Lake discharges its waters, at the place called the Sault, very advantageous in which to perform Apostolic functions, since it is the great resort of most of the Savages of these regions, and lies in the almost universal route of all who go down to the French settlements. It was also on this spot that all these lands were taken possession of in his Majesty's name, in the presence and with the approval of fourteen Nations who had come hither for that purpose.

Toward the other end of the same lake is found the Mission of Saint Esprit, covering both the district known as Chagaoumigong point and the neighboring islands. It will be easy to recognise the rivers and routes leading to various Nations, either stationary or nomadic, located in the vicinity of this same lake, who are somewhat dependent on this Mission of saint Esprit in the matter of trade, which draws them to our Savages' abode.

For it is a Southward course that is taken by the great river called by the natives Missisipi, which must empty somewhere in the region of the Florida sea, more than four hundred leagues hence. Fuller mention of it will be made hereafter. Beyond that great river lie the Villages of the Ilinois, a hundred leagues from saint Esprit point. Still farther away is situated another Nation, of an unknown tongue, beyond which, it is said, lies the Western sea. Again, proceeding toward the West-Northwest, we find the people called Assinipoulac, not far from the North Sea, two weeks' journey from the Mission of saint Esprit.

The reader will also be enabled—on his journey, so to speak—to note all the places on this Lake where copper is said to be found. For the slabs and huge lumps of this metal which we have seen; that great rock of copper, seven or eight hundred livres in weight, seen near the head of the Lake by all who pass; and, furthermore, the numerous pieces found at the water's edge in various places— all seem to force upon us the conviction that somewhere there are parent mines not yet discovered.

Toward the South, on the other side of the Lake, are the territories formerly occupied by various Nations of the Hurons and Outaouacs, who had stationed themselves at some distance from one another, as far as the famous Island of Missilimakinac. In the neighborhood of this island, various Peoples used to make their abode, who now fully intend to return thither if they see that peace is firmly established. It is for this reason that we have already begun to found there the Mission of St. Ignace.

Thence one enters the Lake called Mitchiganous, to which the Ilinois have given their name. Between this lake of the Ilinois and Lake Superior is seen a long bay called the bay des Puans, at the head of which is the Mission of saint François Xavier.

Finally, the remaining tribes, farther distant toward the South and Southwest, are either beginning to draw near to us—for already the Ilinois have reached the bay mentioned above, or else are waiting until we can advance to them. All these matters will be treated more in detail, touching upon what has been found most rare and curious among those newly-discovered countries and Peoples. But first let us see how the King took possession of them this year, and subjected them to Jesus Christ's dominion before placing them under his own.

It is not our present purpose to describe this ceremony in detail, but merely to touch on matters relating to Christianity and the welfare of our missions, which are going to be more flourishing than ever after what occurred to their advantage on this occasion.

When Monsieur Talon, our Intendant, returned from Portugal, and after his shipwreck, he was commanded by the King to return to this country; and at the same time received his Majesty's orders to exert himself strenuously for the establishment of Christianity here, by aiding our Missions, and to cause the name and the sovereignty of our invincible Monarch to be acknowledged by even the least known and the most remote Nations. These commands, reinforced by the designs of the Minister—who is ever equally alert to extend God's glory, and to promote that of his King in every land— were obeyed as speedily as possible. Monsieur Talon had no sooner landed than he considered means for insuring the success of these plans—choosing to that end sieur de saint Lusson, whom he commissioned to take possession, in his place and in his Majesty's name, of the territories lying between the East and the West, from Montreal as far as the South sea, covering the utmost extent and range possible.

For this purpose, after wintering on the Lake of the Hurons,

Monsieur de saint Lusson repaired to sainte Marie du Sault early in May of this year, sixteen hundred and seventy-one. First, he summoned the surrounding tribes living within a radius of a hundred leagues, and even more; and they responded through their Ambassadors, to the number of fourteen Nations. After making all necessary preparations for the successful issue of the whole undertaking to the honor of France, he began, on June fourth of the same year, with the most solemn ceremony ever observed in these regions.

For, when all had assembled in a great public council, and a height had been chosen well adapted to his purpose—overlooking, as it did, the Village of the people of the Sault—he caused the Cross to be planted there, and then the King's standard to be raised, with all the pomp that he could devise.

The Cross was publicly blessed, with all the ceremonies of the Church, by the Superior of these Missions; and then, when it had been raised from the ground for the purpose of planting it, the *Vexilla* was sung. Many Frenchmen there present at the time joined in this hymn, to the wonder and delight of the assembled Savages; while the whole company was filled with a common joy at the sight of this glorious standard of JESUS CHRIST, which seemed to have been raised so high only to rule over the hearts of all these poor peoples.

Then the French Escutcheon, fixed to a Cedar pole, was also erected, above the Cross, while the *Exaudiat* was sung, and prayer for his Majesty's Sacred person was offered in that far-away corner of the world. After this, Monsieur de saint Lusson, observing all the forms customary on such occasions, took possession of those regions, while the air resounded with repeated shouts of "Long live the King!" and with the discharge of musketry—to the delight and astonishment of all those peoples, who had never seen anything of the kind.

After this confused uproar of voices and muskets had ceased, perfect silence was imposed upon the whole assemblage; and Father Claude Allouez began to Eulogize the King, in order to make all those Nations understand what sort of a man he was whose standard they beheld, and to whose sovereignty they were that day submitting. Being well versed in their tongue and in their ways, he was so successful in adapting himself to their comprehension as to give them such an opinion of our incomparable Monarch's greatness that they have no words with which to express their thoughts upon the subject.

"Here is an excellent matter brought to your attention, my brothers," said he to them, "a great and important matter, which is the cause of this council. Cast your eyes upon the Cross raised so high above your heads; there it was that JESUS CHRIST, the son of God, making himself man for the love of men, was pleased to be fastened and to die, in atonement to his Eternal Father for our sins. He is the master of our lives, of Heaven, of Earth, and of Hell. Of him I have always spoken to you, and his name and word I have bourne into all these countries.

"But look likewise at that other post, to which are affixed the armorial bearings of the great Captain of France whom we call King. He lives beyond the sea; he is the Captain of the greatest Captains, and has not his equal in the world. All the Captains you have ever seen, or of whom you have ever heard, are mere children compared with him. He is like a great tree, and they, only like little plants that we tread under foot in walking.

"You know about Onnontio, that famous Captain of Quebec. You know and feel that he is the terror of the Iroquois, and that his very name makes them tremble, now that he has laid waste their country and set fire to their Villages. Beyond the sea there are ten thousand Onnontios like him, who are only the Soldiers of that Great Captain, our Great King, of whom I am speaking. When he says, 'I am going to war,' all obey him; and those ten thousand Captains raise Companies of a hundred soldiers each, both on sea and on land. Some embark in ships, one hundred or two hundred in number, like those you have seen at Quebec. Your Canoes hold only four or five men—or, at the very most, ten or twelve. Our ships in France hold four or five hundred, and even as many as a thousand.

"Other men make war by land, but in such vast numbers that, if drawn up in double file, they would extend farther than from here to Mississaquenk, although the distance exceeds twenty leagues. When he attacks, he is more terrible than the thunder; the earth trembles, the air and the sea are set on fire by the discharge of his Cannon; while he has been seen amid his squadrons, all covered with the blood of his foes, of whom he has slain so many with his sword that he does not count their scalps, but the rivers of blood which he sets flowing. So many prisoners of war does he lead away that he makes no account of them, letting them go about whither they will, to show that he does not fear them. No one now dares make war upon him, all nations beyond the sea having most submissively sued for peace. From all parts of the world people go to listen to his words and to admire him, and he alone decides all the affairs of the world.

"What shall I say of his wealth? You count yourselves rich when you have ten or twelve sacks of corn, some hatchets, glass beads, kettles, or other things of that sort. He has towns of his own, more in number than you have people in all these countries five hundred leagues around; while in each town there are warehouses containing enough hatchets to cut down all your forests, kettles to cook all your moose, and glass beads to fill all your cabins. His house is longer than from here to the head of the Sault"—that is, more than half a league—"and higher than the tallest of your trees; and it contains more families than the largest of your villages can hold."

The Father added much more of this sort, which was received with wonder by those people, who were all astonished to hear that there was any man on earth so great, rich, and powerful.

Following this speech, Monsieur de Saint Lusson took the sword, and stated to them in martial and eloquent language the reasons for which he had summoned them—and especially that he was sent to take possession of that region, receive them under the protection of the great King whose Panegyric they had just heard; and to form thenceforth but one land of their territories and ours. The whole ceremony was closed with a fine bonfire, which was lighted toward evening, and around which the *Te Deum* was sung to thank God, on behalf of those poor peoples, that they were now the subjects of so great and powerful a Monarch.

Tracks

in the Snow

"Sailors' Encampment" sounds like a misnomer, but it was an actuality for many years. The white-winged schooners, upbound through the St. Marys River, waited above Lake Munuscong for a fair wind, and while they waited the sailors left their close foc'sles for a camp on the river bank. Even the early steamers stopped there at nightfall, wanting daylight to run the unlighted channel. Around a campfire the crews had food and drink and storytelling.

One story was of the British schooner *Maria* arriving in the spring of 1803 at Fort St. Joseph, where the commander reported that his mutinous crew had threatened to kill him. He refused to leave the fort without a guard. Night and day, on the return voyage to the Detroit River, sentries patrolled the schooner's deck with muskets primed and loaded.

A grimmer tale was the stark journey of two British soldiers who deserted Fort St. Joseph in midwinter 1810. They started on foot for Mackinac Island, forty-five miles away, and they never reached their destination. The actual incident was recorded in a report of Captain Dawson to Lieutenant-Governor Gore, reprinted in the *Michigan Pioneer Collections*, vol. XXIII.

FORT ST. JOSEPH
21st April 1810

Sir

I have the honor to state for Your Excellencys information the particulars of a plot that has been formed at this Post by some of the soldiery while under my command, and altho I have been so fortunate as to frustrate it—in fact to put it completely down—I think it expedient to acquaint Your Excellency with the particulars at this crisis.—

Upon the 3ʳᵈ day of March last two men of my Detachment Con. Kearey and Patᵏ Myuagh privates deserted about ten o'clock in the morning, about four o'clock the same day Dennis Dogherty Taylor reported to Corporal Pendergart that he saw Kearey and Myuagh going towards the Detour at 10 o'clock that morning on their way to Michilimackinac which is nearly 45 miles distant from this Post.

I immediately ordered Ensign Dawson and Serjeant Drennan to proceed as far as the Detour which is 9 miles from hence, which they did and saw the tracks of those deserters in the snow—but being unprovided with snow shoes—or provisions, bunk &c. they returned, and on the same night Serjeant Drennan and an Indian accompanied by a man of the name of Whiting an Inhabitant pursued the deserters—on the 6ᵗʰ of March Serjeant Drennan returned and reported to me that about 4 o'clock on the morning of the 5ᵗʰ March they found Myuagh frozen dead opposite Goose Island about 30 miles from hence; nearly 9 miles further on they found Kearey quite insensible but still breathing. Their provisions being short they left Kearey in an Indian lodge for the purpose of getting Warmth and housing in charge of Whiting with directions to him to get Myuagh's body and have it drawn along with Kearey in a sleigh to St. Joseph's.

On the 7ᵗʰ of March a party of Indians arrived with Kearey who was much recovered but his hands and feet were frozen in a most dreadful manner since which time he has lost all his fingers and suffered amputation of both his legs, about eleven o'clock the same day another party of Indians arrived with the body of Myuagh, which I ordered to be interred immediately which was accordingly done.—

This disaster not having terminated here, I must now beg leave for Your Excellencys information to state the particulars as they since occurred, minutely—

All the vigilance I could observe did not enable me to find the cause of those mens having deserted—and from their uniformly professing they were perfectly satisfied and happy it was almost incredible the plan they had formed.—

On the 15ᵗʰ of March I was informed by Mary McCowly [wife to one McCowley Private] that she had heard through Drummer James McCahill that a number of men had formed a Plan of desertion and had actually taken a secret Oath to the following purport Viz.—

That they were not to have "discovered upon each other on pain of Death and that "they would support their scheme to the last" to effect their escape—that they were to have "broken open the King's Provision Store and that "if any person or persons were to have "attempted to resist or prevent their putting their plan into execution, "that they would pay no respect to persons, but would put every man "so resisting to" death.—

This I understand to be as near as possible the fact—The Information I received from Private Dogherty I beg leave to enclose a Copy of as taken *verblim* with his signature Witnessed—and a corroboration (if any now could be wanting) I had from Pat Kerr of the Rebellious and wanted dissaffection—which could only be frustrated by the greatest exertion and perspecuity so well had they formed their plan, and with so much caution—

On the 18th day of March I judged it expedient according to the information I had received from Dogherty to order Corpl Coffey and Mr Cadotte an Indian Interpreter with two Indians to take with them two of the ringleaders and another of a suspicious character to a place called the Chenouse 30 miles off where there were several good Indian Lodges which I was told could accomodate them—in order to have them separated as much as possible—and after their departure I immediately secured four more of those concerned.—

On the 20th of March Corporal Coffey arrived with his party; about nine o'clock at night Nesbitt came up to my Room and appeared very desperate—I put him into the Guard House went up to the Barrack Room where I took Byrne who made great resistance with much abusive language and attempted to get his bayonet to run me through but I seized him by the neck and put him into the Guard House.—

In consequence of this business a good deal of provision &c. was issued to the Indians who were employed.—

I cannot sufficiently express my approbation of Mr Cadotte the Indian Interpreters Conduct who took charge of the party as mentioned in the detail to the Chenouse, and was at all times ready to render service to His Majestys Government since I have known him, and I must also beg leave to say that he was at all times perfectly steady, and evinced a readiness and loyalty when employed on duty that I have not before witnessed in persons in his situation.—

I shall now only beg leave to acquaint Your Excellency that altho unfortunately there have been some men of my Company Wantonly Rebellious that I cannot express myself too strongly in the

praise of others—for instance—Serjeant Drennan, Corporals Pendergart, Lee & Coffey, with all the Protestants of my Company have
invariably conducted themselves with the most perfect correctness
and have essentially rendered Service by their alertness and Steadi-
ness in assisting to bring the unfortunate Delinquents to Justice.—

I have the honor to be

[with the greatest Respect]

Your Excellencys

Obedient Servant

THO. DAWSON

Capt 100 Regt

His Excellency Lieutenant-Governor Gore.—

HELEN HARDIE GRANT

Winter

in the North

In 1822 Henry Rowe Schoolcraft was appointed Indian agent on the Northwestern Frontiers, with headquarters at Sault Ste. Marie. There he lived for eleven years.

In the summer he traveled to distant tribes, journeying over Lake Superior in Mackinaw boat or Indian canoe and paddling up rivers that only the Indians knew. He traveled with feeling and imagination, seeing the country with the eyes of a scientist who was also a poet. In fact he wrote poems about the dark woods and the shining waters, and about the birchen canoe, the native craft which white men could imitate but could not improve:

> Its rim was with tender young roots woven round,
> Like a pattern of wicker-work rare;
> And it pressed on the waves with as lightsome a bound
> As a basket suspended in air.

In the long winter season Schoolcraft became another kind of explorer. While snow and cold besieged the little settlement at the Sault, he fed his stove with maple and his mind with literature, history and ethnology. Between wheedling and importunate visits from the Indians, he burrowed into Algonquin language and mythology. So he began his *Algic Researches,* while the ghostly aurora shimmered in the midnight sky and the candlelight gleamed in his study window.

At the Sault he became a warm friend of John Johnston, a cordial, generous Irish aristocrat and trader who had married the daughter of a Chippewa chief. In his second year in the North, Schoolcraft married the charming and delicate Jane Johnston, the first and the favorite of the trader's eight children. In his diary Schoolcraft wrote, "I have stumbled, as it were, on the only family in North West America who could, in Indian lore, have acted as my guide, philosopher and friend."

The following sketch of Schoolcraft's first seasons in the North is taken from a manuscript biography of *Schoolcraft of Old St. Marys* by Helen Hardie Grant of New York. Mrs. Grant has followed her subject through libraries across the country.

NOVEMBER BROUGHT SNOW and cold and icy winds. Huge gray clouds lowered over Lake Superior. The singing birds had gone, followed by swans, brant, cranes and, last of all, the ducks. The last vessel of the season was long since departed, the last mail. Colonel Brady left after the first snowfall, as did every belated visitor, every lingering trader. No one at all remained, the young agent suddenly realized, but the little number whose duty lay there. Soberly he anticipated the months to come.

To his satisfaction he found that the post's library was shelved in the agency beside his own Montreal stove! He read ravenously that first winter in the Upper Country, good Mr. Johnston's copy of the *Edinburgh Review* and his volumes of Johnson's *Lives of the Poets,* as well as various books of travel, Forster's *History of Northern Voyages,* those of Mr. Harmon revised with religious reflections by Mr. Haskell, and journeys as far removed as those of Herodotus and Mackenzie and Mungo Park. Each day at four he dined with the Johnston household and remained for the family worship which followed. It was dark before five o'clock.

But when the river at last froze over and communication became easier the winter's social life began. Mr. Siveright of the North West House gave a large party for the American officers, Schoolcraft, Johnston, and Ermatinger, another well-to-do trader with an Indian wife and a large family. There Henry Schoolcraft heard his first stirring tales of the North West Company and was inspired at last to read Mackenzie's *History of the Fur Trade,* the disputes between Lord Selkirk and the North West Company, and the *Report of Trials* during the contest between the Hudson's Bay Company and the North West that ended in their ultimate union.

Conversation was good, if only between Mr. Johnston and an officer or two gathered in the agency office, for it traveled the complete range of European politics. One day, for example, "Greece, Turkey and Russia, the state of Ireland, radicalism in England, the unhappy variance of the King and Queen, Charles Fox and so forth, were successively the object of remark."

On New Year's Eve an officer at the fort gave a dance which lasted till twelve o'clock; the Indians paid New Year's visits during the three succeeding days from eight o'clock until three; the *métis* messenger, the snowshoe "express," left for Detroit with a hundred outgoing letters in his charge. After several days at twenty-five degrees below zero, the thermometer rose to a mere ten below, and the intrepid Mr. Siveright came on snowshoes from the Canadian shore with dinner invitations for the next day. It is a bit difficult to tell from the circumlocutions of Schoolcraft's diary what really happened on that winter evening, but it is probable that he lost some money in a card game.

I have for some time felt that time devoted to these amusements in which I have never made much advance would be better given up to reading or to some inquiry from which I might hope to derive advantage. An incident this evening impressed me with this truth and I came home with a resolution that one source of them should no longer engross a moment of my time.

Harris, the author of *Hermes*, says, "It is certainly as easy to be a scholar as a gamester or any character equally illiberal and low."

January passed by in the perusal of Thiebault's *Anecdotes of Frederick the Great* and Marshall's *Life of Washington*. DeWitt Clinton had sent his young protégé *British Major's History of the Late War,* whereupon an anonymous eulogy of the character and administration of the governor of New York appeared in the tiny Sault paper, between poetry and prophecy regarding the dissolution of the seventeenth Congress in March and the date of the arrival of the first boat in April or May. Mr. Ermatinger gave a gay caribou dinner for a party of sixteen, Henry Schoolcraft among them.

After several formal and national toasts, we had Mr. Calhoun, Governor Cass, General Brown, Mr. Sibley, the representative of Michigan, Colonel Brady and Major Thayer, superintendent of the military academy. In coming home in the cariole, we all missed the balizes [pole-marker] and got completely upset and pitched into the snow.

An express, arriving at the end of January just before the temperature dropped to twenty-eight below, brought New York papers of as late date as the end of November, but after the garrison library was removed to the fort the agent was reduced at last to Holmes on *The Fulfillment of the Revelation of St. John,* which with its required transpositions of "church and state" for "air," "armies of northern invaders" for "hail storms," a month for thirty years and so forth, must have occupied him for some days. When the weather moderated, a party of gentlemen swung on snowshoes from the British garrison on Drummond's Island, some fifty miles, and there was a round of gaiety, dinners at the Johnstons' and Ermatingers', and at the quarters of Lieutenants Morton and Folger, a dance at Mr. Johnston's, a supper party with Captain Beal.

Late in February the second express arrived and with it the agent received animated inquiries from his sister Maria Eliza in Vernon.

> Who have you at the Sault who writes such pretty poetry as *The Death Song of an Indian Woman at the Grave of her Murdered Husband*? It is equal to your Indian Lament, *The Blackbirds are Singing on Michigan's Shore.* . . .

The poem, in the little newspaper circulated by the settlement, was written by "Captain Thompson's lady," a favorite chaperone, but the astute Maria may already have realized that she should be making inquiries for someone of the feminine persuasion at the Sault!

The end of March several carioles [light Canadian sleighs] of officers and ladies went down the river to Mrs. Johnston's sugar camp, where they watched the sap dripping into ox hides and boiling in twenty kettles over a huge bed of fire. There, too, they ate a picnic lunch augmented by maple sugar in every conceivable form and, with packages of the candy they had pulled, merrily returned to the Sault.

By April snow and ice had grown monotonous indeed. It was the twelfth before "horse trains" were unsafe upon the river. Then suddenly within a fortnight robins, bobolinks, and wild duck arrived and whitefish were caught in the rapids. Spring had come.

By May of 1823 General Brady down at the Madison Barracks did not share in Maria Eliza's mystification, for he was gaily writing Henry Schoolcraft to present his compliments to Mr. Johnston and all the family, and "also to Her." Lieutenant George Whistler had passed through on his way to Fort William and the Lake of the Woods. Charlotte Johnston's beautiful dark eyes had smiled upon them all, but it was with a roguish glance at Henry and Jane that she had sung;

> What is the matter with the young American?
> He crosses the river with tears in his eyes.
> He sees the young Ojibway girl preparing to leave the place.
> He sobs for his sweetheart because she is going away!
> But he will not sigh for long.
> As soon as he is out of sight, he will forget her.

Other young Americans were soon to write home rapturously about the charms of Charlotte and Jane. They found the latter

. . . a little taller and thinner but in other respect precisely like her sister. She has her face precisely. Her voice is feeble and tremulous, her utterance slow and distinct. There is something silvery about it. Mildness of expression and softness and delicacy of manners as well as of voice characterize her. She dresses with great taste and in all respects in the costume of our fashionables but wears leggins of black silk drawn and ruffled around the ankles, resembling those worn by our little girls. I think them ornamental.

You would never judge either from her complexion or language that her mother was a Chippewa. Except that her moderately high cheek bones, her dark and fine eye and breadth of jaw slightly indicate it, you would never believe it. . . . Nor would you, were you to hear her converse or see her beautiful and highly finished compositions in both prose and poetry.

But all of the surviving letters as well as Schoolcraft's published journals fail to note that on October 12, 1823, before another long, monotonous winter had settled down upon the Sault, dark-eyed Jane Johnston was definitely committed to his care by the Reverend Robert McMurtrie Laird, a Presbyterian minister who had just arrived at St. Marys.

But despite the happy marriage, community irritations were magnified as winter came on and the isolation increased. Friction arose between the agent and the commanding officer at the fort, who insisted that Schoolcraft as a justice of the peace prosecute all citizens who settled on the reserve and opened shops for the sale of liquor. On his part, Henry Schoolcraft seemed to feel that such action of his which would forbid the sale of liquor to whites was quite unlawful. By way of retaliation Major Cutler refused to erect until another year the quarters for the Indian agent which he was required to build.

The winter, however, both at the Johnston homestead and the agency office, passed quickly away. At the office, the Indians were frequent visitors until after New Year's, when Schoolcraft again settled down to work upon his travels in the valleys of the Miami and the Wabash. Of the Sault he wrote:

. . . tempests howled about us without diminishing our comforts. We stood often in the clear winter evenings to gaze at the splendid display of the Aurora Borealis. The cariole was sometimes put in requisition. We sometimes tied on the augim or snowshoe and ventured over drifts of snow whose depths rendered them impassable to a horse.

We assembled twice a week at a room to listen to the chaste preaching of a man of deep-toned piety and sound judgment, whose life and manners resembled an apostle's.

Since Jane's tenderness for her husband was mingled with anxiety regarding his want of religious conviction, she took him regularly to these services. Although the Reverend Mr. Laird departed in the spring as abruptly as he had come, his influence upon Henry Schoolcraft lingered. For years his scientific mind wrestled with the Old Testament legend of the creation of the world in seven days.

From Detroit the Rev. Mr. Laird wrote to Schoolcraft about the "truth of the Gospel of Jesus Christ," and the same mail brought word from Governor Cass on mundane matters. The agent had better come down to the city and bring with him his collection of Indian tales and a barrel of cherries for bounce. And enough liquor, he dictated, *must* go into Lake Superior to counteract the advances of the Hudson's Bay Company. The Kickapoos and Potawatomies of Illinois were growing cross and troublesome. Lewis Johnston now began the habit—so soon to be followed by his brothers—of calling upon Henry for a loan. In order further to strengthen the frontier, the adjutant general of the territory sent Schoolcraft a commission as captain of an independent company of militia, a measure which surely cannot have reduced his friction with the fort.

But the agent did not go down to Detroit. Too important an event was pending at St. Mary's: on June 27, 1824, his little son, William Henry was born. He was the idol of the household, the first grandchild, dearest Jane's boy. Old John Johnston's happiness overflowed in the tender little name he gave him, Penachense, the little American eaglet. It was Johnston who went down to Detroit in Henry's place, on his way to Toronto to present his claims to Lieutenant Governor Maitland.

No matter how irritating it may have been to the military to receive orders from a civilian locally entrenched in his position by marriage into the Sault's most influential family, it does seem as though the agent were in the right in that current quarrel of July, 1824. According to instructions, Schoolcraft had asked Major Enos Cutler to post a guard at the head of the portage to examine all traders' boats for liquor and to see their licenses or passports, and to examine the Indian canoes for liquor, too. No one was to enter "the closed lake" (Superior) without proper authority. Major Cutler countered with the fact that a trader was permitted to take in a private store of liquor and said that, while he preferred to post no guard, he would examine what the agent might think were really suspicious loads! Schoolcraft was forced to write again, pointing out that the second section of the Act of 1822 ordered that "the stores and packages of goods of *all* traders be searched."

Major Cutler spent an evening—perhaps in the company of pleasant Robert Stuart—brooding over the instructions of the Indian department, at that time occupied with Indian *trade*.

1. The license of each trader must be shown.
2. Kegs are to be counted and all without license detained.
3. No Indian is to go into the Lake without a passport.
4. No white is to enter the Lake as a hunter or trapper.
5. All liquor contrary to instruction is to be stored for future disposition according to law, but the trader is to be allowed to proceed with his other goods.

Cutler at last reluctantly agreed to post the guard and detain the boats, providing that the agent himself would make the required search, although he still somewhat sulkily maintained that he should know of whom Schoolcraft was especially suspicious. In carrying out his instructions from Washington, the agent was unable also to follow the governor's instructions to let enough liquor go into the Indian country to compete with the liquor of the Hudson's Bay Company. Several times during the succeeding winter he heard from George Johnston up on the Grand Marais that the Whitefish Lake Indians were going north to Fort William to trade, and he wondered if it were the liquor or long habit that took them there.

Meanwhile household life went on beside the rushing river. From a Detroit merchant Schoolcraft ordered a bureau, bed, washstand, dining table, tea table, and work stand, to be shipped on the *Tiger*, once the Indians' iron bars, tobacco, nails, calico, strouds and net twine were safely dispatched.

Woman of the

Bright Foam

To Sault Ste. Marie in 1837 came two notable visitors from England, and each left a record of the place. Captain Frederick Marryat habitually traveled in bad humor. Journeying from Mackinac to the Sault in a *canot du nord* driven by five sweating *voyageurs,* he described his paddlers as "lazy, gluttonous scoundrels." In Sault Ste. Marie he found about fifty houses, mostly of logs, inhabited by half-breeds. Having been entertained at Mackinac by Schoolcraft and his half-Indian wife (Schoolcraft found this Englishman "ill-mannered and conceited beyond all bounds") he stated that "the females generally improve, and the males degenerate, from the mingling of strains." He was as much interested in the horses as the humans at the Soo; the horses, he said, fed upon fish, and one horse habitually patroled the wharves watching for a chance to seize a fish from the canoes and run off with it in his mouth. Returning by canoe to Mackinac, Marryat and a couple of other passengers camped on a river meadow heaped with fresh cut hay. To soften their beds they carried armfuls into their tent, and then found the hay swarming with mosquitoes. Trying to smoke them out, the travelers set fire to the hay and nearly burned down their tent. So, itching and smarting, Marryat left the North country.

A more gracious visitor was Mrs. Anna Jameson, wife of the Attorney General of Upper Canada. To see and report the Lake Superior country she came up the lakes in 1837 in the steamer *Thomas Jefferson,* reading Alexander Henry's *Travels* as an introduction to the primitive North. Her companions included the Bishop of Michigan, a son of Daniel Webster, and General Hugh Brady; a hundred Norwegian and Irish immigrants along with their horses and cattle were traveling on deck. At Mackinac she was delighted to find scores of Indian camps along the half-moon shore and to share the comforts of the rambling agency house with Henry Schoolcraft and his charming half-Chippewa wife. Going on to Sault Ste. Marie, she traveled with Mrs. Schoolcraft whose relatives all lived there.

At the Sault Mrs. Jameson was the guest of the Rev. William MacMurray, missionary to the Indians on the British side; his wife was a sister of Jane Johnston Schoolcraft. During her pleasant stay at the village Mrs. Jameson became the first white woman to run the rapids in a canoe—a trip that won her a name, as she reported with satisfaction in her *Winter Studies and Summer Rambles,* published two years later.

I WAS SITTING LAST FRIDAY, at sultry noon-tide, under the shadow of a schooner which had just anchored alongside the little [Mackinac Island] pier—sketching and dreaming—when up came a messenger, breathless, to say that a boat was going off for the Sault Ste. Marie, in which I could be accommodated with a passage. Now this was precisely what I had been wishing and waiting for, and yet I heard the information with an emotion of regret. I had become every day more attached to the society of Mrs. Schoolcraft—more interested about her; and the idea of parting, and parting suddenly, took me by surprise, and was anything but agreeable. On reaching the house, I found all in movement, and learned, to my inexpressible delight, that my friend would take the opportunity of paying a visit to her mother and family, and, with her children, was to accompany me on my voyage.

We had but one hour to prepare packages, provisions, everything—and in one hour all was ready.

This voyage of two days was to be made in a little Canadian bateau, rowed by five voyageurs from the Sault. The boat might have carried fifteen persons, hardly more, and was rather clumsy in form. The two ends were appropriated to the rowers, baggage, and provisions; in the centre there was a clear space, with a locker on each side, on which we sat or reclined, having stowed away in them our smaller and more valuable packages. This was the internal arrangement.

The distance to the Sault or, as the Americans call it, the Sou, is not more than thirty miles over land, as the bird flies; but the whole region being one mass of tangled forest and swamp, infested with bears and mosquitoes, it is seldom crossed but in winter, and in snow shoes. The usual route by water is ninety-four miles.

At three o'clock in the afternoon, with a favourable breeze, we launched forth on the lake, and having rowed about a mile from the shore, the little square sail was hoisted, and away we went merrily over the blue waves. . . .

I cannot, I dare not, attempt to describe to you the strange sensation one has, thus thrown for a time beyond the bounds of civilized humanity, or indeed any humanity; nor the wild yet solemn reveries which come over one in the midst of this wilderness of woods and waters. All was so solitary, so grand in its solitude, as if nature unviolated sufficed to herself. Two days and nights the solitude was unbroken; not a trace of social life, not a human being, not a canoe, not even a deserted wigwam, met our view. Our little boat held on its way over the placid lake and among green tufted islands; and we its inmates, two women, differing in clime, nation, complexion, strangers to each other but a few days ago, might have fancied ourselves alone in a new-born world.

We landed to boil our kettle, and breakfast on a point of the island of St. Joseph's. This most beautiful island is between thirty and forty miles in length, and nearly a hundred miles in circumference, and towards the centre the land is high and picturesque. They tell me that on the other side of the island there is a settlement of whites and Indians. Another large island, Drummond's Isle, was for a short time in view. We had also a settlement here, but it was unaccountably surrendered to the Americans. If now you look at the map, you will wonder, as I did, that in retaining St. Joseph's and the Manitoulin islands, we gave up Drummond's Island. Both these islands had forts and garrisons during the war.

By the time breakfast was over, the children had gathered some fine strawberries; the heat had now become almost intolerable, and unluckily we had no awning. The men rowed languidly, and we made but little way; we coasted along the south shore of St. Joseph's, through fields of rushes, miles in extent, across Lake George, and Muddy Lake; (the name, I thought, must be a libel, for it was as clear as crystal and as blue as heaven; but they say that, like a sulky temper, the least ruffle of wind turns it as black as ditchwater, and it does not subside again in a hurry,) and then came a succession of openings spotted with lovely islands, all solitary. The sky was without a cloud, a speck—except when the great fish-eagle was descried sailing over its blue depths—the water without a wave. We were too hot and too languid to converse. Nothing disturbed the deep noon-tide stillness, but the dip of the oars, or the spring and splash of a sturgeon as he leapt from the surface of the lake, leaving a circle of little wavelets spreading around. All the islands we passed were so woody, and so infested with mosquitoes, that we could not land and light our fire, till we reached the entrance of St. Marys River, between Neebish island and the mainland.

Here was a well-known spot, a sort of little opening on a flat shore, called the Encampment, because a party of boatmen coming down from Lake Superior, and camping here for the night, were surprised by the frost, and obliged to remain the whole winter till the opening of the ice, in the spring. After rowing all this hot day till seven o'clock against the wind, (what there was of it,) and against the current coming rapidly and strongly down from Lake Superior, we did at length reach this promised harbour of rest and refreshment. Alas! there was neither for us; the moment our boat touched the shore, we were enveloped in a cloud of mosquitoes. Fires were lighted instantly, six were burning in a circle at once; we were well nigh suffocated and smoke-dried—all in vain. At last we left the voyageurs to boil the kettle, and retreated to our boat, desiring them to make us fast to a tree by a long rope; then, each of us taking an oar—I only wish you could have seen us—we pushed off from the land, while the children were sweeping away the enemy with green boughs. This being done, we commenced supper, really half famished, and were too much engrossed to look about us. Suddenly we were again surrounded by our adversaries; they came upon us in swarms, in clouds, in myriads, entering our eyes, our noses, our mouths, stinging till the blood followed. We had, unawares, and while absorbed in our culinary operations, drifted into the shore, got entangled among the roots of trees, and were with difficulty extricated, presenting all the time a fair mark and a rich banquet for our detested tormentors. The dear children cried with agony and impatience, and but for shame I could almost have cried too.

I had suffered from these plagues in Italy; you too, by this time, may probably know what they are in the southern countries of the old world; but 'tis a jest, believe me, to encountering a forest full of them in these wild regions. I had heard much, and much was I forewarned, but never could have conceived the torture they can inflict, nor the impossibility of escape, defence, or endurance. Some amiable person who took an especial interest in our future welfare, in enumerating the torments prepared for hardened sinners, assures us that they will be stung by mosquitoes all made of brass, and as large as black beetles—he was an ignoramus and a bungler; you may credit me, that the brass is quite an unnecessary improvement, and the increase of size equally superfluous. Mosquitoes as they exist in this upper world are as pretty and perfect a plague as the most ingenious amateur sinner-tormentor ever devised. Observe, that a mosquito does not sting like a wasp, or a gad-fly; he has a long proboscis like an awl, with which he bores your veins and pumps the life-blood out of you, leaving venom and fever behind. Enough of mosquitoes—I will never again do more than allude to them; only they are enough to make Philosophy go hang herself, and Patience swear like a Turk or a trooper.

Well, we left this most detestable and inhospitable shore as soon as possible, but the enemy followed us, and we did not soon get rid of them; night came on, and we were still twenty miles below the Sault.

Night on Lake Huron

I offered an extra gratuity to the men, if they would keep to their oars without interruption; and then, fairly exhausted, lay down on my locker and blanket. But whenever I woke from uneasy, restless slumbers, there was Mrs. Schoolcraft, bending over her sleeping children, and waving off the mosquitoes, singing all the time a low, melancholy Indian song; while the northern lights were streaming and dancing in the sky, and the fitful moaning of the wind, the gathering clouds, and chilly atmosphere, foretold a change of weather. This would have been the *comble de malheur*. When daylight came, we passed Sugar Island, where immense quantities of maple sugar are made every spring, and just as the rain began to fall in earnest, we arrived at the Sault Ste. Marie. On one side of the river, Mrs. Schoolcraft was welcomed by her mother; and on the other, my friends, the MacMurrays, received me with delighted and delightful hospitality. I went to bed—oh! the luxury!—and slept for six hours. . . .

This river of St. Marys is, like the Detroit and the St. Clair, already described, properly a strait, the channel of communication between Lake Superior and Lake Huron. About ten miles higher up, the great Ocean-lake narrows to a point; then, forcing a channel through the high lands, comes rushing along till it meets with a downward ledge, or cliff, over which it throws itself in foam and fury, tearing a path for its billows through the rocks. The descent is about twenty-seven feet in three quarters of a mile, but the rush begins above, and the tumult continues below the fall, so that, on the whole, the eye embraces an expanse of white foam measuring about a mile each way, the effect being exactly that of the ocean breaking on a rocky shore; not so terrific, nor on so large a scale, as the rapids of Niagara, but quite as beautiful—quite as animated. . . .

The more I looked upon those glancing, dancing rapids, the more resolute I grew to venture myself in the midst of them. George Johnston went to seek a fit canoe and a dexterous steersman, and meantime I strolled away to pay a visit to Wayish-ky's family, and made a sketch of their lodge, while pretty Zah-gah-see-gah-qua, held the umbrella to shade me from the sun.

The canoe being ready, I went to the upper end of the portage, and we launched into the river. It was a small fishing canoe about ten feet long, quite new, and light and elegant and buoyant as a bird on the waters. I reclined on a mat at the bottom, Indian fashion, (there are no seats in a genuine Indian canoe;) in a minute we were within the verge of the rapids, and down we went with a whirl and a splash!—the white surge leaping around me—over me. The Indian with astonishing dexterity kept the head of the canoe to the breakers, and somehow or other we danced through them. I could see, as I looked over the edge of the canoe, that the passage between the rocks was sometimes not more than two feet in width, and we had to turn sharp angles—a touch of which would have sent us to destruction—all this I could see through the transparent eddying waters, but I can truly say I had not even a momentary sensation of fear, but rather a giddy, breathless, delicious excitement. I could even admire the beautiful attitude of a fisher, past whom we swept as we came to the bottom. The whole affair, from the moment I entered the canoe till I reached the landing-place, occupied seven minutes, and the distance is about three quarters of a mile.

My Indians were enchanted, and when I reached home, my good friends were not less delighted at my exploit: they told me I was the first European female who had ever performed it, and assuredly I shall not be the last. I recommend it as an exercise before breakfast. Two glasses of champagne could not have made me more tipsy and more self-complacent! As for my Neengai, she laughed, clapped her hands, and embraced me several times. I was declared duly initiated, and adopted into the family by the name of Wah, sah, ge, wah, no, qua. They had already called me among themselves, in reference to my complexion and my traveling propensities, O, daw, yaun, gee, the fair changing moon, or rather, the fair moon which changes her place; but now, in compliment to my successful achievement, Mrs. Johnston bestowed this new appellation, which I much prefer. It signifies the bright foam, or more properly, with the feminine adjunct qua, the woman of the bright foam; and by this name I am henceforth to be known among the Chippewas.

JANET LEWIS

The Battle of

the Millrace

The first canal at Sault Ste. Marie was built in 1797 by the fur traders of the North West Company. It was a cleared channel half a mile long leading to a thirty-eight-foot lock, just big enough to float a modern freighter's lifeboat. Birch bark canoes with their four tons of freight were raised nine feet in that stone chamber and towed by oxen to the head of the falls. A small thing but their own, it saved the *voyageurs* many a grunting portage until American troops destroyed it in the War of 1812.

Twenty-five years later, a few months after Michigan's statehood in 1837, young Governor Mason launched a bold program of public improvements, including a canal from Lake St. Clair to the Kalamazoo River linking lower Lake Huron and Lake Michigan in a short cut to Chicago. This grandiose project never got started. Another proposal was a canal at St. Marys with a lock large enough to accommodate the schooners that carried the lake trade. This looked like a sure thing. No one foresaw an armed clash between the State of Michigan and the U.S. Army.

In the path of the projected canal lay a narrow millrace leading to Fort Brady. When the fort was established in 1823 its soldiers built a raceway and a sawmill to provide their lumber. Since then the sawmill had burned down. In 1839 the raceway was quite useless, but it was government property and the commander meant to defend it.

In the clash of authority the canal project was defeated by the U.S. garrison—its chief accomplishment that year. Not until 1855 would a ship canal link Lake Superior with the lower lakes.

The comic opera on a May morning in 1839 is faithfully described by Janet Lewis (Mrs. Yvor Winters) in *The Invasion,* a narrative of the Johnston family of St. Marys.

THE GARRISON of Fort Brady had a way of lounging up and down the inclosure in flannel jackets and shirt sleeves, muskets over their shoulders, looking, as Mrs. Jameson remarked to Charlotte McMurray, more like a troop of plowboys going to shoot sparrows than the defenders of a nation. However, on the morning of May 13, 1839, a company of thirty regulars under Captain Johnson left Fort Brady, fife playing, muskets and bayonets shining, in a rapid and orderly march, and, proceeding in a westerly direction along the Portage road, arrived at a spot near the upper end of the rapids where, on the banks of a small mill race, some fifty workmen with shovels and picks, according to the instructions of Contractors Weeks, Smith, and Driggs, of Buffalo, were making the first excavations for the canal and locks which a sanguine State government had considered warranted by the increasing trade with the upper peninsula. There were to be three locks tandem, each with a lift of six feet, each measuring a hundred feet in length, thirty-two in width, ten in depth, and approached by a canal seventy-five feet wide. These gentlemen had undertaken to do the work for $112,544.80, the estimated cost, and Mr. Weeks had imported his men, implements, rations, and other necessary equipment in the schooner *Eliza Ward*, seventy tons burthen, arriving at the rapids on May 11.

It was a fine day for the inauguration of such an undertaking. The rapids, swollen with melted snow and ice, raced and tumbled and flung their wreaths of foam into the sweet spring air, and at their foot mallards, green-winged teal, helldivers, and little grebe splashed and dove and called to each other. Captain Johnson halted his regiment with drawn swords upon the brink of the mill race and called upon the crew of workmen to disperse. A short but pithy correspondence having passed the previous day, which was Sunday, between Captain Johnson and Mr. Weeks, the issues were well defined, the workmen had received their orders, and were not surprised to be thus interrupted, and, while they stood to their picks, and the thirty regulars flourished their sabers, briefly, the situation was this.

Mr. Weeks, surveying the ground in a leisured stroll on Saturday evening, had observed that the line of the canal which was stipulated in the contract of Smith and Driggs of Buffalo crossed an already existent canal serving as mill race to the United States Army sawmill, and had on Sunday sent a note to the Commander at Fort Brady explaining that it would be necessary to check the flow of water through the mill race in order to construct the lock canal. The Commander, strong in the possession of a certain letter from the War Department, informed Mr. Weeks that he could not tolerate any interference with the highly important mill race. The letter in question was from the Acting Quartermaster General, and read as follows: "It could not, it is presumed, have been the intention of the Legislature of Michigan in contracting for the opening of the canal around the rapids of St. Marys, authorized by that body, to interfere with the improvements made by the United States at your post, amongst which the mill race is regarded as one of the greatest importance. You will therefore apprize the contractor that he cannot be allowed, in the execution of his contract, to interfere in any way with that work." On Monday morning Mr. Weeks instructed his men to commence work at the point of intersection of these disputed waterways. And on Monday morning Captain Johnson, since the foreman of Mr. Week's gang did not disperse his men nor cease work, engaged in a hand-to-hand battle with the foreman, wrested his spade from him, and, resolutely backed by his regiment, drove the fifty workmen from the field. And that was the end of the proposed ship canal and locks, for the year 1839 at least, and for the twelve years to follow.

The driver of an oxcart which was conveying a load of hay and flour to the upper end of the portage, observed the battle and applauded. Before nightfall the action was well known in town, and not so well approved. Mr. Weeks, having been forcibly prevented from fulfilling his contract, considered it canceled, and dismissed his men, who, having nothing else to do, went fishing, and by the first of June were causing not inconsiderable competition and damage to the fishing business of the American Fur Company. For since beaver had grown scarce, the American Fur Company was shipping the incomparable whitefish by the thousand, and the oily and indigestible but none the less valued siscowet, three hundred barrels at a shipment, to Detroit and other ports down the lakes. To the annoyance of disappointment thus was added the annoyance of fifty free-lance fishermen, and members of the American Fur Company were mean enough to remind Captain Johnson that the highly important mill race had been out of use for a number of years, in fact, ever since the sawmill had gone up in flames. The United States Army seemed in no hurry to rebuild the sawmill.

LEWIS MARVILL

Voyage

of the *Independence*

Before the season of 1845 three small schooners, totaling a hundred tons, carried the commerce of the greatest of the lakes. But in that busy summer three sailing vessels and a steamer were hauled around the falls, and the tonnage on Lake Superior was six times greater.

The pioneer steamer on the "closed lake" was the *Independence,* a black little tub with two rotary engines and one sooty mast jutting above the smokestack; she was more pushy and less graceful than the tall white schooners. She had been built, it was said, to load Great Lakes grain for Liverpool, but her bunkers held barely enough coal to get her halfway across the Atlantic. So she splashed up to Lake Superior and became famous there.

The *Independence* survived seven seasons on the lonely, uncharted, unlighted lake, before her boilers blew out in 1853. She made some memorable trips, but none more risky than her first voyage, with a cabin full of miners and a hold full of blasting powder, late in the season of 1845.

One of her crew recalled that trip nearly forty years later. His account was published in the *Detroit Post and Tribune* on March 26, 1882.

I NOTICED A COMMUNICATION from your Marquette correspondent some time ago, in which he referred to the old hulk of the steamer *Julia Palmer,* now lying at that place, and made the remark that she was the first steamer that ever plowed Lake Superior; which is an error, and he has been misinformed. I have waited thus long to see it corrected, but I don't think it has met the eye of the other survivors of that trip—if there are any left.

Therefore, before I too, pass away, and while my memory yet serves me, I will correct the statement and give a short history of that memorable first trip by steam on Lake Superior.

My memory carries me back to the spring of 1845, or more than one-third of a century, and I have a vivid recollection of standing on Dorr & Webb's dock in Detroit early in that spring, watching the process of transforming a little tub of a sloop of about fifteen tons, into a fore-and-after called the *Ocean*. Said sloop had a history, she having capsized once or twice and drowned part of her crew. They thought they could disguise her so as to get a crew to man her. My funds being rather low I determined to ship if I could, and ship I did. We took in a cargo of fish for Sandusky and Milan, Ohio, and in due time sailed for those ports, and returned without any serious mishaps. We then received orders to fit up for Lake Superior, which we accordingly did, but I, being slightly indisposed when we got ready, could not proceed with the vessel, which sailed without me.

Some time in June, I think, the same firm that owned the *Ocean* bought and fitted up the topsail schooner *Merchant* of about seventy-five tons, Captain John Watson, for the same trade, *i.e.*, Lake Superior, and I, being determined to visit that famous lake, shipped on her, with the understanding that I might join my own ship (the *Ocean*) at the Sault if I felt so disposed. In due time we took on board all the necessary materials for taking both vessels over the rapids, *i.e.*, the *Ocean* and *Merchant*, and reached the Sault, where we found the *Ocean* waiting for us. We fell to and jerked her over in short meter, and then tackled the larger one, the *Merchant*. They were both taken over on rollers the same as buildings are sometimes moved. When we had the *Merchant* about half way across, word came that a steamer had just arrived from Chicago, with all the rigging on board, to be taken over the rapids. A few days after, a misunderstanding arose among the crew of the *Merchant*, and a part of them quit and left her. Hearing that they were in want of a porter on board the newly arrived steamer *Independence*, then lying at McKnight's dock getting ready to be hauled over, I applied and got the berth of porter and immediately began my duties as such. Everything being in readiness the ship was hauled out of water, and began its transit across the neck of land forming the rapids. In the meantime I was promoted to head waiter in the cabin. No mishaps occurring, the process of hauling progressed slowly but surely, and in about seven weeks we were again launched in the river at the head of the falls. In the meantime the schooner *Napoleon* of about 150 tons was being put together (her whole works having been got out and shipped there ready) and she was launched a short time before the *Independence*, and so was the *Merchant*, she having stuck in the process of launching, which caused considerable delay. By this time it had got to be quite late in the fall and it began to be feared that we would not be able to make the trip before we were froze in. On the strength of this the steward and cook, both belonging in Philadelphia, quit and went home. I was then left alone to do the cooking and see to the cabin, for two or three days. We then found a cook and everything went lovely again, and I had to fill the place of steward and waiter for the balance of the trip. In due time we got a mixed cargo and were ready to sail for up the lakes, but we didn't just then. The passengers came on board, and among them was a family named Spencer with a very sick child, who lingered a day or two and died, on whose account we delayed sailing until after the burial. We again got ready and this time sailed with a crew of fourteen all told, composed of the following, as near as I can recollect them: Albert Averill, captain; Samuel Moody, chief mate; Thomas Richie, chief engineer; Rufus Durham, assistant engineer; Captain Stanard, pilot; myself as steward, and Stafford (forget given name) as cook, two firemen and six deck hands of mixed nationality, comprised of Greek, Scotch, Irish, Yankee, and English. Only one of these I remember by name, a little Englishman, James Bendrey, who afterwards became well known on the lakes. I do not remember how many passengers we had, but distinctly remember that C. C. Douglass was one of them. He was then in charge of the Cliff mine at Eagle River, the only one of them that was then being worked to amount to anything, and also the Spencer family in the employ of Mr. Douglass.

As was before stated, we steamed up the lake and the first place we touched at was Copper Harbor, or Fort Wilkins (no such place as Marquette being thought of), where we found a small garrison and two or three log huts. The next in order was Eagle Harbor, where there were a few prospectors, and then on to Eagle River, where we discharged the most of our cargo, but before we could throw off some fifty kegs of powder the wind raised from the northwest and kicked up such a sea that we had to weigh anchor and leave. We shaped our course for La Pointe, but made poor headway, the wind being almost ahead. We, however, persevered till we got within sight of the Apostle islands, when the wind freshened into a gale and we had to turn about and run before it and make for the lee of Keweenaw point, the nearest harbor that we dared enter with safety. In the meantime the seas got running so high that it tossed our little steamer like a shell and rolled so heavy that the stoves broke loose from their moorings and tumbled all over the cabin, scattering fire all over the floor. When it is remembered that it was not generally known among passengers and crew that we had 50 kegs of powder aboard it made rather lively work for us straightening things up. We succeeded in reaching our objective point in safety, where we cast anchor and laid by for three or four days, waiting for fair weather, repairing and laying in a stock of wood, which we had to chop and take off in our yawl boat—rather slow but sure work. We again set sail, and this time having favorable weather, we succeeded in reaching Eagle River, where we bade good-by to our dangerous cargo (powder) and where some of us strolled up to the Cliff mine and there saw the first stamp mill (rather a primitive one) in operation in that now famous region. Returning on board we again steamed up the lake to La Pointe, our final destination (no such a place as Ontonagon then being thought of), which we reached in safety and gave the natives a dreadful scare with the appearance of our craft, and the noise of our steam whistle.

Our trip up the lake being now accomplished, we started on our return to the Sault, which we reached in safety. The season being now far advanced we immediately proceeded to dismantle the steamer and laid her up for the winter, in company with the following named crafts, which then constituted the available fleet of that greatest of all great lakes: The *Ocean,* about fifteen tons, the *Chippewa,* about twenty tons, the *Algonquin,* about thirty tons, the *Swallow,* about forty tons, the *Merchant,* about seventy-five tons, the *Napoleon,* about one hundred and fifty tons, and the *Independence* about three hundred and sixty-five tons. The first steamer that ever ploughed Lake Superior thus ended that memorable first trip by steam to the mining regions. We found below the falls the steamer *Baltimore,* which was either hauled over in the winter or early spring. The *Napoleon* was also fitted up the next summer with engines.

So you see that the *Julia Palmer* was not the first nor second, and I doubt the third, steamer on Lake Superior. We were fortunate to find a small topsail schooner, the very last of the season, on which the most of us took passage for Detroit and civilization.

WILLIAM CULLEN BRYANT

Journey

to the Soo

In 1846 the lonely village of Sault Ste. Marie became a stirring place. Discovery of the Cliff Copper Mine, a year before, brought a rush of fortune-seekers on their way to Lake Superior. From the Soo a dozen small vessels, mostly schooners, carried men and goods to Copper Harbor. In the village, restlessly awaiting transportation, were travelers, speculators, surveyors, engineers, financiers (Bryant recognized two men from Wall Street), along with prospectors, packers and footloose adventurers.

With this rush of life the town's two small hotels were overflowing. Tents sprang up around the village and at night the riverbank twinkled with campfires. Above the roar of the rapids rose voices of revelry. Said a traveler, "The boys had to keep up their spirits while waiting for a ride to the copper mines."

All day restless men roamed past the mission church and the log stockade of Fort Brady, past the millrace on the site of the present MacArthur Lock, along Portage Street with its rows of shops and stores and trading posts, and past the Chippewa huts beside the swirling river. Above the rapids lay a steamboat, but she wasn't loading. Earlier that season the *Julia Palmer* had been hauled over the portage; launched in the upper river, she promptly went aground. Now they were awaiting machinery from Cleveland to get her off.

One of the visitors in that lively season was William Cullen Bryant. When he looked at the dark Laurentian Hills across the river, the author of *Thanatopsis* was reminded of the Berkshire forests of his boyhood. But this was a wilder, vaster country.

Bryant could not wait for the *Julia Palmer* to be floated, and so he did not see the copper country. He took the steamer *General Scott* to Mackinac Island and sailed down the lakes on the *St. Louis*. Back in his newspaper office in New York he assembled his *Letters of a Traveller* for publication. They included sketches of France, Italy, Ireland and the West Indies, but no place seemed as distant as Sault Ste. Marie.

SAULT STE. MARIE, *August* 13, 1846

W HEN WE LEFT CHICAGO in the steamer, the other morning, all the vessels in the port had their flags displayed at half-mast in token of dissatisfaction with the fate of the harbor bill. You may not recollect that the bill set apart half a million of dollars for the construction or improvement of various harbors of the lakes, and authorized the deepening of the passages through the St. Clair Flats, now intricate and not quite safe, by which these bulky steamers make their way from the lower lakes to the upper. The people of the lake region had watched the progress of the bill through Congress with much interest and anxiety, and congratulated each other when at length it received a majority of votes in both houses. The President's veto turned these congratulations into expressions of disappointment which are heard on all sides, sometimes expressed with a good deal of energy. But, although the news of the veto reached Chicago two or three days before we left the place, nobody had seen the message in which it was contained. Perhaps the force of the President's reasonings will reconcile the minds of people here to the disappointment of their hopes.

It was a hot August morning as the steamer *Wisconsin,* an unwieldy bulk, dipping and bobbing upon the small waves, and trembling at every stroke of the engine, swept out into the lake. The southwest wind during the warmer portion of the summer months is a sort of Sirocco in Illinois. It blows with considerable strength, but passing over an immense extent of heated plains it brings no coolness. It was such an air that accompanied us on our way north from Chicago; and as the passengers huddled into the shady places outside of the state-rooms on the upper deck, I thought of the flocks of quails I had seen gasping in the shadow of the rail-fences on the prairies.

People here expose themselves to a draught of air with much less scruple than they do in the Atlantic states. "We do not take cold by it," they said to me, when I saw them sitting in a current of wind, after perspiring freely. If they do not take cold, it is odds but they take something else, a fever perhaps, or what is called a bilious attack. The vicissitudes of climate at Chicago and its neighborhood are more sudden and extreme than with us, but the inhabitants say that they are not often the cause of catarrhs, as in the Atlantic states. Whatever may be the cause, I have met with no person since I came to the West, who appeared to have a catarrh. From this region perhaps will hereafter proceed singers with the clearest pipes.

Some forty miles beyond Chicago we stopped for half an hour

at Little Fort, one of those flourishing little towns which are springing up on the lake shore, to besiege future Congresses for money to
build their harbors. This settlement has started up in the woods
within the last three or four years, and its cluster of roofs, two of
the broadest of which cover respectable-looking hotels, already
makes a considerable figure when viewed from the lake. We passed
to the shore over a long platform of planks framed upon two rows
of posts or piles planted in the sandy shallows. "We make a port in
this manner on any part of the western shore of the lake," said a
passenger, "and convenient ports they are, except in very high
winds. On the eastern shore, the coast of Michigan, they have not
this advantage; the ice and the northwest winds would rend such a
wharf as this in pieces. On this side too, the water of the lake,
except when an east wind blows, is smoother than on the Michigan
coast, and the steamers therefore keep under the shelter of this
bank.". . .

It was not till about one o'clock of the second night after leaving
Chicago, that we landed at Mackinaw, and after an infinite deal of
trouble in getting our baggage together, and keeping it together,
we were driven to the Mission House, a plain, comfortable old
wooden house, built thirty or forty years since, by a missionary
society, and now turned into an hotel. Beside the road, close to the
water's edge, stood several wigwams of the Potawottamies, pyramids of poles wrapped around with rush matting, each containing a
family asleep. The place was crowded with people on their way to
the mining region of Lake Superior, or returning from it, and we
were obliged to content ourselves with narrow accommodations for
the night.

At half-past seven the next morning we were on our way to the
Sault Ste. Marie, in the little steamer *General Scott*. The wind was
blowing fresh, and a score of persons who had intended to visit the
Sault were withheld by the fear of seasickness, so that half a dozen
of us had the steamer to ourselves. In three or four hours we found
ourselves gliding out of the lake, through smooth water, between
two low points of land covered with firs and pines into the west
strait. We passed Drummond's Island, and then coasted St. Joseph's
Island, on the woody shore of which I was shown a solitary house.
There I was told lives a long-nosed Englishman, a half-pay officer,
with two wives, sisters, each the mother of a numerous offspring.
This English polygamist has been more successful in seeking solitude than in avoiding notoriety. The very loneliness of his habitation on the shore causes it to be remarked, and there is not a passenger who makes the voyage to the Sault, to whom his house is not
pointed out, and his story related. It was hinted to me that he had a

third wife in Toronto, but I have my private doubts of this part of the story, and suspect that it was thrown in to increase my wonder.

Beyond the island of St. Joseph we passed several islets of rock with fir-trees growing from the clefts. Here, in summer, I was told, the Indians often set up their wigwams, and subsist by fishing. There were none in sight as we passed, but we frequently saw on either shore the skeletons of the Chippewa habitations. These consist, not like those of the Potawottamies, of a circle of sticks placed in the form of a cone, but of slender poles bent into circles, so as to make an almost regular hemisphere, over which, while it serves as a dwelling, birch-bark and mats of bulrushes are thrown.

On the western side of the passage, opposite to St. Joseph's Island, stretches the long coast of Sugar Island, luxuriant with an extensive forest of the sugar-maple. Here the Indians manufacture maple-sugar in the spring. I inquired concerning their agriculture.

"They plant no corn nor squashes," said a passenger, who had resided for some time at the Sault; "they will not ripen in this climate; but they plant potatoes in the sugar-bush, and dig them when the spring opens. They have no other agriculture; they plant no beans as I believe the Indians do elsewhere."

A violent squall of wind and rain fell upon the water just as we entered that broad part of the passage which bears the name of Muddy Lake. In ordinary weather the waters are here perfectly pure and translucent, but now their agitation brought up the loose earth from the shallow bottom, and made them as turbid as the Missouri, with the exception of a narrow channel in the midst where the current runs deep. Rocky hills now began to show themselves to the east of us; we passed the sheet of water known by the name of Lake George, and came to a little river which appeared to have its source at the foot of a precipitous ridge on the British side. It is called Garden River, and a little beyond it, on the same side, lies Garden Village, inhabited by the Indians. It was now deserted, the Indians having gone to attend a great assemblage of their race, held on one of the Manitoulin islands, where they are to receive their annual payments from the British government. Here were log-houses, and skeletons of wigwams, from which the coverings had been taken. An Indian, when he travels, takes with him his family and his furniture, the matting for his wigwam, his implements for hunting and fishing, his dogs and cats, and finds a home wherever he finds poles for a dwelling. A tornado had recently passed over the Garden Village. The numerous girdled-trees which stood on its little clearing, had been twisted off midway or near the ground by the wind, and the roofs had, in some instances, been lifted from the cabins.

At length, after a winding voyage of sixty miles, between wild banks of forest, in some places smoking with fires, in some looking as if never violated either by fire or steel, with huge carcasses of trees mouldering on the ground, and venerable trees standing over them, bearded with streaming moss, we came in sight of the white rapids of the Sault Sainte Marie. We passed the humble cabins of the half-breeds on either shore, with here and there a round wigwam near the water; we glided by a white chimney standing behind a screen of fir-trees, which, we were told, had belonged to the dwelling of Tanner, who himself set fire to his house the other day, before murdering Mr. [James] Schoolcraft, and in a few minutes were at the wharf of this remotest settlement of the northwest.

A crowd had assembled on the wharf of the American village at the Sault Sainte Marie, popularly called the *Soo*, to witness our landing; men of all ages and complexions, in hats and caps of every form and fashion, with beards of every length and color, among which I discovered two or three pairs of mustaches. It was a party of copper-mine speculators, just flitting from Copper Harbor and Eagle River, mixed with a few Indian and half-breed inhabitants of the place. Among them I saw a face or two quite familiar in Wall-street.

I had a conversation with an intelligent geologist, who had just returned from an examination of the copper mines of Lake Superior. He had pitched his tent in the fields near the village, choosing to pass the night in this manner, as he had done for several weeks past, rather than in a crowded inn. In regard to the mines, he told me that the external tokens, the surface indications, as he called them, were more favorable than those of any copper mines in the world. They are still, however, mere surface indications; the veins had not been worked to that depth which was necessary to determine their value with any certainty. The mixture of silver with the copper he regarded as not giving any additional value to the mines, inasmuch as it is only occasional and rare. Sometimes, he told me, a mass of metal would be discovered of the size of a man's fist, or smaller, composed of copper and silver, both metals closely united, yet both perfectly pure and unalloyed with each other. The masses of virgin copper found in beds of gravel are, however, the most remarkable feature of these mines. One of them which has been discovered this summer, but which has not been raised, is estimated to weigh twenty tons. I saw in the propeller *Independence*, by which this party from the copper mines was brought down to the Sault, one of these masses, weighing seventeen hundred and fifty pounds, with the appearance of having once been fluid with heat. It was so pure that it might have been cut in pieces by cold steel and stamped at once into coin.

Two or three years ago this settlement of the Sault de Ste. Marie, was but a military post of the United States, in the midst of a village of Indians and half-breeds. There were, perhaps, a dozen white residents in the place, including the family of the Baptist Missionary and the agent of the American Fur Company, which had removed its station hither from Mackinaw, and built its warehouse on this river. But since the world has begun to talk of the copper mines of Lake Superior, settlers flock into the place; carpenters are busy in knocking up houses with all haste on the government lands, and large warehouses have been built upon piles driven into the shallows of the St. Mary. Five years hence, the primitive character of the place will be altogether lost, and it will have become a bustling Yankee town, resembling the other new settlements of the West.

Here the navigation from lake to lake is interrupted by the falls or rapids of the river St. Mary, from which the place receives its name. The crystalline waters of Lake Superior on their way through the channel of this river to Lake Huron, here rush, and foam, and roar, for about three quarters of a mile, over rocks and large stones.

Close to the rapids, with birchen-canoes moored in little inlets, is a village of the Indians, consisting of log-cabins and round wigwams, on a shrubby level, reserved to them by the government. The morning after our arrival, we went through this village in search of a canoe and a couple of Indians, to make the descent of the rapids, which is one of the first things that a visitor to the Sault must think of. In the first wigwam that we entered were three men and two women as drunk as men and women could well be. The squaws were speechless and motionless, too far-gone, as it seemed, to raise either hand or foot; the men though apparently unable to rise were noisy, and one of them, who called himself a half-breed and spoke a few words of English, seemed disposed to quarrel. Before the next door was a woman busy in washing, who spoke a little English.

"The old man out there," she said, in answer to our questions, "can paddle canoe, but he is very drunk, he can not do it to-day."

"Is there nobody else," we asked, "who will take us down the falls?"

"I don't know; the Indians all drunk to-day."

"Why is that? Why are they all drunk to-day?"

"Oh, the whisky," answered the woman, giving us to understand, that when an Indian could get whisky, he got drunk as a matter of course.

By this time the man had come up, and after addressing us with the customary "*bon jour*," manifested a curiosity to know the nature of our errand. The woman explained it to him in English.

"Oh, messieurs, je vous servirai," said he, for he spoke Canadian French; "I go, I go."

We told him that we doubted whether he was quite sober enough.

"Oh, messieurs, je suis parfaitement capable—first rate, first rate."

We shook him off as soon as we could, but not till after he had time to propose that we should wait till the next day, and to utter the maxim, "Whisky, good—too much whisky, no good."

In a log-cabin, which some half-breeds were engaged in building, we found two men who were easily persuaded to leave their work and pilot us over the rapids. They took one of the canoes which lay in a little inlet close at hand, and entering it, pushed it with their long poles up the stream in the edge of the rapids. Arriving at the head of the rapids, they took in our party, which consisted of five, and we began the descent. At each end of the canoe sat a half-breed, with a paddle, to guide it while the current drew us rapidly down among the agitated waters. It was surprising with what dexterity they kept us in the smoothest part of the water, seeming to know the way down as well as if it had been a beaten path in the fields.

At one time we would seem to be directly approaching a rock against which the waves were dashing, at another to be descending into a hollow of the waters in which our canoe would be inevitably filled, but a single stroke of the paddle given by the man at the prow put us safely by the seeming danger. So rapid was the descent, that almost as soon as we descried the apparent peril, it was passed. In less than ten minutes, as it seemed to me, we had left the roar of the rapids behind us, and were gliding over the smooth water at their foot.

In the afternoon we engaged a half-breed and his brother to take us over to the Canadian shore. His wife, a slender young woman with a lively physiognomy, not easily to be distinguished from a French woman of her class, accompanied us in the canoe with her little boy. The birch-bark canoe of the savage seems to me one of the most beautiful and perfect things of the kind constructed by human art. We were in one of the finest that float on St. Marys river, and when I looked at its delicate ribs, mere shavings of white cedar, yet firm enough for the purpose—the thin broad laths of the same wood with which these are inclosed, and the broad sheets of birch-bark, impervious to water, which sheathed the outside, all firmly sewed together by the tough slender roots of the fir-tree, and when I considered its extreme lightness and the grace of its form, I could not but wonder at the ingenuity of those who had invented so beautiful a combination of ship-building and basket-work. "It cost me twenty dollars," said the half-breed, "and I would not take thirty for it."

We were ferried over the waves where they dance at the foot of the rapids. At this place large quantities of white-fish, one of the most delicate kinds known on our continent, are caught by the Indians, in their season, with scoop-nets. The whites are about to interfere with this occupation of the Indians, and I saw the other day a seine of prodigious length constructing, with which it is intended to sweep nearly half the river at once. "They will take a hundred barrels a day," said an inhabitant of the place.

On the British side, the rapids divide themselves into half a dozen noisy brooks, which roar round little islands, and in the boiling pools of which the speckled trout is caught with the rod and line. We landed at the warehouses of the Hudson Bay Company, where the goods intended for the Indian trade are deposited, and the furs brought from the northwest are collected. They are surrounded by a massive stockade, within which lives the agent of the Company, the walks are graveled and well-kept, and the whole bears the marks of British solidity and precision. A quantity of furs had been brought in the day before, but they were locked up in the warehouse, and all was now quiet and silent. The agent was absent; a half-breed nurse stood at the door with his child, and a Scotch servant, apparently with nothing to do, was lounging in the court inclosed by the stockade; in short, there was less bustle about this centre of one of the most powerful trading-companies in the world, than about one of our farm-houses. . . .

We climbed a ridge of hills back of the house to the church of the Episcopal Mission, built a few years ago as a place of worship for the Chippewas, who have since been removed by the government. It stands remote from any habitation, with three or four Indian graves near it, and we found it filled with hay. The view from its door is uncommonly beautiful; the broad St. Mary lying below, with its bordering villages and woody valley, its white rapids and its rocky islands, picturesque with the pointed summits of the fir-tree. To the northwest the sight followed the river to the horizon, where it issued from Lake Superior, and I was told that in clear weather one might discover, from the spot on which I stood, the promontory of Gros Cap, which guards the outlet of that mighty lake.

ERNEST H. RANKIN

Canalside

Superintendent

In the summer of 1847 after the River and Harbor Meeting in Chicago, the eastern delegates of the convention embarked on the Steamer *St. Louis* for Sault Ste. Marie and Buffalo. Thurlow Weed, editor of the Albany *Evening Journal,* was excited by the north country. In his record of the trip he commented on the little portage town and the great wilderness, the platters of succulent whitefish in the hotel, and the thrill of shooting the rapids in a Chippewa canoe— though three visitors had drowned in that sport a few weeks earlier. He watched a tramcar hauling goods between ships in shouting distance of each other; inevitably he thought of a canal. "I shall be disappointed," he wrote, "if Messrs. Corwin, Butler King, and Schenck, who are with us, do not press this Improvement in the next Congress."

But the Soo was a long way from Washington—it was "beyond the remotest settlement in the United States, if not in the moon," said Henry Clay—and Congress took no action. However, in his first annual message to the legislature in 1851, President Fillmore observed that "a ship canal around the falls of St. Mary of less than a mile in length, though local in its construction, would be national in its purpose and benefits." In August, 1852, a bill was passed, donating to the state of Michigan 750,000 acres of federal land as subsidy for a canal project and granting a 400-foot right of way through the Fort Brady reservation.

At this time a twenty-three-year-old Yankee, Charles T. Harvey, was in the Northwest, talking with traders, prospectors, speculators, and selling Fairbanks scales in the iron and copper towns. In August 1852 he arrived at the Soo, burning with typhoid fever. While recovering he watched the portage car trundling freight down Water Street and he studied the swirling river till he could see it in his sleep. Then he began to burn with another fever. He wrote to the Fairbanks Company in St. Johnsbury, Vermont: "A three quarter mile canal here not costing over $400,000 would enable any lake craft to load at

Buffalo and go through to Fond du Lac, 600 miles west of here, without breaking bulk."

In Detroit with the help of a lawyer for the Michigan Central Railroad, Harvey outlined a canal bill which was passed by the Michigan legislature. It called for a canal with tandem locks 350 feet long, each with a nine-foot lift, to be constructed within two years; a company taking the contract would be awarded 750,000 acres of public land, to be seleced by its agents. That winter Harvey persuaded the Fairbanks brothers to form the St. Mary's Falls Ship Canal Company and apply for the contract. The agreement was signed on April 5, 1853. The Canal Company appointed Harvey general superintendent in charge of work at the Soo.

In his memoirs, years afterward, Harvey gave himself generous credit as a construction engineer, and writers taking him at his word have dramatized the traveling salesman who built one of the great canals of the world. After a fresh look at the sources Ernest H. Rankin, executive secretary of the Marquette County Historical Society, offers another view of Harvey's role and a revised account of the canal construction. This narrative is reprinted from the Summer, 1965 issue of *Inland Seas.*

THE NEED FOR A CANAL with locks, between Lakes Huron and Superior, to bypass the rapids in St. Marys River and overcome the difference in level of eighteen feet between these two Great Lakes, had been a matter of concern for many years. If the industrial progress of the Lake Superior country were to be developed—be it furs, fish or minerals—a canal was needed. The North West Company had built a sluiceway and a small lock on the Canadian side of the river in 1797, only to have it destroyed by United States troops in 1814. In September, 1838, the State of Michigan entered into a contract with a construction company to build a canal. Unfortunately, the State failed to obtain permission from the Federal Government to cross the United States Military Reservation at Fort Brady and the work was stopped by a detachment of soldiers within a week after it was started.

The need for a canal at the Sault was a frequent subject of the editor of the *Lake Superior News and Miners' Journal* in 1846. This journal, a weekly, was the upper peninsula's first newspaper, its first twelve issues being published at Copper Harbor. It was then moved to the Sault where it continued to be published until it folded in 1849. It was followed by the *Lake Superior Journal,* whose first edition appeared on May 1, 1850. This paper was financed by a number of Sault businessmen, some of whom were bound to lose if a canal were built. However, J. Venen Brown, editor of this new journal, was given a free hand, devoting far more space to the need of a canal than Editor Ingersoll had done in his newspaper.

By 1850, Michigan men from both peninsulas were pressuring Congress at Washington for money to build the canal, but without success. The canal promoters then turned their efforts to obtaining a suitable land grant and were turned down several times.

During the Winter of 1851/1852, John Burt and J. Venen Brown headed a delegation to Washington and continued the fight. It was spearheaded by Senator Alpheus Felch of Michigan. Felch carried the fight right on throughout the Summer of 1852 and it was on August 26th that a bill granting 750,000 acres of Michigan's government-owned lands, was approved by President Millard Fillmore.

Without waiting for the Michigan Legislature to accept the land grant, Governor Robert McClelland applied to the Secretary of War for an engineer to make a survey for the canal; however, no money had been appropriated to defray the cost. Upon hearing this, Captain Augustus Canfield, of the United States Topographical Engineers, and William Austin Burt, volunteered their services, which the governor gladly accepted. They arrived at the Sault on October 4, 1852, and a week later were on their way back to Detroit with their field notes.

While in the Lake Superior country and at the Sault during August and September, 1852, Charles T. Harvey, a young salesman for the Fairbanks Scales Company, learned of the long struggle to get a canal built. Some weeks after the passage of the Federal Act of August 26, Harvey wrote a long letter to his employers in Vermont, submitting a plan for securing the contract for the building of the ship canal. The Fairbanks brothers were immediately interested, which interest was quickly spread to Erastus Corning at Albany, New York, John F. Seymour of Utica, John W. Brooks of Detroit and other men of wealth who had money to invest. One cannot deny Harvey any of the credit for this act—it was probably the highest point and the greatest accomplishment in his whole career. Cash money would be needed to build the canal and he set the machinery in rapid motion to secure it.

However, to give full credit to Harvey as being responsible for the inception of the canal is an anachronism, for the need of a canal and the will to build it had been conceived by others long before he appeared on the scene. Even before a company had been formed, the Fairbanks brothers engaged L. L. Nichols of Utica, New York, a civil engineer, who had had experience in canal construction, to return to the Sault with Harvey. They arrived there several weeks after Canfield and Burt had completed their survey, made a visual and cursory examination of the terrain through which the canal would be built, and then returned to Detroit. Here they obtained copies of the plats of the survey and plans of the proposed canal and locks which had been prepared under Canfield's direction. Under date of December 9, 1852, Nichols submitted to the Fairbanks brothers an estimate of the cost for building the canal, the lowest figure being $361,000.00 and the highest, $403,500.00, which figures were based on various factors.

The Canal Act was passed and approved by the State of Michigan on February 5, 1853, and proposals from contractors to build the canal were to be received up to April 1. To say that there was no underhanded work in Lansing in securing the contract for the Fairbanks-Corning-Seymour group would be a misstatement. Under date of April 5, John W. Brooks wrote to Erastus Corning at Albany, "The contract for the construction of the St. Mary Canal has been given to us today. . . ." During May, 1853, the St. Mary's Falls Ship Canal Company was organized in Albany, New York, with Erastus Corning, President; John W. Brooks, Vice-President; John V. L. Pruyn, Treasurer; and Charles T. Harvey, General Agent.

Whether or not this particular group of men received the contract to build the canal, or some other group, the canal would have been built. However, everyone concerned with the building, be they Lake Superior pioneers, or the lower peninsula promoters, was well pleased with the personnel of this company. Corning was a noted merchant, financier and railroad president; Brooks, an outstanding civil engineer, was referred to as "the Napoleon of Railroads;" and Pruyn was an Albany investor, representing a family of great wealth. Among the Directors was James F. Joy of Detroit. He was the counsel for the Michigan Central Railroad, and it was largely through his lobbying at Lansing that the contract was awarded to these men.

About 10 o'clock, Monday evening, June 6, 1853, the steamer *Albany* arrived at the Sault, bringing Harvey, Captain Canfield, Col. James L. Glenn, who was the Michigan State engineer, and about one hundred men, tools, and various supplies and materials. The next day, Harvey filled a wheelbarrow with earth, wheeled it to the site for an embankment, and the building of the canal began in dead earnest. Harvey, as general agent, had been given practically unlimited authority by the canal company to proceed with the work, and $50,000.00 had been placed to his credit in a Detroit bank.

It has been stated by some of the writers on the Sault canal project that because the place was isolated, it was difficult to keep men on the job. This isolation also presented problems in the repairing of tools and equipment, making it necessary to mend them on the spot, or even the devising and making of special tools to meet emergencies. However, sufficient men were secured and repair shops were set up at the Sault, as is quite usual on large construction jobs. It is interesting to note that the bulky gates were fabricated at Detroit and shipped to the Sault. While it is true that the Sault was isolated during the wintertime, as were many other places, it was as close to industrial centers as were all the other locations on the Great Lakes ports during the open season of navigation. It was an era of water transportation, and fast steamers plied the waterways in every direction. There was no want of quick transportation between the Sault and the lower lake ports.

All Summer long and into the Fall and even into the Winter, the human moles dug, wasting the earth along the sides of the canal as there were many feet of embankment to be built, as well as a long, wide ditch to be dug. It was not long before Canfield, representing the United States Government, took exception to some of Harvey's methods, especially in the building of the embankments. Those who have seen dams, both as built by humans as well as by beavers, the dykes of Holland, and the sub-ballasting for railroad and highway grades, would know that an embankment, to retain water and not disintegrate, must be of the highest workmanship. The embankments which Harvey was building on both sides of the canal at its eastern end, were being built up of waste materials—earth and loose, broken rock—indiscriminately piled into heaps, and apparently without puddling. To this careless method of building, Canfield took rightful exception and there was much friction between him and the youthful Harvey during the entire Summer. And these carelessly built embankments were to be the cause of much trouble, not only when the canal was opened, but for several years afterwards. Some portions of them had to be rebuilt.

Years later, when Harvey wrote his memoirs on how he had built the canal almost single handed, he disposed of Canfield in a very brief statement, as "a martinet on military etiquette." To be fair to Canfield the following brief account of his career should be a matter of record.

Augustus A. Canfield was some twenty-eight years older than Harvey, having been born on April 9, 1801, in New Jersey. He was graduated as a second lieutenant, from the United States Military Academy at West Point, New York, on July 1, 1822. At that time West Point was considered to be the leading engineering school in the country. On July 7, 1838, he was promoted to captain, Corps of Topographical Engineers, U.S.A. He was engaged in the survey of rivers and harbors in New York State, 1837–1839; at Sault Ste. Marie, 1840–1841, taking time out in 1841 to visit Europe. He conducted surveys at St. Joseph's Harbor, Michigan, and made the survey for the Waugoshance Shoal, Lake Michigan, in 1847–1848. He was also the engineer of construction of the Waugoshance Lighthouse in 1848–1852.

Such was the career of a man whom Harvey held in contempt during the first season of canal construction. Canfield died during April, 1854, in Detroit.

Not only did Harvey quarrel with Canfield, but with the owner of the stone quarry on Drummond Island. He reported to the officers of the canal company that the Drummond Island stone was unfit for the lock walls and they must look elsewhere. This resulted in obtaining a porous stone from an underwater quarry near Marblehead on Lake Erie. A number of vessels, loaded with this stone were received at the Sault in the Fall of 1853. This waterlogged stone suffered the ravages of a cold winter and many of the stone blocks froze, causing a large number of them to shatter, and thousands of dollars were wasted.

Harvey reported regularly to the canal officials in the East. "The work in its various details has gone steadily forward. . . ." While on the surface the work of building the canal was progressing satisfactorily during the first season of digging, as expressed in Harvey's glowing accounts, such was not actually the case and Brooks and others down in Detroit were badly worried. Not only were the Detroit promoters of the canal disturbed over its slow progress during the first season, but they finally managed to convey the fact to Erastus Fairbanks in Vermont. To satisfy himself Fairbanks visited the Sault, and on June 7, 1854, wrote from there to President Corning at Albany: "The situation of the Canal enterprise is somewhat critical. . . . Mr. Brooks has now been here some two weeks and has done what could be done in putting the works in a shape to be finished this fall. . . . Mr. Brooks will be the master spirit directing the whole, while Mr. Harvey retiring from all responsibilities respecting the construction will find full . . . employ in the general agency of furnishing supplies, disbursing money, etc."

The *Lake Superior Journal,* apparently aware of the change in management, commented in their issue of June 3, 1854, in part, as follows: "J. W. Brooks, Esq., Vice President of the S.M.F.S. Canal Co., has been in town for several days, and appears to have relieved Mr. Harvey considerably from his onerous duties as Canal Agent. . . . Under the present direction, the work is likely to be carried forward in a more systematic and energetic manner. . . .

"The difficulty lies far back in the commencement of this important work, in placing it in charge of a person without a particle of experience or familiarity with such a work; who, as a matter of fact, had to cut and try, and, in this very course, conduct all matters in a penny-wise and pound-foolish manner. A whole year has been spent this way . . . and it will require four times the amount of expenditure that it would, provided it had been properly undertaken."

By the end of May, 1854, Harvey had expended some $385,442.47 and all he had to show for this enormous amount was an unfinished ditch and some badly built embankments. They were now within $18,000.00 of Mr. Nichol's highest estimate of the total cost of the completed canal and it was not yet half finished.

Needless to say, Mr. Brooks took over the job with vigor, two-thirds of the stone for the lock walls was secured from the Drummond Island quarry, and by October, 1854, the canal and locks were completed for all practical purposes. Harvey was left at the Sault during the Winter of 1854/1855 with a skeleton crew to do the cleanup work.

It was on May 21, 1855, that the State Commissioners and officers arrived at the Sault, the editor of the *Journal* writing, in part, "Proceeding at once to the Canal, the Commissioners and Officers traversed its entire extent, scrutinizing with the greatest care every part—walls, locks, gates, embankments and piers. . . . Of course, they could only judge the work by its appearance to the eye, but all seemed to feel, and several expressed surprise at the greatness and permanent character of the work, and apparent fidelity of its execution." After this inspection, they boarded the steamer *Illinois,* and on the return trip to Detroit, formally accepted the St. Marie Ship Çanal.

It must be assumed that the canal and locks were filled with water when this inspection was made and that the water was let out immediately after the departure of the *Illinois.* The records state "that on the 19th of April, 1855, Mr. Harvey had the honor of opening the coffer-dam sluice-gates, which let the waters of Lake Superior flow permanently into the finished canal and locks. . . .". On February 1, 1855, Harvey had written one of his many "private" letters to John F. Seymour at Utica: "Before I let the water in as I have proposed I shall have the ice cleaned off the bottom above the Gate for a proper space and shall put in a couple of Vessel sails to stop the water from running while on our hands. . . ." Thus it would seem that Harvey didn't hesitate to use subterfuge to cover up his careless work.

John Burt took over his duties as first superintendent of the canal on June 1, 1855. On the 16th, he received an order from the State Board of Control for the opening of the Canal on Monday, the 18th. "At 1 o'clock a.m., Monday, the water was let in. The canal filled slowly, but at 11 o'clock a.m. was ready for the reception of boats."

One might well imagine Harvey standing at the side of Captain Jack Wilson in the pilothouse as he guided the *Illinois* into the channel-approach to the lower lock. Quite the contrary. On June 1, Harvey had been relegated to Marquette and his association as general agent of the Ship Canal Co. was terminated on the 13th.

In the 1850's the country was pushing to the westward. Railroads, canals and bridges were being built, machinery and tools of all sorts were being manufactured, copper and iron ore mines were being opened, and there was a great need for experienced and qualified men—leaders—to carry on the general expansion. The Fairbanks Company was expanding, Erastus Corning had consolidated several short rail lines, providing a through railroad between Albany and Buffalo, and John W. Brooks was building up the Michigan Central Railroad between Detroit and Chicago in a desperate effort to keep the Lake Shore & Northern Indiana from securing all the traffic. All of these men knew Harvey and had he been, at the age of twenty-six, "The Greatest Engineer," "Young Mister Big," or one of the "Lost Men of American History," as some of his biographers have acclaimed him, it would seem that he would have been retained by any one of these industrial giants or their companies—and he could have named his own salary. Had his greatness been as profound as expressed by present-day writers, who have described his accomplishments in such elaborate terms, one would expect that contemporary writers would have acclaimed him upon the completion of the canal. Instead of being "the man of the hour" Harvey had been sent to Marquette to open a Canal Land Office, and in less than a year's time he departed, leaving the affairs of the office in a "mess," and this chapter of his life passed into history.

One might further imagine a picture of the *Illinois* being locked through in splendid glory. Such was not the case. One of the lower gates was fouled by a block of wood which had to be removed before the gates could be opened. The ship got through the middle gates without difficulty. However, the upper set of gates was blocked by earth at the miter sill—two feet of earth that had washed down from the embankments and had settled against the bottom of the gates. With the help of the steamer *Baltimore*, which was up above on Lake Superior, and the *Illinois,* and with the use of a winch, the gates were slowly opened and the *Illinois* steamed through to the upper end of the canal. It had required over eleven hours to accomplish this first locking-through of a ship from Lake Huron to Lake Superior.

The

Soo Locks

In 1852 Sault Ste. Marie had no canal but a big argument. Congress had proposed locks 250 feet long; the Lake Superior mining companies wanted locks of 300 feet; and some bold men, like John Burt, who became the canal's first superintendent, urged the building of giant locks 350 feet by 70. At the height of the controversy Captain Eber B. Ward, the leading vessel owner on the lakes, argued that the cramped channels of the St. Marys river would never permit the passage of large steamers; he thought that locks of 260 feet would take the biggest ships that could ever come up from Lake Huron.

The canal that was opened in 1855 included two locks, in tandem, 350 feet long, 70 feet wide, with 11½ feet of water over the miter sills. Each had a lift of nine feet.

Fifty years later the locks that Captain Ward had thought too large were replaced by the 800-foot Poe lock, and now that lock is being supplanted by a huge new lock 1,200 feet long, 100 feet wide, and 32 feet deep.

Captain Ward shrewdly read the manifests of his sailing vessels, but he could not read the future. In January, 1853, he wrote to Judge William A. Burt, arguing for 260-foot canal locks.

THE DEEP ANXIETY I feel in common with the rest of the community for the early completion of the Sault Ste. Marie canal induces me to write to you on the subject.

I fear the defeat of our long cherished hopes.

The legislature in their anxiety to prevent undue speculation by those who would be disposed to contract to do the work are in great danger of going to the opposite extreme, and make such requirements as will deter competent men from taking the contract for the land. The size proposed by the senate bill, 350 by 70 foot locks, is entirely too large for the locks. The crooked, narrow, shallow and rocky channels in the St. Marys river will forever deter the largest class of steamers from navigating these waters. Aside from the impediments in the two lakes George, there are several places where the channel is very narrow, with but 11 feet of water clear of rocks, and the channels too crooked for the large class of steamers to pass in safety.

This I regard as a conclusive argument against making the locks so large as is contemplated.

I do not believe there is the least necessity for making the locks over 260 feet in the clear and 60 feet wide, as no vessels of larger dimensions than could pass such locks can be used there with safety without an expenditure of a very large sum of money in excavating rock at various points along the river, a work that is not likely to be undertaken during the present century.

The value of wild lands may be estimated by ascertaining the amount actually realized by the state for the large grants that have heretofore been made for purposes of improvement when no taxes were collected until lands were sold to settlers. I think it will be difficult to find the value of 25 cents per acre for all such grants made to this state. A well organized company might make the lands worth 75 cents per acre, provided they were not taxed while held by the company. I have no doubt the smallest sized canal required by the act making the grant of land would cost $525,000 or 70 cents per acre. Add eight cents per acre for interest during the construction of the work and 15 cents per acre for selection and location, brings it to 93 cents per acre, a price at which any quantity can now be located without any risk of loss and with much greater chances of making desirable selections. If the legislature will appoint a committee who shall act with the governor to make the best contract for the state they can, holding them responsible for a faithful discharge of their duties, I feel confident we shall succeed in securing the great object of our wishes. But if the bill should materially restrict the governor in his powers I think we have good reason to fear that the most vital interests of the state will be delayed for years to come.

E . B . W I L L I A M S

The New Lock,

1967

First came the tandem lifts of the 1855 canal; then the Weitzel Lock; then the Poe; and then the twin Davis and Sabin Locks, largest in the world. Then, with World War II, the MacArthur Lock yawned on the site of the obsolete Weitzel, and a cycle was completed. With each new construction it seemed the locks were big enough for any future need. But the lakes trade goes on changing.

In 1896 the Poe Lock replaced the original tandem lifts; and now, in the mid-1960s, that lift is giving place to a lock 1,200 feet long, 100 feet wide and 32 feet deep. As the Poe Lock vanishes into memory the sounds of blasting and building may recall some words of seventy years ago. "The wildest expectations of one year," said General Orlando M. Poe, watching the parade of ships outside his window on the canal, "seem absolutely tame the next."

Construction of the Poe Lock set off a surge of shipbuilding; scores of new vessels, of unprecedented tonnage, went into service at the turn of the century. So the 1967 lock, on the site of the vanished Poe and the tandem Harvey Locks before it, will spur the building of a new class of freighters.

In these pages an official of the American Ship Building Company of Cleveland shows the relationship between the new lock and carriers yet to be designed and constructed.

THE WEITZEL LOCK at the Soo, completed in 1881, opened the way for larger and more economical ships to navigate between Lake Superior and the Lower Lakes. The following year, in 1882, the iron steamer *Onoko* was launched in Cleveland, the first ore carrier to be built of iron and the true prototype of the modern lake vessel of today. Her length was 302 feet 6 inches overall, 39 feet 0 inches in beam and 25 feet 0 inches deep, with a capacity of 3,000 tons. In spite of some skeptics who thought an iron vessel could never float, she served in the ore trade for 33 years, finally being lost in Lake Superior in 1915.

With the opening of the Poe Lock in 1896, a tremendous building program was started on the Lakes and a few of the vessels built at the turn of the century are still in existence although they have ceased to operate in the ore trade. In less than a decade, it was evident that even this lock, together with the Weitzel, was inadequate to answer the demands of commerce. Construction of a second canal was therefore started, paralleling the first canal and it was provided with twin locks named the Davis and Sabin Locks. These locks are the longest in the world—1,350 feet each, 80 feet wide and 23 feet in depth. They were opened in 1914 and 1919, respectively. It was thought that these locks would be adequate for all time to come and they could each take two ships in tandem. The depth restriction, however, and the demands of World War II, led to the construction of the MacArthur Lock, completed in 1943, replacing the Weitzel Lock which had served for 60 years. The MacArthur is 800 feet long, 80 feet wide and has a depth of 31 feet.

As this is written, the Poe Lock has been retired and in its place, a new lock is now under construction and will be in service by 1967: This lock, yet unnamed, will be 1,200 feet long, 100 feet wide and 32 feet in depth. The MacArthur Lock is in general the same size as the fifteen locks of the Welland Canal and St. Lawrence Seaway, which limit the vessel size to approximately 730 feet by 75 feet, with a maximum draft of about 26 feet. Under these conditions, the maximum cargo is not over 25,000 long tons.

Seagoing vessels of these dimensions, with increased draft, can carry much greater cargoes—almost double. Consequently, foreign ore delivered to east coast ports in foreign ships, with foreign crews, even with a much longer rail haul to midwest steel centers, presents a serious threat to our domestic Lake Superior ore movement. However, the new lock at the Soo will again release dimensional restrictions and vessel sizes can again increase, this time possibly to 900 feet by 95 feet, with modest increases in draft to carry cargoes up to 40,000 long tons. Such vessels will, of course, be limited to service on Lakes Superior, Michigan, Huron and Erie, but excluded from Lake Ontario and the Seaway.

Thus, we find that lock dimensions were increased from time to time, viz.: the Weitzel Lock in 1881, the Poe Lock in 1896, the twin locks in 1919, the MacArthur Lock in 1943 and the new lock in

1967. These events, together with the increasing demands for iron ore, had a significant effect on vessel sizes. The 5- to 6,000-ton carriers had practically disappeared by the beginning of this century and gave way to the 8- to 10,000-ton carriers, of which a hundred or more were built during the first decade.

Today, nearly all of these vessels are gone, except for a few in special services. Beginning in 1906, some 12,000-ton ships appeared on the scene—the first 600-footers with 58-feet beam. This size continued to be popular until 1916, when 600-footers, with 60-feet beam, became standard. There were two notable exceptions, however, namely the *Col. James M. Schoonmaker* and the *William P. Snyder, Jr.*, built for Shenango Furnace Company in 1912. These vessels are 617 feet overall length, 64 feet beam and 33 feet deep. They carry close to 15,000 long tons each. Construction of the standard "600-footer" began in 1916 and continued through 1938, except for seven depression years when no ships were built on the Lakes. There are 50 vessels of this general size in service today, which were built over that 22-year period.

After three more depression years, 21 ore carriers were built during 1942 and 1943. Five of these are 67 feet in beam and the others are 60 feet, but they are all 35 feet in depth and somewhat longer than their predecessors. This group reflects the value of the MacArthur Lock, particularly its greater depth.

The greatest value of the MacArthur Lock became more significant with the advent of the first 20,000-ton carriers, beginning with the *Wilfred Sykes* in 1949. Twenty-five new or converted U. S. flag vessels, with capacities from 20- to 25,000 tons, have been placed in service since that date. Foreign competition through the Seaway has seriously retarded this program. In fact, the last four in the group, delivered in 1961, probably would not have been built, had it not been possible to buy foreign midbodies to be attached to the ends of former seagoing World War II tankers. Today, most of the Seaway iron ore is delivered in foreign ships and a significant amount of iron ore is coming by rail from the east coast. The new lock at the Soo strengthens the possibility of developing a healthy fleet of Great Lakes ore carriers under the U. S. flag. With such a fleet, it is believed that we will continue to move annual quantities of about 75,000,000 tons. Without such a fleet, the movement may be no more than half that amount. From this point of view, the future of the Lake Superior district depends upon this new lock and it is fortunate that our Government has seen fit to proceed with its construction.

VI

STORM WARNING

In Northwest Canada, between Great Slave Lake and the arc of the Mackenzie River, a low pressure front develops and the wind rises. With the earth's rotation it moves in an accelerating curve, like a weight on a whirled string. It races over the prairies of Saskatchewan and roars through the Minnesota forest. Under a torn sky it lashes Lake Superior. At Coast Guard Stations the storm signals flutter—red flags with a black center—and over the air waves goes a weather warning.

Every year brings storms like this, and some years bring hurricanes that are remembered long after their brief and crushing fury. In November, 1842, a three-day storm destroyed fifty vessels. In 1869 a hurricane raced over the lakes leaving a hundred shipwrecks. The Coast Guard records list thousands of vessels, steam and sail, large and small, loaded and empty, lost on the lakes. A few ran aground in fine weather. Some were victims of fog and collision, like the *Lady Elgin* which went down on a September night in 1860, between Chicago and Milwaukee, with three hundred lives. But most of those lost ships were battered by wind and wave when autumn storms were raging.

The lakes' first victim was their first commercial vessel, on its first and only trip. On the 7th of August, 1679, the *Griffin* steered out of the Niagara River with thirty-four men, including LaSalle, Tonty and Hennepin. Six weeks later, loaded with peltry, she sailed out of Green Bay. Wrote Hennepin:

Though the wind was favorable, it was never known what course they [a pilot and five men] steered, nor how they perished. The ship came to an anchor to the north of the Lake of the Illinois, where she was seen by some savages who told us that they advised our men to sail along the coast and not towards the middle of the lake. . . . But our pilot would steer as he pleased. . . . The ship was hardly a league from the coast when it was tossed up by a violent storm in such a manner that our men were never heard of since, and it is supposed that the ship struck upon a sand and was there buried.

Each of the lakes has its tales of storm and shipwreck. The biggest lake has the longest record of disaster. While a gale rocked the Mackinac forest and water pounded the shore Jacques Marquette wrote: "The winds from the Lake of the Illinois no sooner subside than they are hurled back by the Lake of the Hurons, and those from Lake Superior are the fiercest of all. In the autumn and winter months there is a succession of storms; and with these mighty waters all about us, we seem to be living in the heart of a hurricane."

After twenty-five years in sail and steam Captain John G. Parker told laconically of his first season on Lake Superior. At twenty-one he had left his father's farm in Wisconsin, shipping with Captain Calvin Ripley on the schooner *Fur Trader* in 1845; that fall the vessel was portaged over the Soo, on the Canadian side. The next year, as mate of the *Fur Trader*, he began his career on Lake Superior. In November, 1846, came a day that John Parker never forgot:

When above Parisien Island I fell overboard. Captain Ripley threw me a rope and I managed to catch it. He hauled in and I had a reef-plat. I told him to throw me a board and they threw over a one-inch board twelve feet long and twelve inches wide. I went to it and lashed myself to it with the reef-plat and in about a half hour the boat came and picked me up. It was snowing hard and difficult to see. We had a good passage after that up to L'Anse. Landed our freight and passengers and returned to the Soo and loaded for Ontonagon. Laid the *Fur Trader* up at the Soo on Dec. 6, 1846.

Captain Parker took the first cargo of copper through the St. Marys Falls Canal, but he remembered that trip less vividly than some others.

We left the Soo late in the afternoon of Nov. 20, 1859. I was piloting the *Burlington*. I did not like the looks of the weather so we ran into Taquamenow Bay. Before sundown the steamers *Planet* and *Cleveland* came along and passed outside. They were both bound for Marquette. The clerk persuaded Captain Fish to get under way and follow, which we did over my protests. About midnight it began to snow, with the wind blowing a gale northwest. Captain Fish sent for me saying the wheelsman was sick, and I went to the pilot house and altered the course. The next morning we passed through bales of hay, dry goods, boxes and most anything that would float. The *Planet* got into Marquette with her smokestack gone and she was otherwise badly crippled. The *Cleveland* got into Grand Island little better.

Since Captain Parker's time there are many aids to navigation—lights, buoys, radio, radar, and radio telephones. But blowing snow blots out the lights, and over ice-sheathed decks spray turns the lifeline into an icy hazard. It is still touch and go when the red flags are flat in the wind and the air waves stutter storm warning.

Great Lakes

Mariner

Between his apprentice voyage to Liverpool and his long whaling voyage to the Pacific, Herman Melville made a trip to Illinois in the summer of 1840, sailing over the Great Lakes and returning East by Mississippi and Ohio river steamers. Ten years later, when he was writing his epic *Moby Dick* in a Massachusetts farmhouse, his mind went back to the inland seas of America.

In the chapter entitled "The Town-Ho's Story" he told of the whale ship *Town-Ho*, whose crew included Steelkilt, a Lakeman from Buffalo. Steelkilt came from inland America but he knew the somber stress of great waters. Though no whales swam past Thunder Bay and the Mackinac Straits, the lakes, he said, could match the massive fury of the ocean.

At the end of June, 1840, Melville sailed from Buffalo to Chicago, a week's voyage, fare ten dollars. On the night of July 1 Lake Erie was swept by a storm that threw travelers from their berths and horses across the halfdeck. Steelkilt had learned seamanship in blasts like this—"as direful as any that lash the salted wave."

In Chapter LIV of *Moby Dick*, Melville told of the *Town-Ho* and its lake-bred seaman.

I SHALL PRESERVE THE STYLE in which I once narrated it at Lima, to a lounging circle of my Spanish friends, one saint's eve, smoking upon the thick-gilt tiled piazza of the Golden Inn. Of those fine cavaliers, the young Dons, Petro and Sebastian, were on the closer terms with me; and hence the interluding questions they occasionally put, and which are duly answered at the time.

"Some years prior to my first learning the events which I am

290 · STORM WARNING

about rehearsing to you, gentlemen, the *Town-Ho*, Sperm Whaler of Nantucket, was cruising in your Pacific here, not very many days' sail eastward from the eaves of this good Golden Inn. She was somewhere to the northward of the Line. One morning upon handling the pumps, according to daily usage, it was observed that she made more water in her hold than common. They supposed a swordfish had stabbed her, gentlemen. But the captain, having some unusual reason for believing that rare good luck awaited him in those latitudes; and therefore being very averse to quit them, and the leak not being then considered at all dangerous, though, indeed, they could not find it after searching the hold as low down as was possible in rather heavy weather, the ship still continued her cruisings, the mariners working at the pumps at wide and easy intervals; but no good luck came; more days went by, and not only was the leak yet undiscovered, but it sensibly increased. So much so, that now taking some alarm, the captain, making all sail, stood away for the nearest harbor among the islands, there to have his hull hove out and repaired.

"Though no small passage was before her, yet, if the commonest chance favored, he did not at all fear that his ship would founder by the way, because his pumps were of the best, and being periodically relieved at them, those six-and-thirty men of his could easily keep the ship free; never mind if the leak should double on her. In truth, well-nigh the whole of this passage being attended by very prosperous breezes, the *Town-Ho* had all but certainly arrived in perfect safety at her port without the occurrence of the least fatality, had it not been for the brutal overbearing of Radney, the mate, a Vineyarder, and the bitterly provoked vengeance of Steelkilt, a Lakeman and desperado from Buffalo.

" 'Lakeman!—Buffalo! Pray, what is a Lakeman, and where is Buffalo?' said Don Sebastian, rising in his swinging mat of grass.

"On the eastern shore of our Lake Erie, Don; but—I crave your courtesy—may be, you shall soon hear further of all that. Now, gentlemen, in square-sail brigs and three-masted ships, well-nigh as large and stout as any that ever sailed out of your old Callao to far Manila; this Lakeman, in the land-locked heart of our America, had yet been nurtured by all those agrarian freebooting impressions popularly connected with the open ocean. For in their interflowing aggregate, those grand fresh-water seas of ours,—Erie, and Ontario, and Huron, and Superior, and Michigan,—possess an ocean-like expansiveness, with many of the ocean's noblest traits; with many of its rimmed varieties of races and of climes.

"They contain round archipelagoes of romantic isles, even as the

Polynesian waters do; in large part, are shored by two great contrasting nations, as the Atlantic is; they furnish long maritime approaches to our numerous territorial colonies from the East, dotted all round their banks; here and there are frowned upon by batteries, and by the goat-like craggy guns of lofty Mackinaw; they have heard the fleet thunderings of naval victories.

"At intervals, they yield their beaches to wild barbarians, whose red painted faces flash from out their peltry wigwams; for leagues are flanked by ancient and unentered forests, where the gaunt pines stand like serried lines of kings in Gothic genealogies; those same woods harboring wild Afric beasts of prey, and silken creatures whose exported furs give robes to Tartar Emperors.

"They mirror the paved capitals of Buffalo and Cleveland, as well as Winnebago villages; they float alike the full-rigged merchant ship, the armed cruiser of the State, the steamer, and the beech canoe.

"They are swept by Borean and dismasting blasts as direful as any that lash the salted wave; they know what shipwrecks are, for out of sight of land, however inland, they have drowned full many a midnight ship with all its shrieking crew.

"Thus, gentlemen, though an inlander, Steelkilt was wild-ocean born, and wild-ocean nurtured; as much of an audacious mariner as any."

JACOB BUTLER VARNUM

Gale on

Lake Erie

In the winter of 1864 in a Massachusetts farmhouse an old man began writing. "Confined a large portion of my time to my room by indisposition and the infirmities of age . . . I have recently sought employment in overhauling my papers of more than fifty years." After the statement "I cannot promise to interest you much, for I have not passed an eventful life," he plunged into an account of hazardous travel and adventure on the western frontier.

In 1811 Jacob Butler Varnum was appointed to the Indian Agency at Sandusky on Lake Erie. He arrived there aboard the schooner *Catherine* late in the season. On Sandusky Bay—"one immense rice field darkened by clouds of waterfowl"—he was instructed in the Wyandot language by chief Tarhe, the Crane. The War of 1812 drove him from Sandusky and a prolonged attack of fever sent him, by wagon and horseback, back to Middlesex County, Massachusetts.

In 1815 Varnum went to Chicago to reestablish the Indian Agency there. After a miserable voyage over Lake Erie, he sailed from Detroit to Mackinac on the schooner *Porcupine* with a tyrannical captain who had his men flogged—from a dozen to a hundred lashes—on slight provocation; no more brutal treatment is recorded in the history of the lakes. At Mackinac he spent a pleasant, sociable winter, and in the spring he married a girl from Detroit who had come to the island to visit relatives there. Late the next summer Varnum and his bride arrived at Chicago on the schooner *Tiger* with a load of trade goods. One of Varnum's first tasks at ruined Fort Dearborn was to gather the bones of victims of the massacre four years before. Near that grave he soon buried his wife who died in childbirth.

Varnum stayed on at lonely Chicago, farming, hunting and attending to the Indian trade. On a trip to Detroit in 1819 he married a trader's daughter and brought her back to Chicago. That winter she coughed her lungs out and in the spring of 1820 he buried her—"by the side of my first wife"—on the Lake Michigan shore.

Of Jacob Varnum's many voyages on the empty lakes, none was more strenuous than his first trip, in 1811, from Buffalo to Sandusky, in the schooner *Catherine* on her last run of the season.

Sept. 1811. Buffalo was then but a small village, some forty or fifty wood houses scattered here and there. In the harbor there lay two or three skippers but there was little or no business. I found on my arrival that the schooner *Catherine,* a new and strong craft, was despatched only the day previous, direct for Sandusky, and that encountering adverse winds she was then lying under Point Ebenew about nine miles up the Canada shore.

So fair an opportunity, and the only one by water, was not to be lost, if possible to avoid it. Accordingly I crossed the river early in the morning, hired horses and a negro guide and in two hours was within hailing distance of the vessel; and fortunately got on board just in time, for the wind had shifted and in 15 or 20 minutes we were on our way up the lake. It was with some hesitation that the captain consented to receive me and only with the understanding that I was to shift for lodgings, every nook and corner in the cabin being occupied.

The wind had been setting in all night, and the point affording little protection, the schooner was rolling from side to side in a manner well calculated to produce that deadly nausea so common to those unaccustomed to the sea. The berths were packed with women and children, 5 or 6 in each, and on the tables and lockers were 8 or 10 men stretched at full length, all more or less affected, some heaving and groaning and others too far gone for that and apparently quite ready to give up the ghost. The ladies manifested more patience under their sufferings than the men, but some of them lamented they ever came on board, and wished themselves ashore.

Soon after we got under way and with a fair breeze all these troubles were forgotten and everyone seemed delighted with the prospect. The wind continued fair and we were progressing satisfactorily on our course. The second night our vessel had made such progress as to justify the expectation of reaching our destined haven [Sandusky] early in the morning.

My resting place was under the main hatch, where I had ensconced myself with two other young men in the space between the cargo and deck, of 15 or 18 inches; our blankets spread on the salt barrels. When we had all sunk into sweet repose, of a sudden an indescribable noise and hurly-burly aroused everyone. It seems without premonitory notice or indications, a terrific gale from the southwest had sprung up of such force as nearly to upset the vessel before the officers and crew could make preparations for meeting it. Fortunately the schooner had been hove to and most of the sails taken in, waiting for daylight, to make the harbor. Every effort was made by close reefing to keep her to the wind, but to no effect. It was soon found that our safest course was to let her drift before the wind, which she did under bare poles. In this manner we were driven back to Erie or Presque Isle, considerably more than 100 miles, where mooring her under the lee of the peninsula our anchor fortunately held her fast.

Still we were at the mercy of the furious elements. The wind and waves continued violent for another 24 hours, when they began to abate and the passengers got on shore. Whilst at anchor every sea passed from stem to stern over our decks with such force as to sweep away everything movable, such as caboose, hencoops, and even a small kedge anchor.

During the whole time my companions and myself were hatched down close, without light or food, rolling from side to side at every movement of the vessel. It was the severest bodily trial I had ever encountered, but being young and robust it had no serious effect.

The next morning after replenishing our stores we set sail under a favorable wind, but we were again disappointed in our hopes of reaching Sandusky. After a day's sail up the lake we were again driven back to Erie by a similar gale but less severe and of shorter duration. This was trying to the patience of all on board, and some of the passengers determined to try a land journey.

They hired wagons and proceeded up the lake over new and miserable roads and were 2 weeks on their way. . . . Relieved of so many, the balance of our party were made more comfortable. The third trial proved more successful and we reached Sandusky Bay early in October.

MARY A. W. PALMER

The Short Life

of the *Walk-in-the-Water*

The pioneer steam vessel above Niagara had a short life, making her first run in September of 1818 and her last run three years later.

On her two masts the *Walk-in-the-Water* carried mainsail, foresail and topmast staysail; in a fair wind that spread of canvas gave more propulsion than her engine. Her stack, made of six jointed lengths of stovepipe, reared up thirty feet above the sidewheels in her twin paddle boxes. Forty cords of hardwood on deck supplied fuel for her clattering engine. She carried twenty-nine paying passengers. Her cabins were below deck, as it was thought that exposed cabins could not withstand the lake storms. A carved figurehead of Commodore Oliver Hazard Perry peered from her prow.

After a season of voyaging between Buffalo and Detroit, this pioneer steamer ventured to distant Mackinac and Green Bay. On her second run to the North, in June, 1820, her passengers included General Alexander Macomb; fur merchant Ramsay Crooks; Dr. William Beaumont, who would make medical history; and the Rev. Jedediah Morse, missionary to the Indians, with his son Samuel F. B. Morse, who would give the world the telegraph. Returning from the northern wilds the steamer carried evergreen sprays in her topmasts. A New York paper compared these voyages to "the famous legendary expeditions of the Heroic Ages of Greece." To the Indians she was a thing of dread and wonder; they called her "Scootie-nabbie-quon" and fled from her presence. The vessel was named for a Wyandot chief who died just before the steamer's first voyage.

It happened that one passenger made both the first and the last trips of the *Walk-in-the-Water,* and walked away from her, wrecked hulk on the sands of Point Abino. Mrs. Mary A. Witherell Palmer recalled those two voyages, years afterward, for the Buffalo Historical Society.

THE FIRST STEAMBOAT built on the Upper Lakes was named the *Walk-in-the-Water*, not only from its appropriateness, but from a chief of the Wyandotte Indians, who lived with his band about twelve miles below Detroit, on the margin of the Detroit River. His Indian name was Mier, and signified a turtle, and his Totem, or signature, was the figure of a turtle.

The boat has been so often described that it is needless to repeat it. She was built at Black Rock, which place continued for some time to be her most eastern port and the terminus of her route; Buffalo at that time having no pier or dock to accommodate her.

She was hauled up the rapids by sixteen yoke of oxen, aided by her engine. She made her trial trip in August, 1818. I was a passenger on her first regular trip, as well as her last. She left Buffalo on her first regular trip, as near as I can recollect, on Wednesday morning, September 1st, 1818. She carried at that time considerable freight and a large number of passengers, among whom was the Earl of Selkirk, Lady Selkirk, and two children; Colonel Dixon, the British Indian Agent for the Northwest, Colonel Jno. Anderson, U. S. Engineer, his wife and wife's sister, Miss Taylor; Colonel Leavenworth, U. S. A., wife and daughter, Colonel James Watson of Washington city, Major Abraham Edwards, who subsequently lived in Detroit, and afterwards removed to Kalamazoo, Mich., where he died about two years ago. She reached Detroit at about 9 o'clock on Monday morning, September 5th, 1818, and as she ushered in a new era in the navigation of the Upper Lakes, her arrival was hailed with delight, and announced by the firing of one gun, which custom was continued for many years. Captain Job Fish was, I think, the commander at that time.

It so happened that on my return from New York, in company with my husband, Mr. Thomas Palmer, and his sister, now Mrs. Catherine Hickman, of this city, we arrived in Buffalo just in time to take passage on her last trip. She lay at the pier on the middle ground. We went on board in a yawl. The boat immediately got under way at 4 P.M., the last day of October, A.D. 1821, and steamed up the lake. Before we reached Point Abino the wind came on to blow a gale. Captain Rogers, her commander at that time, made every effort to get behind the Point (Abino), but the wind was too strong ahead. It rained incessantly. The night was very dark, and to add to the danger of the situation, the boat began to leak badly. About eight o'clock, the Captain, finding it impossible to proceed farther, put about and started for Buffalo.

The sailing master (Miller) proposed running the boat into the Niagara River and anchoring, but the Captain said it was so dark that she might strike the pier in the attempt, and in such a case no human power could save a soul on board. The boat was run to within a few miles of the pier, as the Captain supposed, no light from the lighthouse being visible, although as was afterwards learned, it had been kept brightly burning. Three anchors were dropped, one with a chain and two with hempen cables. The boat plunged heavily at her anchorage. This, I think, was about 10 o'clock in the evening. The leak continued to increase. The whole power of the engine was applied to the pumps. The boat dragged her anchors. The night was one of terrible suspense. It was the impression of the greater number on board that we should never see the morning.

The water gained gradually in spite of every exertion, and it became evident, as the night wore on, that the bark must founder or be run on shore, which the Captain concluded, either from the sound of the breakers or from calculations of distances and courses, could not be far off. Most of the passengers were calm. One instance of coolness I remember. A Mr. Thurston, when requested to go on deck and prepare for the worst, replied: "No, I have great confidence in Captain Rogers; he promised to land me in Cleveland, and I know he will do it," wrapped his cloak around him and lay down on a settee.

About half-past four in the morning the Captain sent down for all the passengers to come on deck. He had decided, although ignorant of the exact location, to permit the boat to go on shore. We could see no lights. The chain cable was slipped, and the two hempen ones cut. Drifting before the gale, the *Walk-in-the-Water*, in about half an hour, grazed the beach. The next swell let her down with a crash of crockery and of glass, the third left her farther up the shore, fixed immovably in the sand. The swells made a clean breach over her. Some of the ladies were in their night clothes, and all were repeatedly drenched.

When daylight came, a sailor succeeded in getting ashore in a small boat, with one end of a hawser, which he tied to a tree, the other end being tied on board. By the aid of the hawser, all the passengers were taken ashore in the small boat. I was handed down by the Captain to a sailor in the small boat, who placed me on a seat. My husband was not so fortunate. A swell carried the yawl ahead just as he jumped, and he went into the water shoulder deep.

We found ourselves about a mile above the lighthouse, in dismal plight, but thankful for the preservation of our lives. In company with a Mr. Calhoun, who was the engineer of the steamer, I ran to the lighthouse. After the lapse of so long a time, it seems to me that I almost flew along the beach, my exhilaration was so great.

The lighthouse keeper anticipating wrecks or disasters (I think signal guns had been fired during the night on board the *Walk-in-the-Water*) had a rousing fire in his huge fire-place, by which we remained until carriages came down for us from Buffalo. The citizens had supposed it impossible that the boat could live through the night, and when, at break of day, she was described upon the beach, their efforts were directed to the care of the passengers and crew. All that could be done for our comfort was done. We were taken to the Landen House, a two-story frame building, then the principal hotel at Buffalo. It stood on the brow of the hill as we went up from the creek. We returned to Detroit by wagon through Canada, a trip occupying two weeks.

The day after we got back to Buffalo, Captain Rogers called upon us. In the course of conversation he told me that his assurance of safety during the storm was anything but heartfelt; that during the gale he had secured the boat's papers on his person, thinking that should the boat and he be lost, his body would be washed ashore and the papers recovered.

Among the passengers now remembered were Major or Jed. Hunt, Lieutenant McKenzie, U. S. A., Jno. Hale, Esq., then a merchant of Canandaigua, afterwards merchant of this place, Jason Thurston, Esq., of Michigan, Rev. Mr. Hart, a missionary to Michigan, and wife, John S. Hudson and wife, and a Miss Osborn, who were on their way to Fort Gratiot to establish a mission for the Indians. Mr. and Mrs. Salsmer, of Ohio, Mr. Palmer and myself, and Mr. Palmer's sister, now Mrs. Catherine Hinchman, of this city.

A young gentleman of Buffalo, by name of J. D. Matthies, went down to the beach where the wreck lay, and, being an amateur artist, took sketches of it in two different positions, painted them and sent them to me at this place. They are now deposited among the archives of the Michigan Historical Society.

The deck of the *Walk-in-the-Water* was like that of sailing vessels of the present day. The cabins were beneath the main deck, the after part partitioned off for ladies. The rest was devoted to gentlemen and answered for lodging, dining, and baggage room. The mast ran down through the gentlemen's cabin, and that part in the cabin was set in octagon with small mirrors. In visiting the wreck, a few days after the disaster, I remember that it laid broadside on shore. I could almost walk around it dry shod; the sand had been deposited around it to such an extent, the oakum had worked out of the seams in the deck for yards in a place, and the panel work had become disjointed in many places.

Return

of the *Superior*

After the wreck of the *Walk-in-the-Water* on Abino Point near Buffalo, her salvaged engines were installed in a new and larger steamer, the *Superior*. Ahead of her main cabin the *Superior* had a roomy steerage hold fitted with bunks, stoves, tables and benches for families moving West. She carried emigrant settlers for half the cabin fare.

The *Superior* was the first steamer to stain the skies of the St. Marys River; in 1822 she brought Henry Rowe Schoolcraft to his post as Indian agent at the Soo, along with 250 soldiers who were to erect Fort Brady there. Actually the steamer was stopped by the limestone "flats" at the foot of Lake George, and her company completed their trip to Sault Ste. Marie in three bateaux.

On July 4, 1825, with her signal cannon booming, the *Superior* brought Governor DeWitt Clinton to Cleveland to dig the first spade of earth for the Ohio Canal.

When the *Superior* was broken up, after a dozen years of service, her veteran engines were bought by a Saginaw man to power a sawmill. They were finally destroyed by fire, the result of a Fourth of July celebration in 1854.

One grim voyage was recorded in the eventful log of the *Superior*. Cholera came aboard in the summer of 1832 when she loaded troops in Buffalo for the Black Hawk War. Many of those soldiers were buried in Lake Huron. Nine years earlier, in the fall of 1823 she had made the long trip to Green Bay, and rough weather on Lake Michigan delayed her return. Bad news travels fast. A rumor of shipwreck reached Detroit a few days before the steamer's safe arrival—as recorded in the *Detroit Gazette* on October 24, 1823. The account was given by a passenger on the voyage.

A S AN EVIL REPORT spreads faster than a good one, you probably have heard that the steamboat *Superior* was lost in Lake Michigan, on her passage to Green Bay.

The false rumor probably originated in the circumstance of her having touched at one of the islands to take in wood, at which time some Indian canoes passed at a distance. When they arrived at Mackinac they reported that she had gone ashore; which they really supposed to be the fact, and offered to join a party to go to her aid. The rumor went to Drummond's Island, and so rapid was the spread of the report from thence, that it reached Detroit, thence down Lake Erie, etc., four or five days ahead of the safe-returning boat.

She was absent six days longer than had been advertised, owing to bad weather from Mackinac to the Bay; but she sustained no injury whatever. Returning, she sailed from Detroit on Saturday, the sixth of September, in a storm of rain. The captain would not have left port in such unfavorable weather, but for the anxiety he apprehended would be felt below on account of the rumor afloat that she was lost.

After leaving the mouth of the Detroit river, the storm increased, the captain, with his accustomed prudence, put back and anchored. The storm having abated a little, he got under weigh at eight o'clock in the morning of the seventh, calculating to make Sandusky Bay. The wind soon increased to a violent gale, and it was impossible to make Sandusky. Put-in-Bay was to us, what it had been to many vessels in distress—a harbor of safety; where we rode at anchor till the ninth. We lost some wood, and one of the hands, whose death was caused by a fall; but the boat itself sustained not the least damage, and maintained her character as the *Superior*. In this gale, during the heaviest part of which we were out, there were some of the best schooners that navigate these lakes lost. The *Erie*, Captain Pease, a fine vessel, well manned, a discreet and able captain, was capsized, nearly opposite Cleveland; her masts were cut away, when she righted, and drifted ashore, with fourteen passengers and crew all safe.

The advantage a steamboat has over a vessel, in a gale, is decided, and appears obvious; her steam power enables her to keep off from a lee shore. Perhaps it will be said that the *Walk-in-the-Water* went ashore. True; but had she been well-built (as every vessel, steam or other, should be, to weather the hurricanes of Lake Erie), she would not have gone ashore. The present boat was built upon the knowledge obtained in the disaster of the *Walk-in-the-Water*. A more staunch vessel, of her size, perhaps, was never afloat.

Stormy Passage

In September, 1825, after the great Indian congress at Prairie du Chien, Henry Rowe Schoolcraft headed home to his wife and infant son at the Sault. With his *voyageurs* he paddled up the Wisconsin River and down the Fox; at Green Bay they were provisioned with fresh melons, cabbages and new potatoes. A fair wind hurried them over Lake Michigan while Schoolcraft read a book on *China, Its Arts, Manufactures, etc.* They reached Mackinac in six days. In another day and a half, Schoolcraft thought, he would be at home.

But the weather changed. For two days fog and head winds kept them idle, and then an equinoctial gale lashed their bleak camp on Outard Point. At last they ran the stormy passage to the sheltered St. Marys.

These pages from Schoolcraft's diary were incorporated in his *Personal Memoirs of a Residence of Thirty Years with the Indian Tribes on the American Frontiers,* 1851.

1825. *Sept. 5th* Michilimackinac. I arose at seven, and we had breakfast at half-past seven. I then went to the Company's store and ordered an invoice of goods for the Indian department. This occupied the time till dinner was announced. I then went to my camp and ordered the tent to be struck and the canoe to be put into the water; but found two of my men so ill with the fever and ague that they could not go, and three others were much intoxicated. The atmosphere was very cloudy and threatening, and to attempt the traverse to Goose Island, under such circumstances, was deemed improper. Mr. Robert and David Stuart, men noted in the Astoria enterprise; Mr. Agnew, Capt. Knapp, Mr. Conner, Mr. Abbott, Mr. Currey, &c., had kindly accompanied me to the beach, but all were very urgent in their opinion that I should defer the starting. I ordered the men to be ready at two o'clock in the morning should the weather not prove tempestuous.

6th. I arose at three o'clock, but found a heavy fog enveloping the whole island, and concealing objects at a short distance. It was not till half-past six that I could embark, when the fog began to disperse, but the clearing away of the fog introduced a light head wind. I reached Goose Island, a distance of ten miles, after a march of three hours, and afterwards went to Outard Point, but could go no further from the increased violence of the wind.

Outard Point, 8 o'clock P.M. Here I have been encamped since noon, with a head wind, a dense damp atmosphere, and the lake in a foam. I expected the wind would fall with the sun, but, alas! it blows stronger than ever. I fondly hoped on quitting Mackinac this morning, that I should see home to-morrow, but that is now impossible. How confidently do we hope and expect in this life, and how little do we know what is to befall us for even a few hours beyond the present moment. It has pleased the All-wise Being to give me an adverse wind, and I must submit to it. I, doubtless, exulted too soon and too much. On reaching Mackinac, I said to myself: "My journey is accomplished; my route to the Sault is nothing; I can go there in a day and a half, wind or no wind." This vanity and presumption is now punished, and, I acknowledge, justly. I should have left it to Providence. Wise are the ways of the Almighty, and salutary all His dispensations to man. Were we not continually put in mind of an overruling Providence by reverses of this kind, the human heart, exalted with its own consequence, would soon cease to implore protection from on high.

I feel solitary. The loud dashing of the waves on shore, and the darkness and dreariness of all without my tent, conspire to give a saddened train to my reflections. I endeavored to divert myself, soon after landing, by a stroll along the shore. I sought in vain among the loose fragments of rock for some specimens worthy of preservation. I gleaned the evidences of crystallization and the traces of organic forms among the cast-up fragments of limestone and sandstone. I amused myself with the reflection that I should, perhaps, meet you coming from an opposite direction on the beach, and I half fancied that, perhaps, it would actually take place. Vain sport of the mind! It served to cheat away a tedious hour, and I returned to my tent fatigued and half sick. I am in hopes a cup of tea and a night's rest will restore my equiposie of mind and body. Thus

"Every pang that rends the heart,
Bids expectation rise."

7th. Still detained on this bleak and desolate Point. A heavy rain and very strong gale continued all night. The rain was driven with such violence as to penetrate through the texture of my tent, and fall copiously upon me. Daybreak brought with it no abatement of the storm, but presented to my view a wide vista of white foaming surge as far as the eye could reach. In consequence of the increasing violence of the storm, I was compelled to order my baggage and canoe to be removed, and my tent to be pitched back among the trees. How long I am to remain here I cannot conjecture. It is a real equinoxial storm. My ears are stunned with the incessant roaring of the water and the loud murmuring of the wind among the foliage. Thick murky clouds obscure the sky, and a chill damp air compels me to sit in my tent with my cloak on. I may exclaim, in the language of the Chippewas, *Tyau, gitche sunnahgud* (oh, how hard is my fate.)

At two o'clock I made another excursion to view the broad lake and see if some favorable sign could not be drawn, but returned with nothing to cast a gleam on the angry vista. It seemed as if the lake was convulsed to its bottom.

About three o'clock P.M. there was a transient gleam of sunshine, and, for a few moments, a slight abatement of wind. I ordered my canoe and baggage taken inland to another narrow little bay, having issue into the lake, where the water was calm enough to permit its being loaded; but before this was accomplished, a most portentous cloud gathered in the west, and the wind arose more fierce than before. Huron, like an offended and capricious mistress, seemed to be determined, at last, on fury, and threw herself into the most extravagant attitudes. I again had my tent pitched, and sat down quietly to wait till the tempest should subside; but up to a late hour at night the elemental war continued, and, committing myself to the Divine mercy, I put out my candle and retired to my pallet.

8th. The frowning mistress, Lake Huron, still has the pouts. About seven o'clock I walked, or scrambled my way through close-matted spruce and brambles to get a view of the open lake. The force of the waves was not, perhaps, much different from the day before, but they were directly from the west, and blowing directly down the lake. Could I get out from the nook of a bay where I was encamped, and get directly before them, it appeared possible, with a close-reefed sail, to go on my way. My *engagees* thought it too hazardous to try, but their habitual sense of obedience to a *bourgeoise* led them to put the canoe in the water, and at 10 o'clock we left our encampment on Outard Point, got out into the lake, not without imminent hazard, and began our career "like a racehorse" for the Capes of the St. Marys. The wind blew as if "'twad blawn its last." We had reefed our sail to less than four feet, and I put an extra man with the steersman. We literally went "on the wings of the wind." I do not think myself ever to have run such hazards. I was tossed up and down the waves like Sancho Panza on the blanket. Three hours and twenty minutes brought me to Isle St. Vital, behind which we got shelter. The good saint who presides over the island of gravel and sand permitted me to take a glass of cordial from my basket, and to refresh myself with a slice of cold tongue and a biscuit. Who this St. Vital may have been, I know not, having been brought up a Protestant; but I suppose the Catholic calendar would tell. If his saintship was as fond of good living as some of his friends are said to be, I make no doubt but he will freely forgive this trespass upon his territory. Taking courage by this refreshment, we again put out before the gale, and got in to the De Tour, and by seven o'clock, P.M., were safely encamped on an island in St. Marys Straits, opposite St. Joseph's. The wind was here ahead.

On entering the straits, I found a vessel at anchor. On coming alongside it proved to be the schooner *Harriet*, Capt. Allen, of Mount Clemens, on her way from the Sault. A passenger on board says that he was at Mr. Johnston's house two days ago, and all are well. He says the Chippewa chiefs arrived yesterday. Regret that I had not forwarded by them the letter which I had prepared at the Prairie to transmit by Mr. Holliday, when I supposed I should return by way of Chippewa River and Lake Superior.

I procured from the *Harriet* a whitefish, of which I have just partaken a supper. This delicious fish is always a treat to me, but was never more so than on the present occasion. I landed here fatigued, wet, and cold, but, from the effects of a cheerful fire, good news from home, and bright anticipations for to-morrow, I feel quite re-invigorated. "Tired nature's sweet restorer" must complete what tea and whitefish have so successfully begun.

9*th.* My journal has no entry for this day, but it brought me safely (some 40 miles) to my own domicil at "Elmwood." The excitement of getting back and finding all well drove away almost all other thoughts.

Rough Weather,

1835

The year 1835 saw five steamers added to the Great Lakes trade, but in the last month of the season a score of ships were lost, along with hundreds of lives. The storm of November 11 lashed all the lakes, but commerce was concentrated on Lake Erie and Lake Ontario, and it was there that the wrecks piled up.

One survivor of that storm was Henry Rowe Schoolcraft, voyaging down from Mackinac. His experience provided a cheerful ending for J. B. Mansfield's account of a somber time. This excerpt is from the *History of the Great Lakes*, 1899.

THE SEASON OF 1835 wound up with one of the most terrific gales that ever visited the lake region, and, in proportion to the number of vessels employed, caused a greater destruction of life and property than ever before. It occurred November 11. The wind was west-southwest and, it is said, announced its approach like the sound of an immense train of cars. At Buffalo the creek rose to a height of 20 feet, floating steamers and vessels into some of the main streets, crushing canal boats under bridges, while on the west side of the harbor dwellings were swept away and the occupants drowned.

A vessel called the *Free Trader,* with 13 passengers on board beside the crew, took her departure from Fort Burwell, Canada, for Cleveland, and was struck by the gale and twice capsized, righting each time. After the storm she was discovered drifting off Dunkirk, and was taken into that port with one sailor still alive and clinging to the tiller. Among the passengers was Mr. Richardson, owner of the cargo.

The schooner *Comet,* of Buffalo, left Madison dock, below **Fair-**

port, with fifteen tons of iron and five tons of ashes. The crew consisted of six sailors, and there was one passenger. She is supposed to have foundered off Dunkirk, as two topmasts were afterward seen in that locality, and several articles, recognized as belonging to them, floated ashore.

The steamboat *North America* was driven on the beach at Erie. She was commanded by Capt. G. Appleby. The steamers *Sandusky, Henry Clay* and *Sheldon Thompson* were floated on the bank in Buffalo harbor and seriously damaged. The *North America*, prior to going ashore, had let go her anchors and attempted to ride out the gale at Erie, but the wind, increasing in its fury, soon parted her cables, while the passengers and crew gave themselves up as lost, but it was suggested to scuttle the boat to prevent her jumping over the pier, and to this action the salvation of the boat may be ascribed. The schooner *Two Brothers* was landed on top of the Buffalo pier and became a total loss.

Vessels which were outside, as soon as the cyclone set in, tried to reach the nearest port, and when forced to Buffalo, on entering the harbor an immense amount of damage was done, as the creek at that time was crowded with vessels. Boats were run into and sunk, while the whole extent of the loss of life ranged far into the hundreds. Among the schooners ashore at Buffalo were the *Tecumseh* and the *Col. Benton*. The flood was the highest known since 1816 and the most destructive. Wharves and piers at various lake ports were demolished, and scarcely a vestige left. At Portland harbor two persons were drowned from the pier on account of the sudden approach of high water. The schooner *Godolphin*, freighted with salt, was wrecked at Fairport and crew lost.

The schooner *Lagrange*, a fine vessel, commanded by Captain Chanchois, with a full cargo of merchandise from Buffalo for Detroit, was capsized near Point Pelee and sunk about seven miles from shore. All perished except a man and boy, who were taken off the mast next morning, nearly frozen to death. The vessel was never recovered.

The storm on Lake Ontario was very severe, and the casualties large. On that lake the schooner *Robert Bruce,* which left Kingston, Canada, for some port up the Bay of Quinte, in ballast, was wrecked and all on board were lost. The wreck, after the storm, drifted ashore on Henderson Point, and the coat of a passenger, Elias Everett, was found hanging to a nail, and his wallet, containing $719, was recovered. The schooner *Medora*, owned in Oswego, from up the lake, laden with wheat and walnuts, went ashore at the mouth of Big Sandy creek, and all hands were lost.

Among the vessels lost on Lake Michigan during that storm

were the schooners *Chance, Bridget, Sloan* and *Delaware*. On the *Chance* seven lives were lost; on the *Bridget,* 16; on the *Sloan,* six. The *Bridget* was wrecked near St. Joseph.

Schoolcraft bears testimony to the skill of the old-time captain during this storm. He embarked November 2, 1835, at Mackinac for Detroit, "on board a schooner under command of an experienced navigator (Captain Ward) just on the eve, unknown to us, of a great tempest, which rendered that season memorable in the history of wrecks on the Great Lakes. We had scarcely well cleared the lighthouse, when the wind increased to a gale. We soon went on furiously. Sails were reefed and every preparation made to keep on our way, but the wind did not admit of it. The captain made every effort to hug the shore, and finally came to anchor in great peril, under the highlands of Sauble. Here we pitched terribly, and were momently in peril of being cast on shore. In the effort to work the ship, one of the men fell from the bowsprit, passed under the vessel and was lost. It was thought that our poor little craft must go to the bottom, but owing to the skill of the old lake mariner we eventually triumphed. He never faltered in the darkest exigency. For a day and night he struggled against the elements, and finally entered the strait at Fort Gratiot, and he brought us safely into the port of our destination."

The Christmas Tree
Schooner

Eighty years ago schooners in the northern ports loaded evergreen trees for the last run of the season. Under reefed sails they hurried through sleet and snow toward Chicago, Detroit and Cleveland.

Three schooners in that trade were owned by Hackley Hume of Muskegon—the *Rouse Simmons*, the *Charles Hackley* and the *Thomas Hume*. Each of them met a violent end. Sixty years ago, in the fading light of an autumn afternoon, the *Rouse Simmons* and the *Thomas Hume* cleared Chicago together. They separated on Lake Michigan, and the *Hume* was never seen again. Afterward, Captain Dane of the *Simmons* said there was a light breeze all the way to Muskegon, and he reported some twenty vessels in the Muskegon-Chicago lane that night. None of those vessels sighted the *Hume*, or saw evidence of her distress. But she was gone forever.

During the next few seasons the owners sent Captain Dane to many points where wreckage was cast ashore. He never found a scrap that he could identify. For a time there was a theory that the crew had stolen the *Hume*, changed her name and altered her rig and were sailing her on the lakes. But their families continued to live in Muskegon, and the missing men never returned. The *Hume* had disappeared in total mystery.

A few seasons later the *Charles Hackley* went ashore and was broken up, and the *Rouse Simmons* was bought by the Schueneman brothers of Chicago. They operated the last of the Christmas tree fleet. When the *Simmons* disappeared in a November gale in 1912, there was a shadow on the Christmas season.

Hundreds of sailing vessels were lost and forgotten on the lakes, but this one has been remembered. The wreck of the *Rouse Simmons*, with its Christmas cargo strewn upon the winter coast, has a lasting place in Great Lakes folklore. For half a century it has been told in story and sung in rhyme.

While the *Rouse Simmons* was still fresh in memory, Vincent Starrett wrote a ballad of many quatrains, which begins:

This is the tale of the Christmas ship
That sailed o'er the sullen lake,
And of sixteen souls that made the trip,
And of death in the foaming wake.

More recently, in *The Chicago*, 1942, Harry Hansen recalled the lost schooner, and along with it the memory of a sturdy Lake Michigan family.

CHRISTMAS IN CHICAGO, fifty years ago, was a happy, home festival in a city not yet too rich, too pretentious, to be neighborly. There was usually snow at Christmas; it lay in large heaps in the gutters and was packed solid on the streets. When snow fell it was heavy with moisture; it blocked trains and held up streetcars. The average citizen shoveled his own sidewalks clean and looked after his own fires. A few blocks beyond the Loop, where the gray wooden cottages with their scrollwork porches stretched for miles, householders would be out early in the mornings wielding their shovels, amid shouts to their neighbors, for in those days families lived long enough in one locality to become known to one another.

In the houses on the near North Side, where brick buildings abounded, the windows had little wooden blinds inside through which came the yellow rays of light from gas jets. The air in the streets outside had the close feeling of a low-ceilinged room and shouts rebounded from wall to wall. In that air bells on sleighs jingled in time a long way off and hoofbeats made a dull patter on the packed snow. As the sleigh passed under the light of the gas lamp at the corner you could see the prancing horse, the curved dashboard, the gleam of the nickeled bars across the front, the flash of the runners. The driver would be wearing a wide fur collar and a fur cap; the woman beside him would be tucked under fur robes and look very comfortable in a brown fur neckpiece and toque.

Inside, the house was warm and a bit stuffy with dry air. The carpets had a firm surface and gay curlicues of vine leaves all over them. The hall might be dark; its walls were covered with embossed paper, stained to the color of leather, and the gaslight flickered behind a globe of pink glass ornamented with a trailing vine. You walked quickly past the parlor, which had a mantlepiece of black slate and a mirror over the fireplace and heavy chairs and settees with curved walnut legs, to the back room where all the family gathered. Here the walls were hung with photographs of young and old and there were music racks and bookshelves. If the house was heated by a furnace, the hot air flooded up through a register in the floor, but more likely a big-bellied stove, consuming anthracite coal, gleamed red through mica windows in a corner. And in the bay stood the Christmas tree.

Most likely the father of the family had picked it out and carried it home. Men and women carried their own bundles in those days. Perhaps he walked down to the Clark Street bridge, a week or two before Christmas, to see if the Schuenemanns had come down from Wisconsin with a load of spruce trees. Invariably the two big, brawny lads would be there with a fishing schooner loaded with trees that they themselves had cut in the Michigan woods. They were fine, well-shaped trees and cost so little—for 75 cents you bought a fullsized tree; for $1 you had your choice of the best. Even saplings provided bright decorations for a city where people were making money, but not too much money, and where the average citizen was always fearful of hard times.

As long ago as 1887 the two Schuenemanns, Herman and August, had sailed down in a schooner from Manistique, Michigan, with a load of spruce and tied up beside the dock behind the old red-brick commission houses at the Clark Street bridge. There Chicago found them and bought their stock, and called Herman captain and remembered to look for him the following year. When snow fell on Chicago's streets in December days the father of the family would say, "Guess I'll have to go down to the Clark Street bridge to see if the captain is in and get us a tree."

Fifty years ago the work of providing trees for Christmas was not yet the mass-production business it has become in recent times. No dealer contracted for thousands of trees as a speculation and destroyed great numbers if he had guessed wrong on the demand. No man cut down whole hillsides to satisfy the whims of people who followed a custom but didn't know how to pray. There were plenty of trees for all. The Schuenemanns went into the woods behind Manistique and Thompson, Michigan, where young trees grew on land that had been cut over to make the lumber that went into midwestern houses a generation before. They chose the trees carefully, including some tall ones for which they had orders from churches and hotels. Sometimes they had to work in the snow and when the trees reached Chicago there was still snow on the branches. The brothers thought they had done well when they made a modest profit on a trip that occupied about six weeks of the wintry season, when it was hard to haul other cargoes.

The work was not easy, neither the cutting nor the sailing, for they always came when Lake Michigan kicked up a lot of rough sea. In 1898 August had just set sail with a load of trees when a storm arose and he and his ship were lost. Thereupon Herman determined to carry on alone. In 1899 he was back at the Clark Street dock with his boat, the *Rouse Simmons,* loaded with Christmas trees. He was a jovial man, with a very ruddy complexion and laughing wrinkles around his blue eyes, and everybody liked him.

For eleven years Herman arrived with his cargo and many people depended on him for a tree year after year. Then came the hard season of 1912, with storms and heavy seas on Lake Michigan. Late in November Herman cut his trees in the woods behind Manistique and started for Chicago in the *Rouse Simmons,* with a crew of seventeen men. There were head winds and heavy seas from the start and soon the schooner was struggling in a raging snowstorm. What took place on board we can only guess. The *Rouse Simmons* sailed into the silence that covers all the fine ships that have fallen victim to the gales of Lake Michigan, which have taken the lives of so many, from the days of La Salle's *Griffin* until now.

Long before Chicago missed the *Rouse Simmons* at its dock reports began to come of the ship's distress. A schooner resembling it was said to have been sighted off Kewaunee, Wisconsin, flying distress signals. The steamer *George W. Orr* reported to the revenue cutter *Tuscarora* that she had seen the *Rouse Simmons* three miles offshore, but the captain later admitted that he might have been mistaken. But on December 5, 1912, fishermen off Two Rivers Point, seven miles north of Manitowoc, Wisconsin, found the tops of spruce trees entangled in their nets. Trees had been roped together on the deck of the *Rouse Simmons,* and how could they get into the lake at that point if not off a ship?

On December 13th a watcher on the beach at Sheboygan, Wisconsin, reported that he had picked up a bottle containing a message that came from the captain. It had been written on a page of the ship's log and read:

Friday—Everybody goodbye. I guess we are all through. Sea washed over our deckload Thursday. During the night the small boat was washed over. Leaking bad. Ingvald and Steve fell overboard Thursday. God help us.

Herman Schuenemann

The men referred to were believed to have been Steve E. Nelson, mate, and Ingvald Nylons, seaman. But if there was such a message, it never reached the captain's wife, who was eagerly waiting for scraps of news in her Manistique home. She was a valiant little woman, with a great deal of stamina. When she realized that her three little girls, Elsie and the twins, Pearl and Hazel, were now dependent wholly on her efforts, she resolved to take up her husband's task.

There was no Christmas ship at the Clark Street dock in 1912. But when 1913 came, Chicago residents who looked over the railings of the bridge beheld another schooner, loaded with trees, as in the days when Captain Herman held forth there. On board was the plucky little wife of the captain. She had gone into the woods with the woodcutters and supervised the felling of the trees. With her, too, were her girls, as well as women to weave wreaths and garlands. Chicago was to become well acquainted with the Schuenemanns. They were to come season after season for twenty-two years after the *Rouse Simmons* went down.

For years Chicago friends would ask the captain's wife whether there had been any definite report on the *Rouse Simmons,* and she could only shake her head sorrowfully. Yet the sea, which guards its secrets well, reluctantly gave up tangible evidence fourteen years after the disaster. On April 23, 1924, the wallet of Captain Schuenemann was found at Two Rivers Point, where the spruce trees had been tangled in the fishermen's nets. It still had the original rubber band around it and the cards and clippings inside seemed to be made of plaster. Some of the clippings related to earlier voyages of the Christmas tree ship. Three years after this find a bottle with a note signed by Charles Nelson was picked up. It read:

These lines were written at 10:30 P.M. Schooner R. S. ready to go down about 20 miles southeast Two Rivers Point between fifteen or twenty miles off shore. All hands lashed to one line. Goodbye.

Eventually the family made its last voyage to the Chicago market with Christmas trees. The mother had grown gray; the girls were handsome young women. Forty-seven years had elapsed since Herman, as an 18-year-old lad, had steered his first cargo into Chicago. The ship had become an institution.

Its fame grew. Today when the winds blow hard on the lake and the heavy surf pounds the frozen shore line watchers in the lighthouses recall the *Rouse Simmons.* Long ago it inspired a ballad. When word of its loss reached Chicago newspapers Vincent Starrett, bibliophile and author of many books of fiction and belles-lettres, was a reporter on the *Daily News.* His editor was Henry Justin Smith. "It would make a fine ballad," said Starrett. "Why don't you write it?" replied Smith. So Starrett composed "The Ballad of the Christmas Ship," a poem of many, many quatrains, and Smith found room for it among the crowded columns of the day's news. It may never challenge the efforts of youthful orators as often as "The Wreck of the Hesperus," but the legend is just as moving and the intentions of the poet were as good as Longfellow's.

JULIUS F. WOLFF, JR.

Grim November

In the year 1900, nineteen million tons of iron ore were shipped from Lake Superior, more than twice the tonnage of a decade earlier. Five years later the tonnage nearly doubled again, though not all of it reached the lower lakes. For 1905 was a year of unprecedented shipwreck and destruction.

From newspaper accounts of that grim year Julius F. Wolff, Jr., of the Duluth branch of the University of Minnesota, compiled a record of strandings and collisions, of vessels battered and broken, of men washed overboard from ships with crippled steering gear and flooded engine rooms.

A raging storm swept Lake Superior in the first three days of September. October brought gale winds that strewed the shores with the wreckage of schooners and steamers. The climax came in the last days of November—as recorded in this stormy narrative from volume 18 of *Inland Seas*.

O N NOVEMBER 23, storm warnings were hoisted over Lake Superior, presaging heavy rain, snow, and a frightful gale at Duluth with winds over sixty miles an hour. Caught in this blow, the steamer *Charlemagne Tower* narrowly made Portage, creeping in with considerable damage. Forewarned, most other shipping apparently stayed under shelter. By Saturday, November 25, the worst seemingly had passed, and ships ventured out from all ports. The weekend weather was ominous, yet, big storms seldom follow each other in immediate succession on Lake Superior, so shipping schedules were resumed for the final rush. Thus, dozens of ships were on the open water. Then came the sledge-hammer blow of weather. At 7:00 P.M., November 27, a howling gale out of the northeast, carrying blinding snow, poured over the Lake at

Duluth, moving east. An initial wind velocity of 44 miles an hour gradually increased to 60 miles an hour, then to 70. For more than 12 hours the gale roared in excess of 60 miles an hour, with some gusts unofficially reported up to 80. The results were catastrophic. Close to thirty ships were victimized, including one foundering, 17 strandings, and substantial storm damage to another dozen. At least 32 men lost their lives. The port of Duluth was a shambles. . . .

The gale was at its worst after the early morning hours of November 28 and persisted well into that night. A panoramic view of western Lake Superior the following morning would disclose the following terrible story. Stranded at Duluth were the Pittsburghers *Isaac Ellwood* and *Mataafa* and the Tomlinson steamer *R. W. England*. Seven miles northeast of Duluth harbor, near Lakewood, lay the Pittsburgh steamer *Crescent City*, right up against the cliff-lined shore. At Encampment Island, seven miles northeast of Two Harbors, were the Pittsburghers, the steamer *Lafayette* and the barge *Manila*, both plastered against the shore, the *Lafayette* broken up. Near Split Rock River, 12 miles to the northeast, the Pittsburgher *William Edenborn* was hard ashore and broken in two, with her escaped barge, the *Madeira*, broken in two and sunk at Gold Rock, three miles northeast. At Two Islands, near Schroeder, the scow *George Herbert* was smashed to pieces, while at Thomasville, close to Tofte, the coal-laden wooden steamer *George Spencer* stood hard aground, along with her barge *Amboy*. On the approach to Port Arthur, at Pie Island, the Canadian steamer *Monkshaven* was firmly on the rocks. On the South Shore at Gull Island in the Apostles lay the Pittsburgh flagship *W. E. Corey*, stranded tight; at Fourteen-Mile Point, near Ontonagon, the *Western Star* was in the same predicament, while on the east side of the Keweenaw at Point Isabelle, the Pittsburgh steamer *Coralia* and the barge *Maia* were hung up. Foundered somewhere northeast of Outer Island was the grain steamer *Ira Owen*. Enjoying fantastic escapes, although some with serious storm damage, were the steamers *Angeline, Arizona, Bransford, H. B. Nye, E. C. Pope, Umbria, P. G. Walker, Yosemite*, and the barge *Constitution*.

Only the more destructive accidents will be noted. The worst loss of life occurred in the foundering of the National Steamship Company's 262-foot, 1,753-ton, steel steamer *Ira Owen* under Captain Joseph Hulligan, downbound with a cargo of barley. The *Owen* was last seen by Captain Alva Keller of the steamer *H. B. Nye* blowing distress signals off Outer Island at the height of the storm on November 28. The *Nye*, in distress herself, could lend no help. Wreckage of the *Owen*, including marked life preservers, was sighted December 1 by Captain M. K. Chamberlain of the steamer *William Siemens*, 12 miles east of Michigan Island. No trace was ever found of her 19-man crew.

The *Mataafa* stranding at the Duluth pier head is a well-known tale. The Pittsburgher *Mataafa*, a 430-foot, 4,840-ton vessel, heavily laden with iron ore, attempted to regain the Duluth harbor at 2:15 P.M., November 28, from which she had sailed the preceding day. Tempestuous seas drove the steamer against the north pier, and she fell outside the canal, stranding 100 feet north of the north pier, about 600 feet off the beach. Within an hour she broke in two. The lifesavers of the Duluth station, at the time engaged in rescuing the crew of the stranded *R. W. England* three miles away on Minnesota Point, could not reach the *Mataafa* scene until 5 P.M. They did place lines aboard the bow of the stricken freighter, but due to the storm and icing a breeches buoy could not be rigged. Fifteen men who had taken refuge in the vessel's forward quarters were kept alive by vigorous action of Captain R. H. Humble and the ship's officer. The nine who remained on the stern, however, either froze to death or were swept overboard. At daylight the following morning, when the storm had subsided a little, the Duluth lifesavers courageously launched a lifeboat and rescued the survivors. Nearly eight months later, the *Mataafa* was taken off by veteran salvager Tom Reid of Sarnia and rebuilt at a cost in excess of $100,000.

No lives were lost in the stranding of the 406-foot, 4,213-ton Pittsburgher *Crescent City* which was neatly deposited against the shore at Lakewood, outside Duluth. The crew crawled ashore on a ladder but suffered exposure in obtaining shelter. She likewise was salvaged months later and rebuilt at an expenditure of $100,000.

At Encampment Island one man was lost when the Pittsburgher *Lafayette* was smashed to pieces against the mainland, with the barge *Manila* slapped nearby against the shore with trees protruding through her rigging. Dexterous use of lines by the crews saved all except one fireman. The survivors under Captain D. P. Wright spent an agonizing 24 hours, half-frozen in the forest around bonfires, until they were able to climb back aboard the barge *Manila* the following day, from which they were rescued on November 29 by the tug *Edna G*. The *Lafayette* was a total loss of over $300,000, only a portion of her stern and engines being salvaged seven months later. The *Manila* was taken off without too grave difficulty.

Near Split Rock River, 45 miles northeast of Duluth, the Pittsburgher *William Edenborn* did a thorough job of running ashore early on November 28, actually sticking her bow in the forest. In this position she broke in two, but her crew was able to stay aboard, although third assistant engineer Johnson was killed by falling into an open hatch. Her skipper, Captain Talbot, sent word of his mishap to Two Harbors by fisherman Octave Iverson, who walked for 12 consecutive hours, 18 snow-drifted miles, through the roaring blizzard. The *Edenborn,* a 5,085-ton, 475-foot steel steamer, only five years old, was a $100,000 repair bill. Not as fortunate was the 5,039-ton, 436-foot barge *Madeira,* also built in 1900. The *Madeira* broke her towline from the *Edenborn* about 3:30 A.M. The ravaging gale, however, drove her shoreward so that she smashed into Gold Rock (the next promontory north of modern Split Rock Lighthouse) about 5:30 A.M., November 28, three miles northeast of her disabled steamer. The barge was pounded repeatedly against the rugged outcrop until she broke in two, both halves sinking, yet all except one of her ten-man crew were snatched from the jaws of death by superhuman work on the part of seaman Fred Benson. With a line around his waist, Benson leaped from the stricken barge to a tree on the face of the cliff, then like a human fly scaled the perpendicular escarpment. He induced the remaining bow crew to follow him. Then, by neat manipulation of the line, he assisted the rest on the sinking stern to reach the top of the cliff. Mate John Morrow fell from the mast and drowned, the only fatality. The *Madeira,* a $175,000 loss, was never salvaged.

Forty miles to the northeast, near Tofte, Minnesota, a thrilling ship-to-shore rescue was accomplished by the crews of the wooden 230-foot steamer *George Spencer* and her barge *Amboy,* with the help of shore residents. The two, coal-laden, were swept aground on the one decent piece of beach found for miles. Fishermen and lumberjacks waded into the surf and seized lines floated from the two ships. Then, with the aid of seaman James Gibson of the *Amboy,* who came to shore hand-over-hand on the line above 50 yards of boiling water, they rigged breeches buoys and took off the remaining 22 persons in the two crews. Wreckers salvaged the *Spencer* three weeks later, though the *Amboy,* a 209-foot, 894-ton schooner built in 1874, was a reported total loss. Repairs to the *Spencer* cost $30,000.

A pathetic death for three Duluth sailors occurred at Two Islands River, southwest of Schroeder, when the small 305-ton scow *George Herbert* broke the towline of the tug *Gillette* while anchored in the lee of Two Islands, early on November 28. The scow was hurled ashore immediately, two of the crew saving themselves by jumping to slippery shore rocks and running for their lives. Three others, who apparently lacked the nerve to jump, perished miserably when the shattered vessel disintegrated.

The most northerly accident of the storm was the stranding of the Algoma Central Line's turret steamer *Monkshaven* on Pie Island the evening of November 27. The crew escaped, but the steamer was so badly battered that she was a complete loss. An English-built vessel, she had lasted only one year on Lake Superior.

The other two strandings at Duluth brought no loss of life. An hour before the ill-fated *Mataafa* hit on November 28, the 478-foot, 5,165-ton Pittsburgher *Isaac Ellwood,* deeply laden with ore, smashed into the piers as she reentered the Duluth ship canal. Mortally wounded, she was assisted by tugs into shallow water on the south side of Minnesota Point in Duluth harbor where she settled in 22 feet of water. She was a $50,000 repair job. Shortly after noon on November 28, three miles south of the Duluth ship canal, the new freighter *R. W. England,* a 363-foot, 3,887-ton ore and grain carrier of the England Transit Line (a Tomlinson affiliate), was tossed stern first, completely out of control, on to the beach of Minnesota Point. Her stern came to rest only 100 feet from the water's edge, the vessel being so high on the beach that she escaped the brunt of the waves. Duluth lifesavers brought part of the crew ashore, but most elected to stay aboard. She was taken off three days later and repairs were reported in excess of $60,000.

On the South Shore the 569-foot *William E. Corey,* flagship of the Pittsburgh Steamship Company fleet, a 6,485-ton craft only a few months old, was dangerously stranded in an exposed position on Gull Island Reef, northeast of Michigan Island in the Apostles, while running for shelter on November 28. Captain F. A. Bailey held his crew aboard and all remained safe. The Pittsburgh Company worked feverishly to rescue their $450,000 flagship. President H. Coulby himself came to the scene, along with Captain William Reed of the *Mariposa* (apparently an experienced salvager) and a flotilla consisting of three tugs and four full-fledged ore-carrying steamers, the tugs *Crosby, Edna G.,* and *Gladiator* and the steamers *Douglas Houghton, Manola, Marina* and *William Siemens.* After 12 frantic days the steamers *Houghton* and *Marina* finally pulled the *Corey* free, for a trip to the shipyard and repairs of $100,000. In the course of the salvage job on December 6, the tug *Edna G.* and the steamer *Siemens* also caught bottom, with minor damage.

Another victim of the storm on November 29 was the new steamer *Western Star,* a 412-footer, owned by M. J. Cummings of Oswego, New York, ashore two miles east of Fourteen-Mile Point, not far from Ontonagon. The *Western Star* had been en route light to Fort William to pick up a grain cargo and was actually 125 miles off her course. She was released with little difficulty by the steamer *Viking* on December 1, but sustained injuries to the extent of $20,-

ooo. Also on November 29, two other Pittsburghers, the steamer *Coralia* and the barge *Maia,* grounded at Point Isabelle on the east side of Keweenaw Point. They were both taken off within ten days with damage over $10,000.

Fortuitous escapes were myriad. The barge *Constitution,* a 379-footer, lost off Copper Harbor on November 28 by the steamer *Victory,* drifted all the way southwest to the Porcupine Mountains west of Ontonagon, over 130 miles, before being retrieved by the little passenger steamer *C. W. Moore* and towed to safety in Chequamegon Bay. The steamer *Bransford,* Captain "Doc" Balfour, hit the rocks of Isle Royale at 3:00 P.M., November 28, was released by the high seas, then fought her way clear to Duluth with 50 fractured frames and 27 plates punctured. The Hawgood ship *Umbria* reached Duluth badly mauled, as did the Tomlinson fleet's *Yosemite.* The *F. M. Osborne, Perry G. Walker,* and *E. C. Pope* all entered Duluth harbor much the worse for wear. The grain carrier *H. B. Nye* limped into Two Harbors after the blow, literally in a sinking condition. The small wooden lumber steamer *Arizona* (189 feet, 779 tons) of the Gray Transportation Line actually had one of the most harrowing experiences, being spun around like a top, three times, as she approached within a quarter of a mile of the Duluth ship canal at 1 A.M., November 28. Luckily, after the final spin, she came around with her bow pointing straight into the canal, and Captain Walter Neal drove her into the harbor at full speed. At the eastern end of the Lake the downbound ore carrier *Angeline* fought the gale for two whole days before reaching the Soo, leaking and bedraggled. Her skipper, Captain S. A. Lyons, was on the bridge for 48 hours straight, fighting waves running higher than the smokestack.

Thus ended the tempestuous season of 1905. Never before had Lake Superior acted so violently, and, vessel men would hope, never again. Nineteen vessels were total losses, and damages ran in excess of $2 million, an enormous sum in those days, with at least 78 sailors losing their lives.

FRED M. LANDON

The

Darkest Day

On Friday, November 7, 1913, a message went out from the U.S. Weather Bureau: HOIST SOUTHWEST STORM WARNINGS TEN A.M. . . . WARNINGS ORDERED THROUGHOUT THE GREAT LAKES.

Next day, November 8, a gale swept Lake Superior. It blew all night, and at daybreak the wind went down and the sea heaved under a heavy sky. Ships waiting in the Soo River steered into Lake Huron. The crews battened down, stretched lifelines over the long cargo deck, and watched the leaden sea.

At the weather stations of Detour and Mackinac, at Cheboygan, Bay City and Harbor Beach, storm signals were still flying, the black-centered red flags flat against the gray sky. A new storm was coming.

Over Lake Huron rushed an icy blast and a blizzard of snow. Soon it was a hurricane, howling over groping freighters and pounding them with massive seas. The most violent storm in history had struck the lakes. It raged for sixteen hours.

This was the somber Sunday of November 9, 1913, a day vividly recorded by Fred M. Landon in his *Lake Huron*, 1944.

SUNDAY, November 9, 1913, is the blackest day in the history of navigation on the Great Lakes. The gales which swept the lakes region on that day sent ten stout ships to the bottom, drove more than a score of others ashore and took the lives of 235 sailors. No other storm of such destructive character has ever been recorded on these inland waters.

"Heavy gales" signals were flying in more than a hundred ports as early as the preceding Friday morning, but when November comes around and shipmasters must count every minute before the close of navigation, long chances are taken. Scores of bulk freighters were on the open waters when the storm began. Those most fortunate found shelter. But eight ships went down on Lake Huron and two more on Lake Superior with not a single survivor to tell the story of what had happened.

The storm had its beginnings on Lake Superior early Saturday morning though there had been unsettled conditions there for some hours before. Lake Huron received the full force of the gale on Sunday and it was chiefly there that loss of life and ships took place. In the lower lakes region the storm was accompanied by rain and a heavy fall of moist snow. Throughout large sections of Michigan and Ontario telephone and telegraph communication was completely out before Sunday evening, and it was several days before these services were restored. Trains and electric cars were stalled by the wet snow which in some places was four feet deep. The water rose from four to five feet above normal at the foot of Lake Huron and in the St. Clair River, and it was estimated that damage amounting to $100,000 was done at Port Huron alone. The Fort Gratiot lighthouse at the foot of the lake was badly undermined by the huge waves which came tumbling about its base, and the Huron lightship, about two miles up the lake, was torn loose from its anchor and dragged with its crew to the Canadian shore.

Newspapers published on Monday morning had extensive accounts of the damage done by the storm on land and expressed fears for vessels that might have been caught in the open waters, though as yet there were no reports of disaster. But such word came quickly. On Monday morning Captain Plough of the Lakeview lifesaving station above Port Huron searched the tossing waters with his glass and suddenly saw, far out, what appeared to be the hull of a vessel, without masts or stack, rising and falling with the movement of the waves. He at once telephoned to Captain Tom Reid of the Reid Wrecking Company at Sarnia and a tug was sent out to investigate.

Captain Reid found the strangest wreck that he had ever seen in all his long experience on the lakes. A big steel freighter had turned turtle and was now floating bottom side up. The bow was about thirty feet out of water but the stern was submerged so that it was not possible to tell the length of the vessel. The visible portion of the hull was coated with ice and there was no mark by which its identity could be established. Captain Reid circled about if for hours and even took a diver out with him, but the lake was too rough for a descent. The hull differed not at all from scores of others and the name plate, if it remained, was below the surface. It was a mystery ship and a mystery ship it remained for the next six days.

News of tragedy soon came from another quarter. Robert Turnbull, a farmer living near Grand Bend on the Canadian shore, had
for many years made it a practice to visit the lake shore each day.
He had a great love for the water, and rain or shine he strolled along
the beach. On the Tuesday after the storm he looked out from the
high cliff near his farm and at its base saw the body of a man
drifting in and out with each successive wave. The arms were extended from the elbows and gave a curious impression of pleading
for help.

With considerable difficulty he pulled the body up on the
sand. Help was summoned and members of the Turnbull family
and others soon recovered another body. Two others were also
found farther along the beach. All bore life preservers with the
name *Wexford*. A broken lifeboat was further evidence that this
vessel had been lost.

With telephone lines down and roads made almost impassable
by the heavy snowfall of Sunday and Monday, it was with difficulty
that word could be carried to the nearest railroad and telegraph
point. A railroad conductor brought the news to Sarnia that bodies
were coming ashore "up the lake." Within the next few hours other
messages came from ports farther north along the Canadian shore
that bodies were being washed in, three and four at a time, and that
they had on them life preservers from the *Regina*, the *James Carruthers*, the *Charles S. Price* and other vessels. For more than a
week bodies continued to come ashore, from the ships that have
been mentioned and from others for which some measure of hope
had been at first entertained. In all more than sixty of the dead were
found along the Lake Huron beach.

As soon as the weather permitted, mournful little processions
began to move from farmhouses along the lake shore, wagon after
wagon bearing the bodies to Zurich, Goderich, Thedford and other
towns where inquests were held. These places were thronged with
relatives and friends seeking information as to the fate of those
known to have been on the boats that were believed to be lost. At
Thedford, a small place thirty miles east of Sarnia, the bodies were
taken to the local undertaker's establishment, the usual small-town
combination of furniture store and funeral parlor. All about were
tables, chairs and beds and on the floor the bodies of drowned
sailors. Men and women, some dry-eyed, some in tears, gazed in-
tently at the faces which were revealed when the blankets were
lifted one by one.

A young woman, her face swollen with weeping, her lips blood-
less, moved about the temporary morgue, looked at each body in-
tently and shook her head. She was the wife of Howard Mackley,

the second mate of the *Charles S. Price*. When his boat was passing Detroit early on Sunday morning he had posted a letter to her, and when the *Price* was abreast of his home at St. Clair he pulled the whistle in the customary salute. She was there waiting to wave a greeting. His boat went on up the river and she watched it until it had passed from sight.

There were six bodies in the undertaker's rooms. The undertaker took her gently by the arm and led her to a barn near by where on the concrete floor lay five others just as they had been picked up from the sand. She shook her head—none of them was her husband. But she saw one body which she recognized. The man was still wearing a cook's apron.

"It's Mr. Jones, the steward," she gasped. "The boat is lost."

She had been aboard the *Price* not long before and knew the steward. Later she was able to identify one other from the same vessel. But the body of Howard Mackley was never found.

Milton Smith, of Port Huron, an engineer on the *Price*, left the boat at Cleveland just before it sailed on its last trip. Men hesitate to leave their mates at a time when risks have become greater and he was sorry to be quitting. It was particularly hard to say good-by to his friend Arz McIntosh of St. Clair, because McIntosh, a wheelsman, was having trouble with his eyes and wanted to quit too. But he needed the money for a possible operation and he "guessed he would stick it out for another trip."

Smith went to Thedford to assist in identifying the bodies off the *Price*. The first he looked at gave him a shock. It was John Groundwater, chief engineer on the vessel he had so recently left, the man under whom he had worked.

"That's big good-natured John," he said. "How the boys all liked him."

"Are you sure it is him?" asked Coroner Clarke.

"As sure as I know that my name is Smith," was the reply.

"Well, this man had one of the *Regina's* life preservers wrapped around his body," said the coroner.

And in that fact lies the only clue to what may possibly have happened to these two ships in the storm and darkness of that November Sunday night. Did the *Regina* and *Price* collide, perhaps even hold together in some strange way for a few minutes, so that men passed from one deck to the other and seized any life preserver that was handy? No one knows or will ever know.

Smith looked down at the body of Herbert Jones, the steward, still with his cook's apron. "There he is," he said, "just as he looked hundreds of times when he was about to prepare a meal or just after he had prepared it."

Strangest experience of all was that of young John Thompson, of Hamilton, Ontario, who read in a Toronto paper that his body had come ashore from the *James Carruthers*. He hastened to his home and was astonished to find a coffin in his father's house and preparations being made for a funeral.

A sister of young John, who lived in Sarnia, on learning that bodies were coming ashore from the *Carruthers* and believing that her brother was aboard this vessel, sent word to the family in Hamilton. The father hastened to Goderich and was shocked to find a body which bore every resemblance to his son even to the tattooed initials "J. T." and a remembered scar. He had little hesitation in claiming it, and at Hamilton others also identified it. The return of the son alive was almost as great a shock as the report of his death. He had left the *Carruthers* and had been aboard another vessel at the time of the storm. The body which the father had claimed was sent back to Goderich.

Not all the bodies which came ashore were identified. The graves of five "unknown" sailors may still be seen in the Maitland Cemetery at Goderich. A dark red polished obelisk, with an anchor carved on the top, bears on one side the inscription: "A memorial to the unidentified seamen whose lives were lost in the Great Lakes Disaster of Nov. 9th, 1913." On the other side is the single word "Sailors."

What deeds of heroism and sacrifice marked the last minutes of men aboard the sinking ships can only be conjectured. Mrs. Walker, the stewardess of the *Argus*, perished with that vessel's crew. Her body came ashore wrapped in a heavy coat belonging to one of the engineers and about it the captain's own life preserver. But when the body of Captain Paul Gutch was washed up on the sand it was without a life preserver.

During these anxious days the hull which had been discovered floating upside down near Port Huron was still there. At first it was believed to be the *Wexford*, since wreckage and bodies from that boat were the first to be reported. Later there was reason to believe that it might be the *Regina* or the *James Carruthers*. By Friday there was a strong suspicion that it was the *Charles S. Price* of the Mahoning Steamship Company's fleet. This was confirmed on Saturday, the fifteenth, when William Baker, a Detroit diver, went down and worked his way around the hull, clutching the railings above him until he found the nameplate. There was no indication of a collision and Baker found that the buoyancy of the hull was due to the imprisoned air which was gradually escaping in two streams of bubbles. There was no other vessel under the bow as some had conjectured might be the case. The *Price* finally sank from sight on the morning of November 17, eight days after she had turned over.

The location of the hull was about ten and a half miles from the Fort Gratiot light, east and a little north. When it was examined in June 1915 the bow was only twenty-four feet under water and a possible menace to shipping. A year later the bow was raised to the surface when it was found that all the machinery had dropped out, perhaps while the hull was floating. Deckhouses and superstructure were also broken off clean so that nothing was left but the distorted hull. In 1917 Canadian interests purchased the wreck for $30,000 but it has never been raised. No trace has ever been found of any of the seven other vessels which were lost in the same section of the lake.

The loss on Lake Huron, both of lives and vessels, was so far in excess of that on all the other lakes combined, that the storm of 1913 has since been thought of chiefly in terms of Lake Huron.* On Lake Superior the steamer *H. B. Smith,* of 10,000 tons capacity, and the *Leafield* of 3,500 tons were lost with both crews, forty-one in all. The barge *Plymouth* disappeared on Lake Michigan with seven lives while Lightship No. 82 at Point Abino near Buffalo went down with its crew of six. The steamers *L. C. Waldo, Major* and *Turret Chief* were constructive total losses on Lake Superior as was the steamer *Louisiana* on Lake Michigan, but their crews escaped death after experiences that none would ever forget. Three lives were lost however, when the steamer *Nottingham* was wrecked near Parisian Island on Lake Superior.

The storm of November 9 practically demoralized lake shipping for the remainder of the season. The Lake Carriers' Association

* The loss of life and vessels on Lake Huron was as follows:

TOTAL LOSSES

Name of Vessel	Length in Feet	Carrying Capacity Gross Tons	Value	Lives Lost
Charles S. Price	524	9,000	$340,000	28
Isaac M. Scott	524	9,000	340,000	28
James Carruthers	550	9,500	410,000	19
Wexford	270	2,800	125,000	17
Regina	269	3,000	125,000	15
John A. McGean	452	7,500	240,000	23
Argus	436	7,000	130,000	24
Hydrus	436	7,000	130,000	24

CONSTRUCTIVE TOTAL LOSSES

Name of Vessel	Length in Feet	Carrying Capacity Gross Tons	Value	Lives Lost
H. M. Hanna Jr.	500	8,500	315,000	
Matoa	310	3,104	117,900	

ordered that every vessel on its roll should carry a flag at half mast until navigation ceased for the year. Vessel owners were appalled to think that the products of the best shipyards in America were unable to withstand the force of this storm. And this was true also of British shipbuilding, for the *Wexford* and the *Leafield* were typical British tramps which had sailed salt water and weathered gales in all parts of the world before they came to fresh water.

What happened aboard the various steamers is pure conjecture, though three of them were seen not long before their disappearance. Captain A. C. May headed the big 550-footer *H. B. Hawgood* out of the St. Clair River into Lake Huron early Sunday morning. At noon he saw the *Price* just north of Sand Beach, "making bad weather." Soon after he decided not to take further chances and so turned his vessel, heading back toward the foot of the lake. He met the *Regina* fifteen miles south of Harbor Beach and at three-thirty saw the *Isaac M. Scott* five or six miles north of the Fort Gratiot Light. No one else saw these vessels after that time. Soon Captain May himself ran into trouble, for, shaping his course by the Huron lightship which had broken from its anchorage and gone on the Canadian shore, he too went aground about two miles above the mouth of the St. Clair River.

Masters of vessels which survived the storm were unanimous in declaring that they had never before witnessed such rapid changes in the direction of the wind and such gusts of speed. The duration of the storm was also without a precedent. For sixteen hours there was a continuous gale, the wind averaging sixty miles an hour and even going beyond that intensity. At times the wind was blowing in one direction and the waves, often as high as thirty-five feet, running in another. A tremendous strain was placed upon both the hull and the engines of any vessel caught in such a situation.

Captains reported seeing three huge waves strike their vessels in quick succession. How dangerous this could be was learned in the sinking of the steamer *S. R. Kirby* on May 8, 1914. This boat, regarded as entirely seaworthy, sank almost without warning in midday during a comparatively moderate storm. The investigation revealed that a great wave had come over the port bow, submerging the deck and by its weight tipping the stern high in the air. Before the *Kirby* could right herself a second wave came, and as the boat stood poised with the after hull out of the water a third wave seemed to catch her from beneath. She heaved upward, stood motionless for thirty seconds and then suddenly plunged to the bottom.

Something was learned also from the experience of the men aboard the *Howard M. Hanna Jr.* which went ashore and broke up at Point aux Barques on the Sunday evening of the 1913 storm. Her master, Captain W. C. Richardson, was unable to keep the steamer's head to the sea and she was subjected to heavy rolling and pounding in the trough. Half an hour before she struck the shore her smokestack went overboard and she lost her rudder. The lifesaving crew at Point aux Barques saw the distress signals and were able to rescue all the crew, thirty-two men and one woman. Many other vessels which went ashore had similar if not as severe experiences.

The fate of the *Charles S. Price* caused more concern than that of any other vessel. Here was a boat, built but three years before, thought capable of withstanding any storm and equipped with every known device to ensure its safety. It had not been thought possible that a bulk freighter, with its wide flat bottom, could possibly turn turtle, yet some combination of circumstances had brought this about. Undoubtedly very unusual conditions obtained in the lake regions during that November Sunday of 1913, especially on Lake Huron.

Apart from the *Wexford* all of the boats lost on Lake Huron were comparatively new. Five of the eight had been built within the last six years. The *James Carruthers,* the largest of all, 550 feet in length, had been so short a time on the lakes that it was scarcely more than broken in. The Georgian Bay town of Collingwood had turned out en masse on May 22 to see it launched, and it had made but a few trips before it was lost. It was carrying a cargo of 340,000 bushels of wheat on its last trip.

Three other vessels, the *John A. McGean,* the *Isaac M. Scott* and the *Charles S. Price,* were all recent additions to the lake fleet, having appeared in 1908, 1909 and 1910 respectively. The *Scott* and the *Price* were each 524 feet long, the *McGean* was smaller, 424 feet long.

The *Argus* and *Hydrus* were but ten years old, products of 1903, one of the great shipbuilding years on the lakes. They were in the 400-foot class, owned by the Interlake Steamship Company of Cleveland. The *Regina,* of Canadian registry, had been built in 1907. She was a smaller boat, 269 feet long and with a carrying capacity of 3,000 gross tons.

The *Wexford,* short and squat, usually needing a coat of paint, had been a familiar craft to sailormen for years. She was somewhat similar in build to the *Bannockburn* which was mysteriously lost on Lake Superior in the fall of 1902. She had been built in a British shipyard as long ago as 1883 yet she was regarded as perfectly seaworthy. She had gone through many a storm on salt water but Lake Huron swallowed her up.

CAPTAIN S. A. LYONS

Ordeal

on Sunday

On Saturday evening, Nov. 8, 1913, the big steamer *J. H. Sheadle* locked through the Soo and in intermittent snow squalls crept down the St. Marys River. She entered Lake Huron two hours after midnight. Other vessels steered into Lake Huron in the gusty darkness, but only the *Sheadle* reached her destination.

By noon on Sunday gale winds had risen; two hours later it was a hurricane. Reeling in cross seas, her long deck buried in a tumult of water, the *Sheadle* plunged southward. The shores were blotted out by the blizzard, but Captain Lyons managed to take soundings. At the foot of the lake he turned his ship around in the battering wind and sea. Three times he reversed course, beating up and down till it was safe to enter the St. Clair River.

Captain Lyons' report to the Cleveland-Cliffs Iron Company, where J. H. Sheadle was secretary of the firm, is the most direct and graphic of all accounts of the big storm. It is now in the Wakefield Museum of the Great Lakes Historical Society at Vermilion, Ohio.

WE LOADED grain at Fort William and left there at 8:00 P.M. the night of November 6th. The captain of the *James Carruthers* and I were in the shipping office together and intended to come down together as we were going to get away at about the same time, but evidently he did not get out until some time after I did.

When I left the barometer was below normal but stationary, and the wind had been blowing for some time. After getting outside of Thunder Cape a heavy sea was running from the southwest, and a strong breeze. I went back under Pie Island, letting go anchor at 10:00 o'clock and laying there until 3:30 the morning of the 7th, when the wind went north and we proceeded on our voyage.

On arriving at White Fish Bay it shut in very thick and foggy, which held us there the balance of the night and until about 8:00 o'clock the following morning, November 8th.

There were a number of steamers laying at anchor further down the bay and they, of course, locked down ahead of the *Sheadle*. The *James Carruthers* locked down just ahead of us, then we followed at 8:30 P.M., with the *Hydrus* immediately after us, both of which vessels were lost. It had been snowing, having commenced along in the afternoon. It was snowing some while we were in the lock but had cleared up when we left the lock.

I had wired the office I would not leave, but as it cleared up we continued on down the river, passing out into Lake Huron at 1:53 A.M. the morning of November 9th, with the wind light north northeast. The only variation in our course from that time until practically within two miles of Thunder Bay was one-eighth of a point. As we approached the fuel dock of Messrs. Pickands, Mather & Co., we sighted the *Carruthers* taking fuel; she left the dock, rounded to, and entered Lake Huron shortly before we did.

Before we arrived at Presque Isle, Lake Huron, it commenced to snow some; sometimes it would clear up so that we could pick up the land; we saw Presque Isle, Middle Island, and Thunder Bay. From our soundings when we got to Thunder Bay at 8:35 A.M. We were about two miles outside of our regular course down Lake Huron, having steered southeast by south ⅛ south. The barometer at this time was below normal, but stationary.

In an hour and a half after passing Thunder Bay Island the wind had increased and there was a strong wind from north northeast with snow. The sea kept on increasing, and the wind changed to due north blowing a gale. At 11:30 A.M. the course was changed to south by east ½ east in order to bring the ship more before the sea, and we continued to shift from a half to a point as the sea increased so as to keep the ship running practically dead before it; also to keep the ship from rolling and the seas from breaking over the decks.

We got the regular soundings at Pointe aux Barques that we had been getting on previous trips, and by the soundings and the time we could tell when we were abreast of the point. It was snowing a blinding blizzard and we could not see anything. According to the soundings we got by the deep sea sounding lead we were abreast of Harbor Beach at 4:50 P.M. and three miles outside of the regular course we take during the summer. At this time the wind was due north and at Harbor Beach we changed our course to due south, running dead before the sea and wind.

The bell rang for supper at 5:45 P.M., which was prepared and tables set, when a gigantic sea mounted our stern, flooding the fantail, sending torrents of water through the passageways on each side of the cabin, concaving the cabin, breaking the windows in the after cabin, washing our provisions out of the refrigerator and practically destroying them all, leaving us with one ham and a few potatoes. We had no tea or coffee. Our flour was turned into dough. The supper was swept off the tables and all the dishes smashed.

Volumes of water came down on the engine through the upper skylights, and at times there were from four to six feet of water in the cabin. Considerable damage was done to the interior of the cabin and fixtures. The after steel bulkhead of the cabin was buckled. All the skylights and windows were broken in. A small working boat on the top of the after cabin and the mate's Chadburn were washed away.

It was blowing about 70 miles an hour at this time, with high seas, one wave following another very closely. Owing to the sudden force of the wind the seas had not lengthened out as they usually do when the wind increases in the ordinary way. In about four hours the wind had come up from 25 to 70 miles an hour, but I do not think exceeded 70 miles an hour.

Immediately after the first sea swept over our stern, I ordered the boatswain to take sufficient men and shutters to close all windows in the after cabin. The men forced their way aft, braving the wind, sleet and seas, one hand grasping the life rail and the other the shutters. Reaching the after cabin in safety they began securing the shutters, when another tremendous sea swept over the vessel carrying away the shutters. The men were forced to cling to whatever was nearest them to keep from being washed overboard; immediately a third sea, equally as severe, boarded the vessel, flooding the fantail and hurricane deck. The men attempted to reach the crew's dining room but could not make it, and only saved themselves by gripping the nearest object they could reach. Indeed one of the wheelsmen was only saved from going over by accidentally falling as he endeavored to grope his way to the rail, his foot catching in one of the bulwark braces, preventing him from being swept off. Another monster sea boarded the boat, tearing the man loose from the brace, and landing him in the after tow line which had been washed from its rack and was fouled on deck.

The men finally made the shelter of the dining room and galley. One of the oilers stood watch at the dining room door, closing it when the boat shipped a sea and opening it when the decks were clear to let the water out of the cabins.

The steward and his wife were standing knee deep in the icy water. The steward's wife was assisted into the engine room, the steward remaining in the dining room, securing furniture and silverware. The firemen and seamen were comfortable in their rooms as they were not touched. Some of the outfit of the private dining room was washed into the mess room, the steward's trunk was washed out of his room and stood on end in the galley. The steward's wife had to remain all night in the engine room wrapped in a blanket.

Water through the engine room skylight drenched the two engineers who were throttling the engines; I do not think it ever happened before when these two men had to stand by those two positions constantly. From 2:30 P.M. until 5:00 the engines raced, requiring the greatest care and judgment. At times the ship was so heavily burdened with seas coming over her decks that her revolutions were decreased from 75 to 35 turns per minute. The engineers made their positions more comfortable by rigging up a piece of canvas over the engines.

We continued on our course, following our deep sea soundings, and at 9:00 o'clock had soundings of eighteen fathoms. This carried us well off to the west shore. I called the engineer up at this time and told him that at 10:00 o'clock (the night of November 9th) I was going to turn around head to the sea unless I could locate the land or Fort Gratiot light, and wanted to increase the speed of the ship up to that time so as to enable me to bring the boat around head to on account of the sea running behind us. At 10:00 o'clock we turned, heading north half east; the vessel rolled very heavily but came around all right head to. I should judge that we were ten minutes in turning. At that time we were about ten miles north of Fort Gratiot by the soundings we got—ten fathoms. I had everything lashed before we turned. No one thought of a life preserver. The way the ship was behaving we had every confidence in her. The heavy rolling tore adrift the binnacle on top of the pilot house. After that it was extremely dangerous to be in the house as this heavy object was hurled back and forth across the deck as the ship labored and rolled in the heavy sea.

During this time from Pointe aux Barques to the foot of the lake our log line iced heavily, and the seas at times washed brace and dial inboard over the rail, rendering it useless. We were obliged to depend entirely on the deep sea lead, which was in constant use for 17 hours, at half hour and 15 minute intervals. By the use of the deep sea lead we knew where the ship was at all times. Having the familiar soundings right along through it all was the only thing that kept us from being wrecked, as it gave us confidence as to our location. The men were familiar with the use of the lead, as we had used the machine constantly, but it was a great punishment on them to keep it going at this time.

Just after turning I sent the first mate aft to inspect the wheel chains and quadrant. He telephoned me that they were all right but that he could not get forward again at that time, the seas covering the decks with a solid mass of blue water. The men of the second watch had remained on deck with us, and while we would not let one man go aft alone we did not hesitate to let two go together.

The mate made quite a fight to get forward but was unable to make it then, and crawled back to the engine room half unconscious.

I started back on a vice versa course, which would be north half east for six and one-quarter hours, following my soundings back from ten to twenty-two fathoms. During this time one of the wheelsmen got aft, securing a few pieces of bread, and came forward again with the mate and boatswain. One watchman remained on watch in the galley.

At 4:15 A.M., November 10th, I turned again, heading south one-quarter west. This time we experienced much difficulty in turning, the ship remaining longer in the trough of the sea on account of not getting so much way and running head into it, but she behaved well, handled well in every way and steered well. The rolling was very bad—I was lifted right off my feet. Only by the greatest effort were the second mate and myself able to hold onto the stanchions on the top house, our legs being parallel with the deck most of the time.

Again and again she plunged forward, only to be baffled in her attempts to run before it, sometimes fetching up standing and trembling from stem to stern. She was buffeted about by the tremendous seas, almost helpless, dipping her hatches in the water on either side, barrels of oil and paint getting adrift and smashing out the sides of the paint locker. The men were tossed around the wheel house at will.

I feared her steering gear had given way, but fortunately on examination it proved to be all right. She would gain a half point, only to lose it, but finally after a mighty effort she swung around. I never had seen seas form as they did at this time; they were large and seemed to run in series, one mounting the other like a mighty barrier.

Running back we decreased our speed from "Full" to 55 turns as we got down closer to the river, following back on somewhat different soundings than we got going up. We came back in two hours where it took us six and one-quarter to face the sea.

At 6:30 A.M., November 10th, I called the engineer and told him I was not satisfied with the soundings we were getting, and to be prepared at any moment to give me full power to turn the ship again. We could see nothing on account of the heavy fall of snow.

At 6:45 A.M. we turned for the third time, heading north by west. This time the sea had decreased, and the wind had gone to the northwest in the meantime, so that there was practically no sea to bother us any.

The 70 mile gale lasted from about 10:00 o'clock Sunday morning until about 2:00 o'clock Monday morning, 16 hours of it, with continuous snow all the time. We kept our whistle blowing all the time, but at times we up forward could not hear it ourselves.

At 8:30 A.M. it had cleared up so we could see quite a distance, so we turned around again heading south one-half west, the wind and sea going down. In fifteen minutes we could see the west shore, and sighted what I suppose was the wreck of the *Price*, passing this hull at about a distance of 1,000 feet. We noted what we thought were oil barrels and wreckage floating not over a quarter of a mile to the leeward of her. Just before we arrived abreast of the wreck we cast our deep sea lead to determine what water there was in that locality, and found ten fathoms.

We proceeded on our way over to the location where the Fort Gratiot lightship should have been stationed. We had slowed down to slow speed some time before we got in this locality. I picked up the stack of the lightship, which had drifted two or three miles out of postion. Just at this time it shut in to snow again, and I backed away from the stack three-quarters of a mile or more, letting go my anchor, and waiting there until it cleared up at 12:00 o'clock noon.

When it cleared up we proceeded on our voyage down, passing Detroit at 7:00 o'clock the evening of the 10th. After entering the river the steward served dinner in the galley, which was the first regular meal since Sunday noon, and which consisted of beef and potatoes. Supper was also served in the galley, consisting of ham and potatoes.

The water being low, and we having no provisions, I tied up at Smith's coal dock to take provisions on board the next morning, the 11th, leaving there at 9:00 o'clock when the water came up.

When we arrived at Bar Point the water was unusually low and we grounded there in the west channel. We released ourselves with our own power after some five and a half hours' delay, getting on our way and proceeding on our voyage to Erie, that being our port of destination, where we arrived at 11:10 A.M., November 12th.

Ice-bound

Great storms ravage the lakes once in a decade, but winter comes every year. On the upper lakes it may come suddenly, temperature diving far below zero and blizzards raging across the water. Blown spray freezes quickly; soon the ships are glazed with ice. Bays and rivers freeze over, with steamers locked tight in the channel.

One of these onsets came at the end of November, 1926, catching the big freighter W. E. Fitzgerald on her last run of the season. Weeks later her fortunes were recounted by Captain Elmer Weborg of Manitowac, Wisconsin, to a reporter on the Manitowac Herald-News.

THREE DAYS spent ice-bound in the Soo river while en route to Fort William to load with grain, a two-day battle for life against one of the worst storms seen on Lake Superior since 1913, and a three-day siege against the ice floes of the Soo river while down-bound with the boat coated with tons of ice was an experience of the W. E. Fitzgerald of the D. Sullivan Steamship Company of Chicago, one of the 153-odd boats that were held captive by ice in the Soo river for an eventful period a short time ago. The Fitzgerald, in command of Captain Weborg, was downbound, and was able to get free from the Soo river ice much ahead of the other boats, particularly those of the fleet bound up river, which were freed after nearly two weeks of battling against the ice.

A prologue to what was to follow, the Fitzgerald encountered bad going in the Soo river while up-bound for Fort William. Slush ice carried by the current, packed to the bottom of the river and held the big freighter and many other ships captive for three days, having hit the pack on December 3 and finally being released December 7. The Fitzgerald, carrying hard coal screenings, yielded part of its cargo to other freighters that had run out of fuel. Many of the boats were forced to load with wheelbarrows, a practice seldom heard of in these days of Leviathans.

After negotiating the Soo river, and safely in Fort William, where the coal cargo was discharged and one of storage wheat for Toledo, Ohio, loaded, the *Fitzgerald* cleared Fort William in company with six or seven other big ships. Scarcely half an hour after the fleet had weighed anchor they encountered a fog frost, a miserable weather condition for lake traffic. Sensing something in the wind, all but the *Fitzgerald* turned tail and sought shelter from the impending storm, the *Fitzgerald* continuing however with its cargo. With the fog frost came a sea the like of which has not been seen since 1913, a most disastrous year for navigation. Waves crashed over the bow of the *Fitzgerald* with such a force as to carry away oak molding that was bolted to the rail of the bow. With the receding of each wave the ship was left with a new coating of ice, subzero weather freezing the water instantly. For two days the *Fitzgerald* battled the storm. Plates and seams opened, and the pumps of the big freighter had all they could do to combat the incoming water. Ice covered the boat from stem to stern, having accumulated to the thickness of two and three feet. The pilot house took the aspect of an Eskimo igloo, it becoming necessary to chop away ice from the window that the wheelsman could make out signals. A binnacle and a compass were washed away, and inside the wheelhouse ice to the thickness of a foot or more covered the floor, water having been washed inside. . . .

No shelter was available, and the ship was leaking badly, and there seemed to be no alternative but let the wind blow and take its toll. To take to lifeboats in case of emergency was out of the question. The boats were covered with ice, and the sea at no time during the two days would have permitted their being lowered. Had the *Fitzgerald* sunk, no possible hope could have been held for any of the crew.

Upon having weathered the storm safely, and once in the Soo river, the boat was one frozen mass, the only ship in the marooned fleet of 153 boats that had navigated Lake Superior during those two days. Once in the Soo river, in the down-bound channel, with nine inches of ice, an unusual condition for so early in the year, and the thermometer at temperatures as low as thirty-five degrees below zero, the entire fleet, both up-bound and down-bound, was held fast by the floes that were constantly piled up underneath the ice by the current. The biggest ice-crushing car ferry on the lakes, the *St. Marie,* was summoned to aid the fleet, along with two Canadian tugs and four tugs of the Thompson Tug and Wrecking Company. The tugs met with little success at first, but with the advent of moderate weather the boats were finally freed, first the down-bound fleet and then the boats bound up river.

No suffering took place during the time the 153 boats were held captive by the ice. Many of the boats held in Lake Neebish ran out of provisions and fuel. Others purchased meat and sundry supplies from farmers that drove cutters out to the ship over the ice. Many of the sailors walked to shore over the ice, cigarettes being one of the shortages most felt. Had they been unable to get free, the entire fleet would have had to spend the winter right there.

Before entering the locks, after being freed, it was necessary to use pick and ax in clearing the ice from the *Fitzgerald,* it being necessary to lighten it of the ice which weighed it down and would not permit the boat to pass through the locks. It is estimated that the *Fitzgerald* carried 1200 tons of ice after the storm on Superior, and that the weight added two feet to the boat's ordinary draft when loaded.

VII

THE LONG SHIPS

The most intimate and interesting record of Great Lakes shipping is the work of Captain James Van Cleve of Oswego. As big as an atlas, his book contains a hundred fondly detailed water colors, along with descriptions of hundreds of sloops, schooners and steamships. His narrative begins: "The first sailing vessel built upon any of the great North American Lakes was a small schooner of about 10 tons built at the 'Cabins' where Kingston in Canada now is, on board of which Robert Cavelier-Sieur de la Salle and Father Hennepin with their men embarked on the 18th Nov. 1678 on an exciting and unknown voyage up Lake Ontario." It ends, in 1878, with an account of the vessels on the lakes two hundred years later.

A century ago Captain Van Cleve knew every ship on Lake Ontario. As an eighteen-year-old youth, "drifting on the lee shore financially," he shipped as clerk on the *Ontario,* the first steam vessel on the lakes. He built and commanded the first propeller-driven craft, the *Vandalia.* One of his full-page paintings shows a race—the trim *Vandalia,* sloop-rigged with a jutting bowsprit and a stubby smokestack at the stern, leading the larger two-masted *Ontario* with her cross-beam rocking above the paddle boxes. Watching the contest are two red-shirted boatmen in a yawl named *Juno.*

After forty years of sailing Captain Van Cleve began his *Reminiscences of the Early Period of Sailing Vessels and Steamboats on Lake Ontario with a History of the Introduction of the Propeller on the Lakes and other Subjects;* he included lake scenes from Sackett's Harbor to Sault Ste. Marie along with his sketches of lake vessels. He wrote his book not once but four times, so there were four identical volumes in shaded script with the illustrations faithfully repeated. Now there are three copies, in the Historical Society libraries at Oswego, Buffalo and Chicago; the fourth copy has disappeared.

Captain Van Cleve saw three of the great changes in lake shipping: sail giving way to steam, paddle wheels supplanted by propellers, and the combination vessels with cargo below decks and travelers in the ladies' and gentlemen's cabins replaced by commodious passenger liners and lengthening bulk freighters. The evolution of lake passenger ships culminated in the huge *Seeandbee,* before highway travel laid up the overnight steamers. The bulk freighters are evolving still.

As the mining and movement of iron ore increased, the ships grew longer, wider and deeper. In 1868 the *R. J. Hackett* was the talk of the lakes. She was a new kind of vessel, 211 feet long, with engines aft, navigation quarters in the bow, and a long clear hold for cargo. In 1874 came the *V. H. Ketchum*, four masts and a bowsprit, with a tall black smokestack jutting from her after cabin. She was a wonder, twenty feet more keel than anything afloat, longer than most dock facilities in the seventies. But new docks were coming, and men were talking about iron ships, still longer, broader and deeper, to bring bigger cargoes down to the spreading mills. In 1882 a crowd in Cleveland watched the launching of the big *Onoko*, the first iron freighter on freshwater. Ten years later the *Maritana* made history by loading 4,800 tons of ore at Escanaba. In 1897, with a 5,000-ton vessel, it seemed that the ultimate had come. But the next year brought 6,000-ton ships, and in 1899 the *Superior City* surpassed them. In 1904 the 560-foot *Augustus B. Wolvin* took the lead, and held it for two years. Then in 1906 came the 600-footers, which remained the prototype for nearly fifty years. Those ships carried the massive cargo of World War I, and in the expanding 1920s thirty of them were added to the lakes fleet. Then, with ore movement falling to less than half of normal, depression stilled the shipyards. Just four vessels were built in the 1930s—all of them launched in 1938—the longest silence in the history of lakes shipbuilding.

World War II put every carrier into service, and they were not enough. With a day-and-night din of riveting, twenty-one bulk freighters took shape in 1942 and 1943. No more were added till the end of the decade, though the demand for coal, limestone and iron ore held on at a high level. In 1949 came the first post-war freighter, the *Wilfred S. Sykes*, 678 feet long, 70 feet wide, 37 feet deep, with a speed of 16 miles per hour deep-laden. New in size and speed the *Sykes* remained the prototype for the next four years, while nineteen vessels joined the American cargo fleet. In 1954 appeared the *George M. Humphrey*, 710 feet overall, 75 feet beam and 37½ feet depth, with a carrying capacity of 25,000 tons. Soon five vessels of her class were on the drawing boards.

Now, in the mid-sixties, with a giant new lock in construction at the Soo, the shape of future lake freighters begins to emerge. They will be longer, broader, deeper—the old story in new proportions—and more efficient both under way and at the terminals. So one prototype succeeds another while the long ships pass through the rivers and over the blue horizon.

ELIZABETH T. BAIRD

Windjammer
to Chicago

Most of the early travelers on the lakes were men—explorers, traders, soldiers, miners, missionaries. But there were occasional women among them, like the mother and child who sailed aboard a schooner down Lake Michigan when there was no town on the Chicago River.

Elizabeth Thérèse Baird (1810-1890) was born at Prairie du Chien, Wisconsin, the daughter of a prominent fur trader, Henry Munro Fisher; she was the great granddaughter of an Ottawa chief, Kewinaquot. Most of her youth was spent on Mackinac Island. There at the age of fourteen she was married to Henry S. Baird, a young lawyer from Green Bay.

Elizabeth Baird was a woman of charm and learning, proud of her Indian ancestry and fond of her early memories in the north country. Late in life she vividly recalled her childhood in a series of reminiscences published in the Green Bay *State Gazette*. These sketches, from which is taken the account of an early voyage on Lake Michigan, were later reprinted in the *Collections of the State Historical Society of Wisconsin*, volume XIV.

IN THE FALL of 1815, Madame Marie Chandonée, née Chapoton, with her infant son, left Detroit to join her husband, Jean B. Chandonée, in Chicago. When she reached Mackinac, her child was too ill to travel farther; and when he recovered, it was too late that season to resume the journey. Although it was only October, no vessel would brave the autumnal storms, and there was no alternative for Mme. Chandonée but to make Mackinac her home for the winter with her husband's aunt, Mme. Thérèse Schindler.

Spring came and went, and not until the middle or last of June, 1816, did the first vessel present itself for this route. Then Mme. Chandonée, with her little one, accompanied by my mother and me, embarked again for Chicago. The vessel had the then familiar load of pork, flour, and butter. I know not how long she was in going or coming; I only know she was one month making the round trip, which was thought to be doing well.

There were no ports on the west side of Lake Michigan, at which to stop. But when we reached Chicago, there was considerable delay in getting into the river. It was a very narrow stream, with high banks of white sand. Not far up the river, stood Fort Dearborn, only a few rods from the water's edge. Directly opposite the fort was the Kinzie homestead, with all its comforts. The house was a large, one-story building, with an exceptionally high attic. The front door opened into a wide hall, that hospitably led into the kitchen, which was spacious and bright, made so by the large fire-place. Four rooms opened into the hall, two on each side, and the upper story contained four rooms. The fare of that house was all an epicure of the present day could desire, including game and fish of all sorts; and then the cooking was done by open fire-place, in its best style.

We were entertained by the hospitable inmates of this pleasant home, Mr. and Mrs. Kinzie (father and mother of John H.) being old friends of my mother. Mme. Chandonée was a stranger to the family; but her husband was an inmate of the household, being there in employ of the government. The establishment consisted of Mr. and Mrs. Kinzie, two sons and two daughters, and the men and women retainers, who seemed to be many. This home, the garrison, and the home of Jean Baptist Beaubien, were all there was of Chicago at that time.

The only way of crossing the river was by a wooden canoe or dug-out. My mother, who feared the water very much, forbade me crossing over. The Kinzie children were so accustomed to this mode of crossing, going whenever they wished, that without realizing my mother's fears they took me over with them, and I recall to this day the pleasure the dug-out gave me. The sailors were a little girl about ten years of age, and a boy of eight. With such a crew did I first cross Chicago River in 1816. The other amusements the surroundings offered, were the walks and tumbles about the sand hills.

My mother had an old acquaintance (a beautiful woman, who was married at Mackinac), the invalid wife of an officer at Fort Dearborn. She was a Miss Aiken, one of the five daughters of a Mrs.

Aiken of Montreal, nearly all of whom married army officers; Mrs. Aiken was a sister of Mrs. Michael Dousman of Prairie du Chien.

Mrs. Kinzie had a daughter by a former husband, who was married to a man named Helms. Their home was at some distance, on the fort side of the river, and once my mother went to see this friend. The walk thither was quite long for the children. On our arrival we found a little square house, with no floor, but tarpaulin spread down in lieu of it. Tarpaulin was also hung about the walls. The writer wonders where to-day in all that vast city, is the site of that humble home! In after years, Mrs. Helms, then a widow, went to Fort Winnebago to make her home there with her brother, John H. Kinzie, who was Indian agent at that post. She was, I think, the first white woman who traveled from Fort Winnebago to Green Bay on horseback. She made the journey in the winter of 1833, and wore a mask to protect her face. She afterwards married Dr. Abbott, of the regular Army.

We remained in Chicago for some time, the vessel master seeking for a cargo which was not secured. It was too early for furs, so finally the vessel had to take on a ballast of gravel and sand. Beside ourselves, the party who took passage on this vessel, were Major Baker, and his wife and daughter. The Major was then on his way to Green Bay to take command of Camp Smith. The daughter was an invalid, and had what is commonly called "fits." She was seized with one in the cabin while I sat by her; and such an impression did her fright make that I have never forgotten Miss Jerusha Baker.

Pursuing our journey northward, we coasted along the east side of the lake, stopping where we could, to secure if possible a cargo; but failing, arrived at Mackinac with the same ballast with which we started from Chicago. One of the sailors was a colored man, who was uncommonly kind to me. One great amusement for me during the long trip, was hunting for shells in the sand in the hold of the vessel. This sailor would take me down, and while I played, sit by and mend his clothes, talking all the while to me, and I not understanding a word, as he spoke English, and I only French.

The day before the vessel arrived at Mackinac a storm came up, which increased in violence as night approached, and nearly dismantled the craft, she losing much of her rigging, and being thrown upon one of those rocky points, escape from which I have since heard was most providential. We reached home the following night, and this arrival made a lasting impression upon one so young. My grandparents seemed overwhelmed with joy, after the fears they had endured during the storm, to have restored to them all they held dearest in the world. Their happiness was indeed pathetic. I still have the keenest recollection of it. This trip might, like many other things, have been forgotten if it had not been the marked event of my little life as it was that of my mother's, who had never before been on any water craft save a birch-bark canoe, or a bateau or Mackinac boat.

HARLAN HATCHER

Sails

Before the steamers took over the trade there was a great age of sail on the lakes—hundreds of barks, brigs, sloops and schooners whitening the blue horizons. Leaning in the wind, their bobstays dipping, they had graceful lines and their names were music: *Moonlight, Aurora, Dawn, Swallow, Hesperus, Wanderer, Evening Star, Lady of the Lake.*

The crews of that vanished fleet developed a rich and racy lore. They sang at the halyards, yarned in the foc'sle and repeated their superstitions of mysterious underground channels, of great winds that lifted a bark out of one lake and dropped it in another, of ships that sailed into a fogbank and were never seen again. The long runs, the dependence on wind and weather, the natural hazard of their life bound the old sailormen together. They were proud of their craft and derisive of the barges, scows and lengthening freighters that would drive them off the lakes.

For a generation after the steamers had usurped the ore trade, sailing vessels carried lumber—which could not be handled with scoop bucket and "whirlie" at the big new docks. The lumber trade crested in the 1880s, and the wind-borne fleet reached a peak in the same period. In those years eighteen hundred sailing vessels graced the lakes, six times as many as the big freighters of today.

In *The Great Lakes*, 1944, Harlan Hatcher vividly recalled the most picturesque period of the inland commerce.

THE TOPSAIL SCHOONER *Illinois* sailed out of Sackets Harbor at the foot of Lake Ontario on a fine May day in 1834. She was bound for the faraway port of Chicago. She was stowed to capacity with 104 passengers and their essential gear of wagons, plows, hoes, pots, children, and bedding. The hold was full, the cabins were overcrowded, and the decks piled high. The wagon wheels were lashed to the shrouds like the spinning wheels

347

of the Puritans. Enthusiasm and excitement ran through the ship. For these men and women were headed for the fabulous lands of northern Illinois, where the fur trade had flourished and where the Black Hawk War (1832) had just been fought by the frontiersmen. Now the Indians were cleared from the hunting grounds and the country was open for settlement. A gigantic land boom hit the region. Its headquarters was the little fort and row of log houses near Lake Michigan on the Chicago River. Only 150 people lived there when the year 1832 began; 2,000 scurried along its muddy streets before the year had closed. Twenty thousand people sailed in from Buffalo that season; they passed on through Chicago and spread out over the Illinois land. The entire Lake country stirred with youthful activity. The only highway for this enormous shift in the population and for the commerce west and east which naturally followed was the shipping lanes of the Great Lakes. The call for ships and still more ships was loud and insistent.

The *Illinois* was one of those ships, and her name signified her mission. She had been specially built to the dimensions of the locks on the new Welland Canal (80 x 20 x 8) in order that she might sail from Ontario ports to the Upper Lakes and back at will. The voyage to Chicago in the early 1830's was still a great adventure. It was a full month's cruise: across Lake Ontario, up the Niagara escarpment and around the Falls, up the Niagara River with the "horned breeze," against head winds and choppy Lake Erie waters off Long Point, through the Pelee channel, and up the river to Detroit; then by sail or tow over the shallow Lake St. Clair and through the swift current at Port Huron into Lake Huron; up the rolls and swells of Lake Huron to Mackinac Island; westward through the Straits of Mackinac, and southward with quartering winds to the foot of Lake Michigan to drop anchor outside the sandbar barrier which lay across the mouth of the Chicago River. The weary, seasick, but eager passengers went ashore in the ship's boats. Their plows and wagons were ferried in on rafts. With her draft eased, the *Illinois* was then hauled across the barrier by ropes manned by Chicago citizens and the ship's crew, and she was finally secured at the new wharf on the Chicago River water front.

That scene and that experience were repeated over and over again all around the new ports on the south shores of the Lakes. In 1835, 255 sailing ships arrived in Chicago. Nearly a thousand arrivals of sailing ships and 990 steamships were recorded in Cleveland harbor in 1836. Chicago and Toledo were both incorporated in 1837. At that time there were 8,000 people in Chicago. Detroit had 10,000. Thousands of immigrants disembarked at Sandusky and spread over the fat wheat lands of Ohio. On a single day in October

1838, 285 wagons drove into that little lake port, with produce for the eastern cities.

All this activity, still only a bare portent of what was to come, gave rise to the storied era of the sailing ships. Steam was already on the Lakes; and steam would in a few decades drive away the sails in competition for the ever-increasing tonnage of bulk cargo— grain, coal, and ore, those golden, black, and red rivers that traced their channel across the Lakes. But in the meantime, in the half century cut through the heart and center by the Civil War, when much of the shipping was deflected to the Lakes from the inland waterways, the sailing ships had their era. Even the United States Navy clung to sails down to the 1880's, and the ships of the "White Squadron" built in that late decade used steam as auxiliary to the familiar rigging of sails. Hammers, saws, and adzes pounded and burred and swished in a hundred shipbuilding yards on the Lakes. Every town had one yard or more. Ships slid down the ways at Sackets Harbor, Toronto, and Oswego; at Buffalo, Erie, Cleveland, Lorain, Sandusky, and the little Ontario river and lake towns; at Detroit and Saginaw; at Milwaukee, Manitowoc, and Chicago. Ropes, cables, masts, spars, and acres of canvas lay on the wharves. The smell of tar and sawdust and damp lumber hovered over the water fronts. The harbors and wharves were a forest of masts interwoven with halyards and rigging.

In the shipyard offices the designers and builders worked over plans for new and better models. They studied weather, winds, harbors, and cargo on the Lakes. They discussed captains' reports on keels, hulls, and winddrifts. Just how should a sailing ship be built and rigged for best performance on these Lakes? The harbors were generally very shallow. The *Illinois* couldn't get in over the sandbar at Chicago. The *Walk-in-the-Water* had to anchor well out at Cleveland. The first ship to call at Kenosha, Wisconsin, in 1835 with a cargo of lumber had to stand well out of the harbor. Passengers went ashore in boats, and the lumber was tossed overboard and floated in to the village. The first canals were also shallow affairs, only about four and a half to six feet deep, though they were later increased to eight or nine feet. Before you built a ship in those days, therefore, you had to decide whether it was to operate through the canals and whether it was to unload off shore or go into the new wharves that were being built at Cleveland, Detroit, Chicago, and other key ports. Smart business called for ships with the largest possible pay load that could be moved in the shortest time with the fewest operating crew. Strike a balance of all these points and what kind of a ship do you get?

The answers were various. The ships were generally built by or for small individual owners. Captain-owners were then as now singular personalities with their own pet notions and ideas about the design of ships. Every conceivable type of sailing ship appeared on the Lakes at one time or another.

The old "canallers" were a familiar sight, particularly on Lake Ontario and Lake Erie. They were purely functional. There was nothing trim about them—no rakish sweep of cutwater bow with a carved and ornamented figure under the bowsprit bespeaking the pride of the captain in his vessel. They were heavy, stubby, and square Hollander-type ships. Their bottoms were flat and their bows nearly perpendicular like a box, designed to fit snugly into the tubby locks of the canals. . . .

The old square-riggers had their day on the Lakes. They were the favorite rigs for warships. Barclay's flagship *Detroit*, which he surrendered to Perry on Lake Erie, was a square-sailed three-masted frigate. All three of Perry's larger ships, the *Lawrence*, the *Niagara*, and the *Caledonia*, were brigs with square sails. It was a good rig for fighting ships, because it was made up of twelve to sixteen independent sheets of canvas, with their edges turned toward the enemy's broadside, and a shell tearing through a foresail or a hit on a topgallant yard would still leave the lower and upper topsails intact to keep the ship under way. These rigs were not so good, however, for commercial ships, because too many hands were needed to operate them. Navies with all their man power could handle them, but private commercial ships could not afford it. The square-riggers, however, did sail well coming loaded down the Lakes with the wind constant behind them, and largely for that reason a few were built and kept in service.

The brigantines, or brigs, were more in favor. They were two masters, of all sizes from around 100 tons on up to as much as 500 tons. Like most of the Lake sailing ships they had square sails on the foremast. It was the brigantine *Columbia*, with the U. S. flag flying proudly at the gaff above her huge fore-and-aft mainsail, that brought the first load of Superior ore through the Soo Canal in 1855 and unloaded it at the busy port of Cleveland.

Up at the little town of Manitowoc, Wisconsin, William Bates had a shipyard and also a new idea. He developed the first distinctive type of sailing ship to appear on the Lakes. He was trying to get a ship that would be fast, carry a good cargo, and be easily handled, and yet at the same time one that would draw a limited draft and not yaw about too much in a wind or drift off the leeward. His answer was the trim clipper type schooner, the *Challenge*, that first sailed out on Lake Michigan in 1852. Her shallow draft was equalized by using a centerboard in the keel. It was a simple and effective device. A stout piece of timber about 12 feet long and 6 to 10 feet wide was boxed in the keel and pivoted on a pin at the bow end. A weight was usually attached to the stern end. When the ship had cleared the shallow harbors, or had passed through a canal or lock, the stern end of the centerboard was dropped with a tackle, and this fin acted as a stabilizer.

The *Challenge* had two masts, the foremast square rigged and the main fore-and-aft rigged. The ship easily attained the phenomenal speed of 13 knots and was noted for her agility and regularity of schedule. Her plan was taken over to France as an example of the Great Lakes type of clipper centerboard schooner. Bates constructed a fleet of these schooners. The *Clipper City* of 1853 had a centerboard and square topsails. The *Manitowoc*, a noted Lake clipper, followed the *Clipper City* down the ways, and these Bates-designed ships soon captured and monopolized much of the Lake trade.

The Lake schooners grew in size as more and more tonnage piled up at the ports for transportation to the East or out across the Lakes to the big outlet city of New Orleans. The larger schooners were usually three-masters—fore, main, and mizzen. They generally retained the centerboard, and carried square topsails. While the American clipper ships were making history on the seven seas, the Lake schooners were sailing by the hundreds back and forth over the blue Lakes. The Lakers, as they were often called, were longer and narrower in the beam than the salt-water ships. They were also a little more rakish in silhouette. On an Atlantic "tern-schooner" all three masts were of approximately equal height— about 91 to 93 feet. But a Lake schooner would have a 98-foot foremast, a graceful main that reached up to 102 feet, and a mizzen that dropped down to about 86 feet. And when a Huron breeze swelled the jib, outerjib, and flying jib well out beyond the bow to complete the sweep of the full sail, these Lakers were about the finest examples of harmony and grace of movement to be seen on any body of water anywhere.

Some minor modifications of rigging were introduced from time to time. The *Moonlight* of Milwaukee, embodying the theories of the early 1870's, was rigged with a billowing triangular topsail or raffe above the square lower sail on her mainmast. This type of sail, which seems to have originated on the Great Lakes, was fairly common in the closing years of the sailing-ship era. But the schooner or barquentine rig proved over the years to be the best for the peculiar natural and economic requirements of the Great Lakes.

Unlike the square rigger, their running gear was easy to store, and the booms could be quickly swung round out of the way while loading or unloading.

These two- or three-masted schooners became standard in the great days of the sailing ships. They performed all sorts of feats astonishing to their age. The little schooner *St. Clair,* as we have noted, was taken from Detroit down the Erie to New York, the first ship to sail to the sea from the Upper Lakes. When the stampede of '49 was on, and the typically American mass rush shifted for the moment from the grain fields of the Great Lakes hinterland to the gold fields of California, the *Eureka* took on 59 passengers and sailed out of Cleveland bound for San Francisco. She crossed Lake Erie, locked through the Welland Canal, ran with the wind down Lake Ontario, threaded her way down the St. Lawrence and through the canals, and, just as though she were a salt-water clipper from Gloucester, Mass., she sailed down the Atlantic, rounded the Horn, beat up the Pacific, and safely deposited her fortune seekers at the Golden Gate.

Other Lake schooners crossed the Atlantic. The *Sophia* of Kingston, rigged as a topsail Lake schooner, sailed from her home port to Liverpool in 1850. Several others followed from Great Lakes ports in the ensuing decade. In fact it was a profitable enterprise to build ships on the Great Lakes and sell them to English firms for salt-water traffic about the Empire—a portent of the desperate days that were to come nearly a century later when these same yards from Kingston to Port Arthur would be furiously building submarines, frigates, and corvettes to protect the North Atlantic shipping lanes against the Nazis.

The *Sea Gull* out of Toronto opened still another market for the Great Lakes when she sailed out of Lake Ontario with a cargo of farm machinery, wagons, buggies, and flour for the new community of Durban, South Africa, and its farms in the back lands. The *Sea Gull* made the round trip in record time and was back in Lake Ontario before the ice closed in on the navigation season. The schooner *Dean Richmond* loaded a cargo of wheat at Milwaukee in 1856 and sailed directly to Liverpool—the first through shipment between those ports. These schooners even reached Lake Superior in the decade before the Soo Canal (1855) was opened. It was an accomplishment not incomparable to that of sailing round the Horn. The schooners had to be hauled out below the Sault, placed on sleds, skids, or rollers, and dragged up to the Superior level of the St. Mary's River. There they were re-launched and sailed off to pick up the trade in the little communities already springing up on the south and west shores of Lake Superior. . . .

At the Buffalo wharves the efficient bustle of getting under way began. The anchor was hove short by drawing the ship by her cables until she was directly over the anchor. The capstan was turned and clicked to the rhythmic chant of sailors' voices. Then the "mudhook" broke out and was hove up and secured. From the quarter-deck by the wheel came the shouted order, "All hands make sail." On the Lake ships that would mean a couple of mates and a dozen sailors or less. The mates take charge, hands scurry up to loose the sails aloft, others man the ropes. The jibs and spankers stretch up to take the first wind and aid the wheelsmen to steer the ship out into the lake. As she begins to make way, the staysails go up with a flap. The ship hastens forward and leans gracefully over on the lee rail. Then the sails are trimmed to the Lake Erie wind and the ship, spreading out a half acre or more of canvas, crowds her way up toward Detroit, Mackinac, Milwaukee, Chicago. At the canals, or when passing through the joining rivers and Lake St. Clair, the sails generally had to come down while the ships were towed in long columns by the steam tugs. But that indignity was soon over, the sails were set again, and the ship sailed on as before.

Generally the hands sang as they worked the ropes and halyards. Singing while you work was one of the traditions on the Lakes. The voyageurs had sung mournful ballads and lively chanties for two centuries as they dipped their paddles into the rivers and lakes. Songs lightened the toil and shortened the hours, and, under their magic, men would paddle eighteen to twenty hours at a single stretch. Good singers got extra pay. Boatmen carried on the custom. Governor Lewis Cass, that rugged, tireless, and great statesman of the Northwest, read the classics while his men sang and rowed him up and down the lakes and rivers to treat with the Indians. On one occasion it is reported that a Chicago citizen at breakfast heard singing in an approaching boat and, without even looking, announced the approach of the Governor. He was right. A Mackinaw boat hove in sight on the Chicago River with twelve oarsmen and a steersman singing a chanty, and Cass himself sitting in the stern to make the fourteenth. These singing men had been rowing him sixty to seventy miles a day. On the sailing ships sailors chanted the rhythm of the capstan weighing the anchor, and the haul on the halyards as they mastheaded the yards to the beat of "A-hay! A-high! A-ho-yo!" And, like their Nova Scotia and deepwater brethren, they set sails to the solo chant of

Haul on the bowlin', the fore and maintop bowlin'—

while all joined in the chorus

Haul on the bowlin', the bowlin' haul!

Most of these old songs, like the libretti of forgotten musical comedies, sound harsh or feeble in the cold print of collectors' albums. But when the watch was aloft belaying a mainsheet off Milwaukee harbor, or when one big sail was spread to port and the other to starboard with a lubber's wind dead aft down Lake Huron and the watch had a moment to smoke and relax, even the most limping of the songs sounded good in the ear. The nearest they can be carried back to their proper setting in our time is when an old sailor, now retired and sitting on a bench on the water front at Sarnia watching the 625-footers go down the channel, recalls the sailing days and rolls out one or two old favorites like "Blow the man down. Give us some wind to blow the man down," as you offer him a cigar and indicate your interest. Or when, too rarely, you go aboard a fishing boat on Lake Erie and find a sailor who remembers the days when song accompanied the slap of the waves against the bow off Bass Island.

There was no time for singing, however, when the cold frontal storms broke over the Lakes or a squall struck at the taut canvas with devastating fury. The master and his men had to be prepared for these crises. They had to know the harbors and how to read the skies and make their own predictions. There were no weather maps, no sequence reports, no forecasts or long-range prediction. Every man was his own aerologist. A few seasons on the Lakes made sailors good weather prophets. The lives of the crew and the safety of the ship depended upon how well the master read the storm warnings of the sky. That first sailing ship on the Upper Lakes, the *Griffin*, most likely went down in one of the sudden Lake Huron storms. The *Ontario* foundered on the lake for which she was christened when she was hit by a storm in 1780, and 172 souls perished at a time when that many people were a large proportion of the white population of the Lakes. Year by year others went down: the schooner *Lexington* with a cargo of whiskey sank between Detroit and Toledo in 1846; the *New Brunswick* in 1859 with a load of walnut and oak timber; the *Fay* plummeting to the bottom of Saginaw Bay with a cargo of steel—and they continue to go down. For the Lakes, though spacious, are still shore lined. Ships cannot run indefinitely with the wind. Moreover, they were navigated near the shore and many were cast up on the rocks.

Disasters like these make men weatherwise. The captains knew nothing of air masses, weather fronts, or millibars, but they did know that cirrus clouds sifting out like spindrift high in the western sky and a halo of cirro-stratus around a golden moon meant storm and trouble over the Lakes on the morrow. They could not chart the vertical and roll currents in a swift-charging cold-front thunderstorm, but when the waves began to kick up and the wind died down for a few minutes, then shifted 180 degrees, these captains knew that the topgallants must come down fast and that even the main lower topsail had better come in. In their own practical way they summed up a chapter of modern scientific meteorology in two handy sayings:

> *If the clouds seem scratched by a hen,*
> *Better take your topsails in.*

> *When the wind shifts against the sun,*
> *Watch her, boys, for back she'll come.*

The hen-scratched clouds, the wind shift, and other natural weather flags were almost constantly hung out on the Great Lakes sky. The big freighters may generally ignore them but the smaller ships must still take care. These storms can roar down over Michigan and hit the long, exposed strip of Lake Huron with terrific force. The plumes and tufts of the first warning high cirrus have hardly reached Georgian Bay before the anvil-headed cumulo-nimbus sweep over the pine forests and hit the waterways. The waves roll and the fresh gale wind at 40 miles per hour carries their crests forward and banners the lake with scud or foam streaks. The smaller craft race to shelter in protected bays and harbors. On the rocky promontory of Presque Isle, Michigan, stands one of the first few lighthouses to be erected on the Upper Lakes. It was built of stone in 1819. It is now privately owned. The top is floored and the proprietor has placed deck chairs up there behind the protective banisters of stone. The view is superb. A half mile to the northwest the tall new beacon flashes signals to passing ships; they see it 16 to 20 miles away and check their course. Below it is the all but abandoned Presque Isle harbor. Off shore you may count eight, ten, seventeen ships spaced and passing. And as the wind sweeps down, you hold on to the stone railing and watch tugs and small fishing boats scurry in from open Huron to the quiet of the protected bay to drop anchor and wait out the blow.

The sailing captains often employed that technique. For many decades there were no aids to navigation. The Lakes were not surveyed and charted until 1889, though this work had been started for certain Canadian waters as early as 1817 by the Royal navy, and for the entire Lake system by the United States Army in 1841. Few lighthouses flashed any warning or direction. There were no red and black buoys carefully marking the channel through dredged or hazardous waters, no ship-to-shore radio, no system of harbor lights and fog horns to warn of coast dangers or pilot the ship to its wharf. There were a few lights on the Canadian shore of Lake Ontario in the pre-1812 days. The Americans added their first lights at Buffalo and at Erie in 1818, and built one at the treacherous Lake Huron entrance to the St. Clair River in 1825. The first light on Lake Michigan appeared at Chicago in 1832; and the first on Lake Superior was set up at Whitefish Point in 1847. You sailed by contact or by dead reckoning, and perhaps put into a harbor at nightfall. But the ships, nearly 2,000 of them in the peak years, sailed with phenomenal regularity and with relatively few losses carrying their endless cargoes of lumber and grain and men up and down the chain of lakes.

It was a colorful era, those sailing decades. It has passed. The last of the schooners was built at Manitowoc in 1875. She served the trade for over half a century, and was wrecked in Lake Michigan in 1929. The yachts and small fishing boats that put out on Sunday morning from Toronto, Cleveland, Detroit, and Chicago, with their tall white sails flashing in the sun and leaning over with a fresh breeze, give only a bare and imperfect suggestion of the picture of the Lakes when 2,000 ships lifted their masts full of canvas from Duluth to Kingston. Only a few aged and retired captains still remember the time when they sailed independently about from port to port, chartering their ships for the voyage, picking up here a load of grain, there a cargo of lumber, and a hold full of coal to take back to Kenosha or the Sault. Volumes could be filled with the names of ships, the personalities of their captains, mates, and crews, the adventures of the voyages through ice, storms, fire, and collisions. They held on toughly against the lengthening bulk-cargo ships of steel and steam, which little by little stole their trade. By the 1890's the sails were dropped to mould on the wharves, the masts were pulled down, and the once-proud sailing ships were reduced to tow barges under the dirty streamer of smoke from their conquerors.

The

Historic *Onoko*

Writing his encyclopedic *History of the Great Lakes* in 1899, John Brandt Mansfield looked back at the rapid development of lake vessels and forward to developments to come. The opening of the Weitzel Lock at the Soo, in 1881, made the old ships obsolete; in twenty years freighters doubled in length and tripled in cargo capacity. In this expansive period ships that were marvels in their first season became "back numbers," as Mansfield remarked, a few years later.

But the *Onoko,* built at the foot of West Fifty-fourth Street in Cleveland in 1882, was remembered. For ten years this leviathan, far ahead of the competition, brought record cargoes down the lakes. Not the first iron merchant ship—that distinction belongs to the *Merchant* launched at Buffalo in 1862—the *Onoko* was the first iron freighter built for bulk cargo.

When young Harry Coulby, fresh from England, arrived in Cleveland in 1884, he tried to ship on the *Onoko.* The mate shook his head; he had no room for a green hand. Despite that rejection, or perhaps because of it, Harry Coulby became in twenty years the "Master of the Lakes," in charge of the vessels of the Pittsburgh Steamship Division and the Interlake Steamship Company. In 1927 he saw the launching of the *Harry Coulby,* with six times the tonnage of the historic *Onoko.* In 1915 that famous ship had foundered in a storm on Lake Superior.

THE STEAMER *Onoko,* 282 feet long, is one of the most remarkable steamers on the lakes, notwithstanding she is of the canal-boat style of naval architecture. She has run on the lakes for sixteen seasons, and has earned money enough to load her down. For ten of the sixteen years that she has run she carried the largest cargoes of any boat afloat on fresh water, and has had business in ore at $3 per ton, and wheat from Port Arthur at 14 cents per bushel. She was the first of the modern iron freighters.

Less then ten years ago the iron steamer *Onoko* was pointed out by marine men as being a marvel. She carried the largest cargo of any ship on the lakes—110,000 bushels of corn. In 1897 the schooner *Amazon* carried out of South Chicago 230,000 bushels of corn, and nothing was thought of it. Every year has seen an average growth of from ten to twenty feet in the length of vessels, with a corresponding increase in the beam and depth. At every advance vesselmen said the boats were as big as they could be economically handled, but generally the next contract showed them to be mistaken. In 1897 it was announced that the Zenith Transportation Company, of Duluth, had given an order for a steamer 450 feet long to the Cleveland Shipbuilding Company; old-time vesselmen again said it was the limit of size for a successful lake carrier. The Bessemer Steamship Company has since added twenty-five feet.

The prediction that within ten years 600-foot vessels will be built on the lakes is made by the Detroit *Free Press*. Experiments are being made with a central arch of steel running fore and aft, as it is in the length not width that weakness is shown in a seaway. Then it is thought that girders will be so changed in position and composition as to give greater strength, and that strakes will not only be made stronger but better fastened as the method improves with experiment. The limit as to depth is certainly reached now, though fifty-five feet, and even a little greater, may be attained in width. Therefore it would be necessary to introduce the arch and other means of strengthening. Not only the seas but the action of the engine gives the long hull the snake-like motion that is plainly perceptible if one stands at the after end and looks towards the bow. A steel arch, running amidships the length of the vessel, and well braced, would so strengthen the modern steel vessel hull as to allow of the 550-foot length and greater, and at the same time not handicap the vessel with dead weight, giving it great draught when with light cargo.

For ten years past it had been impossible to get a strictly modern boat on the lakes. Size and style changed between the laying of the keel and the launching of the ship. Nowhere in the world has the progress in marine architecture been so pronounced as on the Great Lakes, where a greater tonnage was launched in 1896 than in all the rest of the United States.

Three years ago the biggest load ever carried on the lakes was about 4,000 tons, and it was a year before such loads became common. Two years ago came the first 5,000-ton vessel, and it was supposed the limit had been reached. In a year the lakes were dotted with vessels that carried over 5,000 tons, and this season there are half a dozen that load over 6,000 tons. Six years ago the 2,500-ton freighters of the Great Northern road were leaders in size and equipment. To-day such ships are back numbers, though most efficient vessels. There never has been a time when nor a waterway where progress has been so rapid as in the past half dozen years on the Great Lakes.

RALPH D. WILLIAMS

All in a

Lifetime

Over the unchanging lakes moved a changing commerce. White-winged sloops and schooners were followed by smoking little steamers. In the steamers paddle wheels gave way to propellers, wooden hulls gave way to iron, and iron hulls to steel. Meanwhile the channels and harbors were deepened, the docks grew longer. On the docks the old block and tackle gave place to the "whirlie" derrick dexterously lifting tubs of cargo, and that led to the giant electric dippers hunching over the long freighters at the end of their run.

Always in this evolution the ships took the lead. In 1869 the *R. J. Hackett* steamed up the lakes and the iron ports saw a new kind of vessel, 211 feet long, with engines aft and navigation quarters forward. For her was built the 213-foot *Forest City,* as her consort. (For half a century this oddly elegant term designated tow barges on the lakes.) In 1874 came the *V. H. Ketchum,* with a leaning bowsprit, a spread of canvas and a tall funnel smoking abaft her mizzenmast; she was larger than the dock facilities of her time, though they would soon catch up. In 1882 appeared the iron-hulled *Onoko,* 300 feet overall with a single cavernous hold of 3,000 tons capacity—and the long ships were on the way. As the carriers grew the cost of transporting iron ore decreased—from three dollars a ton in 1855 to sixty cents a ton half a century later.

In this half-century one man saw all the changes in the trade. As a youth he had furled sails on the graceful schooners; he lived to see his name on a 600-foot steamer loading 10,000 tons of cargo. Peter White's memory spanned the bark canoes of the Indians and the parade of freighters through the Sault. The evolution of lake shipping in his lifetime was sketched in 1906 by Ralph D. Williams in his eventful biography, *The Honorable Peter White.*

HAT HAS this man seen? He wrote the bill of lading for one of the earliest, if not the first, shipments of ore to leave the Lake Superior country. He saw it carried away in a little schooner to be portaged over the falls and to be loaded again upon equally tiny vessels. He saw it carried in sailing vessels because steamers were largely at that time passenger craft and such a thing as a steamer for bulk freight purposes exclusively was not even dreamed of. It was a period of unlighted channels and navigation was therefore impossible by night. He saw these little sailing craft delayed by current and unfavorable winds in the rivers and he saw the old steamer *Gore*, an old-fashioned British-built paddle craft, lash a sailing vessel on each side of her and carry them through the rivers.

He saw this sytem of towing speedily abandoned in favor of the astern towing by the handier propeller and he saw the *Hamilton Morton*, *Peck Castle* and *John Martin* built for this purpose. Then the tug *Champion* followed with double engines and power sufficient to tow seven or eight sailing vessels. Occasionally an increasing north wind would compel the *Champion* to release one of her tows so as to make headway with the rest against the current and then great would be the profanity of the skipper so abandoned, a cyclone being but a summer's breeze to his vast and awful bluster. In 1869 he saw the steamer *R. J. Hackett* built to carry the ore of the Jackson mine. She was the first steamer to be built exclusively for the ore trade. She was the first to be built with machinery aft with a continuous hold and hatches spaced 24-ft. centers. The next year her consort, the *Forest City,* was constructed. They are the parents of a very numerous and much improved family. This system of a steamer and its consort began gradually to displace the sailing vessel and to counteract its effect the owners of sailing vessels frequently employed the tugs to tow them all the way between upper and lower lake ports.

He saw iron supplant wood as a shipbuilding material in the construction of the *Onoko* in 1882 at the Globe Iron Works, Cleveland. The *Onoko* was 287 ft. long and 38 ft. beam, and was the largest dead-weight carrier on the lakes for many years. He saw steel supplant iron in ship construction by the building of the *Spokane* for the Wilson Transit Co. by the Globe Iron Works, Cleveland, in 1886, until now it is the only material used of which to build them. The *Spokane* was 310 ft. long, 38 ft. beam and 24 ft. deep. He saw the one great departure in the construction of the ore carrier made by Alexander McDougall in 1888, when he conceived a form of construction known as the whaleback, and built No. 101 and thirty like it only to discover after all that the type did not embody the points of highest efficiency for ore carriage. He saw how cautious was the growth in the size of the ore carrier, the main dimensions even as late as 1894 being under 300 ft. He saw in 1895 the first of the 400-footers, the *Victory* and the *Zenith* appear, and in 1897 noted that the Bessemer Steamship Co. gave orders for a steel steamer and two consorts larger than anything previously built, the steamer being 475 ft. over all and the barges 450 ft. These dimensions stood until 1900, when Mr. A. B. Wolvin placed an order for four 500-footers. These vessels are the *John W. Gates, Wm. Edenborn, Isaac L. Ellwood* and *J. J. Hill.* They are called 500-footers because they approach it so nearly, being less than 2 ft. short of 500 ft.

He saw in Mr. Wolvin the boldest experimenter in ship construction, not only in the size of ships but in the method of building them. The unit of construction spacing for an ore ship is the length of the ore car in use on Lake Superior. This car is 24 ft. long. The dock pockets are therefore 12 ft. wide center to center and, therefore, the ship has her hatch openings 24-ft. centers. With these openings she could load from every other pocket and when a series of pockets was emptied, a 12-ft. shift along the dock would put the hatchways in front of another series. Now the human ore handler is wedded to strike and holidays when the pressure on the docks is greatest, and the new type of ship's deck was demanded with opening sufficient to permit the unloading machines to operate all over the interior of the vessel. Mr. Wolvin accordingly built the steamer *James H. Hoyt* in 1902 with nineteen hatches all spaced 12-ft. centers. She took on her cargo of 5,250 tons of ore in the record-breaking time of 30.5 minutes, and unloaded it by means of the Hulett unloading machine in 3 hours and 52 minutes. These records have since been superseded by those obtained on the steamers *Wolvin* and *George W. Perkins.* Mr. Wolvin then went a step further—a considerable one, it must be admitted. He built in 1904 the steamer *Augustus B. Wolvin,* 62 ft. longer than any other ship ever constructed on the lakes. She is 560 ft. over all, 540 ft. keel, 56 ft. beam and 32 ft. deep with thirty-three hatches spaced 12-ft. centers. In constructing the *Wolvin* hold stanchions were dispensed with and a system of girder arches were substituted in their place to support the deck as well as the sides of the ship. This system, first introduced on the *Sahara,* built a few months prior to the *Wolvin,* has since become the accepted mode of modern construction since it leaves the hold entirely free from any obstruction which might interfere with the unloading machines. Another novelty lies in the shape of her cargo hold. This is built in the form of a hopper with sides that slope from her main deck down to the tank top and the ends built on the same slopes. The hopper extends in one continuous length of 409 ft. without bulkheads or divisions of any kind and in width measures at the top 43 ft. and at the bottom 24 ft.

Recent, however, as is the construction of the *Wolvin*, she has already been greatly superseded in size. Mr. Harry Coulby, president and general manager of the Pittsburgh Steamship Co., which is the corporate name under which the ships of the United States Steel Corporation are operated on the Great Lakes, placed orders with the American Ship Building Co. for four steamers 9 ft. longer than the *Wolvin*. Their names are *Elbert H. Gary*, *Wm. E. Corey*, *Henry C. Frick* and *George W. Perkins*. Scarcely had they been built before he placed orders for eight ships of even greater dimensions—the *J. Pierpont Morgan*, *A. H. Rogers*, *P. A. B. Widener*, *Norman B. Ream*, *Thomas Lynch*, *George F. Baker*, *Thomas F. Cole* and *Henry Phipps*—all of them being 600 ft. overall with the exception of the *Cole* which is 605 ft. 5 in. Even these were hardly in the water before they were outstripped by W. M. Mills' three ships—the *W. B. Kerr*, *W. M. Mills* and *L. S. DeGraff*, with their overall length of 607 ft. and beam of 60 ft. These are the record cargo carriers of the lakes, moving in a single trip over 12,000 tons.

How vivid this recital is by contrast. A single full cargo of one of these steamers represents seven times the movement of ore through the Sault Ste. Marie canal in 1855, and one of these vessels could alone have carried the entire ore commerce of the lakes for a number of years thereafter. Progress has been rapid on the Great Lakes during the past few years but it has nevertheless been cautious. Even as late as 1897 two big consorts were constructed for a steamer then building. The year 1897 is not so very far in the past, but it is reasonably assured that no one to-day would place an order to build a consort. The highest economy of operation is reached by the single steamer of large carrying capacity and low power. There was justification for the consort system in the days of wooden ship building because a fleet of sailing ships was in existence whose natural destiny in the evolution of trade was that of consort. But it was not economy to build a new vessel for consort purposes. It took the vessel owners a long time to come to the conclusion that it was really expensive business to put machinery of high power in a steamer for the purpose of enabling her to tow a consort. She burned a great deal of fuel, and moreover lost considerable of her own time in port waiting for her consort. The *Elbert H. Gary* has the same engines that the *Manola* had which was built by Pickands, Mather & Co. in 1890. The *Manola* could carry 3,000 tons of ore; the *Gary* over 10,000 tons.

In 1905 the Cleveland Cliffs Iron Co., the same old Cleveland company changed in title a bit but not a whit in its fine character, named one of its great steamers in honor of *Peter White*. She was built by the Great Lakes Engineering Works of Detroit. She is of large carrying capacity and low power and represents the highest type of modern ore freighter.

The

Whaleback Fleet

In his long career Captain Alexander McDougall commanded some famous lake vessels, including the liner *Japan* with a carved Japanese figure peering from the roof of its pilot house. That patient lookout saw many changes on the lakes, and one of them was McDougall's own invention.

According to legend, Captain McDougall woke one morning excited by a dream in which he had seen a cigar-shaped freighter nosing steadily through tossing seas. For years that dream drove him, until he had completed plans and drawings for a revolutionary vessel. On his drawing board was a ship of rounded sides and bulbous bow, with forward and after cabins mounted on heavy stanchions above the tubular hull. McDougall had never seen a whale, but he called this ship a whaleback; lakemen called it a pig. With financial backing in New York, two ends of the first whaleback barge were built at Brooklyn. Shipped to Duluth they were joined to a center section that McDougall had built there. This first pigboat was loaded with iron ore at Two Harbors in June of 1888.

With a flat bottom giving stability, a rounded upper structure offering little resistance to wind and waves, and a pig nose that made steering easy, the first whaleback made exciting news up and down the lakes. In the next eight years forty of these arresting craft were launched at Duluth-Superior. Many of them were barges; it was common to see a whaleback steamer towing two or three whaleback barges. That ponderous procession ran smoothly through rough seas and drifting ice fields. But the pigboats were unhandy at the docks and their narrow hatches hampered cargo handling. No new ones were built after 1898.

McDougall's fleet attracted great attention, and was vastly publicized when the whaleback passenger steamer *Christopher Columbus* was built to carry World's Fair visitors at Chicago. The following account accompanied a three-page picture spread in the weekly *Graphic,* for December 31, 1892.

NO MORE interesting achievement in marine architecture has been witnessed than is presented in the Whaleback. As the title indicates the vessel is quite like a whale, round-decked and flat-bottomed. It has but little bulk above the water to catch the sea, the waves dashing over it. The whalebacks are all constructed on the same general plan, the ends being pointed and turned upward. Since the first of these boats were launched, about two years ago at Superior, Wisc., they have grown rapidly in favor, as their many special merits have become known. They promise a radical change in transportation, and have already demonstrated their merits in competitive tests. The whaleback is cheaper of construction than the ordinary vessel, is less expensive to run and carries a considerably larger cargo. The general introduction of these boats into the lake traffic will mean an enormous reduction in the expenses attending the transfer of commodities from producers to the large centers of trade.

The plan of the whaleback is the invention of Mr. Alexander McDougall of Superior, Wisc., an old lake vessel owner, who is now at the head of the shipyard from which they are turned out.

The peculiar advantages of the whaleback attract attention to it as a means of steamship transportation from Chicago to Jackson Park during the World's Columbian Exposition, and the World's Fair Transportation Company of Chicago had built for this service the large steel passenger whaleback *Christopher Columbus*, which was constructed under the supervision of the inventor in the yards of the American Steel Barge Company. This is the first effort made to adapt the whaleback for passenger traffic, and the large size of the vessel makes the innovation in this field especially interesting. The *Christopher Columbus* was launched at West Superior, Wisc., on December 3rd in the sight of 15,000 people. The great vessel does not differ in any essential from the regulation whaleback. It is designed to carry 5,000 passengers. The vessels previously built have only two turrets, one forward and one aft, but the new vessel has seven turrets. These rise 7½ feet above the deck and are elliptical in form. They extend the full length of the vessel and are occupied by the windlass, stairways to the saloon deck above and between decks below, air fans, stacks, ash-hoists, engine room and machinery.

The spacious refreshment rooms are located amidships. Four gangways on either side are provided for entering and leaving the vessel. The *Christopher Columbus* is 362 feet in length, has a beam of 42 feet and a depth of 24 feet. It has one screw 14 feet in diameter, and a speed of 20 miles an hour is promised. Practically the entire deck supported by the turrets is devoted to the saloon proper. It is 225 feet long and 30 feet wide. The vessel has electrical equipment for lighting, and steam heating apparatus.

A promenade deck 4 feet wide runs around the saloon, with more than 30 feet of space at the bow and stern. The promenade deck proper is above the saloon and is 257 feet long with a skylight 15 by 138 feet in the center. An elaborate fountain in the center of the grand cabin will be one of the principal features of the boat. It is said that the run from the Lake Front at Chicago to the World's Fair grounds, a distance of seven miles, will be made in half an hour.

Attention has been called to the whaleback as a most formidable boat for naval warfare, the round deck and the absence of bulk above the water forming an excellent recommendation for it in this service.

MILO M. QUAIFE

Parade

on the River

The St. Marys River is more properly a strait, an intricate and beautiful waterway that broadens and narrows for forty-two miles between Detour and the Soo. Though its deep-dredged channels carry a prodigious commerce, the shores are wild and silent. On Sugar Island some Indians live in tar-paper shanties, dark huts among the white birch trees. From the doorway they watch without wonder the great procession of lake shipping.

Once it was an Indian commerce that moved on the river. Every spring the canoe caravans came, and the tribesmen pitched their camps beside the gleaming water. At night their fires twinkled on the shore and the darkness throbbed with the beat of drums. Now the hills echo with deep-throated whistles and the big ships glide past.

An unbroken line of evolution links the bark canoe and the seven-hundred-foot ore carrier. So that in the eyes of memory another parade passes—canoe, bateau, sloop, schooner, sidewheel steamer, propeller, wooden freighter, iron freighter, steel freighter. In a century and a half the vessels have grown from ten tons capacity to twenty-five thousand tons. That parade was pictured by Milo M. Quaife in *River of Destiny*, 1955, a narrative of changing times on the wilderness river that the French explorers named for the Blessed Virgin.

FOR UNCOUNTED CENTURIES before the white man came to America the Indians journeyed in canoes. In the latitude of Lake Superior, where the white birch abounds, the canoes were made of birch bark. These were the conveyances of all the early explorers, and they were marvelously adapted to the purpose they were contrived to serve. Jean Nicolet in 1634, seeking in the Wisconsin wilderness the domain of the Emperor of China, journeyed in a bark canoe propelled by seven dusky companions.

368

Radisson and Grosseilliers two decades later embarked upon a 500-league journey "not in great galleons or large-oared barges, but in little gondolas of bark." Louis Jolliet and Father Jacques Marquette in 1673 departed from Saint Ignace with five *voyageurs* and a little smoked meat and Indian corn in two bark canoes on a voyage "whose duration they could not foresee." As late as 1820 Governor Cass conducted his 4,000-mile exploration of Lake Superior and the upper Mississippi in bark canoes.

"The utility and artistry of the birch-bark canoe of the savage," wrote William Cullen Bryant in 1846, "seems to me one of the most beautiful and perfect things of the kind constructed by human art. I could not but wonder at the ingenuity of those who had invented so beautiful a combination of ship-building and basket-work." And Henry W. Longfellow, another poet, deriving his information from Henry R. Schoolcraft, wrote that

> The forest's life was in it,
> All its mystery and magic,
> All the lightness of the birch tree,
> All the toughness of the cedar,
> All the larch's supple sinews;
> And it floated on the river
> Like a yellow leaf in autumn,
> Like a yellow water lily.

In recent decades much has been written about the influence on American life exerted by the automobile. Whether the Indian canoe, invented centuries earlier, did not exert a greater influence may reasonably be questioned. The canoe made possible the French advance over the Great Lakes and the Mississippi Valley. It was responsible for the development of the fur trade, over whose control France and England waged more than a hundred-years war. In like fashion, it was essential to the waging of the uncounted tribal wars, on whose outcome the rise and fall of the Indian nations depended.

On the interior rivers where portages are common, the narrow light canoes, sixteen feet in length, called by the *voyageurs canots du nord,* were used. But the fur traders employed, from Montreal to the Sault and on the Great Lakes, the *canots du maître,* vessels thirty or more feet long and five or six feet wide, capable of carrying, in addition to the crew of eight or ten men, two or more tons of cargo. In such canoes as these the Cass expedition of 1820 was conducted. The Chippewas were marvelous swimmers and paddlers, as much at home in the water as on land. The Canadian *voyageurs,* mainstay of the fur trade, were no less remarkable for their endurance of hardship and their patient submission to a life of extraordinary exposure and toil. Furs were packed for transportation in packs weighing ninety pounds. Two such packs were the common load of a *voyageur* across a portage, however long or difficult of passage it might be. On occasion, they were known to carry twice as many. . . .

Intermediate between the bark canoe and the sailing ship were the bateau and the Mackinaw boat. These were sturdier vessels than the red man's canoe. The bateau, in fact, was merely the white man's adaptation of the bark canoe, designed for use in open or navigable water. Constructed of red cedar, with a flat bottom and pointed ends, it was closely related to the Mackinaw boat, which was a flat-bottomed barge with blunter ends, constructed of red or white oak boards. Both bateaux and Mackinaw boats were equipped with mast and sail which could be easily erected and was used whenever circumstances permitted to supplement the man power of the crew. With a favoring wind such craft could sail sixty or more miles in a day carrying as many as twenty persons, with their baggage and supplies.

The first, and for long the only, decked vessel on Lake Superior was the one maintained by the Sieur de La Ronde for several years beginning in 1734. Soon after the conquest of Canada in 1760 the British began constructing sailing vessels for use on the upper lakes and by the early 1770's they were commonly navigating the Saint Marys as far as the Sault. They were very small craft, and energetic John Askin at Mackinac, as we have seen, devised a means of passing them around the rapids into and from Lake Superior. This practice was repeated two generations later, when sailing vessels and their cargoes were laboriously hauled or propelled on rollers around the American side of the rapids.

The hazards encountered in navigating the Saint Marys were enough to try the soul of even the sturdiest mariner. "The strait of St. Marys to the falls," relates Blois' *Gazetteer of Michigan,* published in 1838, "is the most difficult to navigate. Its common sailing channel is a perfect labyrinth, devious and circuitous, around islands and sunken rocks, passing across channels and shoals. It is ascended by a southwest wind only, and then none but the most experienced can pilot a vessel either up or down it." Until the latter half of the nineteenth century the tortuous channels remained wholly unmarked, and most captains of sailing ships were compelled to employ pilots to conduct them through the river. One noted pilot—of a tugboat—was Captain William Greenough of Sault Sainte Marie, who was known as the "nighthawk," since he alone would undertake to pilot a vessel after dark.

The limestone bar at the foot of Lake George, with its six-foot depth of water, was long a serious deterrent to navigation of the river. Although it offered no obstacle to the smaller sailing craft it proved a more serious matter for the heavier steamboats. The first one ever to attempt the navigation of the Saint Marys was the *Superior,* which in 1822 conveyed the troops sent to establish Fort Brady. Since the vessel drew eight feet of water, her voyage ended at the bar, and the soldiers were compelled to complete the journey in Northwest canoes.

The experience of the *Superior* was repeated uncounted times during the ensuing third of a century, until the government dredged a twelve-foot channel through Lake George. Commonly, of course, vessels having a greater draft than six feet made no effort to cross the bar. What might happen when some misguided skipper did make the attempt is pointedly described by Gabriel Franchère, Sault agent of the American Fur Company, in a letter written to the company's agent at Detroit on June 17, 1836, from which we quote:

On Monday last towards evening the schooner *Lodi* came in and reported the *Ramsay Crooks* on the bar below, demanding lighters. I lost no time in dispatching a boat under the command of Mr. Livingston with seven men. . . . I cannot but recommend never to overload a vessel bound for this place. 7½ feet is all the water we have on the bar and there is a loss instead of a gain by loading them 8 feet or over. The vessel comes in with a fair wind, strikes, and it takes ½ a day for some of the crew to come up and give us notice. Boats of course must be sent down with 10 or 12 men at six shillings per diem [and] another half day is employed before they can get there, the distance being 21 miles. If they have to carry part of the loading on shore, as was the case in this instance, it is not easily accomplished in a gale of wind—then everything must be brought back on board after the vessel is over the bar. Add to that, the loss of a fair wind, which may possibly detain the vessel a week or more below. Upon the whole, you will no doubt agree with me that there is more loss than gain.

The Erie Canal, completed in 1825, opened a flood-tide of migration into the states adjoining the upper lakes. Although many of the migrants came by land, thousands of others, upon reaching Buffalo, continued their journey by vessel around the lakes. Both steam and sailing ships increased rapidly in number as the century advanced, to accommodate the ever-increasing demands for transportation. The earlier steamboats were side-wheelers, relatively small, and poorly constructed. As in the subsequent case of the early automobiles, their engines were painfully weak, and frequently incapable of making headway against a contrary gale. The vessels, too, were floating firetraps, giving rise to frequent appalling disasters. Charles Dickens, who traveled in one of them on Lake Erie in 1842, was moved to record that he felt as if he were seated in a powder mill.

Vastly more numerous, for many years, than the steamboats were the sailing ships, of many types and sizes. Dependent upon the winds, they encountered particular difficulty in navigating such river channels as the Saint Marys and the Detroit. This led to the employment of steam tugs to tow them in and out of harbors and in the rivers. Tugs were employed to tow sailing vessels from the head of Lake Munuscong, or even from Detour, to the Sault, and eventually to tow strings of several vessels throughout the length of the Great Lakes. The passage of the age of sails was accompanied by a marked decline in the use and number of the tug boats; although these still perform essential services, their glory departed when the white sails ceased to dot the lakes. Prior to their advent, upbound sailing vessels were often deterred, sometimes for weeks, by adverse winds from negotiating the Saint Marys above Lake Munuscong. This circumstance gave rise to the name "Sailors Encampment," applied to both Canadian and American shores for a distance of one or two miles, where the river is narrowest. According to one report, the name was first applied when the crew of a schooner, caught in the river, wintered here in 1817.

Captains of upbound vessels always endeavored to reach Sailors Encampment before dark, since only rarely was the navigation of the river after sundown attempted. Many vessels carried traveling salesmen, who from the fur-trading days were still called "traders," and displayed their wares and took orders wherever the vessel stopped. Passenger boats, and sometimes other vessels, carried a band of musicians, and after the transaction of business was concluded, a dance—always attended by the settlers—was frequently arranged, either aboard ship or at one of the nearby homes. So prevalent was this custom that the masters of most sailing vessels refused to hire a man unless he were a musician or a singer or an entertaining story teller.

The latter half of the nineteenth century witnessed the heyday of the sailing ships on the Great Lakes. Prior to 1869 they carried practically all the bulk freight, while steamers conveyed the passengers and package freight. In 1871, 10,000 sailing ships and 1,000 steamboats entered or left the port of Chicago. In the sixties the side-wheelers averaged 680 tons and the propellers 478 tons. By present-day standards these were pigmy ships, of course. The crews of the sailing ships were professional sailors who spoke contemptuously of the steamboats and their crews as "iron ships and wooden men." Prior to 1890, steamboat men were not permitted to join the sailors' unions.

Today no sailing ships whiten the lakes, and the day is fast approaching when the last of the passenger steamers will have vanished. Yet throughout the eight-months season of navigation a steady procession of huge freighters plies the Saint Marys bearing a commerce which is vastly more valuable and important than the river in bygone generations ever knew.

The Great Lakes freighter has no counterpart elsewhere in the world. It is a highly specialized craft, no less admirably designed for the function it serves than was the birch-bark canoe of the red man. The Providence which designed the world saw fit to surround Lake Superior with a fabulous store of timber and mineral wealth and to provide on the prairies of interior Canada and the United States perhaps the world's most extensive and important grain-producing area. Separated by a thousand miles of distance from the head of Lake Superior, it placed the no-less fabulous coal deposits contiguous to Lake Erie and the upper Ohio Valley. To and fro between Lake Superior and the lower lakes during eight months of the year, the world's most extensive waterborne commerce is carried; grain and lumber, dairy products and iron ore downbound to the mills and markets of the world, and coal and articles of use and consumption of almost countless kinds required to satisfy interior America's needs upbound. Before the little town of Amherstburg at the mouth of the Detroit River 29,700 vessels passed in 1941, an average rate of one every 12½ minutes throughout the season of navigation.

Key to all this vast commerce are the freighters and the river channels—Saint Marys, Saint Clair, and Detroit—which bear them. The size and cargo of the freighters is limited only by the capacity of the harbors and the connecting river channels to float them. Ship construction presses hard upon river and harbor improvement, therefore, and the demands of business for the deepening of the river channels are constant.

The first steel ship built for Great Lakes service was the *Spokane* in 1886. Her tonnage of 2,357 and length of 249½ feet would render her insignificant today, yet she initiated a revolution in Great Lakes shipping which still continues. The year 1906 saw the advent of the first 600-foot freighter. Although no engineering obstacles prevent the building of 1,000-foot vessels, the capacity of the channels still prevents their construction. The urgent demand for steel created by World War II led to the launching of several 640-foot freighters, and by 1953 two of 714-foot length were in operation.

The one economic reason for the existence of the Great Lakes freighters is their ability to transport freight as rapidly and cheaply as possible. This involves, of course, not merely the size of the cargo but the number of cargoes carried each season. To keep the freighters in motion on their water highways as much of the time as possible, and to load and discharge their cargoes as quickly as possible, is therefore a prime economic consideration. The return of each Easter season heralds the awakening of Nature from her sound sleep. Once more "the flowers appear on the earth, the time of the singing of birds is come." But around the Great Lakes an earlier harbinger of spring is the hum of activity in the shipyards. On Erie, Huron, and Michigan the great drab vessels lie restlessly at their docks in readiness for instant departure, while from captain downward, their crews eagerly await the word that the channels of the Saint Clair and the Saint Marys, along with the Straits of Mackinac and Whitefish Bay, are open, to begin their northward dash for such distant ports as Marquette and Duluth. By way of an assist to Mother Nature, the world's greatest fleet of ice-breakers leads the procession, hurling their ponderous bulk in repeated onslaughts upon ice fields twenty or more inches thick in the stern determination to clear the channels at the earliest possible moment.

So the unending race against time and the elements continues, and on its outcome depends the wealth and prosperity of uncounted millions of people. When the great ships shuttle in constant procession from end to end of the lakes, fires glow in the steel mills and labor is everywhere in demand; when they lie idly at anchor, despair and industrial stagnation grip the heart of the nation. Before the eyes of the dweller beside the Saint Marys, throughout the annual season of navigation the great long ships parade in almost unbroken procession. Frequently several are in sight at one time, their capacious holds transporting the ore whose abundance and cheapness unite to make America the world's foremost industrial power. So closely are the cargoes adjusted to the capacity of the channels to bear them, that a clearance of only a few inches between the vessel and the river bottom is provided and the speed of the ship is tempered to maintain the necessary clearance.

Between the bark canoe of the red man and the steel leviathan which today plies the Saint Marys the differences are vast. Yet the great long ship today fulfills its function no less admirably than did the bark canoe of a former era. In time, we venture to predict, an artist will arise endowed with imagination to picture it as a thing of beauty no less than of utility.

ROBERT H . FOLKERT

Towed from

Baltimore

During World War I, shipyards on the lakes worked day and night building freight vessels for ocean service. At the close of navigation in 1917 scores of new ships hurried toward the Welland Canal and the St. Lawrence before winter should lock them in. They were a new kind of lakes-built vessel—stubby, high-riding with a raised foc'sle and a raised poop and a tall stack jutting from the 'midship cabins. Two hundred and sixty-one feet long, they were built to squeeze through the old St. Lawrence locks. More than two hundred of them went out to war-time merchant duty. After the war scores of those "lakers" sailed from Chesapeake Bay in the Gulf and the coastal trades.

Thirty years later, in the surge of industrial growth following the second World War, the lakes shipyards were clamorous with construction of new lake freighters, while a backlog of orders piled up. To obtain additional new capacity lake shipping companies turned to salt water.

While the lakes trade needed new tonnage there was a surplus of ocean vessels; scores of war freighters lay idle on the coasts. In 1951 the Cleveland-Cliffs Iron Company purchased from the U. S. Department of Commerce, Maritime Administration, the 454-foot *Notre Dame Victory*, then moored in the James River. The ship went into a graving dock in Baltimore where the decks were removed and the hull was cut in two. A midships section 165 feet long, constructed at the Sparrows Point yard, was inserted. Pilot house, bow and cabin were hoisted into place, and the ship, now the *Cliffs Victory*, made her trial runs. Then the big freighter was stripped of her superstructure to clear inland bridges on her roundabout way to the Great Lakes.

On April 2, 1951, a deep sea tug took her lines and started the journey. Down the coast she went, around the Florida Keys and across the Gulf, up the winding Mississippi and into the Illinois waterway. At Joliet schools were dismissed to let the children watch the passing of the first ocean-to-lakes freighter; church bells rang as she glided under the Joliet bridges. In Chicago multitudes saw the big ship creep through the canyoned river. On May 9 the first salt water cargo ship joined the fleet of Great Lakes freighters.

Meanwhile at the Sparrows Point shipyard on Chesapeake Bay rivets were racketing into three big freighters for the lakes trade. They were identical vessels, 626 feet long, with a capacity of 18,000 tons; their geared turbines could generate 7,700 horsepower, driving the loaded vessels at 16.5 miles per hour. Oil-fired and electric powered, they had electric engines on deck and deepfreeze units and a disposal system in the galley. The old hiss and clank of steam winches and the cry of gulls swooping for refuse would not be heard on these ships.

Two of them, the *Sparrows Point* and the *Johnstown*, were built for the Bethlehem Transportation Company; the *Elton Hoyt 2nd* joined the Pickands Mather & Co. Interlake fleet. The *Elton Hoyt 2nd* was lengthened to 698 feet and now has a per-trip carrying capacity of 23,200 gross tons.

After trial runs in Chesapeake Bay the ships were prepared for the long trip, by tow, to the lakes. To clear bridges on the inland waters their superstructure was removed. It made a novel deckload—the pilothouse, the texas and the after penthouse covering the first eight hatches; then the twin sections of the funnel and two more deckhouses from the after end. The spars were laid on deck; the rudder and five-bladed propeller were lashed in the hold. In fine summer weather seagoing tugs took their lines and the big ships, with maintenance crews aboard, began the three-thousand mile journey, down the Atlantic, across the Gulf, up the Mississippi and the Illinois waterway and through the Chicago River, to Lake Michigan.

The journey of the *Elton Hoyt 2nd* from Baltimore to Chicago was recorded by Robert H. Folkert, her chief engineer, for the *Interlake Log*, from which it is reprinted.

WEATHER ON THE Atlantic Coast was mild, with a light easterly breeze. The *Hoyt* followed the tug sort of sidewise without any turning or yawing back and forth and for the first four days rolled steadily in a ground swell. We were in sight of land almost all the time.

We were trying to get some work done but the first sight of sea turtles, porpoises, flying fish and so forth continually interrupted us.

I left Baltimore without any fishing tackle and was forced to improvise by beating a fish hook out of a steel packing hook. I used a white rag for bait which turned rust-colored every half hour in the salt water, a copper wire leader and a coil of heaving line for a fish line. I did catch a fish, however, and that quieted all the smart cracks about my "fishing."

Around the Keys the shrimp boats and stations were interesting to see, as well as the coral bottom that we saw under us for miles at a time.

We used the 15 feet of cool salt water in No. 7 side tank for a swimming pool. With portable lights strung up it was a popular place for days. Also, it was the first salt water swimming for several of our crew.

The lower Mississippi was muddy water, mud banks, willow brush and levees, some near the river and some a mile back.

At New Orleans, the *Tenaru River* fastened two barges loaded with gravel and one loaded with sulphur alongside, then took her position behind the barges and kept pushing along day and night for almost two weeks. They handled their "tow" surprisingly well, too, around bends and shoal spots and through bridges. One pilot stood on the bow of the *Hoyt* with a telephone connection to the pilot on the pusher.

Nearly everyone went naked from the waist up, getting a real tan, and slept out on deck with just one sheet for cover, hoping the mosquitoes wouldn't be bad.

One of the river boats' crew remarked, after looking all through the *Hoyt* and looking down at his own boat, that to someone on the river bank "this outfit must look like an ant pushing a loaf of bread."

We passed through several of the most interesting places at night, or, as it seemed to the cooks, at mealtime. The Mississippi was surprisingly clean after passing the mouth of the Missouri River.

As we got further up the Illinois, there was less clearance through and under bridges. Closest top clearance under a bridge was 13 inches, and the closest lock looked like the *Hoyt* could not have been built one foot longer and made it through O.K.

There were no storms other than hard rains on the trip. It was a once in a lifetime chance to make the trip and nobody was sorry they made it, but not many would go out of their way to make another.

Now the *Hoyt* is back together and performing as though she likes fresh water best.

E. B. WILLIAMS

The

New Carriers

In the 1960s, for the first time in its history, the Great Lakes trade faces foreign competition. Ships of all nations come through the Seaway, and the lake freighters with their high costs and high wages are under threat. Foreign construction costs and insurance are, roughly, 50 per cent of U.S. costs; foreign seamen's wages average less than 25 per cent of wages paid on lake vessels.

To survive, the lakes fleet must reduce the costs of operation. Proposed measures are: the use of larger ships allowed by the 1967 lock at the Soo; the reduction of crews through shipboard automation; the lengthening of the navigation season by ice-crushing design of freighter hulls and air-bubble installation to prevent freeze-up of channels and harbors.

Most immediate and imperative is the building of ships of massive capacity. At a meeting of the Society of Naval Architects and Marine Engineers in Duluth in 1962, E. B. Williams, consultant to the American Ship Building Company, traced the evolution of lake freighters and pointed to revolutionary developments ahead.

IT HAS BEEN KNOWN for the past ten years and more, that some rather basic changes have been approaching in the Great Lakes ore trade. In the first place, it has been apparent that this fleet of sturdy, reliable and reasonably efficient bulk carriers is at last getting old. These ore, coal, grain and stone carrying vessels do not last forever, even though many of them already are more than fifty years old and still in active service. In the second place, big changes have been taking place in the Lake Superior mining area. Some people were afraid that we were running out of iron ore. To be sure, the most ominous predictions came from business magazine "experts," but there was some cause to worry because, after all, iron ore, like any other natural resource, once mined is gone forever. That's pretty basic. We have learned, however, as mining men knew all along, that there is still a great deal of high grade ore in the Lake Superior country and low grade ore is virtually unlimited in supply. The competitive picture in the world market, however, is another matter, but even this troublesome problem is reaching a satisfactory solution. In the years to come, we will continue to move vast quantities of raw materials over these Lakes, but the iron ore will be of a considerably different nature and the ships themselves will also change. The long ships will still be passing . . . but the old ships will soon move out of the picture and a new fleet will be taking on a stature of great importance in the drama taking place here in the industrial heart of this nation.

In this section of the paper, we will examine the existing Great Lakes bulk fleet—iron ore, coal, stone and grain carriers—to determine, if possible, which of these vessels may be expected to continue in the ore trade from 1965 into the future. We shall also attempt to determine the need for additional tonnage and some of the probable design features of the new fleet. The problem is very complicated, to say the least, and there are a great many facets because, in the old days, sixty years ago, almost any vessel capable of carrying a few thousand tons of ore could make money; today, the trade is very competitive, both locally and world-wide. . . .

In considering the design features of ore carriers of the future, it is first necessary to establish how much of the existing fleet is likely to continue in active service over an extended number of years— say, for twenty years or more. There are several assumptions to be made which, if correct, will give us a basis on which to make reasonable predictions for the future.

1. The ore trade, even today, is so competitive that only the larger, more efficient vessels can hope to compete. These vessels must show a profit when loaded downbound only. Return cargoes in the ore trade cannot be counted upon as a rule.

2. The total movement of Lake Superior ore will be in the order of 75,000,000 gross (long) tons, annually. Many will disagree with this figure, believing it too high. On the other hand, considering the population growth of this country, the development of low grade concentrates in Michigan and Minnesota and a more efficient operation throughout the industry—mines, ships, railroads and mills—this figure does not seem unreasonable. Our total require-

ments are already twice this amount and estimated by steel company executives to continue to grow to over 200,000,000 tons per year.

3. If the above assumptions are correct, all Great Lakes bulk freighters built prior to 1916 will cease to operate in the ore trade. There may be some exceptions for a few years, but on the other hand, a number of carriers built after that date will probably be converted to other trades.

4. There is a strong indication that the new fleet may be self-unloading or largely so. Such vessels would possibly have shore-based unloading booms.

In this complex world of constant change, there is nothing really new—or so they say. And before we take up the possible characteristics of the 40,000-ton Great Lakes ore carrier, we must admit that it is not a new idea. In fact, such a ship was conceived (possibly in jest) no less than 64 years ago. In the May 5, 1898 issue of *Marine Review*, there appeared an article in which it was imagined how the fleet would look in 1940. Here are a few excerpts from that article:

There are few of the old fleet of '97 still in existence. What a change is here! Most of the fleet now are 1,000-footers, some of them 100 feet wide and 50 feet deep. . . . I find there are practically only three corporations owning boats, where there used to be many, not counting the individual owners. Ships of the big concerns are all of the largest and most approved type. Electricity is the motive power and most of them have triple screws. A few of the older class have twin screws. . . . A voyage on one of these ships is delightful. You get up in the morning and have a trolley car ride to breakfast aft. After spending the day with the Captain forward you put on your dress suit and attend a grand opera at the midship theater in the evening, or pass a pleasant time in the 10-story roof garden over the theater.

In determining the design characteristics of an iron ore carrier for Great Lakes service, there is every indication that at least the first five or ten such vessels should be of maximum capacity, within the physical limitations of the new Soo lock. Such vessels will be best able to compete with foreign ore delivery. Based on the premise that clearances prevailing in the case of the MacArthur Lock will be adequate for the new lock, the dimensions of the new vessel could be about 900-feet length overall by 95-feet beam.

As this is written, however, the maximum dimensions contemplated by the Corps of Engineers are 850-feet length overall by 90-feet beam. The difference between these dimensions represents an additional carrying capacity of about 5,000 long tons, nearly 15 percent, and the Corps has been urged by representatives of industry to give every consideration to the larger set of dimensions. Design studies for the present, however, have been restricted to the 850-feet by 90-feet size.

As previously stated, a number of ore carriers for the future may be of MacArthur Lock size. Current designs for such ships are already well-established and will not be given further consideration. Of course, many of the design concepts of the maximum size ship are readily applicable to any new Great Lakes vessel.

In developing lines for a vessel 850 feet by 90 feet, it is first recognized that the design draft is limited to 25 feet 6 inches at low water datum. For freeboard purposes and considering seasonal drafts, a somewhat deeper summer load line will be incorporated into the design. At 25 feet 6 inches, however, we have a beam-draft ratio of 3.53 which is unusually high. Furthermore, it is desirable to have the load water line as long as possible and to maintain a high block coefficient for maximum deadweight. This concept leads us to exceedingly full water lines with correspondingly easy buttocks and diagonals, from which a twin-screw arrangement is indicated. With either single or twin-screws, modified tunnel-type stern lines will probably be adopted. Recent model experiments for a single-screw, 75-foot beam ore carrier and trial results of twin-screw LST's have confirmed this concept.

Another important consideration is the fact that Great Lakes ore carriers must be highly maneuverable to navigate narrow channels and restricted harbors. They must be moored at docks every day or two and worked through the Soo lock both upbound and downbound. The tremendous mass of 45 or 50,000 long tons is not easily stopped or started. Conventional wire rope mooring lines, already overloaded on 700-foot ships, are even more inadequate on these proposed giants. Major improvements are essential.

With this in mind, bow and stern lateral thrusters offer a possible solution. Bow thrusters, fitted in tunnels, have recently shown marked success and additional installations of this type are continuing. On a ship of this size, perhaps two thrusters forward and two aft would be needed. However, this requires additional auxiliary power far beyond usual requirements.

Pursuing this line of thinking, the retractable type of motor-driven thruster unit might be considered. Such units can be trained and used for steering and maneuvering at docks. Possibly a group of such units—say three at each end, two of which would be fixed and one, directional, could provide the main propulsion. Existing units are low in power, but studies are being made as to the practicability of 2,000 h.p. units. Since these units are motor-driven, they will be wheelhouse controlled and, accordingly, the machinery location is flexible. No rudder would be required unless one or possibly two active rudders were used. Here, at least, is a challenge for some research and development.

The powering of a huge ore carrier for Great Lakes service offers a wide variety of choices in the fields of diesels, gas turbines, steam turbines, etc. Electric drive is attractive not only because of its flexibility but also because of the demands for auxiliary power when pumping ballast and using deck machinery. Self-unloaders, if using ship power, depend on electric motors aggregating possibly 2,000 h.p. Controllable pitch propellers, now firmly established, further extend the possibilities of various prime movers. Automation must be seriously considered in the selection of main machinery. . . .

Great Lakes bulk carriers, traditionally, and for very practical reasons, have always had deckhouses at the extreme ends. Unobstructed decks are necessary and houses are tapered back from the sides to clear loading spouts when in the raised position and to facilitate fast loading when the spouts are lowered into the regularly spaced hatches. The ship and the docks are a part of the overall system. Recent developments in dock design and in communications, generally, offer opportunities to break away from these traditional arrangements and to reduce some of the expensive cost items inherent in designs of the recent past.

With machinery located aft, the most logical location for all accommodations would likewise be aft, including the wheelhouse. If necessary for navigation in narrow channels, a control station located at the forward end would be indicated. Possibly a closed TV circuit, having cameras at fixed, critical positions, would be even better. A lookout, stationed at the bow and in constant communication with the officer on the bridge, could keep him informed of conditions while approaching the dock. . . .

It is only through increased overall transportation efficiency that the Lake Superior iron ore industry can retain its rightful prominent position during the years ahead. Savings must be made in all segments—mining, land transportation, docks and ships. As to the ships themselves, their relative cost is low considering longevity and tremendous annual tonnages carried, but there is much more we can do to reduce the cost per ton. The actual round trip voyage time is only about six days from the head of the Lakes to a Lake Erie port and return. The loading and unloading time, however, is about a day and a half—25 percent. A self-unloading vessel could cut the port time in half. This situation favors a trend toward self-unloaders; the larger the ship, the stronger the trend. Taconite is readily handled in self-unloaders. . . .

The revolutionary changes in the Lake Superior mining areas and the equally basic changes in the making of iron and steel, present a challenge to all who are responsible for transporting the raw material to the blast furnaces. Our Government has cleared the way for longer ships with deeper drafts. The old fleet can still carry us along for a few years.

It is therefore up to the naval architects and vessel operators of this generation to come through with bold, new thinking, economically and technically sound; to produce a new Great Lakes fleet which will again be the envy of the world.

VIII

CITIES AND
SEAWAY

In the summer of 1827 a startling handbill circulated in the town of Buffalo: "The pirate ship *Michigan* with cargo of furious animals will pass over the Falls of Niagara on the 8th of September." Some local men had bought the old topsail schooner, and they meant to collect cash for the grim spectacle. Wrote Captain James Van Cleve, historian of Lake Ontario: "The announcement of sending her over the great cataract was heralded over the country and in foreign countries for some months, and drew a vast concourse of people to the Falls."

On the eighth of September in full canvas the vessel sailed down the Niagara with two bears, a dog, and some geese and chickens on deck. Captain Rough and his crew pulled away at the last moment, beaching their yawl on the Canadian side. One smart bear jumped overboard and swam ashore. With topmasts swaying, the *Michigan* swept over.

Two years later the bizarre event was repeated, with the schooner *Superior* sailing to destruction.

In 1837, when Canadian "patriots" tried to join their province of Ontario to the United States, the American steamer *Caroline* brought supplies from Buffalo to the rebels. On December 29 Canadian loyalists seized the steamer, raked fire onto her deck and sent her toward the Falls. At the brink of the cataract, her hull and rigging ablaze, the vessel wedged in the rocks. Days later her blackened timbers plunged over. The bowsprit was brought ashore at Fort Niagara, where for many years a tavernkeeper used it as a hitching post.

By 1829, when the *Superior* made the plunge, there was another way to Lake Ontario. That year the first vessel passed through the Welland Ship Canal. During the next century, by successive enlargements, the canal grew with the lengthening lake freighters. But between the lakes and the Atlantic there remained the St. Lawrence rapids, skirted by narrow canals. Commerce between Lake Ontario and Montreal was confined to small "canalers"; the twenty-two St. Lawrence locks limited them to 295 feet of length, 43 feet beam, and 14 feet draft. Meanwhile a potential ocean commerce waited for the future.

When the St. Lawrence Seaway was opened in 1959 the biggest lake freighters could steam out to tidewater, and ocean ships could bring their cargoes two thousand miles inland. The minimum channel depth was twenty-seven feet. The seven Seaway locks—St. Lambert, St. Catherine, the Beauharnois Twin Flight, Grasse River, Eisenhower, Iroquois—

measured 859 by 80 feet, with 30 feet of water on their sills. They affected cities thousands of miles away.

To Chicago's harbors on the lakefront and in the Chicago and Calumet rivers, Seaway ships bring whisky from Scotland, toys from Germany and Japan, glass from Venice and Gothenburg, Spanish olives, Norwegian herring, Swiss, Dutch and French cheeses, Dutch tulips and jonquil bulbs; they carry away machinery, oils, fats, lard and many other agricultural products. Milwaukee's new terminals handle a diversified Seaway commerce, with a large export of heavy machinery.

The port of Detroit is second to Chicago in direct Great Lakes-overseas trade. Sixty years ago a writer described two streams of traffic through the Detroit River: the old-time "rabbits" and "coffins"—with their cargoes of salt, coal and stone and their deckloads of shingles, lath and posts—and the "modern" vessels—liners with tourists crowding the rails and freighters loaded deep with coal and iron ore. Now Detroit's two streams of traffic are the long lake freighters and the ocean ships unloading glass, liquors, tools and hardwood. Back to the Old World they take motor vehicles, machinery and agricultural products.

Toledo, Cleveland and Buffalo have expanded port facilities to handle ocean ships and cargoes. In one recent month 72 foreign ships rounded the Cleveland breakwater with cargo bound to 85 ports in 49 countries. Foreign flags are now familiar in all the Lake Erie harbors.

Lake Ontario is shaped like the track of a moccasin. A little more of that big footprint is in Canada than is in the United States, and its northern shores are the more populous. In the Canadian counties bordering the lake live one-seventh of the Dominion's people.

Ontario's north shore is vitalized by Canadian ports and cities—a dozen of them between Kingston and Hamilton. The most important are the two lake ports at the western end, near the north portal of the Welland Canal. Both Toronto and Hamilton have roomy harbors, improved and deepened for Seaway trade, and both conduct a growing ocean commerce. Toronto, especially, has looked forward to Seaway traffic. For years its port developments have progressed in anticipation of foreign trade; Toronto has large and efficient terminals, with room for ships of many nations.

On April 25, 1959, the Seaway was open. The first ship through was the Dutch freighter *Prins Wilhelm George Frederick*. Dressed in all her pennants, with a fresh gray hull and cream superstructure, she steamed past Montreal and into the shipway. A mile farther, with engines at Dead Slow, she crept into the St. Lambert lock, leaving a smear of gray paint on the guide wall. The currents were tricky. The first American ship was the Grace Line steamer *Santa Rosa*, inaugurating a general cargo trade between the Great Lakes and South America. At the formal opening on June 26 President Eisenhower joined Queen Elizabeth on the royal yacht *Britannia*, while guns, sirens, trumpets and church bells sounded over the St. Lawrence.

Despite the festive opening the Seaway was having troubles. It was a late spring (1959) and while the ice broke up a hundred vessels had waited below Montreal. In the Seaway canals and locks ocean captains met unfamiliar problems. While their vessels crept through narrow channels and shifting currents, owners fumed over delay. At the Welland Canal scores of ships waited for passage, and operating costs went on at $1,500 a day. Finally, at their inland destinations, ocean freighters found shallow harbors and inadequate docks. Of all the lake ports only Toronto, Hamilton, Milwaukee and Chicago had adequate dockage, and only Toronto, Hamilton and Milwaukee had harbor depth equal to the twenty-seven-foot Seaway channels. When the first season ended the Seaway traffic totaled a disappointing twenty million tons, five million short of official estimates.

But the next season was better. The arrival of foreign trade spurred harbor dredging and construction of terminals on all the lakes. Iron ore from Labrador came down to the Midwest mills. Inland consumers benefited from reduced rates on many imports, and farmers profited up to ten cents a bushel on grain shipped through the Seaway.

Meanwhile improvements were made in the canals, lock approaches and lock controls, and foreign ships came equipped with tension winches, controllable pitch propellers and stern anchors. There were fewer accidents and shorter delays. The second and third seasons brought increased trade through the Seaway in fewer ships; this trend toward larger vessels, both domestic and foreign has continued. In its fourth season the Seaway handled a record commerce, 25,593,000 tons of bulk and general cargo. On June 4, 1963, an all day fog lifted at the head of Lake Superior and a parade of fifteen ships passed into Duluth harbor. Among them was the Liberian-registered *Transporter,* the one thousandth ocean vessel to reach the lakehead since the Seaway had opened in 1959. While the traffic still falls short of expectations, shipping men foresee an annual fifty million tons of cargo moving through the Seaway by 1968. So time may bring fulfillment of the prophecy made by a geographer ninety years ago, that "all the lake ports on both sides of the 'Inland Seas,' like the Baltic and Black Seas, or the Mediterranean, will form one continued line of seaports, from which can be shipped, at a low rate, all the agricultural and mineral wealth of a vast region of country teeming with all the products that go to enrich nations."

ROWLAND W. MURPHY

The Four

Welland Canals

Lake Erie is less than thirty miles from Lake Ontario, but it lies 326 feet higher. Half of that height is descended by the spectacular Niagara cataract, but all of it had to be climbed by the old portage trail. Over the portage explorers lugged their canoes, their baggage and their presents for the Indians. Up the steep path went all the materials for the building of LaSalle's *Griffin*—axes, sledges, saws, a forge, an anvil, bar iron, rigging, guns and canvas.

The nine-mile portage was used until 1829, when the first canal was built around the falls and rapids of the Niagara. That was strenuous labor too; a flight of forty wooden locks climbed the escarpment. The first vessels passed through the canal in November, 1829.

From that time there has been a growing traffic between Lake Ontario and the upper lakes—a traffic that required repeated enlargement of the channel and the locks. Within a hundred years after 1829 there were four successive Welland canals, each one using segments of new channel along with some of the old. In volume XV of *Inland Seas* Rowland W. Murphy of Toronto sketched the evolution of the canal and gave a seaman's account of the problems of its modern Seaway traffic.

Since his writing, the Canadian government has announced a five-year $180 million project to complete the duplication of the eight Welland Canal locks. (The flight locks at Thorold are already duplicated—three up-bound and three down-bound.) The projected "twinning" of the other locks will increase by 60 per cent the canal's capacity.

TO DEVELOP the Lake Ontario trade with the Upper Lakes and to obviate the steadily increasing cost of transportation of men, gear and goods over the Niagara Portage, the first Welland Canal was built from 1825 to 1829 by a private Canadian company. The leader of this enterprise was the great William Hamilton Merritt of St. Catharines, whose initiative and enthusiasm ensured a successful conclusion to a public work of this importance.

As the total rise of lockage, or difference of the level of Lake Erie above Lake Ontario, (326¾ feet) is greater than in any other Great Lakes or St. Lawrence canal, the First Welland Canal was an outstanding contribution to Great Lakes navigation. The actual work was carried out by pick-and-shovel men, horses and scoops, and by drilling, blasting and sawing through the limestone of the Niagara Peninsula.

As the Niagara Peninsula contains many rivers complete with beautiful waterfalls, the Welland Canal Company made good use of the large valley of the 12-mile Creek (12 miles from Niagara), from the Lake Ontario entrance at Port Dalhousie to Merritton. Port Dalhousie was named for a former governor of Upper Canada, Lord Dalhousie, and Merritton for William Hamilton Merritt. Port Maitland is named for Sir Peregrine Maitland.

This still beautiful waterway was deepened and widened where necessary, and was of great assistance to the canal builders. Then, by the use of locks and cuts the canal reached up the Niagara Escarpment from Merritton to the Summit Reach at Port Robinson, where the level was higher than that of Lake Erie. For this steep climb, 40 locks of wood, 110 feet long, 22 feet wide and with 8-foot draught, were well-built.

From Port Robinson the canal turned easterly and followed the Welland River to Chippawa where it joined the Niagara River. Chippawa was a port used in the days of the Niagara Portage. There the really hard towing job began as the strong current of the upper Niagara River made necessary the use of additional teams of horses. (This towing was too much for *Griffin's* crew on the east bank in 1679, who had to wait for a strong NNE wind as auxiliary power.)

Chippawa Creek is the old name for the Welland River, and on its banks, west of Chippawa Village, was the shipyard where H. M. S. *Tecumseth* and *Naiwash* were built during the winter of 1814.

As the strong current of the Niagara River from Chippawa to Lake Erie became an increasing cause of delay, the First Canal was extended south from Port Robinson to a new port on Lake Erie, known as Port Colborne (after Sir John Colborne, Governor of Upper Canada). This approximately 12-mile extension of the canal was completed in 1833, making the new total length of the canal 27½ miles.

As the level of the Summit Reach was higher than that of Lake Erie, with strong north winds, there was sometimes insufficient water for canalling, especially as at that date (as at present) vessels were usually loaded to the greatest permitted draught. So an entirely new canal, named the Feeder Canal, was built from the two ports on the Grand River, Port Maitland and Dunnsville, a distance of 21 miles, to ensure a sufficient supply of water at this point.

Due to the continual increase in the size of lake vessels (which still continues) it became necessary to enlarge the canal for nine-foot draught. This enlargement, known as the Second Canal, was completed in 1850. The 27 locks were built of stone and were 150 feet long and 27 feet wide. In 1853, the draught was increased to ten feet by lowering the bottom of the Summit Reach and raising the lock walls and banks of the levels.

Canalling was again improved at the Summit Reach between 1846 and 1887 by dredging, so that all necessary water was continually available from Lake Erie. For some years, however, the Feeder Canal, which now imparts a beautiful memento of the past, was used for navigation. Now it could be the scene of a pleasant canoe cruise.

Again an enlargement of the Second Welland Canal was imperative, so the Third Canal was built between 1871 and 1887. It followed the route of the First Canal from the Welland River to Allanburg, and of the Second Canal from Port Colborne to Allanburg, which is 15 miles. From here, however, much new construction was used, as it descended the Niagara Escarpment by a different course, and took a direct line to Port Dalhousie. Its 24 stone locks and one guard lock were 270 feet in length, 45 feet wide and had an original draught of 10 feet, which later was necessarily increased to 14 feet, from 1872 to 1887. The length of the canal was reduced to 26¾ miles.

The traffic through this canal increased greatly, and since 1902, when the writer first met it, the weekly canal jam at both ends caused a picturesque but costly delay. This was due to the observance of Sunday, as the canal closed at midnight on Saturdays and opened at 9 P.M. Sundays, except during the grain rush in the Fall, when from October until the ice made canalling impossible in December, it was in operation continually.

There never was a more interesting or colourful period than during the years mentioned, on the Third Canal. The days of sail were still with us and about twelve or more big three-masted schooners were still to be seen. There were many more which had been cut down to tow barges, and some very elderly relics of the days of wooden steamers, interspersed with older iron steamers and the latest from Great Lakes yards, the Tyne and the Clyde. Twelve canal tugs were kept busy towing schooners and barges and it took eight horses to tow the cut-down four-masted schooner *Minnedosa* before she was lost with all hands in Lake Huron October 21st, 1905. The aristocrat of tow barges, which carried sail, was the splendid *No. 57* of New York, with four masts, owned by the Standard Oil Company, towed on the Lakes by the big steel tug *S. O. Co. No. 2*, of New York.

Up to 1905 all gates and valves were operated by hand on the 24 locks, yet some remarkable speed records were made through the canal by various vessels. The famous upper lakers *India, China* and *Japan*, at this time (1905) under Canadian registry as the *City of Ottawa, City of Hamilton* and *City of Montreal* carried cargo and passengers, and once the *City of Ottawa* was locked through the 24 locks in six and one half hours by human sweat, with three men on each winch handle for opening and closing gates.

This canal, as well as its predecessors, was first lighted by oil lamps, but by 1905 was fitted with electric lights of exceptional power and clarity. Not long after this, lock gates were swung by power from electric motors, as in the early days of Niagara power the cost was so low that some street lights were left burning continually.

In the years the writer knew this canal rather well, there was a steady increase in the usually generous number of canal passages, so that again relief was necessary. This was effected by the commencement of the present Fourth Welland Canal in 1913. The first World War, with necessity for steel and building materials, seriously interrupted the progress of building, but it was in operation by 1932.

In order to cause no interruption or delay to canal traffic, this canal again took a different course, using only a part of any former canal. It is therefore quite proper to speak of the *four* Welland Canals, as each has or had a distinct and different character and direction, though using part of a former canal.

The Fourth Canal took a different course from Thorold, or above Thorold, to an entirely new harbour, Port Weller, on Lake Ontario, four miles east of Port Dalhousie. The seven locks and one guard lock in this canal are 859 feet in length, 80 feet wide, with a draught permitted of 30 feet. The present limit of length of vessels is 715 feet.

The six flight locks at Thorold, three upbound and three downbound (north) have a most impressive appearance and provide a speedy passage with safety. As this Fourth Canal is the really vital link of the St. Lawrence Seaway between the Upper and Lower Lakes, it has needed duplication of other locks throughout its length. Due to active winter construction, the levels between the locks have been widened suitably, so that the addition of an extra lock alongside those of Lock 1, Lock 2, Lock 6, and Lock 7 should not provide any serious difficulty or interruption of vessel passages.

According to the July 18, 1959 issue of *Toronto Telegram*, the announcement has been made that Canada's Transport Department has already taken under advisement a proposal to build a new canal between Port Maitland on Lake Erie and Jordan Harbor on Lake Ontario. The route would parallel the present Welland Canal but would deviate ten to eighteen miles west of it. Proponents of the route say that only two or three lift locks would be required as the route is through gradually rising country.

This seems a suitable time to mention that the troubles in canalling on the Fourth Welland Canal since the opening of the Seaway have been caused mainly by indifference to the technique of canalling, or to the Rules of the Road at Sea, which has been the cause of much unnecessary damage. As all of the writer's early seagoing training, before going to salt water, was acquired in Great Lakes vessels, Welland Canal tugs, etc., he wishes to record the necessity for each stranger on the Lakes to carry a qualified Great Lakes pilot.

A Great Lakes freighter of our day has the proper canalling gear developed by 139 years of experience. This gear consists of a big steel checking cable on a suitable reel (cable strong enough to hold the whole ship when going ahead dead slow), a compressor, suitable chocks, fair-leads, bitts and deck winches, landing booms, fenders, etc.—not to mention the watch having had training and experience.

To see nearly the whole ship's watch on deck dragging heavy manila lines along canal banks or locks and checking the ship's way (or attempting to) with turns around the bitts, is alarming and dangerous for those so employed and for lock walls and gates and other vessels in the vicinity. This is "Niagara Portage" stuff! Equally harmful is attempting to check a vessel's way by going astern on the engines, as the wash of a propeller is hard on lock sills and walls and should be cut to a minimum.

There is, however, a comic element. The master of a big foreign tanker steamed into a Welland Canal lock not realizing that his bridge was six feet too wide to clear the lock walls! Fortunately no one was injured, but this incident made more work for the already overworked Port Weller shipyards!

The foregoing remarks, which are only personal opinions from observation and experience, do not naturally apply to those great seamen who fly the flags of Holland, Sweden, Norway, Denmark and others of equal ability and experience on salt and fresh water. Many readers will realize from experience or observation that on deep water there is generally more than enough sea room; but on entering harbour these deep water men often use tugs to get them alongside—a help in tide water.

A school for foreign shipmasters coming to the Great Lakes for the first time would be valuable and very useful. Too bad some of the time wasted in the Welland Canal or at anchor off Port Weller or Port Colborne could not have been used for such worth-while activity.

For historical education it should be mentioned that several deep water vessels have traded up the Lakes through the St. Lawrence and Welland Canals since 1898 when the writer remembers seeing his first British vessel unloading here, and ships from foreign countries were not uncommon sights in the Third Welland Canal. So only the size of the present Seaway is new, not the idea!

CARLTON MABEE

Sailing

the Seaway Route

The seaway route, from Lake Erie through the Welland Canal, over Lake Ontario, around the St. Lawrence rapids and down the tidal St. Lawrence, is older than the St. Lawrence Seaway. For more than a century small vessels have come and gone from the upper lakes to salt water—their size determined by the locks that bypass the rapids above Montreal.

In the long-ago spring of 1842 Charles Dickens made a trip from Sandusky, Ohio to Montreal. In the St. Lawrence his steamer wallowed through the upper rapids but was stopped at the Long Sault, where canals were then in construction; a stage coach carried passengers along the canal works to the foot of the rapids. Two years later the brigantine *Pacific* sailed out of Cleveland with a cargo of wheat for Liverpool. The route to the sea was open.

In 1955, while dynamite was blasting and earth-movers were gouging out the Seaway, Carlton Mabee traveled the route in a 250-foot Canadian "canaller." In seasons soon to come the new Seaway trade would bring ships of many nations into the North American heartland. This narrative is taken from chapter 4 of *The Seaway Story,* 1961.

MORE THAN A HUNDRED YEARS after Dickens' trip I too boarded a Great Lakes ship. Like Dickens I boarded it in Sandusky, Ohio, and like him I was on my way to Montreal. Passenger ships having almost vanished from the lakes by 1955, my ship was a freighter. I watched an automatic loader put coal into its holds. From a slight rise behind the dock, Chesapeake and Ohio cars were sliding down, one by one, each with a brakeman riding on its end, toward the loading tower. A "pig-pusher" shoved the car up into the base of the tower, where the brakeman got off; then steel claws seized the car and emptied it into a hopper from which the coal slid into our ship.

I sat on a curb near where the loaded train cars stopped before entering the loading tower: "How long does it take to load this ship?" I asked one of the brakemen.

"Only an hour and a half," he replied; "we can put forty-seven cars into your ship."

On the dock beside the ship the captain was talking with a dock agent. They looked at the water-level mark at the prow of the boat, then again at the stern, directing the placing of the last tons of coal in the proper hatchways to balance the load. The captain explained that the St. Lawrence canal guards would not let our ship in if the water at either end went above the fourteen-foot mark.

Some of our crew were leveling out the coal on top of one of the hatchways, their faces and chests streaked with sweat and coal dust. A burly one among them complained: "Christ, how many more tons?"

His buddy from the stern upper deck called an obscene reply. The burly one menaced him with his shovel and returned to work.

By 4:25 P.M. the last carload of coal was dumped on top of the hatch boards, making a twelve-foot pile in front of my cabin door, and five minutes later the winches drew in our mooring lines.

"We pull out the instant the loading is done," said the captain. "We have to save money for Uncle," as he called the boss of the line. Some of the sailors complained to me that the quicker the loading, the less time in port for them, and the less desirable the St. Lawrence-Great Lakes run becomes.

As our ship passed out of the harbor, the hands were swinging booms and cleaning the deck. I heard them taunt each other, some in French, some in English. Like most of these St. Lawrence-Great Lakes canallers, this was a Canadian ship, and the crew of twenty-four, including seven officers, were all Canadians. One chesty sailor, rolling his large, clear eyes to see if he was being watched, teased a winchman on the deck above him. When the winchman noisily gathered spit in his mouth to reply, the sailor fled, hurling badly aimed spit and more French taunts after him, and at a safe distance holding his stomach in laughter.

We were moving on those vast St. Lawrence waters which more than four hundred years ago the Indians introduced to the French as a highway into the continent.

At the foot of Lake Erie we entered the Welland Canal. Enlarged three times since Merritt first built it, since 1932 it had been twenty-five feet deep and needed to be made only two feet deeper to be ready for the Seaway.

In the early daylight we approached a lock. Another ship was inside. We tied up outside to await our turn.

The monstrous ship inside was an upper laker, as the sailors called the larger boats in the trade. Usually upward of seven hundred feet long, they could go through the canals from Lake Superior to Lake Ontario, but not through the smaller St. Lawrence canals between Prescott and Montreal. She carried grain, the sailors said, to upper St. Lawrence ports like Kingston or Prescott for transshipment in smaller canallers like our 250-foot ship, which could go on through the St. Lawrence canals, to Montreal or Quebec, perhaps for transshipment once more to Europe. The Seaway would eventually make such transshipments unnecessary.

The upper laker was dropping. Soon we could see only its funnel and masts behind the lock gates. Presently it moved out of the lock, and after a pause the lock gate swung open for us.

The captain took the wheel, as he always did when difficult maneuvers were required, the wheelsman going down to the main deck rail, and the mate on duty going out to the bridge. We were moving.

"Eight feet," sang out the wheelsman below, reporting his estimate of what the distance from ship to lock side would be if we continued our present course into the lock.

"Eight feet," repeated the mate on the bridge.

"Eight feet," echoed the captain. Our nose was almost in the lock.

"Five feet."

"Five feet."

"Five feet." We were preparing to tie up on the right side of the lock. When water is let in or out, it thrashes so violently that the ship might strike against the lock sides or gates if it were not tied up. Sailors had ropes, their ends tied to cables, ready.

"Two feet all along," called out the wheelsman, and the mate and captain repeated it. Now we were halfway in.

"Coming up," came the call as we were finally well in. The deck hands threw out their ropes. The lock guards pulled in the cables, and looped them over the snubbing posts. One lock guard on the wall to the front waved us on to exactly the right position. Our steam winches drew the cables taut, the ship was fast, the gates at our stern closed. At once we could see the ship was dropping.

As we came level with the lock walls, there were few people about. "Too early. No 'goils,' " said one of the hands. In twenty minutes we were at the bottom of a concrete canyon, and presently the gate before us opened, and we moved slowly out of the lock.

We passed in the canal within seven feet of an upper laker. As we watched one sailor walking its astonishingly long deck, one of our men said, "He's probably still walking back from last night's supper."

By afternoon we saw youngsters swimming in the canal and sunning themselves on the banks. The captain would take his glasses to see if the bridge or lock lights were green for us, and then turn his glasses toward the shore to inspect the girls in their bathing suits. "Not bad," he said once, "but nothing to stop a clock with."

In one of the double locks we found ourselves opposite a white German ship, from Hamburg. Like most of these small foreign ships on the St. Lawrence-Great Lakes run, this one had some of its housing midship, instead of at the bow and stern, like ours; it had a longer and more pointed bow, and was more strongly built to withstand heavy seas. Since the deepening of the St. Lawrence canals to fourteen feet, such small ocean ships had been coming into the lakes, and a limited Seaway functioning.

A sailor from this ship called out to us. We couldn't understand his version of English at first. He was startlingly blond, but wore, like our sailors, dirty pants and a dirty shirt.

The sailor called out again and again. Finally we understood that he was trying to tell us that our mast lights were on.

"Those sailors are so poor," said one of our mates, "it's no wonder they worry about lights." Canadian and Amerian sailors resent having to compete with poorly paid European sailors on the Great Lakes and St. Lawrence. After a studied pause, the mate reluctantly climbed to the pilothouse and cut off our lights.

Up on the bridge our English-born captain was looking over the trim German ship too. "Those bloody foreign boats don't even buy fresh milk over here," he said. "The only thing we get out of them is, they have to use our pilots." Foreign ships are required to use pilots in the St. Lawrence, in canals, and in harbors, he said, but most American and Canadian captains do their own piloting.

In the Welland Canal, the captain explained, all ships pay the same fees, $25 for canallers, and $60 for the larger upper lakers.

"That's reasonable," I ventured.

"Reasonable!" roared the captain. "We pay taxes for these canals, but why should foreign ships get through here for $25? That doesn't even pay the wages of the lock guards."

Forty-eight hours out from Sandusky we were approaching the entrance to the St. Lawrence River proper, at the eastern end of Lake Ontario. We could see nothing but fog ahead. In the whirling radar image I made out a shore line, but it was so indented, I told the captain, that I could not find where the river channel began. The captain was merely amused. But I, not being able to find the channel even with radar, found my respect for the captains of Dickens' pre-radar days growing.

In a few minutes we broke through the fog and were in the river among a myriad of islands, dotted with a myriad of cottages, and here and there a millionaire's summer home in the form of a monstrous castle. "The castles will soon burn down for the insurance," said the captain. "It keeps happening every year or so." Being in a Dickensian mood, I had to admit it would be a blessing.

Beyond Alexandria Bay the channel twists among shoals. One of them near our channel was marked on our chart as only two feet deep. "There," said the captain, "in 1914 a new ship was wrecked." There was no trace of strain in his voice as he gave his orders to the wheelsman: "Port," "a little more to port," "steady." We followed the channel markings, keeping, as we were downbound, the black stakes and buoys on the right, the red on our left. The channel is much better marked now, the captain said, than when he first navigated the river thirty years ago; and soon with the Seaway, sailing the St. Lawrence will be "like driving on a four-lane highway."

As we left the Thousand Islands, the river began to narrow. In the evening, watching the lights on both sides of the river, we noticed more lights on the Canadian side, which here is the more heavily populated and industrialized. We passed a gigantic nylon factory, and then saw the lights of the grain elevator town, booming Prescott; and opposite, the only American city on the St. Lawrence, not-so-prosperous Ogdensburg.

It was foggy again as we prepared to stop for fuel in Ogdensburg. We dropped below the city, then turned and crept back against the swift current along the shore, surrounded by the confused lights of ferries, buoys, and the city itself, with all their shivering reflections. For a long time we followed a distant red light. When we neared it, the light suddenly moved, and I, astonished, looked at the captain. He seemed as serene as ever. Then I realized that I was listening to the sound of an outboard motorboat moving away from us. The captain hadn't been steering by *that* red light after all.

We tied up at 11:25; the sailors bought cigarettes and candy and picked up laundry at a store on the dock; and by midnight we were refueled and off again. I went to bed, and the captain went back to the pilothouse to choose his way among the quivering lights and shadows of the swirling St. Lawrence.

The next morning, our third out of Sandusky, we ran into a traffic jam: there were three ships tied up in the canal ahead of us waiting to get into a lock. When we had tied up too, some of our sailors dropped to the pier and dived into the canal. As they splashed, just across the river we could see earth-movers gouging out the Seaway canals that were to make such refreshing delays unlikely in the future.

Eventually we moved toward the lock.

"Five feet," a hand cried out.

"Five feet," repeated the mate on the bridge.

"Five feet," repeated the captain at the wheel, with ritualistic intonation.

At our left was Highway 2, the main highway from Toronto to Montreal. Trailer trucks, our competitors in transport, thundered past. Some cars stopped, and tourists with wonder-eyed children came to gape at us.

On deck two sailors were loosening the landing boom as they usually did for the St. Lawrence canal locks. A rope hung loose from its end.

"Two feet."

"Two feet."

"Two feet." Our nose was now well in the lock. We were moving very slowly. One of the men grasped the landing boom rope with both his hands and feet, and some others swung the boom out over the side of the ship. He dangled a moment in the air, then dropped onto the lock entrance wall.

Another hand threw out a coil of rope to him. He caught it and pulled, drawing the first steel cable out of the ship, while the winches rattled.

"One foot." The man on the dock slipped a loop of the cable over one of the snubbing posts.

"Move it up the next one," shouted the captain.

"Move it up the next one," repeated the hand on the dock, dragging the cable forward.

The motor of the ship had stopped now. Another hand swung out on the boom and dropped. Soon four cables were tied to the dock, and the winches were drawing the ship further in. We came within three feet of the lock gate ahead.

"Hang onto it," said the mate.

"Hang onto it," intoned a winchman. The spring snub tightened; all the winches tightened, and we tied up in the lock.

After the grand canyon of the Welland locks, these St. Lawrence locks seemed to be bathtubs: they were only about 270 feet long, just long enough for our ship to get in. They were not long enough for most Great Lakes ships, not to mention most ocean ships.

Half an hour later the canal led us away from the furious Long Sault into a lake, where we could see, twisting along the lake shore, the brush-covered 1848 canal banks, remains of Merritt's first-version St. Lawrence canals, which Dickens had seen under construction. In a few minutes, slipping along in the 1900 second-version St. Lawrence canals, we saw the lower tip of Barnhart Island crawling with monstrous earth-movers at work on the third-version canal system, the Seaway.

After a few more locks we came out of the Cornwall Canal into Lake St. Francis. In the haze to the south were the Adirondacks. On the lake, Seaway dredges were at work. One had a drag line with a barge next to it for dumping; another had a long suction pipe, resting on pontoons, that snaked its way to an island, where it vomited its waste in a heap.

The next morning in the Lachine Canal, surrounded by factories and grain elevators, we passed through the last Lachine lock into Montreal Harbor, the biggest port of Canada. Ocean ships were all around us, making our canaller seem small. To the right, just a little downriver, was the Jacques Cartier Bridge, which was to be permanently lifted for Seaway ships to pass under it. To the left in the distance loomed Mount Royal, much the same as it had loomed over the river when others had sailed the St. Lawrence: the Iroquois and the French, Morris, Merritt, and Dickens too.

We turned into a backwash of the harbor, flanked by acres of coal, and tied up. The chief engineer climbed down the ladder to the dock, astonishingly clean in a well pressed gabardine suit—the French-Canadians no longer wear the colorful costumes of Dickens' day—and picked his way among the dusty coal heaps toward his home in the city. Two hands followed him, on their way to find "four cool beers and a floor show." And at last, on our fourth day out of Sandusky, great clams began to snatch the coal out of our ship.

We had docked in that traditional center of Seaway opposition, the ocean-canal transfer port of Montreal.

North

to Salt Water

For more than a hundred years the freighters steamed north and west to the iron ore ports of Michigan and Minnesota. But in the 1950s geologists found a new iron range in the rugged region of the Newfoundland-Labrador border. When the Seaway was ready the new mines were producing, and from the ports of Lake Erie freighters headed in a new direction.

For half a century the silver and black funnels of the Pittsburgh Steamship fleet of the United States Steel Corporation have been a familiar sight in the Detroit River and the Soo Canal. In the summer of 1862 the first ship of the lakes' biggest fleet made the run to salt water—through the Welland Canal and the Seaway to Port Cartier in the Gulf of the St. Lawrence. The story of that voyage was told by Jack C. Yewell in *Sidelights*, Autumn, 1962.

AT SIX MINUTES AFTER SIX on the gray morning of August 14, the Steamer *Arthur M. Anderson* passed the piers at Conneaut, Ohio. Four minutes later she hauled to course 49°. As the big ship swung northeastward, wheelsman Bert Johnson feigned difficulty in handling the wheel. Captain Olsen smiled. "By golly," he said. "She doesn't want to head this way."

For the past half century, Pittsburgh ships have moved northwestward for iron ore from the Mesabi Range. This morning, one of them was heading the other way toward the Gulf of the St. Lawrence, where whales and porpoise play—north to saltwater.

The sailing orders posted under glass in the pilothouse read: When unloaded, proceed to Port Cartier, load ore for Gary. . . .

Out across Lake Erie, past Long Point the *Anderson* ran, to places no Pittsburgh ship has ever been. At eleven that morning she reached Port Colborne, the entrance to the Welland Canal.

Locking through the guard lock at Port Colborne, she began her passage through the narrow, gently curving man-made waterway that skirts the great falls at Niagara to link Lake Erie with Lake Ontario. All afternoon the *Anderson* passed through a summer countryside on a trip more like a train-ride than a cruise. Past highways, vineyards, towns, factories, fruit and dairy farms, the masts of ships that ply the seven seas glide silently. The ships move slowly in a steady stream of traffic, their crews exchanging greetings with men on ships which pass less than fifty feet away, or waving to motorists or children who brave a dip in this bustling waterway.

At dinnertime the *Anderson* tied up at the approach wall of Lock 6 at Thorold, Ontario, perched at the edge of the Niagara escarpment, some eight miles from the famous falls. Then, when the lock was clear, she eased into position between the gates of Lock 6 on the top rung of a spectacular water stairway.

Below them in the twilight, the crew could see the famous Flight Locks that raise and lower ships 139.5 feet; and beyond, Lake Ontario, 326 feet below. The lights of Toronto, 40 miles away, flickered on the far shore.

Darkness came as the *Anderson* locked through each of the twin locks. Crewmen off watch put away their cameras and stayed to view the transit which raises ships 60 feet higher than the 85-foot rise of the Gatun Locks of the Panama Canal.

In the small hours of the morning, Captain Olsen moved the big ship through the three remaining locks, and by the time Chief Cook Don Wojcieszak made the breakfast coffee and had buttermilk pancakes off the grill, the Silverstacker was crossing Lake Ontario.

There was no fanfare over this trip, but there was the spirit of a hardworking outfit anxious to do another job, and do it right, but this was no pleasure cruise.

At midday the long ship passed abreast Psyche Shoal and False Duck Island to enter the St. Lawrence River. From here to the Iroquois Lock, where the St. Lawrence Seaway begins, ocean going ships pass close by cottages that line the river or balance nimbly on tiny spits of rock that rise above the water. These are the Thousand Islands, summer Mecca for vacationers and small boat enthusiasts.

At Iroquois, the ship passed over ground that once had been a town, moved now, stone by board, to higher ground.

In the twilight of Wednesday, August 15, the *Anderson* eased out of the Iroquois Lock, past the power dam, and on into the darkness. She locked through the Eisenhower and Snell locks about ten o'clock, shuddered momentarily in the surge of current at Polly's Gut, and steamed on, leaving the lights of Massena, New York, behind her. When dawn came, she had transited the Upper and Lower Beauharnois Locks and was on her way to the diked passage that sweeps majestically around Montreal.

And from this canal which skirts the Lachine Rapids, Montreal does indeed look like a royal mountain. The dome of St. Joseph's on the far side can be seen for miles, and then, as the ship reached the St. Catherine's Lock, crewmen had their first glimpse of the city skyline. The St. Lambert Lock marks the spot where downriver ships leave the Seaway and re-enter the St. Lawrence River.

Leaving the lock and teeming harbor, the busy docks and elevators of Montreal behind her, the long ship of United States Steel's iron ore fleet headed into the broad reaches of the St. Lawrence. Below Montreal the river is wide, the land flat. Towns dot the shoreline, each one stamping the landscape with a church steeple rising high above the treetops. Farms line the river and horses graze in sight of passing ships.

The sky is as wide as the river here, the clouds like banks of snow, the sun a pale cast of pink, for this is truly north country. The channel is marked as clearly as a path through the woods, but fog comes quickly. Each black buoy and stake off the *Anderson's* port side has a pine branch lashed to its top, an innovation of the river pilots who guide the heavy traffic through all kinds of weather. The little trees make channel markers easier to see on the radar screen.

Well below Three Rivers, the gang meets in the galley. Over coffee and some bit of baking artistry, the officers and crew exchange ideas about this run. Their conversation is good to hear. Talk runs from Communism to girls, from the stock market to anecdotes of days gone by. To listen is to feel a sense of pride in men who speak of God and country, their families and friends, their hopes, their jobs with a tart thriftiness of words that are rich in meaning.

The *Anderson* steams on through the night toward Quebec, the radio in her pilothouse spewing bits of French, German, Norwegian, Danish, Dutch, Italian and British; the talk of mariners plying their trade from every corner of the earth. Thursday the 16th of August is nearing its end, and while the long lake ship slips silently through saltwater, her crewmen smoke, regard the blackness of the night and think about the future.

Passing under the maze of steelwork that is the Quebec Bridge, the long ship came in sight of the chateau on the promontory which marks the Plains of Abraham. During the Seven Years War (in 1759) General Wolfe led his British troops around the western approach to capture the strongest French position in the New World, and turn the tide against the French in the struggle to control the Ohio Valley and the Great Lakes.

The channel at Quebec takes ships around the south end of Ile d'Orleans. On the north side are Mont Morency Falls and St. Anne de Beaupre, a famous religious shrine.

In the darkness of the early morning, the *Anderson* passed Murray Bay and the Saguenay River. From here to Port Cartier, the *Anderson* would make her way to the mouth of the River, past Point des Monts out into the Gulf of St. Lawrence.

The Gulf is a wide expanse of shoreless sea. On Friday, August 17, it greeted this Pittsburgh ship with its characteristic cloudy haze and gray, swelling seas. At her bow, the ship pushed a bone of foaming, frothing sea, and off her stern lay a ribbon of salt-water wake, three times the beam of the ship.

On the northern leg of the run to Port Cartier, a little land could be seen to port, but all hands were more intent on what lay ahead— a new port of call.

About 4:30 P.M. the *Anderson* ran out of a squall in time to see Port Cartier on the horizon. Two sleek tugs came out to meet the stranger and guide her into the loading dock, bringing with them the President of Quebec-Cartier and a party of officials to welcome the men of another segment of United States Steel.

Loading of cargoes is fast at this modern facility, one conveyor doing the job with efficient ease. The processed ore is steel-gray, and from a distance looks as fine as face powder. It is heavy, about 12 cubic feet to the ton, and looks so rich that one would guess it is only necessary to melt and form it to make steel. Its silica glitters in the light and gives the roads around the dock a festive look as truck headlights reflect its sparkle.

A foreign flag ship tied up behind the *Anderson* and our crewmen had a full-face look at a kind of competition they had not seen—a huge brute of a ship that moves nearly 60,000 tons of cargo in her hold.

At ten o'clock that Friday night, the little tugs, performing like trained seals, moved the *Anderson* out of the loading dock and pointed her towards home. On the return run, her crew would see black whales above Escoumains, and white porpoises playing near Murray Bay. They would see some other things they had missed in the darkness of the downriver run.

But the whole picture, the facts of this run were already plain. They had opened a trade route to saltwater for the Pittsburgh ships. They had worked carefully and hard. They had seen the face of competition flying from the mast of every ship they passed. And more, they had seen themselves in a new environment, a clean-cut crew on a modern, trim ship whose bulk dwarfed the locks they squeezed her into. In these surroundings, the *Anderson* looked strong, lean and competent, her crew keen and skilled. One thing more, that if they didn't see, this writer did—another somewhat overlooked resource—the raw material of American crewmen, a sharp, good-humored lot, educated, experienced, confident in their faith, their traditions, their loyalties, ready in an instant to grapple with a challenge and gain a foothold in the future.

HUGH MACLENNAN

Time

and the River

Kebec in Algonquin means "the place where you go back," but it was the place where the French went forward to the wilds. The rock of Quebec stood up 330 feet from the cold St. Lawrence tides. It cast a shadow all the way to the Mississippi.

At the foot of the rock French ships stood at the quay. French seamen with flashing teeth and brass rings in their ears strolled the streets of the lower town. Down by the quayside, where birch canoes bobbed against the hulls of French merchantmen, a circle of Indians squatted around a fire. They boiled Indian corn—Turkey wheat, the French sailors called it—with a fish tossed into the pot for flavor. The French stared at the brown-skinned Hurons and the blanketed Chippewas. The savages stared back. Under the shadowed rock the Old World was meeting the New.

In *Shadows on the Rock*, Willa Cather told of the arrival, nearly three centuries ago, of the ships from France. After the long winter word came down by land that five tall ships had passed Tadoussac, beating up the river. In Quebec the whole town, except for the cloistered nuns, gathered on the waterside. Around Ile d'Orléans the first sails appeared; from the citadel a cannon boomed the governor's salute, and all the watchers shouted a great welcoming cry. Soon the ships were in the roadstead, their anchors roaring down, and a small boat came ashore with post-bags full of news and letters. Other boats would follow, with food, wine, cloth, medicines, tools, firearms, prayer books, vestments, altars for the missions, everything to comfort the body and the soul.

Since then the North American colonies have grown to nations, and the ships of the St. Lawrence have sustained their industry and commerce.

Reflecting on time and the river, the Canadian novelist Hugh MacLennan watched the changing shores from the rail of an ocean freighter. He saw a river haunted with memories and alive with Seaway commerce. The old and the new still meet on the St. Lawrence. This sketch is from *The Rivers of Canada*, 1961.

THE FREIGHTER FELT the tug of the current flowing through the gorge between Quebec and Lévis, and looking around I felt the excitement this famous scene always gives me. The sky over the purple-grey city was turbulent, and the distant mountains were streaked with patches of brightness as the sun struck through clouds. Here, as everywhere in the central and lower St. Lawrence, was visible the perpetual Canadian frontier, the rocky hills of the Shield.

Travelling along the St. Lawrence aboard a working freighter is still the best way to know this river. On the upper reaches where the Seaway now runs it can be very intimate, the ocean-going ships sailing through farms and villages. Once years ago, before the Seaway was built, stealing past the little Ontario town of Cardinal, I seemed to be looking into everyone's home. We slipped noiselessly along in the dark virtually between the United States and Canada, and I will never forget the startling beauty of a lighted window behind which a young girl, smiling secretly to herself, was brushing her hair. Nor again another night in 1940, the month that France fell, the feeling of hope and security when I looked across the river-frontier to the lights shining in the most powerful country in the world. Standing now on the freighter below the pile of Quebec City, I wondered how anyone could believe that a nation containing a city like this is really young at heart.

Quebec, to me at least, has the air of a city that never was young. No community in America, few in Europe, give out such a feeling of intense, rain-washed antiquity. A little like Calais, perhaps, but far nobler on its rock with the wilderness behind it and the great river at its foot. Those stern grey walls with their Norman and Mediterranean roofs two centuries ago sheltered an embattled, isolated people who lived as long and as hard in a decade as most communities live in a century. Even their religion contributed to their tensions, for the Quebec of Bishop Laval was a product of the fierce intolerance of the Counter Reformation, in turn a riposte to the equally fierce intolerance of Protestantism.

I looked up at the palisade of the Citadel polished smoothly grey by wind, rain, snow and ice with the river sheer below it, and remembered an evening not long before when I had stood on the grass of the King's Bastion beside a famous English statesman with whom we had been playing croquet. A corporal's guard had marched round the corner of the blockhouse to the flagstaff. Wind tossed the clouds and across the river rain was falling on Lévis. The soldiers were guardsmen in red coats and bearskins, and as the flag came down one of them sounded the British Last Post over the river whence, two centuries ago, British shells had whirred into the Lower Town and smashed it to a shambles. I saw tears in the eyes of the English statesman and heard him murmur:

"If Winston could see this, he'd talk of it for hours."

Our host said with a quiet smile: "If he knew those guardsmen spoke French, I fancy he might talk about it half the night." . . .

The ship turned into the channel leading round the southern tip of the Ile d'Orléans, the sun broke through the clouds and slowly set, and I found myself recalling Conrad's chapter at the opening of *Heart of Darkness*. Conrad's scene was a river even more famous, the Thames, but the thoughts it evoked in the novelist seemed to fit the St. Lawrence better than any of my own:

"The old river rested in its broad reach unruffled at the decline of day, after ages of good service to the race that people its banks, spread out in tranquil dignity to a waterway leading to the uttermost parts of the earth."

Ages of good service! At least three centuries of varied service the St. Lawrence has given, and not the least of its gifts has been the knowledge the problems it created have taught the people who have been involved in its story. The chief lesson of all is that history is invariably ironical, that the greatest men of action seldom understand the true meaning of what they do, that the results that flow from their lives are seldom as they planned them. Irony has been connected with the St. Lawrence from the very beginning.

Jacques Cartier seems to have been as practical a mariner as ever sailed from a Brittany port, but when he entered that enormous estuary in 1534, when he sailed on and on up the firth, what else could he have assumed than that the St. Lawrence was the Northwest Passage? What importance he attached to the wild grapes he found in abundance on the Ile d'Orléans! Was he disappointed, or was he stricken with awe when he stood on Mount Royal after his ship had been halted by the rapids and stared into the unpeopled land into which the great river disappeared? And why did his own government, when he returned with the news of his discovery, do nothing about it for nearly a full century? Had France moved promptly then, the whole of North America would have been hers.

Irony has haunted most of the great lives connected with the St. Lawrence. LaSalle, seeing the rapids boiling past his seigneury on the southern shore of Montreal Island, may not have been as naïve as the jokers who called the rapids "Lachine" in mockery of his dream, but China seems to have been his dream-goal when he paddled and portaged all the way to the delta of the Mississippi. The meaning of the river's future was clearly closed to Jean Talon, or at least to the French government who employed him, when he established along its banks a replica of a European feudal system. Was it not in America that the first decisive blow against the old privileged classes was struck? Laurentian facts quite baffled Laval's dream of a Catholic-American empire with a cross on every hill from the Gaspé to the Gulf of Mexico. The same river which led the French canoes into the interior also invited the Royal Navy in behind them, and at Quebec the French were trapped.

Irony also haunted the Europeans who thought about the St. Lawrence. The cleverest man in the eighteenth century is remembered in Canada chiefly for one epigram which is repeated only to make a fool of him, namely that along the St. Lawrence two empires were fighting for a few acres of snow.

But what of the English conquerors of Quebec—what did their victory on the St. Lawrence achieve for *them*? The English experience with the river was the most exquisitely ironical of all.

In the middle eighteenth century when Lord Chatham studied his maps in London, it seemed very clear to him that if Britain could become master of the St. Lawrence, the whole of North America would be hers permanently. The river was the sole avenue into the Ohio Territory from which the English of the Thirteen Colonies were barred by the Appalachians. Imperial France was in a bad condition internally with a corrupt government, a weak navy and a worthless king. So Pitt made his decision and mounted the greatest overseas armada in the history of Europe up to that time. Louisbourg fell and the American auxiliary troops razed it. The St. Lawrence was open, no longer did a French fortress lie across the British lines of communication, and the French at Quebec were cut off from a discouraged and (for the moment) decadent motherland. Whether or not Wolfe would have preferred to be the author of a minor poem than to have taken Quebec is a matter in some dispute. He certainly took Quebec, and four years later the government of France ceded Canada to England.

This was the most fatal victory England ever won. For now that the Laurentian threat was removed, the American revolutionary movement grew rapidly. When the Quebec Act, the most liberal document ever granted to a conquered people up to that time, came into effect in 1775, it fired the mine in the southern colonies. The French Canadians had been the enemies of the British Americans for a century and a half. The French Canadians were as militantly Catholic as the Americans were militantly dissenting Protestants. The Revolutionary War broke out and the Americans, as everyone knows, won it.

So came about the greatest irony of all: at the end of the war the chief North American region flying the British flag was Laurentia, the home of Britain's ancient enemy. And as a component part of *that* irony, the Protestant United Empire Loyalists, ousted from their American homes, now had to trek north to build in the wilderness along the upper river, and from then on were doomed to share the river with a people they had always accounted their enemies. Their foolish attempts to dominate the French in the next century and a half served only to make their own lot more difficult. For the French waited. The endless patience enforced upon them enabled them to wait and wait until now, in the mid-twentieth century, Quebec is theirs. It was said in ancient times: "Greece, captive, led captive her captors." The French Canadians have been too shrewd to say as much in public, but they say it in private many times, and so they should. By waiting, by enduring, by yielding again and again on small issues but never on a vital one, they have seen their concept of a dual culture accepted by the English-speaking compatriots whose ancestors considered them a conquered people.

An imperial river—the St. Lawrence has always been that. After the first commercial empire of the St. Lawrence withered, the empire of timber took its place. Then came the railway empire, and soon the prairies discovered by the voyageurs became virtual provinces of the Laurentian cities, their tribute manifest in the Victorian castles which still survive on the southern slopes of Mount Royal. With the coming of hydro-electricity, empire moved from the railway barons and the forest industries to the manufacturers. Now the power bred out of the St. Lawrence system has changed in a few decades the whole nature of traditional French-Canadian life, turning an erstwhile race of simple folk into one of the most highly organized industrial communities on the continent, with results to their character as yet unpredictable.

Finally, with the opening of the International Seaway, the rapids were conquered and ocean-going ships of more than 20,000 tons began moving into the continent's heart. The Power Project connected with the Seaway is sure to create still another Laurentian empire along the former agricultural reaches of the upper river. What course this one will take I would not presume to guess; there have been enough bad guesses connected with the St. Lawrence as it is. But already it seems certain that the St. Lawrence, breeder of nations though she has been, will never tolerate a narrow nationalism in North America. Just as the French and English have had to sink their differences in order to share the river, so now, more closely than ever, Canada and the United States are permanently tied together by the river which theoretically divides them.

Yet the St. Lawrence has changed its appearance very little over the years. The lower Thames is overwhelmed by London, the lower Hudson is utterly dominated by the towers of Manhattan, the Elbe disappears into Hamburg. But when you fly out of Dorval on the London or Halifax plane, the river below you is so enormous that even the seaway excavations look no more than a trivial scar along the south bend of Laprairie Basin. At night Montreal is a scintillating wash of coloured lights pouring in a sluice of brightness down the long slope of the mountain to the stream. But in a matter of minutes you leave it behind. The river is still too big to be dominated in its landscape by anything human connected with it. Below Quebec there are long reaches which look exactly as they did to Cartier. Even along the upper river, even in the section of the old International Rapids where the engineering work connected with the Seaway and Power Project has been most spectacular, the changes wrought in the landscape are still relatively small compared to the landscape's vastness.

My freighter turned into the channel round the Ile d'Orléans and an incoming ship broke out her lights. We passed her and went on into the gathering darkness of the stream. After dinner I came out on deck and began counting the ships we passed, but as I could see nothing but their lights I could only guess at their nationalities. For hours I walked around the decks looking at the lights of the old parishes slipping by, and leaning over the side I could hear the hiss of brine along the plates of the ship. The water was almost entirely salt now, but we were still many miles inland from Father Point. I went to bed and slept eight hours, and in the morning we were still in what the maps call the river. A school of white porpoises flashed about us very close and a deckhand told me they were unique to this region. A steward contradicted him and said they can also be found in the estuary of the River Plate and probably he was right, for he was torpedoed there in the war. We passed Anticosti and entered the Gulf, but we were still, in a sense, within the St. Lawrence system as we passed slowly north along the flank of Labrador where yet another empire connected with the St. Lawrence is a-building. Newfoundland appeared on the starboard bow as I was going to bed. The next morning broke cold and foggy, I dressed and saw the icebergs in the Strait of Belle Isle. Some time in the forenoon we rounded Cape Bon and were out of the St. Lawrence system at last.

HENRY BESTON

Quebec

to the Sea

Tide comes far into the St. Lawrence. At Quebec, five hundred miles from Cape Gaspé, the river tastes of salt. Beyond Ile d'Orléans the stream widens to twenty miles, and beyond Tadoussac and the mouth of the Saguenay it becomes a gulf. Through these waters pass ships of many flags, but the rugged shores show few signs of habitation. Still a land of Indians and trappers, it now has iron mines and concentrating plants. At Sept Iles and Port Cartier big freighters load Labrador ore for the Midwest mills.

In *The St. Lawrence*, 1942, Henry Beston described the vastness of the rivermouth. Past Father Point flow the waters that came from Nipigon and Nipissing, from Minnesota and Wisconsin. After two thousand miles the streams that gathered in the Great Lakes basin find their way to sea.

THE CONTINENT has broken apart. North and eastward lies an immense and widening rift into which the river has found its way, disputing it with the sea. To one side, far mountains descend in a sidelong wall to the stream, their crests notching an emptiness of sky, to the other, a fair twelve miles across, stands a confronting and lower rim of blue. Day after day this is a blue country, river and far coasts becoming all one panorama of a blue which is part of the huge and vaporous air. The blue of the St. Lawrence is not a blue of the sea or the sky, it is a blue of earth, a terrestrial mystery one in being with these huge shores and the great earth stream, a blue of the lower atmosphere floating over the dark green of North America. So vast a manifestation of nature has a strangeness of beauty together with that impressiveness inherent in aspects of earth on so great a scale, but one must not look for warmth. Changing in terms of light, paling or darkening with day and hour, it is fundamentally one mood of color, one dusk of blue gathering a whole continental region into its composure and austerity.

Some twenty miles to the east of Quebec rock, looming above the northern shore, the Laurentians begin with a bold headland rooted in the stream. It is Champlain's Cap Tourmente, the dark and outpost tower of the mountains, little changed in aspect, one imagines, since the day when a fury of water at its base gave it an enduring name some three hundred years ago. Enclosed between its sudden lift and the high rock of the city, narrowed between the St. Lawrence and the more rugged wilderness country which has fallen back to the north, lies Quebec plain, an open agricultural country spilling down to the river like the fan of a glacier reaching the sea. It is uplifted on ancient rocks which are grey to black in color, and over their edge, between a greenery of trees, the Montmorency pours its sunlit cataract. Villages sprawling into suburbs occupy the shore, each with its great church of stone and coldly-silvered spire.

Leaving Quebec reach, the ship channel swerves to the south to follow the pleasant rural shores of the Isle of Orleans.

So Quebec falls behind, a narrows of rushing water and a rock, an old city and a new, a place of ships and modernity, a place of cannon and walls and a noble sound of bells, the north and the wilderness fixed at its gates, and the clouds beyond it tinted pale to the far shores of Hudson's Bay.

It is again the morning. The beginning day is pleasant with sunshine and midsummer warmth, the river is busy, and the enormous scale of the broken continent to the east invests the entire scene with a quality of drama. Every great landscape imposes something of its own measure of earthly time, and there is something here of that debatable mystery.

Field beside striped field, farmhouse and barn, church spire and tiny summer villa, the pleasant shore and broad upland top of the Isle of Orleans sail along beside the ship. To the south another upland stands with mainland fields and farms above, and a fine precipitous shore of cliffs and trees. One by one, incoming ships pass flying astern the colors of many nations; a churning sound, a smell of oil and iron, an exchange of casual stares, and they are gone towards the narrows and Montreal or the wharves of Quebec. Island and island-passage ending, the width of the river opens ahead, a sidereal stream now, almost a part of space and the sky.

The Laurentian mass has risen above the river to the north. It is as a coastal wall that the higher country begins at Tourmente, shoulder after shoulder of grey archaic rock fronting the new immensity of the river, with occasional small glens or forested gullies hid between. Save for a next-to-invisible railroad managed at the base, there are few signs of human occupation, and one goes as along a local solitude. The channel now holding a northern course, the south shore dims to a blueness withdrawn into a serenity of dream. Far across, islands lie atop the stream like the crests of all but submerged mountains, their blue-black lengths melting into one appearance with the blue of the southern coast.

A first break in the northern wall, a first river mouth at Baie St. Paul, and the traveler has a glimpse of the farming country inland, and of the mountain rims and valley contours of so huge an earth. Still following close below the Laurentian scarp, the ship channel now enters the narrow passage between the mainland and the eight-mile length of the pleasant Isle aux Coudres. The stream races, a darkness descends from the towering shore; one might be at the beginning of a fjord. Mountain shapes and Laurentian domes, trees dark and austere, have replaced the wall, their forest colors and earth blues lifted between the passage and an increasingly colder sky.

A second opening at Murray Bay, ninety miles from Quebec, discovers the hidden country of the ranges to the north. Like blue mountains out of a fairy tale they rise, outposts of the wilderness rolling mile upon empty mile to the end of earth and of all human things.

Beyond the bay, its beautiful vesture of cleared and planted fields overlaid with cold Laurentian air, lies the great ridge of the open coast which the farmer has made his own. Like a long mountain it stands compact of other mountains, the colored crops climbing its pale sides, one road of villages leading eastward along it in a succession of metallic spires. A curtain of spruce hides the half slope, half precipice of the actual shore, covering with a green which seems here more sylvan the monstrous confusion of grey and tumbled rock confronting the wide St. Lawrence stream. As one passes, the same ridge takes on to the east a growing look of the frontier, clearings, cuttings, and the forest mingling together on the slopes above in traditional hostility. Seen from a ship, the coast on the level of the eye seems to present a grim and unbroken front of rock. Concealed by the perspective, however, are wild crannies and inlets and amphitheater coves: plunging rivers descend to them, their green silence is broken only by the sound of cataracts and the confused wash of waves in a confusion of rock, and sea birds swim all untroubled in their peace.

Now fourteen, now eighteen, now a long twenty miles across, the river is widening in its giant path. Distant but substantial still, at once a part of illusion and the solid reality of earth, the south coast remains in sight, continuing to the east its blue and impressive parallel. An island lies midstream, flat as a shadow on the river and overgrown from end to end with trees—the uninhabited Isle aux Lièvres. Mountain shapes and the forest now take over the north, a lighthouse marking all that seems left of man. Presently from the shore comes a new gleam of light on cliffs of sand, and a vast discoloration overside. The traveler has reached Tadoussac, the mouth of the Saguenay.

The coastal lift of the Laurentians is dying out of the scene. A new country lies ahead, falling off to the ever-widening east, a coast of bold terraces and rock occasionally widened below with tidal flats and salt-hay fields. It is a frontier country of frontier fishermen, farmers and cutters of pulp, a thread of human life along one adventuring road.

Fifty miles beyond Tadoussac and a fair hundred and fifty beyond Quebec, the road comes to its present end at the Portneuf River. Sand bars, miles long and lying parallel to the coast, lead the tributary forth into the greater stream, and half conceal a valley which might have emerged but yesterday from under the glaciers and their sands. The caribou drift here betimes, moving down through the ragged firs to the river plain with its bog vegetation and winding miles of scrub. The coast beyond (La Côte Nord) is the coast of wilderness America. An inconceivable shore of the chaos and savagery of rock topped with a stunted savagery of trees, it remains the country of the trapper and the Indian.

The south coast has vanished out of one's consciousness. Far away, certain of its hills rise in the east like blue and solitary isles, very beautiful in their shapes of earth. All else is the St. Lawrence, and the long wilderness to the north with its brow of green and its surges breaking below. Miles to the east and north will lie the Point des Monts and the white tower of the light, the sudden turn of the coast to the north'ard, and the vast opening of the waters of the gulf. White whales appear, swimming well in toward shore. A change has come over the look of the river. It has put off its earthly coldness of white and the cold of steel, its strange colorlessness as of level miles of rain. Having broken free of earth, it has come to an end as a presence of earth. This is the sea and the north and the cold, final blue of the sea.

Coda

Certain decades have been times of change in the Great Lakes commerce. Like the 1820s when steam came to the lakes, the 1850s when the Soo Canal unlocked Lake Superior, and the 1900s when lake freighters grew to ten thousand tons capacity, the 1960s are a time of transition. A chapter is ending in the history of lakes transport, and while it ends a new chapter is beginning to unfold.

A century after the first ladings of Lake Superior ore, the 1960s see the end of direct-shipping iron ore cargoes from Lake Superior. One after another the famous mines close down as steam shovels bite bottom in the yawning pits. Vast deposits of jasper and taconite remain, and this iron-bearing rock can be concentrated into a rich feed for the blast furnaces. But the agglomerating is a complex process, with production limited to the capacity of crushers, separators, and sintering and pelletizing plants. Meanwhile increasing cargoes of foreign ore come into coastal ports and more than ten million tons annually pour down the Seaway from new ranges in Labrador.

Competition of American freighters with foreign shipping through the Seaway is a hard new reality on the lakes. Foreign shipbuilding costs are less than half the cost in this country, and there is a still greater difference in costs of vessel operation. On a British ship under the Liberian flag Chinese seamen are paid fifty cents a day. At four hundred dollars a month a deckhand on an American freighter draws more than a captain on many foreign vessels. In 1961 the Canadian government granted a 40 per cent construction subsidy to owners of ships built in Canada. Since then twenty-three huge freighters—the last word on the lakes—have come from Canada, while American shipyards stand idle. Construction and insurance costs in the United States have prohibited new shipbuilding in this decade.

Meanwhile the old plodding freighters are leaving the lakes. Between 1958 and 1963 age and obsolescence removed 78 vessels from the United States fleet; in 1963 the Lake Carriers Association reported the smallest number of steam vessels—though the largest tonnage capacity—in the twentieth century. Each year big freighters of the early 1900s are taken out of service. In the summer of 1963 the veteran *Crete* arrived in the harbor of Leghorn, Italy—at the end of a towline. A few months earlier the W. *Wayne Hancock* sank in heavy weather thirty miles southeast of the Azores. She was the third Great Lakes freighter to be lost in the Atlantic while being towed to European scrapyards.

In 1965, seventy-five years after their launching, just four of the famous whaleback freighters were still afloat—three under Canadian and one under United States registry—and they were about to go. In May of that year the whaleback barges *Alexander Holley* and *137* were tied up at Hamilton, Ontario, and dismantled for scrap. Meanwhile the steamer *John Ericsson* was out of service and awaiting disposition. That left one whaleback, the last of a storied fleet, still working. As the *Frank Rockefeller* it had carried grain and iron ore; as the *South Park*, decked over, it had loaded automobiles; now it is the tanker *Meteor,* carrying petroleum products out of Cleveland. When it has made its final run, the whaleback, like the vanished sloops and schooners, will become a memory.

In 1962 two obsolete freighters, the *William Edenborn* and the *James J. Hill,* were towed from Lorain to Cleveland and anchored off the foot of East Fifty-fifth Street. They were stationed there and sunk, to serve as a breakwater for Cleveland's east harbor. From Gordon Park they look deepladen, the *Edenborn* nudging the *Hill*—and both of them going nowhere. They make twelve hundred feet of solid breakwall. In 1965 two veteran freighters, the *Amasa Stone* and the *Charles S. Hebard,* were converted into an offshore loading dock for the cement trade in Cleveland.

Another use was found for the aging *Horace S. Wilkinson.* In 1963 this thirteen-thousand-tonner, built in 1917, was stripped of its superstructure and converted to a barge. Barges were commonplace fifty years ago; many a steamer crept down the lakes with a "consort," or a pair of them, in tow. But the *Wilkinson* is an unmanned barge, pushed at nine miles an hour by a tugboat with a high-rise pilot house. A crew of twelve on the tug replace thirty-six men on the freighter, which with increased capacity—its number 4 hold was extended into what had been the boiler room—carries ore from Lake Superior to steel plants on Lake Erie.

The economy of that operation led to other conversions from steamer to unmanned barge. Meanwhile a number of old freighters have been fitted with automated boiler controls. To cut the cost of vessel operation, owners replace men with mechanical devices. Each year the Great Lakes trade employs fewer seamen, and in the lake ports the old shipping halls are empty.

But renovation and automation are not enough. The future calls for bold new ship dimensions and designs. To compete with foreign carriers and to keep Lake Superior's agglomerated iron ores competitive with foreign ore the American lakes fleet must have larger, faster, more efficient ships and a longer navigating season.

Now the historic Poe lock at the Soo is a scene of tumult. Where the long freighters rose and fell, men and machines are moving earth and rock within a huge cofferdam. In 1967 a new lock will open on that site—a chamber 1,200 feet long, 110 feet wide and 32 feet deep. It will accommodate ships a thousand feet long with forty thousand tons of cargo in their holds. Operating for a nine-month season, such a giant carrier could transport two million tons of iron ore. Taconite pellets can be handled by conveyor belt in all kinds of weather. De-icing equipment can combat winter on the ships, in the locks, and at the terminals. Air-bubbling systems can keep harbors open in zero temperature. These are items in the next chapter of Great Lakes transportation. On June 25, 1963, the U.S. Senate authorized an extended study of de-icing methods on the St. Lawrence Seaway and the lakes.

In 1679, from the bow of the lakes' first commercial vessel, Father Hennepin dimly foresaw the "inconceivable commerce" that would come to the empty waters. On the unchanging lakes moves a changing trade and traffic. Over the same horizons that the *voyageurs* knew, will pass the long ships of the future.